The Collected Works
of Abraham Cowley

The Collected Works of Abraham Cowley

GENERAL EDITORS

Thomas O. Calhoun
Laurence Heyworth
Robert B. Hinman
William B. Hunter
Allan Pritchard

GENERAL TEXTUAL EDITOR

Ernest W. Sullivan II

The Collected Works of Abraham Cowley

VOLUME 2: Poems (1656)
PART 1: *The Mistress*

EDITED BY

Thomas O. Calhoun

Laurence Heyworth

J. Robert King

TEXTUAL CONSULTANT

Ernest W. Sullivan II

Newark: University of Delaware Press
London and Toronto: Associated University Presses

© 1993 by Associated University Presses, Inc.

All rights reserved. Authorization to photocopy items for internal or personal use, or the internal or personal use of specific clients, is granted by the copyright owner, provided that a base fee of $10.00, plus eight cents per page, per copy is paid directly to the Copyright Clearance Center, 27 Congress Street, Salem, Massachusetts 01970.
[0-87413-408-0/93 $10.00 + 8¢ pp, pc.]

Associated University Presses
440 Forsgate Drive
Cranbury, NJ 08512

Associated University Presses
25 Sicilian Avenue
London WC1A 2QH, England

Associated University Presses
P.O. Box 39, Clarkson Pstl. Stn.
Mississauga, Ontario,
L5J 3X9 Canada

The paper used in this publication meets the requirements
of the American National Standard for Permanence of Paper
for Printed Library Materials Z39.48-1984.

Library of Congress Cataloging-in-Publication Data

(Revised for vol. 2)

Cowley, Abraham, 1618-1667.
 The collected works of Abraham Cowley.

 Includes bibliographical references.
 Includes indexes.
 Contents: v. 1. Poetical blossomes, The puritans lecture, The puritan and the papist, The civil war—v. 2. Poems (1656). pt. 1. The mistress.
  I. Calhoun, Thomas O. II. Heyworth, Laurence.
 III. Pritchard, Allan. IV. Title.
 PR3370.A5C35   1989   821'.4   87-40005
 ISBN 0-87413-282-7 (v. 1: alk. paper)
 ISBN 0-87413-408-0 (v. 2)

PRINTED IN THE UNITED STATES OF AMERICA

Contents

Preface	7
Introduction to *The Collected Works*, Volume 2	9
The Text	15
The Mistress	17
Textual Introduction, Analysis, Collations, and Textual Notes	127
Editorial Principles, Sigla, Abbreviations	129
Textual Introduction	132
Textual Analysis	160
Collations and Textual Notes	175
Critical Commentary and Explanatory Notes	205
References Consulted	207
The Mistress: Commentary	219
Explanatory Notes	237
The Musical Settings of Poems from *The Mistress*	303
Editorial Principles	305
The Composers	311
Settings of Poems from *The Mistress*	317
Music Copy Texts: Sigla and Descriptions	556
Collations and Notes to the Musical Settings	568
Index	643

Preface

The Collected Works of Abraham Cowley, in six volumes, includes works in English and Latin, the letters, and edited scores of seventeenth-century musical settings. General editors for the series are Thomas O. Calhoun, Laurence Heyworth, Robert B. Hinman, William B. Hunter, and Allan Pritchard. Ernest W. Sullivan is general textual editor; Peter Beal is the manuscript consultant; J. Robert King is music editor. The first volume of *The Collected Works*, published in 1989, contains Cowley's juvenilia and political poems. Volume 2, including the contents of Cowley's *Poems* (1656), is in two parts. Part 1 contains *The Mistress*, which was first published in 1647, independent of other contents in the collected *Poems*. Part 2 will contain Cowley's *Miscellanies, Pindarique Odes*, and the *Davideis*.

For volume 2, part 1, the text of *The Mistress* has been prepared by Thomas Calhoun and Laurence Heyworth. Ernest Sullivan reviewed the texts and textual apparatus. Thomas Calhoun, with the assistance of Laurence Heyworth, prepared the critical commentary and notes. J. Robert King edited the musical settings and, with the assistance of Thomas Calhoun, prepared notes to the settings. The settings are printed following the text and commentary, and the scores appear in a sequence that follows the order of poems in *The Mistress*.

We owe a debt of gratitude to many kind professionals at libraries in the United States and Britain who have helped in the gathering of manuscript and early printed materials for this volume. Special thanks go to Melanie Wisner at the Houghton, Hilton Kelliher at the British Library, and Susan Clermont at the Library of Congress. We are also grateful to Cedric Brown, Allan Pritchard, Martin Butler, Thomas Roche, John Carey, David Foxon, Curtis Price, and Richard Luckett for their criticism and advice; to Alex Lindsay, Patience Phillips, and Kat Patrick for checking manuscript materials and collations; to Robert Shay for checking the music and Michael Morgan for printing the musical scores; and to Catherine Norman for her hospitality.

The editors acknowledge the Bodleian Library for permission to publish photographs of the title page and section title taken from the presentation copy of Cowley's *Poems* and the Chatsworth Trustees for permission to publish a photograph of Inigo Jones's drawing showing Queen Henrietta Maria in costume for her role in *Salmacida Spolia*.

Introduction
The Collected Works of Abraham Cowley Volume 2: Poems (1656)

Copy Text

Most of the contents of this volume were first printed in the authorized folio collection *Poems*, published in 1656. Therein Cowley and his publisher, Humphrey Moseley, gathered together texts under the section titles *Miscellanies, The Mistress, Pindarique Odes*, and *Davideis*. The author added a prose preface, and for the finished volume these contents were framed with two Latin poems: a dedicatory elegy to Cambridge at the beginning and at the end *Davideidos, Liber Primus*. The 1656 edition, designated F1, is described below. It will be referenced in textual introductions to the four titled sections, where any departures from or emendations to the 1656 text are discussed. Cowley donated a copy of *Poems* to the Bodleian Library (C 2.21 Art, here numbered copy i). This is the copy text for the present edition.

F1 [within a double-rule border] POEMS: / Viz. [a bracket { is set to the left of the first three titles] I. MISCELLANIES. / II. *The Mistress*, or, *Love Verses.* / III. PINDARIQUE ODES. / And IV. / Davideis, / OR, A / SACRED POEM / OF THE / TROUBLES / OF / DAVID. / rule / Written by *A.* COWLEY. / rule / VIRG. GEORG. 3. / ———*Tentanda via est quà me quoq; possim / Tollere humo, victórq; virûm volitare per ora.* / rule / LONDON, / Printed for *Humphrey Moseley*, at the Prince's / Arms in St *Pauls* Church-yard, M.DC.LVI.

Title page: copy i see photocopy, p. 14.

Collation: 2° (in fours): [unsigned]1 A2 (a)-(b)4 B-F4 [unsigned]1 2A-2K4 3A2 3B-3I4 3K2 4A-4T4 [unsigned]1 5A-5C4 [$2 signed (-A2, 2A1, 3A1, 3K2, 4A1); 2B1, 2 missigned B1, 2; 3G1 missigned G; 3H1 missigned H1; 5A1, 2 missigned A1, A2], 197 leaves, pp. [i-xxii] 1-41 [42; 1-2] 3-80 [4] 1-58 61-70 (copies i-v misnumbering 65 as 63, 66 as 64; Perkin reports a copy with the numbering corrected—we have not found such a copy) [1-2] 3-154 (*var.* copies iv and v [1-2] 3-67, 70-71, 70-154; *var.* University of London, Senate House, Sterling Library [1-2] 3-66 69-72 71-154; all copies misprint 57 as 75) [1] 2-23 [24 blank]

Bound folio, copy i measuring 21.8 cm × 32.8 cm on large paper; copy iii, representing the ordinary-sized folio, measures 18 cm × 28 cm; watermarks: copy i large, ornate design with figure of a bird in the center, measuring c.150 mm top to bottom, alternating with another, very similar watermark; sigs. 4A–4T4 show a smaller ornamented design with a diagonal band in the center; copy iii and the British Library copy show a cardinal's hat watermark, c. 60 mm × 60 mm, but for sigs. 2A–2K4 and 4A–4T4, which are marked with an urn surmounted with a crescent, c. 50 mm × 100 mm, and another, similar watermark.

Contents: [*unsigned* 1]^r title, [*unsigned* 1]^v blank, A1^r rule / headpiece / HT] ELEGIA / DEDICATORIA, ad ILLUSTRISSIMAM / Academiam / *CANTA-BRIGIENSEM.*, A2^v blank, (a)1^r THE / PREFACE, (b)4^r Errata, (b)4^v blank, B1^r headpiece / rule / HT] Miscellanies. / rule / THE / MOTTO. / rule, [second *unsigned* 1]^v blank, 2A1^r section title: THE / MISTRESS; / OR, / SEVERAL COPIES / OF / LOVE-VERSES. / rule / Written by *A. Cowley.* / rule / VIRG. Æn. 4. / ——*Hæret lateri lethalis arundo.* / two rules / *LONDON:* / Printed for *Humphrey Moseley*, and are to be sold at / his shop at the *Princes Arms* in St. *Pauls* / Church-yard. 1656. (photocopy, section title page, copy i, see p. 18), 2A1^v blank, 2A2^r headline / HT] THE / MISTRESS: / OR, / SEVERAL COPIES / OF / Love-Verses. / rule, 3A1^r section title: Pindarique / ODES, / Written in Imitation of the / STILE & MANER / OF THE / ODES / OF / PINDAR. / rule / by *A. Cowley.* / rule / HOR. EP. L. I. 3. / *Pindarici fontis qui non expalluit haustus.* / rule / *LONDON:* / Printed for *Humphrey Moseley*, at the sign / of the Princes Arms in St. *Pauls* / Church-yard. 1656. (photocopy in vol. 2, pt. 2), 3A1^v blank, 3A2^r headline ornament / PREFACE, 3B1^r headline ornament preceding texts, 4A1^r section title: Davideis, / A / SACRED POEM / OF THE / TROUBLES / OF / DAVID. / rule / *In FOUR BOOKS.* / rule / VIRG. GEORG. 2: / *Me verò primum dulces ante omnia Musæ, / Quarum sacra fero ingenti percussus amore, / Accipiant, Cœliq; vias ac Sidera monstrent.* / rule / *LONDON:* / Printed for *Humphrey Moseley,* a the Princes Arms in / St. *Pauls* Church-yard. 1656. (photocopy in vol. 2, pt. 2), 4A1^v blank, 4A2^r headline ornament / THE / CONTENTS., 5A1^r headline ornament / HT] DAVIDEIDOS, / *LIBER PRIMUS.* / rule / Authore A. COWLEY. / rule, 5C4^v blank.

CW] A2 The [THE], (a)4^v may, (b)3^v *Miscellany.* [(b)4 = Errata; B1 = Miscellanies.], B1^v Hence [3. Hence], B2 In [8. In], B4 The [4: The], B4^v *On*, C1^v Again [Again;], C2^v Twas ['Twas], C4^v Silent, D1 Hence, [Hence], D2^v He [4. He'], D3^v When [6. When], D4 If [12. If], D4^v So, E1^v Taste [2. Taste], E2 *Visions* [2. *Visions*], E3^v *Ana-* [Anacreòntiques:], E4 *Drinking.* [II. *Drinking.*], E4^v What, F1 *Age* [V. *Age.*], F2 *The* [VIII. *The*], F3 *The*

Introduction   11

[XI. The], F3ᵛ Elegie, [ELEGIE], F4 Love [Love], F4ᵛ And, 2A2 If [3. If],
2A4ᵛ You, 2B3 'Tis [2. 'Tis], 2B4ᵛ The, 2C2ᵛ Wisdom [Wisdom.] 2C3
Never, [Never,], 2C4ᵛ What [4. What], 2D2ᵛ Counsel [Counsel.], 2D4ᵛ
Thou'rt, 2E1 Yet [3. Yet], 2E3 copies i–iv Well fare; copy v Welfare [Well
fare], 2E4 Will [2: Will], 2E4ᵛ The, 2F3 You [3. You], 2F4 Beauty [Beauty.],
2F4ᵛ The, 2G2ᵛ Hearts [4. Hearts], 2G3ᵛ Ah [2. Ah], 2G4ᵛ Or, 2H2 Say
[5. Say], 2H2ᵛ In [6. In], 2H4ᵛ Her, 2I1ᵛ Joynture, [2. Joynture,], 2I2 Three
[3. Three], 2I4ᵛ The, 2K1 Honour [Honor.], 2K2 Dialogue: [DIALOGUE,],
2K2ᵛ Who [6. Who], 2K3 'Tis [2. 'Tis], 2K3ᵛ Why [2. Why], 3A2ᵛ The
[THE], 3B1 The [4 The], 3B1ᵛ But [4. But], 3B2ᵛ To [9. To], 3B4 Ιδοῖσα
[5. Ιδοῖσα], 3B4ᵛ Virg., 3C1ᵛ The [THE], 3C3ᵛ Notes. [NOTES.], 3C4ᵛ
eximium, 3D1ᵛ Lo [4. Lo,], 3D2 Διθυ. [Διθυραμβοποιῶν], 3D3ᵛ The [The],
3D4ᵛ For [2. 1. For], 3E2ᵛ Corpore [——Corpore], 3E3 Destiny: [Destinie.], 3E3ᵛ Me [3. Me], 3E4 Notes. [NOTES.], 3E4ᵛ Brutus [Brutus.], 3F2
The [3. The], 3F3 Hannibal [4. Hannibal], 3F4ᵛ The [The], 3G1 Through
[5: Through], 3G1ᵛ Thus [10. Thus], 3G2 Sowrenes [Sowreness], 3G2ᵛ Notes
[NOTES:], 3G3 My [2. My], 3G3ᵛ Notes. [NOTES.], 3G4 The [The], 3G4ᵛ
With, 3H1 The [6. 2 The], 3H1ᵛ V. 8. And [And], 3H4 What [3 What],
3H4ᵛ Lo, [8. Lo], 3I2ᵛ The [16. The], 3I4ᵛ And, 3K2 is [is], 4A2 Davideis.
[DAVIDEIS.], 4A4ᵛ She, 4B2 Round [28 Round], 4B2ᵛ Whil [Whilst], 4B3
When [Psal.114 41 When], 4B4 In [1 Sam.19 14. In], 4B4ᵛ That 4C1 For
[48 For], 4C1ᵛ Some [57 Some], 4C4 The [NOTES], 4C4ᵛ [Geor-]gicks,
[Sed](copies i–iv); Sed [Sed](copy v), 4D4 The [23 The], 4D4ᵛ And, 4E2
Scaliger [33 Scaliger], 4E2ᵛ The [38 The], 4E4ᵛ upon, 4F2 and [And], 4F2ᵛ
The [THE], 4F3 Davideis [DAVIDEIS,], 4F4ᵛ Hither, 4G4 From [2 Sam.5.
From], 4G4ᵛ In, 4H2 The [2 Kin.23. 11. 84 The], 4H4 Notes [NOTES],
4H4ᵛ Pherecides, 4I1ᵛ For [14 For], 4I2ᵛ Gen. [24 Gen.], 4I4 I Sam. [37 I
Sam.], 4I4ᵛ of, 4K2ᵛ 2 Kings [64 2 Kings], 4K3 con- [concerning], 4K3ᵛ
The [77 The], 4K4 L I. [L.I.], 4K4ᵛ Jehoiachin [87 Jehoiachin,], 4L2 The
[THE], 4L2ᵛ Davideis [Davideis,], 4L3ᵛ Asahel, [9 Asahel,], 4L4ᵛ Swift
[21 Swift], 4M1 Abraham [Gen. 14.13. Abraham], 4M3ᵛ Twice [51 Twice],
4M4ᵛ As, 4N4ᵛ All [64 All], 4O1 But [74 But], 4O1ᵛ Notes [NOTES], 4O2
Fatal, [3 Fatal,], 4O3 Edom; [14 Edom:], 4O3ᵛ For [19 For], 4O4ᵛ Cheder-
[28 Chedor-], 4P1 The [31 The], 4P2 This [37 This], 4P2ᵛ Fleecy [41 Fleecy],
4P4 If [60 If], 4P4ᵛ The [68 The], 4Q1 The [THE], 4Q1ᵛ Davideis
[Davideis,], 4Q3 In [I Sam.7. In], 4Q4 He [I Sam.8.6. He], 4Q4ᵛ Was,
4R4 Again [Ver.15. Again], 4R4ᵛ Whose, 4S4ᵛ What, 4T1 Notes [NOTES],
4T1ᵛ Religionem [religionem], 4T2 The [12 The], 4T2ᵛ See [15 See], 4T3
The [19 The], 4T3ᵛ Psal. [Psalm], 4T4ᵛ yet, unsigned1 Hom. [44. Hom.],
5A2 Vir- [Virgineoque], 5A3 Divi- [Divisum], 5A4ᵛ Non, 5B4ᵛ Nil

RT] (a)1ᵛ–(b)3ᵛ The Preface.; B1ᵛ–unsigned1 MISCELLANIES.; 2A2ᵛ–
2K4ᵛ The MISTRESS.; 3B1-3K2ᵛ PINDARIQUE ODES.; 4A3-4A4ᵛ

DAVIDEIS.; 4B1–4C4 verso RT Davideis, *A Sacred Poem* Book I. (4C1ᵛ reads Book I͟), recto RT Book I. *of the Troubles of* David.; 4D1–4F2 *Notes upon the first Book.*; 4F3 Book II.; 4F4–4H4 verso RT Davideis, *A Sacred Poem* Book II., recto RT Book II. *of the Troubles of* David. (4G3, 4G4, 4H2 and 4H4 read . . . *Of the Troubles* . . .); 4I1–4L2 *Notes upon the second Book.*; 4L2ᵛ–4L3 Book III.; 4L3ᵛ–4O1 verso RT Davideis, *A Sacred Poem* Book III., recto RT Book III. *of the Troubles of* David. (4M1, 4M3, 4N1 and 4N3 read . . . *Of the Troubles* . . .; 4M3 and 4N3 read David͟); 4O1ᵛ Davideis, *A Sacred Poem, &c.* Book III.; 4O2ᵛ–4Q1 *Notes upon the third Book.*; 4Q1ᵛ–4Q2 Book IV.; 4Q2ᵛ–4T1 verso RT Davideis, *A Sacred Poem* Book IV., recto RT Book IV. *of the Troubles of* David. (4R3, 4R4, 4S3 and 4S4 read . . . *Of the Troubles* . . .); 4T2–*unsigned*1ᵛ *Notes upon the fourth Book.*; 5A1ᵛ–5C4 verso RT *DAVIDEIDOS.* Lib.I. (5C2ᵛ and 5C3ᵛ omit Lib.I.), recto RT Lib.I. *DAVIDEIDOS.* (5C1, 5C2 and 5C3 omit Lib.I.).

Copies collated: i Bodleian C 2.21 Art (large-paper presentation copy); ii Cambridge University Library (large-paper copy); iii University of Delaware, Morris Library; iv Liverpool University (Thomas Flatman's copy); v Yale, Beinecke Rare Book and MS Library. *Copies consulted*: British Library 116071. 1; Newberry Library; University of London Library, Senate House, Sterling Library; Pforzheimer copy; Princeton University Library, Taylor Collection (presentation copy signed "For My Lady Hanmer From Her Ladisps most humble and most obedient servant The Author").

The Collected Works
of Abraham Cowley

POEMS:

Viz. {
I. *MISCELLANIES.*
II. *The Mistress,* or, *Love Verses.*
III. *PINDARIQUE ODES.*
}

And IV.
Davideis,
OR, A
SACRED POEM
OF THE
TROUBLES
OF
DAVID.

Written by *A. COWLEY.*

VIRG. GEORG. 3.
----*Tentanda via est quà me quoq; possim*
Tollere humo, victorq; virûm volitare per ora.

LONDON,
Printed for *Humphrey Moseley,* at the Prince's
Arms in St *Pauls* Church-yard, M.DC.LVI.

The Text

Queen Henrietta Maria in costume for *Salmacida Spolia* (1640). Sketch by Inigo Jones, from the Devonshire Collection, Chatsworth. Reproduced by permission of the Chatsworth Settlement Trustees.

The Mistress

THE
MISTRESS;
OR,
SEVERAL COPIES
OF
LOVE-VERSES.

Written by *A.* COWLEY.

VIRG. Æn. 4.
——*Hæret lateri lethalis arundo.*

LONDON:
Printed for *Humphrey Moseley*, and are to be sold at his shop at the *Princes Arms* in St. *Pauls* Church-yard. 1656.

THE MISTRESS:

OR,

SEVERAL COPIES

OF

Love-Verses.

1. *The Request.*

1.

I'Have often wisht to love; what shall I do?
   Me still the *cruel Boy* does *spare*;
   And I a double task must bear,
First to woo *him*, and then a *Mistress* too.
   Come at last and strike for shame;
   If thou art any thing besides a *name*.
   Ile think Thee else no *God* to be;
But *Poets* rather *Gods*, who first *created Thee*.

2.

I ask not one in whom all beauties grow,
   Let me but *love*, what ere she be,
   Shee cannot seem *deform'd* to *me*;
And I would have her seem to *others* so.
   Desire takes wings and strait does fly,
   It stays not *dully* to inquire the *Why*.
   That *Happy* thing a *Lover* grown,
I shall not see with *others* Eyes, scarce with *mine own*.

Poems numbered 1-84] numbers are editorial; Text: F1

3.

If she be coy and scorn my noble fire,
   If her chill heart I cannot move,
   Why I'le *enjoy* the very *Love*,
And make a *Mistress* of mine own *Desire*.   20
   Flames their most vigorous heat do hold,
   And purest light, if compast round with *cold*:
   So when sharp *Winter* means most harm,
The springing Plants are by the *Snow* it self kept warm.

4.

But do not touch my heart, and so be gon;   25
   Strike deep thy burning arrows in:
   Lukewarmness I account a sin,
As great in *Love*, as in *Religion*.
   Come arm'd with flames, for I would prove
   All the extremities of mighty Love.   30
   Th' excess of heat is but a fable;
We know the *torrid* Zone is now found *habitable*.

5.

Among the Woods and Forrests thou art found,
   There *Bores* and *Lyons* thou dost tame;
   Is not my heart a nobler game?   35
Let *Venus, Men*; and *Beasts, Diana* wound.
   Thou dost the Birds thy *Subjects* make;
   Thy nimble *feathers* do their *wings* o'retake:
   Thou all the *Spring* their Songs dost hear,
Make *me Love* too, I'll *sing* to'thee all the *year*.   40

6.

What service can *mute Fishes* do to Thee?
   Yet against them thy Dart prevails,
   Piercing the armour of their *Scales*;
And still thy *Sea-born Mother* lives i'th' Sea.
   Dost thou deny onely to mee   45

The no-great priviledge of *Captivitie*?
   I *beg* or *challenge* here thy Bow;
Either thy *pitty* to me, or else thine *anger* show.

          7.

Come; or I'll teach the world to scorn that Bow:
   I'll teach them thousand *wholesome arts*   50
   Both to resist and cure thy darts,
More then thy skilful *Ovid* ere did know.
   Musick of sighs thou shalt not hear,
   Nor drink one wretched *Lovers* tasteful *Tear*:
   Nay, unless soon thou woundest me,   55
My Verses shall not onely *wound*, but *murther* Thee.

2. *The Thraldome.*

          1.

I *Came*, I *Saw*, and was *undon*;
  Lightning did through my bones and marrow run;
A *pointed pain* pierc'd deep my heart;
A swift, cold trembling seiz'd on every part;
   My head turn'd round, nor could it beare   5
   The *Poyson* that was enter'd there.

          2.

   So a *destroying Angels breath*
Blows in the *Plague*, and with it hasty *Death*.
   Such was the pain, did so begin
To the poor wretch, *when Legion* entred in.   10
   Forgive me, *God*, I cry'd; for I
   Flatter'd my self I was to *dye*.

3.

But quickly to my *Cost* I found,
'Twas cruel *Love*, not *Death* had made the wound:
   Death a more generous rage does use; 15
Quarter to all he conquers does refuse.
   Whilst *Love* with barbarous mercy saves
   The vanquisht lives to make them *slaves*.

4.

I am thy *slave* then; let me know,
Hard *Master*, the great task I have to do: 20
   Who pride and scorn do undergo,
In tempests and rough *Seas* thy *Galleys* row;
   They pant, and groan, and sigh, but find
   Their sighs encrease the angry wind.

5.

Like an *Egyptian Tyrant*, some 25
Thou weariest out, in building but a *Tombe*.
   Others with sad, and tedious art
Labour i'the' *Quarries* of a *stony Heart*;
   Of all the works thou does assigne
   To all the several slaves of thine, 30
Employ me, mighty *Love*, to dig the *Mine*.

3. *The Given Love.*

1.

I'll on; for what should hinder mee
From *Loving*, and *Enjoying* Thee?
Thou canst not those exceptions make,
Which *thin-sould, under-mortals* take;
That my Fate's too mean and low;
'Twere pity I should love thee so,
If that dull cause could hinder mee
In *Loving*, and *Enjoying* thee.

2.

It does not me a whit displease,
That the rich all honours seize;
That you all *Titles* make your owne,
Are *Valiant, Learned, Wise* alone.
But if you claim o're *Women* too
The power which over *Men* ye do;
If you alone must *Lovers* be;
For that, Sirs, you must pardon me.

3.

Rather then lose what does so neare
Concern my *Life*, and *Being* here,
I'll some such crooked ways invent,
As you, or your *Fore-fathers* went:
I'll flatter or oppose the *King*,
Turn *Puritan*, or *Any Thing*;
I'll force my *Mind* to arts so new:
Grow *Rich*, and *Love* as well as *You*.

4.

But rather thus let me remain,
As Man in *Paradise* did reign;
When perfect *Love* did so agree
With *Innocence* and *Povertie*.
Adam did no *Joynture* give,
Himself was *Joynture* to his *Eve*:
Untoucht with Av'arice yet or Pride,
The *Rib* came freely back to 'his *side*.

5.

A curse upon the man who taught
Women, that *Love* was to be bought;
Rather dote onely on your *Gold*;
And that with greedy av'arice hold;
For if *Woman* too submit
To that, and sell her self for it,
Fond Lover, you a *Mistress* have
Of her, that's but your *Fellow-slave*.

6.

What should those *Poets* mean of old
That made their *God* to woo in *Gold*?
Of all men sure *They* had no cause
To bind Love to such *costly Lawes*;
And yet I scarcely blame them now;
For who, alas, would not allow,
That *Women* should such gifts receive,
Could They, as He, *Be* what *They* give.

7.

If thou, my Dear, Thy self shouldst prize,
Alas, what value would suffize?
The *Spaniard* could not do't, though he
Should to both *Indies joynture thee*.

The Mistress

Thy beauties therefore wrong will take,
If thou shouldst any *bargain* make;
To *give All* will befit thee well;
But not at *Under-Rates to sell*.

8.

Bestow thy *Beauty* then on me,
Freely, as *Nature* gave't to *Thee*;
'Tis an exploded *Popish* thought
To think that *Heaven* may be *bought*.
Prayrs, Hymns, and *Praises* are the way;
And those my thankful *Muse* shall pay;
Thy *Body* in my verse enshrin'd,
Shall grow *immortal* as thy *Mind*.

9.

I'll fix thy title next in fame
To *Sacharissas* well-sung name.
So faithfully will I declare
What all thy wondrous beauties are,
That when at the last great *Assise*,
All *Women* shall together rise,
Men strait shall cast their eyes on Thee
And know at first that *Thou art Shee*.

3.61. *Hymns,*] ~ ; F1

4. *The Spring.*

1.

THough you be absent here, I needs must say
The *Trees* as beauteous are, and *flowers* as gay,
    As ever they were wont to be;
    Nay the *Birds* rural musick too
    Is as Melodious and free,   5
    As if they sung to pleasure you:
I saw a *Rose-Bud* o'pe this morn; I'll swear
The blushing *Morning* open'd not more fair.

2.

How could it be so fair, and you away?
How could the *Trees* be beauteous, *Flowers* so gay?   10
    Could they remember but last year,
    How *you* did *Them, They you* delight,
    The sprouting leaves which saw you here,
    And call'd their *Fellows* to the sight,
Would, looking round for the same sight in vain,   15
Creep back into their silent *Barks* again.

3.

Where ere you walk'd, trees were as reverend made,
As when of old *Gods* dwelt in every shade.
    Is't possible they should not know,
    What loss of honor they sustain,   20
    That thus they smile and flourish now,
    And still their former pride retain?
Dull *Creatures*! 'tis not without Cause that she,
Who fled the *God of wit*, was made a *Tree*.

4.10. so gay] sogay F1

4.

In ancient times sure they much wiser were,
When they rejoyc'd the *Thracian* verse to heare;
    In vain did *Nature* bid them stay,
    When *Orpheus* had his song begun,
    They call'd their wondring *roots* away,
    And bad them silent to him run.
How would those learned trees have followed you?
You would have drawn *Them*, and their *Poet* too.

5.

But who can blame them now? for, since you're gone,
They're here the *onely Fair*, and *Shine alone*.
    You did their *Natural Rights* invade;
    Where ever you did walk or sit,
    The thickest Bows could make no *shade*,
    Although the Sun had granted it:
The fairest *Flowers* could please no more, neer you,
Then *Painted Flowers*, set next to them, could do.

6.

When e're then you come hither, that shall bee
The time, which this to others is, to *Mee*.
    The little joys which here are now
    The name of Punishments do beare;
    When by their sight they let us Know
    How we depriv'd of greater are.
'Tis you the best of *Seasons* with you bring;
This is for *Beasts*, and that for *Men* the *Spring*.

5. *Written in Juice of Lemmon.*

1.

WHilst what I write I do not see,
 I dare thus, even to *you*, write *Poetrie*.
Ah foolish Muse, which do'st so high aspire,
 And know'st her judgement well
  How much it does thy power excell,
Yet dar'st be read by, thy just doom, the *Fire*.

2.

 Alas, thou think'st thy self secure,
Because thy form is *Innocent* and *Pure*:
Like *Hypocrites*, which seem unspotted here;
 But when they sadly come to dy,
  And the last *Fire* their Truth must try,
Scrauld o're like thee, and *blotted* they appeare.

3.

 Go then, but reverently go,
And, since thou needs must *sin, confess* it too:
Confes't, and with humility cloth thy shame;
 For thou, who else must burned bee
  An *Heretick*, if she pardon thee,
May'st like a *Martyr* then *enjoy* the *Flame*.

4.

 But if her *wisdom* grow severe,
And suffer not her *goodness* to be there;
If her large mercies cruelly it restrain;
 Be not discourag'd, but require
  A more gentle *Ordeal Fire*,
And bid her by *Loves-Flames* read it again.

5.

  Strange power of heat, thou yet dost show
Like winter earth, *naked*, or *cloath'd* with *snow*,
But, as the quickning *Sun* approaching near,
  The *Plants* arise up by degrees,
  A sudden paint adorns the trees,
And all kind *Natures Characters* appear.

6.

  So, nothing yet in Thee is seene,
But soon as *Genial heat* warms thee within,
A new-born *Wood* of various Lines there grows;
  Here buds an A, and there a B,
  Here sprouts a V, and there a T,
And all the flourishing *Letters* stand in *Rows*.

7.

  Still, seely *Paper*, thou wilt think
That all this might as well be writ with *Ink*.
Oh no; there's sense in this, and *Mysterie*;
  Thou now maist change thy *Authors* name,
  And to her *Hand* lay noble claim;
For as *She Reads*, she *Makes* the words in Thee.

8.

  Yet if thine own unworthiness
Will still, that thou art mine, not Hers, confess;
Consume thy self with Fire before her Eyes,
  And so her *Grace* or *Pitty* move;
  The *Gods*, though *Beasts* they do not Love,
Yet like them when they'r burnt in *Sacrifice*.

5.32. *lineation*] *Line 32 is aligned with line 31 in Fl.* 48. in] In Fl; ln O1

6. *Inconstancy*.

Five years ago (says *Story*) I lov'd you,
   For which you call me most *Inconstant* now;
Pardon me, Madam, you mistake the *Man*;
For I am not the same, that I was than;
No *Flesh* is now the same 'twas then in Mee;   5
And that my *Mind* is chang'd your self may see.
The same *Thoughts* to retain still, and *Intents*
Were more inconstant far; for *Accidents*
Must of all things most strangely '*Inconstant* prove,
If from one *Subject* they t'another move;   10
My *Members* then, the *Father Members* were
From whence *These* take their birth, which now are here.
If then this *Body* love what th'other did,
'Twere *Incest*; which by Nature is forbid.
You might as well this *Day* inconstant name,   15
Because the *Weather* is not still the same,
That it was yesterday: or blame the *Year*,
Cause the *Spring, Flowers*; and *Autumn, Fruit* does bear.
The *World's* a *Scene* of *Changes*, and to be
Constant, in *Nature* were *Inconstancie*;   20
For 'twere to break the *Laws* her self has made:
Our *Substances* themselves do fleet, and fade;
The most fixt Being still doth move and fly,
Swift as the wings of *Time* 'tis measur'd by.
T'imagine then that *Love* should never cease   25
(*Love* which is but the *Ornament* of these)
Were quite as senseless, as to wonder why
Beauty and *Colour* stays not when we dy.

7. *Not Fair*.

'Tis very true, I thought you once as faire,
   As women in th' *Idea* are.
Whatever here seems beauteous, seem'd to bee
   But a faint *Metaphor* of *Thee*.

But then (methoughts) there something shin'd within, 5
    Which cast this *Lustre* o're thy *skin*.
Nor could I choose but count it the *Suns Light*,
    Which made this *Cloud* appear so bright.
But since I knew thy falshood and thy pride,
    And all thy thousand faults beside; 10
A very *Moor* (methinks) plac'd near to Thee,
    White, as his *Teeth*, would seem to bee.
So men (they say) by hells delusions led,
    Have ta'ne a *Succu'bus* to their bed;
Believe it fair, and themselves happy call, 15
    Till the *cleft Foot* discovers all:
Then they start from't, half *Ghosts* themselves with fear;
    And *Devil*, as 'tis, it does *appear*.
So since against my will I found Thee *foul*,
    Deform'd and crooked in thy *Soul*, 20
My *Reason* strait did to my *Senses* shew,
    That *they* might be *mistaken* too:
Nay when the world but knows how false you are,
    There's not a man will think you faire.
Thy shape will monstrous in their fancies bee, 25
    They'l call their *Eyes* as *false* as *Thee*.
Be what thou wilt; *Hate* will present thee so,
As *Puritans* do the *Pope*, and *Papists Luther* do.

8. *Platonick Love.*

1.

INdeed I must confess,
  When *Souls* mix, 'tis an *Happiness*;
But not compleat till *Bodies* too do joyne,
And both our *Wholes* into one *Whole* combine;
But half of Heaven the *Souls* in glory tast, 5
    'Till by Love in Heaven at last,
      Their *Bodies* too are plac't.

2.

  In thy immortal part
 Man, as well as I, thou art.
But something 'tis that differs *Thee* and *Me*; 10
And we must *one* even in that *difference* be.
I Thee, both as a *man*, and *woman* prize;
  For a perfect *Love* implies
  Love in *all Capacities*.

3.

  Can that for true love pass, 15
 When a fair *woman* courts her *glass*?
Something *unlike* must in *Loves likeness* be,
His wonder is, *one*, and *Varietie*.
For he, whose *soul* nought but a *Soul* can move,
  Does a new *Narcissus* prove, 20
  And his own *Image* love.

4.

  That *souls* do beauty know,
 'Tis to the *Bodies* help they ow;
If when they know't, they strait abuse that trust,
And shut the *Body* from't, 'tis as injust, 25
As if I brought my dearest *Friend* to *see*
  My *Mistris*, and at th' instant *Hee*
  Should steal her quite from *Mee*.

9. *The Change.*

1.

Love in her Sunny Eyes does basking play;
Love walkes the pleasant Mazes of her Haire;

The Mistress

Love does on both her Lips for ever stray;
And *sows* and *reaps* a thousand *kisses* there.
In all her outward parts *Lov's* always seen;
    But, oh, He never went within.

2.

Within *Loves* foes, his greatest foes abide
    Malice, Inconstancy and Pride.
So the Earths face, Trees, Herbs and Flowers do dress,
    With other beauties numberless:
But at the *Center, Darkness* is, and *Hell*;
There wicked *Spirits*, and there the *Damned* dwell.

3.

With Me alas, quite contrary it fares;
Darkness and *Death* lies in my weeping eyes,
Despair, and Paleness in my face appeares,
And Grief, and Fear, Loves greatest enemies;
But, like the *Persian-Tyrant, Love* within
    Keeps his proud *Court*, and ne're is seen.

4.

Oh take *my Heart*, and by that means you'll prove
    Within too stor'd enough of *Love*:
Give me but Yours, I'll by that change so thrive,
    That *Love* in all my parts shall live.
So powerful is this change, it render can,
My *outside Woman*, and your *inside Man*.

9.20. Within] ~ , F1

10. *Clad all in White.*

1.

Fairest thing that shines below,
Why in this robe dost thou appear?
Wouldst thou a *white* most perfect show,
Thou must at all *no garment* wear:
Thou wilt seem much whiter so,   5
Then *Winter* when 'tis *clad* with snow.

2.

'Tis not the *Linnen* shews so fair:
Her skin shines through, and makes it bright;
So *clouds* themselves like *Suns* appear,
When the *Sun* pierces them with Light: 10
So *Lillies* in a glass enclose,
The *Glass* will seem as white as those.

3.

Thou now *one heap* of *beauty* art;
Nought outwards, or within is foul:
Condensed beams make every part;   15
Thy *Body's Cloathed* like thy *Soul*.
Thy *soul*, which does it self display,
Like a *star* plac'd i'th *Milky* way.

4.

Such robes the *Saints* departed weare,
Wooven all with *Light* divine;   20
Such their exalted *Bodies* are,
And with such full glory shine.
But they regard not mortals pain;
Men *pray*, I fear, to *both* in vain.

5.

Yet seeing thee so gently pure,
My hopes will needs continue still;
Thou wouldst not take this garment sure,
When thou hadst an intent to *kill*.
Of *Peace* and *yielding* who would doubt,
When the white *Flag* he sees hung out?

11. *Leaving Me, and then loving Many.*

SO Men, who once have cast the *Truth* away,
Forsook by *God*, do strange wild lusts obay;
So the vain *Gentiles*, when they left t'adore
One *Deity*, could not stop at thousands more.
Their zeal was senseless strait, and boundless grown;
They worshipt many a *Beast*, and many a *Stone*.
Ah fair *Apostate*! couldst thou think to flee
From *Truth* and *Goodness*, yet keep *Unitie*?
I reign'd alone; and my blest *Self* could call
The *Universal Monarch* of her *All*.
Mine, mine her fair *East-Indies* were above,
Where those *Suns* rise that chear the world of Love;
Where beauties shine like gems of richest price;
Where *Coral* grows, and every *breath* is *spice*:
Mine too her rich *West-Indies* were below,
Where *Mines* of gold and endless treasures grow.
But, as, when *the Pellœan Conqueror* dy'd,
Many small *Princes* did his *Crown* divide,
So, since my *Love* his vanquisht world forsook,
Murther'd by poysons from her falshood took,
An hundred petty *Kings* claim each their part,
And rend that glorious *Empire* of her *Heart*.

12. *My Heart discovered.*

HEr body is so gently bright,
Clear, and transparent to the sight,
(Clear as fair *Cristal* to the view,
Yet soft as that, ere *Stone* it grew;)
That through her flesh, methinks, is seen   5
The brighter *Soul* that dwells within:
Our eyes the subtile *covering* pass,
And see that *Lilie* through its *Glass.*
I through her *Breast* her *Heart* espy,
As *Souls* in *hearts* do *Souls* descry,   10
I see't with gentle *Motions* beat;
I see *Light* in't, but find no *Heat.*
Within, like *Angels* in the sky,
A thousand *guilded thoughts* do fly:
Thoughts of bright and noblest kind,   15
Fair and chaste, as *Mother-Mind.*
But, oh, what other *Heart* is there,
Which sighs and crouds to hers so neere?
'Tis all on flame, and does like *fire,*
To that, as to its *Heaven,* aspire.   20
The wounds are many in't and deep;
Still does it bleed, and still does weep.
Whose ever wretched Heart it be,
I cannot choose but grieve to see;
What *pitty* in my Breast does raign?   25
Methinks I *feel* too all its pain.
So torn, and so defac'd it lyes,
That it could ne're be known by th'eyes;
But, oh, at last I heard it grone,
And knew by th'*Voyce* that 'twas *mine owne.*   30
So poor *Alcione,* when she saw
A shipwrackt body tow'ards her draw
Beat by the waves, let fall a Tear,
Which onely then did *Pitty* wear:
But when the Corps on shore was cast,   35

12.8. its] it's F1   12.20. its] it's F1   aspire.] ~ , F1   12.26. its] it's F1
12.35. was] were F1

The Mistress

Which she her *Husband* found at last;
What should the wretched widow do?
Grief chang'd her strait; away she flew,
Turn'd to a *Bird*: and so at last shall I,
Both from my *Murther'd Heart*, and *Murth'rer* fly.   40

13. *Answer to the Platonicks.*

SO Angels love; so let them love for me;
When I'am *all soul*, such shall *my Love* too be:
Who nothing here but like a *Spirit* would do,
In a short time (believ't) will *be* one too:
But shall our Love do what in Beasts we see?   5
E'ven *Beasts* eat too, but not so well as *Wee*.
And you as justly might in thirst refuse
The use of *Wine*; because *Beasts Water* use:
They taste those pleasures, as they do their food;
Undrest they tak't, devour it *raw*, and *crude*:   10
But to us *Men*, *Love Cooks* it at his fire,
And adds the *poignant sawce* of sharp desire.
Beasts do the same: 'tis true; but ancient fame
Says, *Gods* themselves turn'd *Beasts* to do the same.
The *Thunderer*, who, without the female bed,   15
Could *Goddesses* bring forth from out his *head*,
Chose rather *Mortals* this way to create;
So much he'esteemed his *pleasure*, 'bove his *state*.
Ye talk of fires which shine, but never burn;
In this *cold world* they'll hardly serve our turn;   20
As useless to despairing Lovers grown,
As *Lambent flames*, to men i'th' *Frigid Zone*.
The *Sun* does his pure fires on earth bestow
With nuptial warmth, to bring forth things below;
Such is *Loves* noblest and divinest heat,   25
That *warms* like his, and does, like his, *beget*.
Lust you call this; a name to yours more just,
If an *Inordinate Desire* be *Lust*:
Pygmalion, loving what none can enjoy,
More *lustful* was, then the hot youth of *Troy*.   30

14. *The vain Love.*

Loving one first because she could love no body, afterwards loving her with desire.

WHat new-found *Witchcraft* was in thee,
With thine own *Cold* to *kindle Mee*?
Strange art! like him that should devise
To make a *Burning-Glass of Ice*;
When *winter*, so, the Plants would harm,   5
Her *snow* it self does keep them *warm*;
Fool that I was! who having found
A rich, and *sunny Dyamond*,
Admir'd the *hardness* of the *Stone*,
But not the *Light*, with which it shone: 10
Your brave and haughty scorn of all
Was stately, and *Monarchical*.
All *Gentleness* with that esteem'd
A *dull* and *slavish virtue* seem'd;
Should'st thou have yielded then to mee,   15
Thou'dst lost what most I lov'd in thee;
For who would *serve* one, whom he sees
That he can *Conquer* if he please?
It far'd with me, as if a *slave*
In *Triumph* lead, that does perceave   20
With what a gay majestick pride
His *Conqu'eror* through the streets does ride,
Should be *contented* with his wo,
Which makes up such a comely *show*.
I sought not from thee a return,   25
But without *Hopes* or *Fears* did burn;
My *Covetous Passion* did approve
The *Hoording* up, not *Use* of Love.
My *Love* a kind of *Dream* was grown,
A *Foolish*, but a *Pleasant* one: 30
From which I'm *wakened* now, but, oh,
Prisoners to *dye* are *wakened* so.
For now th'*Effects* of *Loving* are
Nothing, but *Longings* with *Despare*:
Despair, whose torments no men sure   35
But *Lovers*, and the *Damn'd* endure.

The Mistress

Her *scorn* I doted once upon,
Ill *Object* for *Affection*,
But since, alas, too much 'tis prov'd,
That yet 'twas *something* that I lov'd;   40
Now my desires are worse, and fly
At an *Impossibility*:
Desires, which whilst so high they soare,
Are *Proud* as that I love'd before.
What *Lover* can like me complain,   45
Who first *love'd vainly*, next *in vain*?

15. *The Soul.*

1.

IF mine *Eyes* do e're declare
They'have seen a second thing, that's *fair*;
Or *Ears*, that they have *Musick* found,
Besides thy *Voyce*, in any *Sound*;
If my *Taste* do ever meet,   5
After thy *Kiss*, with ought that's *sweet*;
If my 'abused *Touch* allow
Ought to be *smooth*, or *soft*, but *You*;
If, what seasonable Springs,
Or the Eastern Summer brings;   10
Do my *Smell* perswade at all
Ought *Perfume*, but thy *Breath* to call;
If all my *senses Objects* be
Not *contracted* into *Thee*,
And so through *Thee* more powe'rful pass,   15
As *Beams* do through a *Burning-Glass*;
If all things that in *Nature* are
Either soft, or sweet, or fair,
Be not in Thee so *'Epitomiz'd*,
That nought *material's* not compriz'd;   20
May I as worthless seem to *Thee*
As all, but *Thou*, appears to *Mee*.

2.

If I ever *Anger* know,
Till some *wrong* be done to *You*;
If *Gods* or *Kings* my *Envy* move,   25
Without their *Crowns crown'd* by thy *Love*;
If ever I an *Hope* admit,
Without thy *Image* stampt on it;
Or any *Fear*, till I begin
To find that *You'r* concern'd therein;   30
If a *Joy* ere come to mee,
That *Tastes* of any thing but *Thee*;
If any *Sorrow* touch my Mind,
Whilst You are *well*, and not *unkind*;
If I a minutes space debate,   35
Whether I shall curse and hate
The things beneath thy hatred fall,
Though all the *World, My self* and *all*;
And for *Love*; if ever I
Approach to it again so nigh,   40
As to allow a *Toleration*
To the least *glimmering Inclination*;
If thou alone do'est not controul
All those *Tyrants* of my Soul,
And to thy Beauties *ty'est* them so,   45
That constant they as *Habits* grow;
If any *Passion* of my Heart,
By any *force*, or any *art*,
Be brought to move one step from *Thee*,
Maist Thou no *Passion* have for *Mee*.   50

3.

If my busie *'Imagination*
Do not *Thee* in all things fashion;
So that all fair *Species* bee
Hieroglyphick marks of *Thee*;
If when Shee her sports does keep   55
(The lower Soul being all asleep)
She play one *Dream* with all her art,

The Mistress 41

    Where Thou hast not the longest part;
    If ought get place in my *Remembrance*,
    Without some badge of thy resemblance,   60
    So that thy parts become to me
    A kind of *Art* of *Memorie*;
    If my Understanding do
    Seek any *Knowledge* but of You,
    If she do near thy *Body* prize   65
    Her *Bodies* of *Philosophies*,
    If Shee to the *Will* do show
    Ought *desirable* but You,
    Or if *That* would not *rebel*,
    Should she'another doctrine tell;   70
    If my *Will* do not resigne
    All her *Liberty* to thine;
    If she would not follow *Thee*,
    Though *Fate* and *Thou* shouldst *disagree*;
    And if (for I a curse will give,   75
    Such as shall force thee to believe)
    My *Soul* be not entirely Thine;
    May thy dear *Body* ne're be Mine.

16. *The Passions.*

1.

FRom Hate, Fear, Hope, Anger, and Envy free,
    And all the *Passions* else that bee,
    In vain I boast of *Libertie*,
    In vain this *State* a *Freedom* call;
    Since I have *Love*, and *Love* is *all*:   5
Sot that I am, who think it fit to bragge,
That I have no *Disease* besides the *Plague*!

15.58. part;] ~ . F1   15.60. resemblance,] ~ ; F1   62. *Memorie*;] ~ . F1

2.

So in a zeal the Sons of *Israel*,
    Sometimes upon their *Idols* fell;
    And they depos'd the powers of Hell,   10
    Baal, and *Astarte* down they threw,
    And *Accaron* and *Molock* too:
All this *imperfect Piety* did no good,
Whilst yet, alas, the *Calf* of *Bethel* stood.

3.

Fondly I boast, that I have drest my *vine*   15
    With painful art, and that the *wine*
    Is of a taste rich and divine,
    Since *Love* by mixing *Poyson* there,
    Has made it worse then *vinegere*.
Love even the taste of *Nectar* changes so,   20
That *Gods* choose rather *water* here below.

4.

Fear, Anger, Hope, all Passions else that be,
    Drive this one *Tyrant* out of Me,
    And practice all your *Tyrannie*.
    The change of ills some good will do: 25
    Th'oppressed wretched *Indians* so,
Be'ing slaves by the great *Spanish Monarch* made,
Call in the *States* of *Holland* to their ayde.

17. *Wisdom*.

'Tis mighty *Wise* that you would now be thought
    With your grave *Rules* from musty *Morals* brought:
Through which some streaks too of *Divin'ity* ran,
    Partly of *Monk*, and partly *Puritan*;
With tedious *Repetitions* too y'ave tane   5
Often the name of *Vanity in vaine*.

The Mistress

Things, which, I take it, friend, you'd ne'r recite,
Should she I love, but say t'you, *Come at night*.
The *wisest King* refus'd all pleasures quite,
Till *Wisdom* from above did him enlight; 10
But when that gift his igno'rance did remove,
Pleasures he chose, and plac'd them all in *Love*.
And if by 'event the counsels may be seen,
This *wisdom* 'twas that brought the *Southern Queen*.
She came not, like a good *old Wife*, to know 15
The wholesome nature of all *plants* that grow:
Nor did so far from her own Countrey rome,
To cure scall'd heads, and broken shinns at Home;
She came for that, which more befits all *Wives*,
The art of *Giving*, not of *Saving Lives*. 20

18. *The Despair.*

1.

BEneath this gloomy shade,
By Nature onely for my sorrows made,
    I'll spend this *voyce* in cryes,
    In tears I'll wast these *eyes*
        By *Love* so vainly fed; 5
So *Lust* of old the *Deluge* punished.
    Ah wretched youth, said I!
Ah wretched youth! twice did I sadly cry:
Ah wretched youth! the fields and floods reply.

2.

    When thoughts of Love I entertain, 10
I meet no words but *Never*, and *In vain*.
    Never (alas) that dreadful name,
    Which fewels the infernal flame:
        Never, my time to come must wast;
In vain, torments the present, and the past. 15

18.14. *lineation*] *Line 14 is aligned with line 15 in F1.*

In vain, in vain! said I;
In vain, in vain! twice did I sadly cry;
In vain, in vain! the fields and floods reply.

3.

    No more shall fields or floods do so;
For I to shades more dark and silent go: 20
        All this worlds noyse appears to me
        A dull ill-acted *Comedie*:
        No comfort to my wounded sight,
In the *Suns* busie and imperti'nent Light.
        Then down I laid my head;   25
Down on cold earth; and for a while was *dead*,
And my freed *Soul* to a strange *Somewhere* fled.

4.

    Ah sottish *Soul*; said I,
When back t'his *Cage* again I saw it fly:
        Fool to resume his *broken chain*!   30
        And row his *Galley* here again!
        Fool, to that body to return
Where it condemn'd and destin'd is to *burn*!
        Once *dead*, how can it bee,
Death should a thing so pleasant seem to Thee,   35
That thou shouldst come to *live it o're again* in *Mee*?

19. *The Wish.*

1.

WEll then; I now do plainly see,
    This busie world and I shall ne'r agree;
The very *Honey* of all earthly joy

The Mistress

  Does of all meats the soonest *cloy*,
  And they (methinks) deserve my pity,
Who for it can endure the stings,
The *Crowd*, and *Buz*, and *Murmurings*
  Of this great *Hive*, the *City*.

2.

  Ah, yet, ere I descend to th'grave
May I a *small House*, and *large Garden* have!
And a *few Friends*, and *many Books*, both true,
  Both wise, and both delightful too!
  And since *Love* ne'r will from mee flee,
A *Mistress* moderately fair,
And good as *Guardian-Angels* are,
  Onely belov'd, and loving mee!

3.

  Oh, *Fountains*, when in you shall I
My self, eas'd of unpeaceful thoughts, espy?
Oh *Fields*! Oh *Woods*! when, when shall I be made
  The happy *Tenant* of your shade?
  Here's the Spring-head of *Pleasures* flood;
Here's wealthy *Natures Treasury*,
Where all the *Riches* lie, that she
  Has coyn'd and stampt for good.

4.

  Pride and *Ambition* here,
Onely in *far fetcht Metaphors* appear;
Here nought but *winds* can hurtful *Murmurs* scatter,
  And nought but *Eccho flatter*.
  The *Gods*, when they descended, hither
From heav'n did always choose their way;
And therefore we may boldly say,
  That 'tis the *way* too *thither*.

19.22. —] 01-2; *line om* F1

5.

How happy here should I,
And one dear *Shee*, live, and embracing dy?
She who is all the world, and can exclude   35
　In *desarts Solitude*.
I should have then this onely feare,
Lest men, when they my pleasures see,
Should hither throng to live like Mee,
　And so make a *City* here.   40

20. *My Dyet*.

1.

Now *by my Love*, the greatest *Oath* that is,
　None loves you half so well as I:
　I do not ask *your Love* for this;
But for heave'ns sake *believe me*, or I dy.
　No *Servant* ere but did deserve   5
His *Master* should believe that he does serve;
And I'll ask no more *wages*, though I *sterve*.

2.

'Tis no *luxurious Dyet* this, and sure
　I shall not by't too *Lusty* prove;
　Yet shall it willingly endure,   10
If't can but keep together *Life* and *Love*.
　Being your *Priso'ner* and your *slave*,
I do not *Feasts* and *Banquets* look to have,
A little *Bread* and *water*'s all I crave.

19.34. Shee,] ~ ∧ F1   20.13. lineation] Line 13 is aligned with line 12 in F1.

The Mistress

3.

O'n a *sigh* of Pity I a year can live,   15
    One *tear* will keep me twenty at least,
    Fifty a gentle *look* will give;
An hundred years on one *kind word* I'll feast:
    A thousand more will added bee,
If you an *Inclination* have for Mee;   20
And all beyond is vast *Æternitie*.

21. The Thief.

1.

THou rob'st my *Days* of bus'ness and delights,
    Of sleep thou rob'st my *Nights*;
    Ah, *lovely Thief* what wilt thou do?
    What? rob me of *Heaven too*?
    Thou even my *prayers* dost steal from me.   5
    And I, with wild *Idolatrie*,
Begin, to *God*, and end them all, to *Thee*.

2.

Is it a *Sin* to *Love*, that it should thus,
    Like an *ill Conscience* torture us?
    What ere I do, where ere I go,   10
    (None *Guiltless* ere was haunted so)
    Still, still, methinks thy face I view,
    And still thy *shape* does me pursue,
As if, not *you Me*, but *I* had *murthered You*.

3.

From *books* I strive some remedy to take,   15
    But thy *Name* all the *Letters* make;
    What ere 'tis writ, I find That there,
    Like *Points* and *Comma's* every where;

>   Me blest for this let no man hold;
>   For I, as *Midas* did of old,   20
>   *Perish* by turning ev'ry thing to *Gold*.

4.

>   What do I seek, alas, or why do I
>   Attempt in vain from thee to fly?
>   For making thee my *Deity*,
>   I gave thee then *Ubiquity*.   25
>   My pains resemble *Hell* in this;
>   The *Divine presence* there too is,
>   But to *torment* Men, not to give them *bliss*.

22. All-over, Love.

1.

> TIs well, tis well, with them (say I)
>   Whose short-liv'd *Passions* with *themselves* can dye:
>   For none can be unhappy, who
>   'Midst all his ills a time does know
> (Though ne'r so long) when he shall not be so.   5

2.

>   What ever *parts* of Me remain,
> Those *parts* will still the *Love* of thee retain;
>   For 'twas not onely in my Heart,
>   But like a *God* by pow'rful Art,
> 'Twas *all* in *all*, and *all* in *every Part*.   10

3.

>   My' *Affection* no more perish can
> Then the *First Matter* that compounds a Man.

The Mistress

    Hereafter if one *Dust* of Mee
    Mixt with anothers *substance* bee,
'Twill *Leaven* that whole *Lump* with Love of Thee.   15

4.

    Let Nature if she please disperse
My *Atoms* over all the *Universe*,
      At the last they easi'ly shall
      Themselves know, and together call;
For thy *Love*, like a *Mark*, is stamp'd on all.   20

23. *Love and Life.*

1.

NOw sure, within this twelve-month past,
I'have *lov'd* at least some twenty years or more:
    The account of *Love* runs much more fast
    Then that, with which our *Life* does score:
So though my *Life* be *short*, yet I may prove   5
    The great *Methusalem* of *Love*.

2.

    Not that *Loves* Hours or Minutes are
Shorter then those our *Being*'s measur'ed by:
    But they'r more close *compacted* far,
    And so in lesser room do ly.   10
Thin airy things extend themselves in space,
    Things *solid* take up little place.

3.

    Yet *Love*, alas, and *Life* in Me,
Are not two several things, but purely one,

    At once how can there in it be 15
      A double *different Motion*?
O yes, there may: for so the self same *Sun*,
      At once does slow and swiftly run:

4.

    Swiftly his *daily* journey' he goes,
But treads his *Annual* with a statelier pace; 20
      And does three hundred Rounds enclose
      Within one yearly Circles space.
At once with *double course* in the same *Sphære*,
      He *runs* the *Day*, and *Walks* the *year*.

5.

    When *Soul* does to *my self* refer, 25
'Tis then my *Life*, and does but slowly move
      But when it does relate to her,
      It swiftly flies, and then is *Love*.
Love's my *Diurnal* course, divided right
      'Twixt *Hope* and *Fear*, my *Day* and *Night*. 30

24. *The Bargain.*

1.

'TAke heed, take heed, thou lovely Maid,
  Nor be by *glittering ills* betraid;
Thy self for *Money*? oh, let no man know
      The *Price* of Beauty faln so *low*!
      What dangers ought'st thou not to dread, 5
When *Love* that's *Blind* is by *blind Fortune* led?

The Mistress

2.

    The foolish *Indian* that sells
    His precious Gold for beads and bells,
Does a more wise and gainful traffick hold,
    Then thou who sell'st thy self for *gold*.
    What gains in such a bargain are?
Hee'l in thy *Mines* dig better *Treasures* far.

3.

    Can *Gold*, alas, with *Thee* compare?
    The *Sun*, that makes it's not so fair;
The *Sun* which can nor *make*, nor ever *see*
    A thing so beautiful as *Thee*,
    In all the journeys he does pass,
Though the Sea serv'ed him for a *Looking-glass*.

4.

    Bold was the wretch that *cheapned* Thee,
    Since *Magus*, none so bold as he:
Thou'rt so divine a thing that *Thee to buy*,
    Is to be counted *Simony*;
    Too dear hee'l find his sordid price,
H'as forfeited *that*, and the *Benefice*.

5.

    If it be lawful Thee to *buy*,
    There's none can pay that rate but *I*;
Nothing on earth a fitting price can bee,
    But what on earth's most *like* to *Thee*.
    And that my *Heart* does onely bear;
For there *Thy self, Thy very self* is there.

6.

So much *thy self* does in me live,
    That when it for *thy self* I give,
'Tis but to change that piece of *Gold* for this,
    Whose *stamp* and *value* equal is.
And that full *Weight* too may be had,   35
My *Soul* and *Body*; two *Grains* more, I'll add.

25. *The Long Life.*

1.

Love from *Times* wings hath stoln the *feathers* sure,
    He has, and put them to his *own*;
For *Hours* of late as long as *Days* endure,
    And very *Minutes, Hours* are grown.

2.

The various *Motions* of the turning *Year*,   5
    Belong not now at all to Mee:
Each *Summers Night* does *Lucies* now appear,
    Each *Winters* Day *St. Barnabie.*

3.

How long a space, since first I lov'd, it is?
    To look into a *glass* I fear;   10
And am surpriz'd with wonder when I miss
    Grey-hairs and *wrinkles* there.

24.35. *lineation*] Line 35 is aligned with line 36 in *F1.*
25.11. miss] ~ , F1

The Mistress

4.

Th'old *Patriarchs age* and not their *happi'ness* too,
    Why does hard fate to us restore?
Why does *Loves Fire* thus to *Mankind* renew,
    What the *Flood washt* away before?

5.

Sure those are happy people that complain,
    O'th' *shortness* of the days of man:
Contract mine, Heaven, and bring them back again
    To th'ordinary *Span*.

6.

If when your gift, *long Life*, I disapprove,
    I too ingratefull seem to bee;
Punish me justly, Heaven; make Her to love,
    And then 'twill be *too short* for Mee.

26. *Counsel.*

1.

GEntly, ah gently, Madam, touch
    The wound, which you your self have made;
That pain must needs be very much,
    Which makes me of *your hand* afraid.
Cordials of *Pity* give me now,
For I too weak for *Purgings* grow.

2.

Do but a while with patience stay;
    For *Counsel* yet will do no good,
'Till *Time*, and *Rest*, and *Heav'n* allay

    The vi'olent burnings of my blood,   10
For what effect from this can flow,
To chide men *drunk*, for being so?

3.

Perhaps the *Physick*'s good you give,
    But ne'r to me can useful prove;
Med'cines may *Cure*, but not *Revive*;   15
    And I'am not *Sick*, but *Dead* in Love.
In *Loves Hell*, not his *World*, am I;
At once I *Live*, am *Dead*, and *Dy*.

4.

What new found *Rhetorick* is thine?
    Ev'n thy *Diswasions* me *perswade*,   20
And thy great power does clearest shine,
    When thy *Commands* are *disobey'd*.
In vain thou bidst me to forbear;
Obedience were *Rebellion* here.

5.

Thy *Tongue* comes in, as if it ment   25
    Against thine *Eyes* t'assist my *Heart*;
But different far was his intent:
    For straight the *Traytor* took their part,
And by this new foe I'm bereft
Of all that *Little* which was left.   30

6.

The act I must confess was wise,
    As a dishonest act could be:
Well knew the *Tongue* (alas) your *Eyes*
    Would bee too strong for *That*, and *Me*,
And part o'th' *Triumph* chose to *get*,   35
Rather then *be a part* of it.

26.28. part,] ~ . F1   34. *Me*,] ~ . F1

27. *Resolved to be beloved.*

1.

'Tis true, I'have lov'd already three or four,
    And shall three or four hundred more;
    I'll love each fair one that I see,
Till I find one at last that shall *love Mee*.

2.

That shall my *Canaan* be, the fatal soil,
    That ends my wandrings, and my toil.
    I'll settle there and happy grow;
The *Countrey* does with *Milk* and *Honey* flow.

3.

The *Needle* trembles so, and turns about,
    Till it the *Northern Point* find out:
    But constant then and fixt does prove,
Fixt, that his dearest *Pole* as soon may *move*.

4.

Then may my *Vessel* torn and shipwrackt be,
    If it put forth again to *Sea*:
    It never more abroad shall rome,
Though't could next voyage bring the *Indies* home.

5.

But I must sweat in *Love*, and labour yet,
    Till I a *Competency* get.
    They'r slothful fools who leave a Trade,
Till they a moderate Fortune by't have made.

6.

  Variety I ask not; give me One
    To live perpetually upon.
   The person *Love* does to us fit,
  Like *Manna*, hath the *Taste* of all in it.

28. *The Same.*

1.

 FOr Heavens sake, what d'you mean to do?
 Keep me, or *let me go*, one of the two;
Youth and *warm hours* let me not idlely loose,
  The *little Time* that Love does choose;
  If always here I must not stay,   5
   Let me be gone, whilst yet 'tis *day*;
Lest I faint, and benighted lose my way.

2.

  'Tis dismal, *One so* long to love
In vain, till to love *more* as vain must prove:
To hunt so long one nimble prey, till we   10
  Too weary to take others be;
  Alas, 'tis folly to remain,
  And waste our *Army* thus in vane,
Before a *City* which will ne'r be tane.

3.

  At several hopes wisely to fly,   15
Ought not to be esteem'd *Inconstancy*;
'Tis more *Inconstant* always to *pursue*,
  A thing that always *flies* from you;
  For that at last may meet a bound,
  But no end can to this be found,   20
'Tis nought but a perpetual fruitless *Round*.

28.10. one] on F1

The Mistress

4.

> When it does *Hardness* meet and *Pride*,
> My *Love* does then *rebound* t'another side;
> But if it ought that's *soft* and *yielding* hit;
>   It lodges there, and stays in it.   25
>   Whatever 'tis shall first love me,
>   That it my *Heaven* may truly be;
> I shall be sure to giv't *Eternity*.

29. *The Discovery.*

1.

> **B**Y 'Heaven I'll tell her boldly that 'tis Shee;
> Why should she asham'd or angry bee,
>   To be belov'd by Mee?
>   The Gods may give their Altars o're;
>   They'l smoak but seldom any more,   5
> If none but *Happy Men* must them adore.

2.

> The *Lightning* which tall *Oaks* oppose in vain,
>   To strike sometime does not disdain
>   The humble *Furzes* of the Plain.
>   She being so *high*, and I so *low*,   10
>   Her power by this does greater show,
> Who at such *distance* gives so *sure* a blow.

3.

> Compar'd with her all things so worthless prove,
>   That nought on earth can tow'ards her move,
>   Till't be *exalted* by her *Love*.   15
>   Æqual to her, alas, there's none;
>   She like a *Deity* is growne;
> That must *Create*, or else must be *alone*.

29.9. humble] humbly F1

4.

>If there be man, who thinks himself so high,
>>As to pretend *æquality*,   20
>>>*He* deserves her less, then *I*;
>>>For he would *cheat* for his relief;
>>And one would give with lesser grief,
>To'an *undeserving Beggar*, then a *Thief*.

30. *Against Fruition.*

NO; thou'rt a fool, I'll swear, if ere thou grant:
Much of my *Veneration* thou must want,
When once thy *kindness* puts my *Igno'rance* out;
For a *learn'd Age* is always least devout.
Keep still thy distance; for at once to me   5
Goddess and *Woman* too, thou canst not be;
Thou'rt *Queen* of all that sees thee; and as such
Must neither *Tyrannize*, nor *yield* too much;
Such *freedoms* give as may admit *Command*,
But keep the *Forts* and *Magazines* in thine hand.   10
Thou'rt yet a *whole world* to me, and do'est fill
My large ambition; but 'tis dang'rous still,
Lest I like the *Pellæan Prince* should be,
And weep for *other worlds* hav'ing conquer'd *thee*;
When *Love* has taken all thou hast away,   15
His strength by too much *riches* will decay.
Thou in my *Fancy* dost much higher stand,
Then *Women* can be plac'd by *Natures* hand;
And I must needs, I'm sure, a loser be,
To change *Thee*, as *Thou'rt there*, for *very Thee*.   20
Thy sweetness is so much within me plac'd,
That shouldst thou *Nectar* give, t'would spoil the taste.
Beauty at first moves wonder, and delight;
'Tis *Natures juggling trick* to cheat the sight,
We 'admire it, whilst unknown, but after more   25
Admire our selves, for liking it before.
Love, like a greedy *Hawk*, if we give way,
Does overgorge himself, with his own *Prey*;

30.10. the] rhe F1

> Of very *Hopes* a surfeit hee'll sustain,
> Unless by *Fears* he cast them up again: 30
> His spirit and sweetness dangers keep alone;
> If once he lose his *sting*, he grows a *Drone*.

31. *Love undiscovered.*

1.

> I; Others may with safety tell
>   The moderate Flames, which in them dwell;
> And either find some *Med'icine* there,
> Or cure themselves ev'en by *Despair*;
> My Love's so great, that it might prove   5
> Dang'erous, to tell her that I Love.
> So tender is my wound, it must not bear
> Any salute, though of the kindest ayr.

2.

> I would not have *her know* the pain,
> The Torments for her I sustain: 10
> Lest too much *goodness* make her throw
> Her *Love* upon a *Fate* too low.
> Forbid it Heaven my *Life* should be
> Weigh'd with her least *Conveniencie*:
> No; let me *perish* rather with my grief,   15
> Then to her *disadvantage* find *relief*.

3.

> Yet when I dye, my last breath shall
> Grow bold, and plainly tell her all.
> Like covetous Men who ne'r descry,
> Their dear hid *Treasures* till they *dy*.   20

31.10. sustain:] ~ . *(or a lightly inked italic colon)* F1

Ah fairest Maid, how will it chear
My *Ghost*, to get from *Thee* a *tear*!
But take heed; for if me thou *Pitiest* then,
Twenty to one but I shall *live* agen.

32. *The given Heart.*

1.

I Wonder what those *Lovers* mean, who say,
    They have giv'en their *Hearts* away.
  Some good kind *Lover* tell me how;
For mine is but a *Torment* to me now.

2.

If so it be, one place both hearts contain,
    For what do they complain?
  What courtesie can Love do more,
Then to *joyn Hearts*, that *parted* were before?

3.

Wo to her stubborn *Heart*, if once mine com
    Into the self same room;
  'Twill tear and blow up all within,
Like a *Granado* shot into a *Magazin*.

4.

Then shall *Love* keep the ashes, and torn parts,
    Of both our broken *Hearts*:
  Shall out of both *one* new one make,
From hers, th'*Allay*; from mine, the *Mettal* take.

The Mistress

5.

For of her heart, he from the flames will find
    But little left behind:
    Mine onely will remain entire;
No *dross* was there, to perish in the *Fire*.   20

33. *The Prophet.*

1.

TEach *me* to *Love*? go teach thy self more wit;
    I chief *Professor* am of it.
    Teach craft to *Scots*, and thrift to *Jews*,
    Teach boldness to the Stews;
In *Tyrants* Courts teach supple *flattery*,   5
Teach *Jesuits* that have *travell'd* far, to Ly.
    Teach fire to burn, and winds to blow,
    Teach restless fountains how to flow,
    Teach the dull earth, fixt, to abide,
Teach *Woman-kind* inconstancy and Pride.   10
See if your diligence here will useful prove;
    But, pr'ithee, teach not *me* to *Love*.

2.

The *God* of *Love*, if such a thing there be,
    May learn to love from *Me*.
    He who does boast that he has bin   15
    In every Heart since *Adams* sin,
I'll lay my *Life*, nay *Mistress* on't, that's more;
I'll teach him things he never knew before;
    I'll teach him a *Receipt* to make
    Words that *weep*, and *Tears* that *speak*,   20
    I'll teach him *Sighs*, like those in *Death*,

33.2. *lineation*] *Line 2 is aligned beneath the* E *in line 1 in F1.*   6. Jesuits] Jesuit's F1.   12. *lineation*] *Line 12 is aligned with line 11 in F1.*

At which the *Souls* go out too with the *breath*:
Still the *Soul stays,* yet still does from me *run*;
    As *Light* and *Heat* does with the *Sun.*

    3.

'Tis I who *Loves Columbus* am; 'tis I,   25
    Who must new *Worlds* in it descry:
    Rich *Worlds,* that yield of *Treasure* more,
    Then all that has bin known before.
And yet like *his* (I fear) *my Fate* must be,
To find them out for *others*; not for *Me.*   30
    Mee Times to come, I know it, shall
    Loves last and greatest *Prophet* call:
    But, ah, what's that, if she refuse
To hear the wholesome *Doctrines* of my *Muse*?
If to my share the *Prophets fate* must come;   35
    Hereafter *Fame,* here *Martyrdome.*

34. *The Resolution.*

    1.

THe *Devil* take those foolish men,
    Who gave you first such pow'rs;
    We stood on even grounds till then;
If any *odds, Creation* made it *ours.*

    2.

For shame let these weak chains be broke;   5
    Let's our slight bonds, like *Sampson*, tear;
    And nobly cast away that yoke,
Which *we* nor our *Forefathers* ere could bear.

33.33. refuse] ~, F1

The Mistress

3.

French Laws forbid the *female Raign*;
    Yet *Love* does them to *slavery* draw,   10
    Alas, if wee'll our rights maintain,
'Tis all *Mankind* must make a *Salique Law*.

35. *Called Inconstant.*

1.

HA! ha! you think y'have *kill'd* my *fame*;
By this not *understood*, yet *common Name*:
A *Name*, that's *full* and *proper* when assign'd
    To *Womankind*:
    But when you call *us* so,   5
It can at best but for a *Met'aphor* go.

2.

    Can you the shore *Inconstant* call,
Which still as *Waves* pass by, embraces *all*?
That had as leif the same waves always love,
    Did they not from him *move*?   10
    Or can you fault with *Pilots* find
For changing course, yet never blame the *wind*?

3.

    Since *drunk* with vanity you fell:
The things turn *round* to you that stedfast dwell;
And you your self, who *from us* take your flight,   15
    Wonder to find us out of sight.
    So the same errour seizes you,
As *Men in motion* think the *Trees* move too.

35.3. *Name,*] ~ ; F1

36. *The Welcome.*

1.

GO, let the *fatted Calf* be kill'd;
  My *Prodigal's* come home at last;
With noble resolutions fill'd,
    And fill'd with sorrow for the past.
    No more will burn with *Love* or *Wine*:   5
But quite has left his *Women* and his *Swine*.

2.

Welcome, ah welcome my poor *Heart*;
    Welcome; I little thought, I'll swear,
('Tis now so long since we did part)
    Ever again to see thee here: 10
    Dear *Wanderer*, since from me you fled,
How often have I heard that Thou wer't *dead*.

3.

Hast thou not found each womans brest
    (The *Lands* where thou hast travelled)
Either by *Savages* possest,   15
    Or wild, and *uninhabited*?
    What joy couldst take, or what repose
In *Countreys* so *unciviliz'd* as those?

4.

Lust, the scorching *Dog-star*, here
    Rages with immoderate *heat*;   20
Whil'st *Pride* the rugged *Northern Bear*,
    In others makes the *Cold* too great.
    And where these are temp'rate known,
The Soyl's all barren *Sand*, or rocky *Stone*.

The Mistress

5.

When once or twice you chanc'd to view
    A rich, well-govern'd Heart,
Like *China*, it admitted You
    But to the *Frontier-part*.
    From *Par'adise* shut for evermore,
What good is't that an *Angel* kept the *Door*?

6.

Well fare the *Pride*, and the *Disdain*
    And *Vanities* with *Beauty* joyn'd,
I ne'r had seen this Heart again,
    If any *Fair one* had been kind:
    My *Dove*, but once let loose, I doubt
Would ne'r return, had not the *Flood* been out.

37. *The Heart fled again.*

1.

FAlse, foolish *Heart*! didst thou not say,
    That thou wouldst never leave me more?
Behold again 'tis fled away;
    Fled as far from me as before.
    I strove to bring it back again,
I cry'd and hollow'd after it in vain.

2.

Even so the gentle *Tyrian Dame*,
    When neither *Grief* nor *Love* prevail,
Saw the dear object of her flame,
    Th'ingrateful *Trojan* hoist his sail:
    Aloud she call'd to him to stay;
The wind bore *him*, and her lost *words* away.

3.

The doleful *Ariadne* so,
    On the wide shore forsaken stood:
False Theseus, *whither dost thou go*?   15
    Afar false *Theseus* cut the flood.
    But *Bacchus* came to her relief;
Bacchus himselfe's too weak to ease my grief.

4.

Ah senseless *Heart*, to take no rest,
    But travel thus eternally!   20
Thus to be *froz'n* in every *breast*!
    And to be *scorcht* in every *Eye*!
    Wandring about like wretched *Cain*,
Thrust out, *ill us'd* by all, but by none *slain*!

5.

Well; since thou wilt not here remain,   25
    I'll ev'en to live without Thee try;
My *Head* shall take the greater pain,
    And all *thy duties* shall supply;
    I can more easi'ly live I know
Without *Thee*, then without a *Mistris Thow*.   30

38. *Womens Superstition.*

1.

OR I'm a very *Dunce*, or *Womankind*
   Is a most unintelligible thing:
I can no *Sense*, nor no *Contexture* find,
    Nor their loose parts to *Method* bring,
    I know not what the *Learn'd* may see,   5
But they'r strange *Hebrew things* to *Mee*.

2.

By *Customs* and *Traditions* they live,
And foolish *Ceremonies* of antick date,
We *Lovers*, new and better *Doctrines* give.
    Yet they continue obstinate;
    Preach we, *Loves Prophets*, what we will,
    Like *Jews*, they keep their *old Law* still.

3.

Before their *Mothers Gods*, they fondly fall,
Vain *Idol-Gods* that have no Sense nor Mind:
Honour's their *Ashtaroth*, and *Pride* their *Bâal*,
    The *Thundring Bâal* of Woman-kind,
    With twenty other *Devils* more,
    Which *They*, as We do *Them*, adore.

4.

But then, like Men both *Covetous* and *Devout*,
Their costly *Superstition* loath t'omit,
And yet more loath to issue Moneys out,
    At their own charge to furnish it.
    To these expensive *Deities*,
    The *Hearts* of Men they *sacrifice*.

38.15. *Bâal*] *Baal* F1   16. *Bâal*] *Báal* F1   Woman-kind,] ~ . F1

39. *The Soul* [II].

1.

SOme dull *Philos'opher* when he hears me say,
    My *Soul* is from me fled away;
Nor has of late inform'd my *Body* here,
    But in anothers breast does ly,
    That neither *Is*, nor *will* be *I*,
As a *Form Servient* and *Assisting* there;

2.

Will cry, *Absurd*! and ask me, how I live:
    And *Syllogisms* against it give;
A curse on all your vain *Philosophies*,
    Which on weak *Natures Law* depend,
    And know not how to comprehend
Love and *Religion*, those great *Mysteries*.

3.

Her *Body* is my *Soul*; laugh not at this,
    For by my *Life* I swear it is.
'Tis that preserves my *Being* and my *Breath*,
    From that proceeds all that I *do*,
    Nay all my *Thoughts* and *speeches* too,
And *separation* from it is my *Death*.

---

39. *title.* [II] *ed.*   6. there;] ~ . F1

40. *Eccho.*

1.

Tir'ed with the rough denials of my prayer,
From that hard she whom I obey,
I come, and find a *Nymph*, much gentler here,
    That gives *consent* to all I say.
    Ah gentle *Nymph* who lik'st so well,   5
In hollow, *solitary Caves* to dwell,
    Her *Heart* being such, into it go,
And do but once from thence answer me *so*.

2.

Complaisant Nymph, who do'est thus kindly share
    In griefs, whose cause thou do'est not know!   10
Hadst thou but *Eyes*, as well as *Tongue* and *Ear*,
    How much *compassion* wouldst thou show!
    Thy *flame*, whilst *living*, or a *flower*,
Was of less beauty, and less rav'ishing power;
    Alas, I might as easilie,   15
Paint thee to *her*, as *describe Her* to *Thee*.

3.

By repercussion *Beams* engender *Fire*,
    Shapes by reflexion *shapes* beget;
The *voyce* it self, when stopt, does back retire,
    And a new *voyce* is made by it.   20
    Thus things by *opposition*
The gainers grow; my barren *Love* alone,
    Does from her stony breast rebound,
Producing neither *Image, Fire,* nor *Sound*.

41. *The rich Rival.*

1.

THey say youre angry, and rant mightilie,
    Because I love the same as you;
    Alas! you're very *rich*; 'tis true;
But prithee Fool, what's that to *Love*, and *Mee*?
        You' have *Land*, and *Money*, let that serve;
And know you' have more by that then you *deserve*.

2.

When next I see my *fair One*, she shall know,
    How worthless thou art of her bed;
    And wretch, I'll strike thee *dumb* and *dead*,
With noble *verse* not understood by you;
        Whilst thy sole *Rhetorick* shall be
Joynture, and *Jewels*, and *Our Friends agree*.

3.

Pox o' your friends, that dote and Domineere:
    Lovers are better *Friends* then they:
    Let's those in other things obey;
The *Fates*, and *Stars*, and *Gods* must govern here.
        Vain names of *Blood*! in *Love* let none
Advise with any *Blood*, but with their *owne*.

4.

'Tis that which bids me this bright *Maid* adore;
    No other thought has had access!
    Did she now *beg* I'd love no *less*,
And were she' an *Empress*, I should love no *more*;
        Were she as just and true to Mee,
Ah, simple soul, what would become of *Thee*!

42. *Against Hope*.

1.

HOpe, whose weak *Being* ruin'd is,
Alike if it *succeed*, and if it *miss*;
Whom *Good* or *Ill* does æqually confound,
And both the *Horns* of *Fates Dilemma* wound!
    Vain *shadow*! which dost vanish quite,   5
    Both at full *Noon*, and perfect *Night*!
The stars have not a *possibility*
    Of blessing Thee;
If things then from their *End* we happy call,
'Tis *Hope* is the most *Hopeless* thing of all.   10

2.

    Hope, thou bold *Taster* of Delight,
Who whilst thou shouldst but *taste, devour'st* it quite!
Thou bringst us an *Estate*, yet leav'st us *Poore*,
By clogging it with *Legacies* before!
    The *Joys* which we *entire* should wed,   15
    Come *deflowr'd Virgins* to our bed;
Good fortunes without gain imported bee,
    Such mighty *Custom's* paid to Thee.
For *Joy*, like *Wine*, kept close does better taste;
If it take air before, his spirits waste.   20

3.

    Hope, Fortunes cheating *Lotterie*!
Where for one *prize* an hundred *blanks* there be;
Fond *Archer, Hope*, who tak'st thy aim so far,
That still or *short* or *wide* thine arrows are!

42.4. wound!] *In F1, the exclamation mark is italic and inverted.*

>   Thin, empty *Cloud*, which th'eye deceives 25
>   With shapes that our own *Fancy* gives!
>   A *Cloud*, which gilt and painted now appears,
>   But must drop presently in *tears*!
>   When thy false beams o're *Reasons* light prevail,
>   By *Ignes fatui* for *North-Stars* we sail. 30

4.

>   *Brother* of *Fear*, more gaily clad!
>   The *merr'ier Fool* o'th' two, yet quite as *Mad*:
>   Sire of *Repentance, Childe* of fond *Desire*!
>   That blow'st the *Chymicks*, and the *Lovers* fire!
>   Leading them still insensibly'on 35
>   By the strange *witchcraft* of *Anon*!
>   By *Thee* the one does changing *Nature* through
>   Her endless *Labyrinths* pursue,
>   And th'other chases *Woman*, whilst She goes
>   More ways and turns then *hunted Nature* knows. 40

43. *For Hope.*

1.

> Hope, of all Ills that men endure,
> The onely cheap and *Universal Cure*!
> Thou *Captives freedom*, and Thou *sick Mans Health*!
> Thou *Losers Victo'ry*, and thou *Beggars wealth*!
>   Thou *Manna*, which from Heav'n we eat, 5
>   To every *Taste* a several *Meat*!
> Thou strong *Retreat*! thou sure *entail'd Estate*,
>   Which nought has power to *alienate*!
> Thou pleasant, *honest Flatterer*! for none
> *Flatter unhappy Men*, but thou alone! 10

The Mistress

2.

    Hope, thou *First-fruits* of *Happiness*!
Thou gentle *Dawning* of a bright *Success*!
Thou good *Prepar'ative*, without which our Joy
Does *work* too strong, and whilst it cures, destroy;
        Who out of *Fortunes* reach dost stand,   15
        And art a blessing *still in hand*!
Whilst *Thee*, her *Earnest-Money* we retain,
        We certain are to gain,
Whether she'her *bargain* break, or else fulfill;
Thou onely *good*, not worse, for *ending* ill!   20

3.

    Brother of *Faith*, 'twixt whom and Thee
The joys of *Heav'n* and *Earth* divided bee!
Though *Faith* be *Heir*, and have the *fixt estate*,
Thy *Portion* yet in *Moveables* is great.
        Happiness it self's all one   25
        In *Thee*, or in *possession*!
Onely the *Future's Thine*, the *present His*!
        Thine's the more hard and noble bliss;
Best *apprehender* of our joys, which hast
So long a *reach*, and yet canst hold so *fast*!   30

4.

    Hope, thou sad *Lovers* onely *Friend*!
Thou *Way* that maist dispute it with the *End*!
For *Love* I fear's a fruit that does delight
The *taste* it self less then the *Smell and Sight*.
        Fruition more deceitful is   35
        Then *Thou* canst be, when thou dost *miss*;
Men leave thee by *obtaining*, and strait flee
        Some other way again to *Thee*;
And that's a pleasant *Countrey*, without doubt,
To which all soon return that travel out.   40

44. *Loves Ingratitude.*

1.

I Little thought, thou fond *ingrateful Sin*,
   When first I let thee in,
   And gave thee but a part
   In my unwary *Heart*,
   That thou wouldst ere have grown,   5
So *false* or *strong* to make it all thine own.

2.

At mine own *breast* with care I fed thee still,
   Letting thee suck thy fill,
   And daintily I nourisht Thee
   With *Idle thoughts* and *Poetrie*!   10
   What ill returns do'st thou allow?
I *fed thee* then, and thou dost *sterve me* now.

3.

There was a time, when thou wast *cold* and *chill*,
   Nor had'st the power of doing ill;
   Into my *bosom* did I take,   15
   This frozen and benummed *Snake*,
   Not fearing from it any harm;
But now it *stings* that brest which made *it warm*.

4.

What cursed *weed's* this *Love*! but one *grain* sow,
   And the whole *field* 'twill overgrow;   20
   Strait will it choak up and devour

44.11. do'st] do st F1.

The Mistress

Each wholesome *herb* and beauteous *flour*!
Nay unless something soon I do,
'Twill kill I fear my very *Lawrel* too.

5.

But now all's gon, I now, alas, complain, 25
  Declare, protest, and threat in vain.
  Since by my own *unforc'd consent*,
  The *Traytor* has my *Government*,
  And is so settled in the *Throne*,
That 'twere *Rebellion* now to claim *mine owne*. 30

45. *The Frailty.*

1.

I Know 'tis *sordid*, and 'tis *low*;
  (All this as well as you I know)
  Which I so hotly now pursue;
  (I know all this as well as you)
  But whilst this cursed flesh I beare, 5
And all the *Weakness*, and the *Baseness* there,
Alas, alas, it will be always so.

2.

  In vain, exceedingly in vain
  I rage sometimes, and bite my *Chain*;
  For to what purpose do I bite 10
  With Teeth which ne'r will break it quite?
  For if the chiefest *Christian Head*,
Was by this sturdy *Tyrant buffeted*,
What wonder is it, if *weak I* be *slain*?

---

45. *title.* Frailty.] ~ , F1
45. *A third stanza, printed in 01–2, reads:* As, when the Sunne appeares, / The Morning thicknesse cleares; / So, when my thoughts let sadnesse in, / And a new Morning does begin, / If any Beauties piercing ray / Strike through my Trembling Eyes a suddaine day; / All those grave sullen Vapours melt in Teares.

46. *Coldness.*

1.

As *water* fluid is, till it do grow
    Solid and fixt by *Cold*;
So in *warm Seasons Love* does loosely flow,
    Frost onely can it hold.
A *Womans rigour*, and disdain,   5
Does his swift course restrain,

2.

Though *constant*, and *consistent* now it bee,
    Yet, when kind beams appear,
It melts, and glides apace into the Sea,
    And loses it self there.   10
So the *Suns* amorous play
Kisses the *Ice* away.

3.

You may in *Vulgar Loves* find always this;
    But my *Substantial Love*
Of a more firm, and perfect *Nature* is;   15
    No weathers can it move:
Though *Heat* dissolve the *Ice again*,
The *Crystal* solid does remain.

46.11. play] ~ , F1

47. *The Injoyment.*

1.

THen like some wealthy *Island thou* shalt ly;
    And like the *Sea* about it, *I*;
Thou like fair *Albion*, to the Sailors Sight,
Spreading her beauteous Bosom all in *White*:
    Like the kind *Ocean* I will bee,
With loving *Arms* for ever clasping Thee.

2.

But I'll embrace Thee gentli'er far then so;
    As their fresh *Banks* soft *Rivers* do,
Nor shall the *proudest Planet* boast a power
Of making my *full Love* to *ebb* one hour;
    It never *dry* or *low* can prove,
Whilst thy unwasted *Fountain* feeds my Love.

3.

Such Heat and Vigour shall our *Kisses* bear,
    As if like *Doves* we'engendred there.
No *bound* nor *rule* my pleasures shall endure,
In Love there's none too much an *Epicure*.
    Nought shall my hands or Lips controul;
I'll kiss Thee *through*, I'll kiss thy *very Soul*.

4.

Yet nothing, but the *Night* our sports shall know;
    Night that's both *blind* and *silent* too.
Alpheus found not a more secret trace,
His lov'd *Sicanian Fountain* to embrace,
    Creeping so far beneath the Sea,
Then I will do t'*enjoy*, and *feast* on Thee.

5.

 Men, out of *Widsom*; *Women*, out of *Pride*,   25
  The pleasant Thefts of Love do *hide*.
That may secure thee; but thou'hast yet from Me
A more *infallible Securitie*.
   For there's no danger I should tell
The Joys, which are to Me *unspeakable*.   30

48. *Sleep.*

1.

IN vain, thou drousie God, I thee invoak;
 For thou, who dost from fumes arise,
  Thou, who *Mans Soul* dost overshade
  With a thick *Cloud* by Vapours made,
 Canst have no power to shut his eyes,   5
  Or passage of his *Spi'rits* to choak,
Whose *flame's* so pure, that it sends up no *smoak*.

2.

Yet how do *Tears* but from some *Vapours* rise?
 Tears, that bewinter all my Year?
  The fate of *Egypt* I sustain,   10
  And never feel the dew of *Rain*,
 From *Clouds* which in the Head appear,
  But all my too much *Moysture* ow,
To *overflowings* of the *Heart* below.

48.5. lineation] *Line 5 is set from the left margin in F1.*

The Mistress

3.

Thou, who dost *Men* (as Nights to *Colours* do)   15
   Bring all to an *Equality*:
     Come, thou *just God*, and *æqual mee*
     A while to my disdainful *Shee*;
   In that condition let me ly;
     Till *Love* does the same favour shew;   20
Love æquals all a better way then *You*.

4.

Then never more shalt thou be'invoakt by me;
   Watchful as *Spirits*, and *Gods* I'll prove:
     Let her but grant, and then will I,
     Thee and thy *Kinsman Death* defy.   25
   For betwixt *Thee* and them that *love*,
     Never will an agreement bee;
Thou scorn'st th'*Unhappy*; and the *Happy*, Thee.

49. *Beauty*.

1.

BEauty, thou wilde fantastick Ape,
   Who dost in ev'ry Country change thy shape!
Here black, there brown, here tawny, and there white;
Thou *Flatt'rer* which compli'st with every sight!
     Thou *Babel* which confoundst the Ey   5
With unintelligible *variety*!
     Who hast no certain *What*, nor *Where*,
But vary'st still, and dost thy self declare
   Inconstant, as thy *she-Possessors* are.

48.17. *God*,] ~ ; F1.   49.9. lineation] *Line 9 is irregularly aligned, as above, in F1.*

2.

  Beauty, Loves Scene and *Maskerade*,   10
So gay by *well-plac'd Lights*, and *Distance* made;
False *Coyn*, with which th'*Impostor* cheats us still;
The *stamp* and *Colour* good, but *Mettal* ill!
  Which *Light*, or *Base* we find, when we
Weigh by *enjoyment* and examine Thee!   15
  For though thy *Being* be but *show*,
'Tis chiefly *Night* which men to Thee allow:
And choose *t'enjoy* Thee, when *Thou lest art Thou*.

3.

  Beauty, Thou *active, passive* Ill!
Which *dy'st* thy self as fast as thou dost *kill*!   20
Thou *Tulip*, who thy stock in paint dost waste,
Neither for *Physick* good, nor *Smell*, nor *Taste*.
  Beauty, whose *Flames* but *Meteors* are,
Short-liv'd and low, though thou wouldst seem a *Starre*,
  Who dar'st not thine own *Home* descry,   25
Pretending to dwell richly in the *Eye*,
When thou, alas, dost in the *Fancy* lye.

4.

  Beauty, whose *Conquests* still are made
O're Hearts by *Cowards* kept; or else *betray'd*!
Weak Victor! who thy self destroy'd must bee   30
When *sickness storms*, or *Time besieges* Thee!
  Thou'unwholesome *Thaw* to *frozen Age*!
Thou strong *wine*, which youths *Feaver* dost enrage,
  Thou *Tyrant* which leav'st no man free!
Thou subtle *thief*, from whom nought safe can be!   35
Thou *Murth'rer* which hast *kill'd*, and *Devil* which wouldst *Damn me*.

50. *The Parting.*

1.

AS Men in *Groen-land* left beheld the *Sun*
    From their *Horizon* run;
      And thought upon the sad half year
Of *Cold* and *Darkness* they must suffer there:

2.

So on my parting *Mistress* did I look,
    With such swoln eyes my farewel took;
      Ah, my fair *Star*! said I;
Ah those blest Lands to which *bright Thou* dost fly!

3.

In vain the Men of *Learning* comfort me;
    And say I'm in a warm *degree*;
      Say what they please; I say and swear
'Tis beyond *eighty* at least, if you'r not here.

4.

It is, it is; I tremble with the *Frost*,
    And know that I the *Day* have lost;
      And those wilde things which *Men* they call,
I find to be but *Bears* or *Foxes* all.

50.4. there:] ~ . F1

5.

Return, return, gay *Planet* of mine *East*,
    Of all that shines Thou much the *Best*!
    And as thou now *descend'st to Sea*;
More fair and fresh *rise* up from thence to Mee.   20

6.

Thou, who in many a Propriety,
    So truly art the *Sun* to Mee,
    Adde one more *likeness*, which I'm sure you can,
And let *Me* and *my Sun* beget a *Man*.

51. *My Picture.*

1.

HEre, take my *Likeness* with you, whilst 'tis so;
    For when from hence you go,
    The next Suns rising will behold
    Me pale, and lean, and old.
    The Man who did this *Picture* draw,   5
Will swear next day my face he never saw.

2.

I really believe, within a while,
    If you upon this *shadow* smile,
    Your *presence* will such vigour give,
    (Your *presence* which makes all things live)   10
    And *absence* so much alter *Me*,
This will the *substance*, *I* the *shadow* be.

51.9. lineation] *Line 9 is aligned with line 7 in F1.*

The Mistress

3.

When from your well-wrought *Cabinet* you take it,
    And your bright looks *awake it*;
    Ah be not frighted, if you see,
    The *new-sould Picture* gaze on Thee,
    And hear it breath a sigh or two;
For those are the first things that it will do.

4.

My *Rival-Image* will be then thought blest,
    And laugh at me as dispossest;
    But *Thou*, who (if I know thee right)
    I'th *substance* dost not much delight,
    Wilt rather send again for *Me*,
Who then shall but my *Pictures Picture* be.

52. *The Concealment*.

1.

NO; to what purpose should I speak?
    No, wretched *Heart*, swell till you *break*!
    She cannot love me if she *would*;
And to say truth, 'twere pity that she *should*.
    No, to the *Grave* thy sorrows bear,
    As *silent*, as they will be *there*:
Since that lov'd hand this mortal wound do's give,
    So handsomely the thing contrive,
    That she may *guiltless* of it live.
    So perish, that her killing Thee
May a *Chance-Medley*, and no *Murther* be.

51.23. *Me*,] ~ . F1

2.

'Tis nobler much for me, that I
   By'her *Beauty*, not her *Anger* dy;
   This will look justly, and become
An *Execution*; that, a *Martyrdome*.   15
   The censuring world will ne'r refrain
   From judging men by *Thunder slain*.
She must be angry sure, if I should be
   So bold to ask her to make me
   By being *hers, happi'er then she*.   20
   I will not; 'tis a milder fate
To fall by her *not Loving*, then her *Hate*.

3.

And yet this death of mine, I fear,
   Will *ominous* to her appear:
   When, sound in every other part,   25
Her *Sacrifice* is found without an *Heart*.
   For the last *Tempest* of my death
   Shall sigh out *that* too, with my *breath*.
Then shall the world my noble ruine see,
   Some *pity*, and some *envy* Mee,   30
   Then *She* herself, the *mighty Shee*,
Shall grace my fun'rals with this truth;
Twas onely Love destroy'd the gentle Youth.

53. *The Monopoly.*

1.

WHat *Mines* of *Sulphur* in my breast do ly,
   That feed th'æternal burnings of my heart?
Not *Ætna* flames more fierce or constantly,
The sounding shop of *Vulcans* smoaky art;
   Vulcan his shop has placed there,   5
   And *Cupids Forge* is set up here.

The Mistress

2.

Here all those *Arrows* mortal Heads are made,
That flye so thick unseen through yielding ayr;
The *Cyclops* here, which labour at the trade
Are Jealousie, Fear, Sadness and Despair.   10
        Ah cruel *God*! and why to me
        Gave you this curst *Monopolie*?

3.

I have the *trouble*, not the *gains* of it;
Give me but the *disposal* of one *Dart*;
And then (I'll ask no other benefit)   15
Heat as you please your furnace in my *Heart*.
        So sweet's *Revenge* to me, that I
        Upon my foe would gladly dy.

4.

Deep into'her bosom would I strike the dart;
Deeper then *Woman* e're was struck by *Thee*;   20
Thou giv'st them small wounds, and so far from th'*Heart*,
They *flutter* still about, inconstantly.
        Curse on thy *Goodness*, whom we find
        Civil to none but *Woman-kind*!

5.

Vain God! who *women* dost thy self *adore*!   25
Their wounded Hearts do still retain the powers
To travel, and to wander as before;
Thy broken Arrows 'twixt that sex and ours
        So'unjustly are distributed;
        They take the *Feathers, we* the *Head*.   30

54. *The Distance.*

1.

I'Have followed thee a year at least,
And never stopt my self to rest.
  But yet can thee o'retake no more,
Then this *Day* can the *Day* that went before.

2.

  In this our *fortunes* æqual prove
  To *Stars*, which govern them above;
  Our *Stars* that move for ever round,
With the same *Distance* still betwixt them found.

3.

  In vain, alas, in vain I strive
  The *wheel* of *Fate* faster to drive;
  Since if a round it swiftlier fly,
She in it mends her pace as much as *I*.

4.

  Hearts by *Love*, strangely *shuffled* are,
  That there can never meet a *Pare*!
  Tamelier then *Worms* are *Lovers* slain;
The *wounded Heart* ne'r turns to *wound* again.

55. *The Encrease.*

1.

I Thought, I'll swear, I could have lov'd no more
Then I had done before;
But you as easi'ly might account
'Till to the *top* of *Numbers* you amount,
  As cast up my *Loves* score.
Ten thousand millions was the sum;
Millions of endless *Millions* are to com.

2.

I'm sure her *Beauties* cannot greater grow;
  Why should my *Love* do so?
  A *real* cause at first did move;
But mine own *Fancy* now drives on my Love,
  With *shadows* from it self that flow.
  My *Love*, as we in *Numbers* see,
By *Cyphers* is encreast æternallie.

3.

So the new-made, and untride *Sphæres* above,
  Took their first turn from th'hand of *Jove*;
  But are since that beginning found
By their own Forms to move for ever round.
  All *violent Motions* short do prove,
  But by the length 'tis plain to see
That Love's a *Motion Natural* to Mee.

56. *Loves Visibility.*

1.

With much of *pain*, and all the *Art* I knew
    Have I endeavour'd hitherto
To *hide* my *Love*, and yet all will not do:

2.

The world perceives it, and it may be, *she*;
    Though so discreet and good she be,   5
By hiding it, to teach that skill to *Me*.

3.

Men without *Love* have oft so cunning grown,
    That something like it they have showne,
But none who had it ever seem'd t'have *none*.

4.

Love's of a strangely open, simple kind,   10
    Can no arts or disguises find,
But thinks none *sees* it 'cause it *self* is *blind*.

5.

The very *Eye* betrays our inward smart;
    Love of himself left there a part,
When thorow *it* he past into the *Heart*.   15

6.

Or if by chance the *Face* betray not it,
    But keep the secret wisely, yet,
Like *Drunkenness*, into the *Tongue* t'will get.

57. *Looking on, and discoursing with his Mistress.*

1.

THese full two hours now have I gazing been;
    What comfort by it can I gain?
To look on *Heav'en* with *mighty Gulfs* between
    Was the great *Misers* greatest pain:
    So neer was he to *Heavens* delight,
    As with the blest converse he might,
Yet could not get one *drop* of water by't.

2.

Ah wretch! I seem to *touch* her now; but, oh,
    What boundless spaces do us part?
Fortune, and *Friends*, and all earths empty show,
    My *Lowness*, and her high *Desert*:
    But these might conquerable prove;
    Nothing does me so far remove,
As her hard *Souls aversion* from my *Love*.

3.

So *Travellers*, that lose their way by night,
    If from afar they chance t'espy
Th' uncertain glimmerings of a *Tapers* light,
    Take flattering hopes, and think it *nigh*;
    Till wearied with the fruitless pain,
    They sit them down, and weep in vain,
And there in *Darkness*, and *Despair* remain.

57.1. been;] ~ , F1   13. *lineation*] *Line 13 is aligned with line 14 in F1.*

58. *Resolved to Love.*

1.

I Wonder what the *Grave* and *Wise*
      Think of all us that *Love*;
Whether our *pretty Fooleries*
      Their *Mirth* or *Anger* move;
They understand not *Breath*, that *Words* does want;   5
Our *Sighs* to them are *unsignificant*.

2.

One of them saw me th'other day,
      Touch the dear hand, which I admire;
My *Soul* was melting strait away,
      And *dropt* before the *Fire*.   10
This *silly Wiseman*, who pretends to *know*,
Askt why I look'd so pale, and trembled so?

3.

Another from my Mistress' dore
      Saw me with eyes all watry com;
Nor could the hidden cause explore,   15
      But thought some *smoak* was in the room;
Such *Igno'rance* from *unwounded Learning* came;
He knew *Tears* made by *Smoak*, but not by *Flame*.

4.

If *learn'd* in other things you be,
      And have in *Love* no skill,   20
For Gods sake keep your arts from me,

---

58. *stanza number 4.*] om in F1

    For I'll be *ign'orant* still.
Study or *Action* others may embrace;
My *Love's* my *Business*, and my *Books* her *Face*.

5.

These are but *Trifles*, I confess,
    Which me, weak Mortal, move;
Nor is your *busie Seriousness*
    Less trifling then my Love.
The wisest *King* who from his sacred brest
Pronounc'd *all Van'ity*, chose it for the *best*.

59. *My Fate*.

1.

GO bid the *Needle* his dear *North* forsake,
    To which with trembling rev'erence it does bend;
Go bid the *Stones* a journey upwards make;
    Go bid th'ambitious *Flame* no more t'ascend:
And when these false to their *old Motions* prove,
Then shall I cease *Thee, Thee alone* to *Love*.

2.

The fast-link'd *Chain* of everlasting *Fate*
    Does nothing tye more strong, then *Me* to *You*;
My fixt *Love* hangs not on your *Love* or *Hate*;
    But will be still the same, what e're you do.
You cannot *kill* my Love with your *disdain*,
Wound it you may, and make it *live in pain*.

59.1. dear] deer F1

3.

Mee, mine example let the *Stoicks* use,
    Their sad and cruel doctrine to maintain,
Let all *Prædestinators* me produce,   15
    Who struggle with *æternal bonds* in vain.
This *Fire* I'm *born* to, but 'tis she must tell,
Whether't be *Beams* of *Heav'en*, or *Flames* of *Hell*.

4.

You, who mens *fortunes* in their faces reade,
    To find out *mine*, look not, alas, on *Mee*;   20
But mark *her Face*, and all the features heed;
    For onely there is writ my *Destinie*.
Or if stars shew it, gaze not on the skyes;
But study the *Astrol'ogy* of her *Eyes*.

5.

If thou find there kind and propitious rays,   25
    What *Mars* or *Saturn* threaten I'll not fear;
I well believe the *Fate* of mortal days
    Is writ in *Heav'en*; but, oh *my heav'en* is there.
What can men learn from *stars* they scarce can *see*?
Two great Lights rule the *world*; and *her* two, *Mee*.   30

60. *The Heart-breaking.*

1.

IT gave a piteous *groan*, and so it broke;
    In vain it something would have spoke:
    The Love within too strong for't was,
Like *Poyson* put into a *Venice-Glass*.

60.2. lineation] *In F1, line 2 is aligned beneath the* g *in* gave, *line 1.*

2.

I thought that *this* some *Remedy* might prove,
    But, oh, the mighty *Serpent Love*,
    Cut by this chance in pieces small,
In all still *liv'd*, and still it *stung* in all.

3.

And now (alas) each little broken part
    Feels the whole pain of all my *Heart*:
    And every smallest corner still
Lives with that torment which the *Whole* did *kill*.

4.

Even so rude *Armies* when the field they quit,
    And into several *Quarters* get;
    Each *Troop* does spoil and ruine more,
Then all joyn'd in one *Body* did before.

5.

How many *Loves* raign in my bosom now?
    How many *Loves*, yet all of you?
    Thus have I chang'd with evil fate
My *Monarch-Love* into a *Tyrant State*.

61. *The Usurpation.*

1.

THou'hadst to my *Soul* no *title* or *pretence*;
    I was mine own, and *free*,
    Till I had *giv'n* my self to Thee;
But thou hast kept me *Slave* and *Prisoner* since.
    Well, since so insolent thou'rt growne,

Fond *Tyrant*, I'll *depose* thee from thy throne;
    Such outrages must not admitted be
        In an *Elective Monarchie*.

2.

Part of my *Heart* by *Gift* did to Thee fall;
    My Countrey, Kindred, and my best   10
        Acquaintance were to share the rest;
But thou, their *Cov'etous Neighbour*, drav'est out all:
    Nay more; thou mak'st me worship *Thee*,
And would'st the rule of my *Religion* bee;
Was ever *Tyrant* claim'd such power as you,   15
        To be both *Emp'rour*, and *Pope* too?

3.

The *publike Mise'ries*, and my *private fate*
    Deserve some tears: but greedy Thou
        (*Insatiate Maid*!) wilt not allow
That I one drop from thee should *alienate*.   20
    Nor wilt thou grant my sins a part,
Though the sole cause of most of them thou art,
Counting my *Tears* thy *Tribute* and thy *Due*,
        Since first mine *Eyes* I gave to *You*.

4.

Thou all my *Joys* and all my *Hopes* dost claime,   25
    Thou ragest like a *Fire* in mee,
        Converting all things into *Thee*;
Nought can resist, or *not encrease* the *Flame*.
    Nay every *Grief* and every *Fear*,
Thou dost devour, unless thy stamp it bear.   30
Thy presence, like the crowned *Basilisks* breath,
        All other *Serpents* puts to death.

61.29. *Fear,*] ~ . F1

5.

As men in *Hell* are from *Diseases* free,
    So from all other ills am I;
    Free from their known *Formality*:   35
But all pains *Eminently* lye in *Thee*.
    Alas, alas, I hope in vain
My conquer'd Soul from out thine hands to gain,
Since all the *Natives* there thou'st overthrown,
    And planted *Gar'isons* of thine own.   40

62. *Maidenhead*.

1.

THou *worst estate* even of the *sex* that's *worst*;
    Therefore by *Nature* made at first,
    T'attend the weakness of our birth!
Slight, outward *Curtain* to the *Nuptial Bed*!
Thou *Case* to buildings not yet finished!   5
    Who like the *Center* of the Earth,
    Dost heaviest things attract to thee,
Though Thou a *point imaginary* bee.

2.

A thing *God* thought for *Mankind* so unfit,
    That his *first Blessing* ruin'd it.   10
    Cold *frozen Nurse* of fiercest *fires*!
Who, like the parched plains of *Africks* sand,
(A steril, and a wild unlovely Land)
    Art always scorcht with hot desires,
    Yet *barren* quite, didst thou not bring   15
Monsters and *Serpents* forth thy self to sting!

3.

Thou that bewitchest men, whilst thou dost dwell
    Like a close *Conj'urer* in his *Cell*!
    And fear'st the days discovering Eye!
No wonder 'tis at all that thou shouldst be   20
Such tedious and unpleasant *Companie*,
    Who liv'st so *Melancholily*!
    Thou thing of subtil, slippery kind,
Which *Women lose*, and yet no *Man* can *find*!

4.

Although I think thou never found wilt be,   25
    Yet I'm resolv'd to search for thee;
    The search it self rewards the pains.
So, though the *Chymick* his *great secret* miss,
(For neither it in *Art* nor *Nature* is)
    Yet things well worth his toyle he gains: 30
    And does his Charge and Labour pay
With good *unsought exper'iments* by the way.

5.

Say what thou wilt, *Chastity* is no more
    Thee, then a *Porter* is his *Dore*.
    In vain to honour they pretend,   35
Who guard themselves with *Ramparts* and with *Walls*,
Them onely fame the truly valiant calls,
    Who can an *open breach* defend.
    Of thy quick loss can be no doubt,
Within so *Hated*, and so *Lov'd without*.   40

62.31. *lineation*] *Line 31 is aligned with line 32 in F1.*   33. more] ~ , F1

63. *Impossibilities.*

1.

I*Mpossibilities*? oh no, there's none;
    Could mine bring thy *Heart Captive* home;
As eas'ily other dangers were *o'rethrowne*,
    As *Cæsar* after vanquish't *Rome*,
His little *Asian* foes did overcome.

2.

True Lovers oft by *Fortune* are envy'd,
    Oft *Earth* and *Hell* against them strive;
But *Providence* engages on their side,
    And a good end at last does give;
At last *Just Men* and *Lovers* always *thrive*.

3.

As *stars* (not powerful else) when they *conjoyne*,
    Change, as they please, the Worlds estate;
So thy *Heart* in *Conjunction* with mine,
    Shall our own fortunes regulate;
And to our *Stars themselves* prescribe a *Fate*.

4.

'Twould grieve me much to find some bold *Romance*,
    That should two kind *examples* shew,
Which before us in wonders did advance;
    Not, that I thought that *story true*,
But none should *Fancy more*, then *I would Doe*.

5.

Through spight of our *worst Enemies, thy Friends*,
    Through *Local Banishment* from *Thee*;
Through the loud thoughts of less-concerning *Ends*,
    As easie shall my passage bee,
As was the *Amo'rous Youth's* ore *Helles Sea*.   25

6.

In vain the *Winds*, in vain the *Billows* rore;
    In vain the *Stars* their ayd deny'd:
He saw the *Sestian Tower* on th'other shore;
    Shall th'*Hellespont* our Loves divide?
No, not th'*Atlantick Oceans* boundless Tide.   30

7.

Such *Seas* betwixt us eas'ly conquer'd are;
    But, gentle *Maid*, do not deny
To let thy *Beams* shine on me from afarre;
    And still that *Taper* let me'espy:
For when *thy Light* goes out, I sink, and dy.   35

64. *Silence.*

1.

CUrse on this *Tongue*, that has my *Heart* betray'd,
    And his great *Secret* open laid!
For of all persons chiefly *She*,
Should not the ills I suffer know;
Since 'tis a thing might dang'rous grow,   5
    Onely in *Her* to *Pity Me*:
Since 'tis for *Me* to *lose* my *Life* more fit,
Then 'tis for *Her* to *save* and ransome it.

2.

Ah, never more shall thy unwilling ear
    My helpless story hear.
    Discourse and *talk* awake does keep
    The rude unquiet pain,
    That in my Brest does raign;
    Silence perhaps may make it *sleep*:
I'll bind that *Sore* up, I did ill reveal;
The *Wound*, if once it *Close*, may chance to *Heal*.

3.

No, 'twill ne'r heal; my *Love* will never *dye*,
    Though it should *speechless lye*.
    A *River*, ere it meet the *Sea*,
    As well might stay its source,
    As my Love can his course,
    Unless it joyn and mix with *Thee*.
If any end or stop of it be found,
We know the *Flood* runs still, though *underground*.

65. *The Dissembler.*

1.

UNhurt, untoucht did I complain;
    And terrifi'd all others with the pain:
    But now I feel the *mighty evil*;
    Ah, there's no *fooling* with *the Devil*!
So wanton men, whilst others they would fright,
    Themselves have met a real *Spright*.

64.20. its] it's F1

2.

    I thought, I'll swear, an handsome ly
Had been no *sin* at all in *Poetry*:
      But now I suffer an *Arrest*,
      For words were spoke by me in *jest*.   10
Dull, sottish *God* of *Love*, and can it be
      Thou understand'st not *Raillerie*?

3.

    Darts, and *Wounds*, and *Flame*, and *Heat*,
I nam'd but for the *Rhime*, or the *Conceit*.
      Nor meant my verse should raised be,   15
      To this sad fame of *Prophesie*;
Truth gives a *dull Propriety* to my stile,
      And all the *Metaphors* does spoile.

4.

    In things, where *Fancy* much does reign,
Tis dangerous too cunningly to *feign*.   20
      The *Play* at last *a Truth* does grow,
      And *Custom* into *Nature* go.
By this curst art of begging I became
      Lame, with *counterfeiting Lame*.

5.

    My Lines of amorous desire   25
I wrote to kindle and blow others fire:
      And 'twas a *barbarous delight*
      My *Fancy* promise'd from the sight;
But now, by *Love*, the mighty *Phalaris*, I
      My *burning Bull* the first do try.   30

66. *The Inconstant.*

1.

I Never yet could see that face
    Which had no dart for me;
From fifteen years, to fifties space,
    They all victorious be.
Love thou'rt *a Devil*; if I may call thee *One*,
For sure in Me thy name is *Legion*.

2.

Colour, or *Shape*, good *Limbs*, or *Face*,
    Goodness or *Wit* in all I find.
In *Motion* or in *Speech* a grace,
    If all fail, yet 'tis *Womankind*;
And I'm so weak, the *Pistol* need not be
Double or *treble charg'd* to murder *Me*.

3.

If *Tall*, the Name of *Proper* slays;
    If *Fair*, she's pleasant as the *Light*;
If *Low*, her *Prettiness* does please;
    If *Black*, what *Lover* loves not *Night*?
If *yellow hair'd*, I Love, lest it should be
Th'excuse to others for not loving *Me*.

66.12. *lineation*] Line 12 is aligned with line 10 in F1.

4.

    The *Fat*, like *Plenty*, fills my heart;
        The *Lean*, with *Love* makes me too so.   20
    If *Streight*, her *Bodie's Cupids Dart*
        To me; if *Crooked*, 'tis his *Bow*.
    Nay *Age* it self does me to rage encline,
    And strength to *Women* gives, as well as *Wine*.

5.

    Just half as large as *Charitie*   25
        My richly-landed *Love's* become;
    And judg'd aright is *Constancie*,
        Though it take up a larger room:
    Him, who loves *always one*, why should they call
    More *Constant*, then the Man loves *Always All*?   30

6.

    Thus with unwearied wings I flee
        Through all *Loves Gardens* and his *Fields*;
    And, like the wise, industrious *Bee*,
        No *Weed* but *Honey* to me yields!
    Honey still spent this dili'gence still supplies,   35
    Though I return not home with *laden Thighs*.

7.

    My *Soul* at first indeed did prove
        Of pretty strength against a Dart;
    Till I this *Habit* got of *Love*;
        But my consum'd and wasted Heart   40
    Once burnt to *Tinder* with a strong Desire,
    Since that by every *Spark* is set on Fire.

67. *The Constant.*

1.

GReat, and wise *Conqu'rour*, who where ere
Thou com'st, dost *fortifie*, and *settle* there!
   Who canst *defend* as well as *get*;
And never hadst one *Quarter* beat up yet;
   Now thou art in, Thou ne'r wilt part
   With one inch of my vanquisht Heart;
For since thou took'st it by assault from Mee,
'Tis *Garison'd* so strong with *Thoughts* of *Thee*,
   It fears no *beauteous Enemie.*

2.

   Had thy charming strength been less,
I'had serv'd ere this an hundred *Mistresses.*
   I'm better thus, nor would compound
To leave my *Pris'on* to be a *Vagabound*:
   A *Pr'ison* in which I still would be,
   Though every *door* stood op'e to Me.
In spight both of thy *Coldness* and thy *Pride*,
All Love is *Marriage* on thy *Lovers side*,
   For onely *Death* can them *divide.*

3.

   Close, narrow *Chain*, yet soft and kind,
As that which *Spi'rits* above to *good* does bind,
   Gentle, and sweet *Necessitie*,
Which does not *force*, but *guide* our *Libertie*!
   Your love on Me were spent in vain,
   Since *my Love* still could but remain
Just as it is; for what, alas can be
Added to that which hath *Infinitie*
   Both in *Extent*, and *Qualitie*?

67.13. *Vagabound*:] ~ . F1

68. *Her Name.*

1.

With more then *Jewish Reverence* as yet
    Do I the *Sacred Name* conceal;
When, ye kind *Stars*, ah when will it be fit
    This *Gentle Myst'ery* to reveal?
When will our Love be *Nam'd*, and we possess   5
That *Christning* as a *Badge* of *Happiness*?

2.

So bold as yet no verse of mine has been,
    To wear that *Gem* on any *Line*;
Nor, til the happy *Nuptial Muse* be seene,
    Shall any *Stanza* with it shine.   10
Rest, mighty *Name*, till then; for thou must be
Laid down by *Her*, e're *taken up* by *Me*.

3.

Then all the fields and woods shall with it ring;
    Then *Ecchoes* burden it shall be;
Then all the *Birds* in sev'eral notes shall sing,   15
    And all the *Rivers* murmur Thee;
Then ever'y *wind* the Sound shall upwards bear,
And softly whisper't to some *Angels* Ear.

4.

Then shall thy *Name* through all my *Verse* be spread,
    Thick as the *flowers* in *Meadows* lye,   20
And, when in future times they shall be read,

68.14. lineation] *Line 14 is indented one letter space from the margin of line 13 in F1.*

The Mistress

(As sure, I think, they will not dye)
If any *Critick* doubt that *They be mine*,
Men by that *Stamp* shall quickly know the *Coyn*.

5.

Mean while I will not dare to *make* a *Name* 25
    To represent thee by;
Adam (*Gods Nomenclator*) could not frame
    One that enough should *signifie*.
Astræa' or *Cælia* as unfit would prove
For *Thee*, as 'tis to call the *Deity*, *Jove*. 30

69. Weeping.

1.

SEE where she sits, and in what comely wise,
    Drops *Tears* more fair then others *Eyes*!
Ah, charming Maid, let not *ill Fortune* see
    Th'attire thy *sorrow* wears,
    Nor know the *beauty* of thy *Tears*: 5
For she'll still come to dress her self in *Thee*.

2.

As *stars* reflect on *waters*, so I spy
    In every drop (methinks) her *Eye*.
The *Baby*, which lives there, and always playes
    In that illustrious *sphære*, 10
    Like a *Narcissus* does appeare,
Whilst in his *flood* the lovely *Boy* did gaze.

68.30. *lineation*] Line 30 is indented, as line 28, in F1.

3.

Nere yet did I behold so glorious weather,
    As this *Sun-shine* and *Rain* together.
Pray Heav'en her *Forehead*, that pure *Hill* of *snow*,   15
    (For some such *Fountain* we must find,
    To waters of so fair a kind)
Melt not, to feed that beauteous *stream* below.

4.

Ah; mighty Love, that it were *inward Heat*
    Which made this precious *Limbeck* sweat!   20
But what, alas, ah what does it avail
    That she weeps Tears so wondrous *cold*,
    As scarce the *Asses hoof* can hold,
So *cold*, that I admire they fall not *Hail*.

70. *Discretion.*

1.

Discreet? what means this word *Discreet*?
    A Curse on all *Discretion*!
This *barbarous term* you will not meet
    In all *Loves-Lexicon*.

2.

Joynture, Portion, Gold, Estate,   5
    Houses, Houshold-stuff, or Land,
(The *Low Conveniences* of Fate)
    Are *Greek* no *Lovers understand*.

3.

Believe me, beauteous one, when Love
    Enters into a brest,
The two first things it doth remove,
    Are *Friends* and *Interest*.

4.

Passion's half blind, nor can endure
    The careful, scrup'lous *Eyes*,
Or else I could not love, I'm sure,
    One who in *Love* were *wise*.

5.

Men, in such tempests tost about,
    Will without grief or pain,
Cast all their *goods* and *riches* out,
    Themselves their *Port* to gain.

6.

As well might *Martyrs*, who do choose,
    That *sacred Death* to take,
Mourn for the *Clothes* which they must lose,
    When they're bound *naked* to the *Stake*.

71. *The Waiting-Maid*
(*Suspected to Love her*).

1.

THy *Maid*? ah, find some nobler theame
    Whereon thy doubts to place;
Nor by a low suspect *blaspheme*
    The glories of thy face.

2.

Alas, she makes Thee shine so fair,   5
    So exquisitely bright,
That her dim *Lamp* must disappear
    Before thy potent *Light*.

3.

Three hours each morn in dressing Thee,
    Maliciously are spent;   10
And make that *Beauty Tyrannie*,
    That's else a *Civil Government*.

4.

The'adorning thee with so much art,
    Is but a barb'arous skill;
'Tis like the *poys'oning* of a *Dart*   15
    Too apt before to kill.

---

71. subtitle] O1-2; *om in F1*

5.

The *Mini'string Angels* none can see;
    'Tis not their beauty'or face,
For which by men they worshipt bee;
    But their high *office* and their *place*.
        Thou art my *Goddess*, my *Saint, Shee*;
I pray to *Her*, onely to pray to *Thee*.

72. *Counsel* [II].

1.

AH! what advice can I receive?
    No, satisfie me first;
For who would *Physick*-potions give
    To one that dyes with *Thirst*?

2.

A little puff of breath we find,
    Small fires can *quench* and *kill*;
But when they're great, the adverse wind
    Does make them *greater* still.

3.

Now whilst you speak, it moves me much;
    But strait I'm just the same;
Alas, th'effect must needs be such
    Of *Cutting* through a *Flame*.

---

72. *title*. [II] *ed.*

73. *The Cure.*

1.

COme, *Doctor*, use thy roughest art,
    Thou canst not cruel prove;
Cut, burn, and torture every part,
    To heal me of my *Love*.

2.

There is no danger, if the pain   5
    Should me to'a *Feaver* bring;
Compar'd with *Heats* I now sustain,
    A *Feaver* is so *Cool* a thing,
        (Like *drink* which feaverish men desire)
That I should hope 'twould almost *quench* my *Fire*.   10

74. *The Separation.*

1.

ASk me not what my *Love* shall do or bee
    (*Love* which is *Soul* to *Body*, and *Soul* of Mee)
        When I am *sep'arated* from thee;
        Alas, I might as easily show,
What after *Death* the *Soul* will do;   5
Twill *last*, I'm sure, and that is all we know.

2.

The thing calle'd *soul* will never stir nor move,
But all that while a liveless *Carkass* prove,
        For 'tis the *Body* of my *Love*;
        Not that my *Love* will fly away,   10
But still continue, as, they say,
Sad troubled *Ghosts* about their *Graves* do stray.

75. *The Tree.*

1.

I Chose the flour'ishingst *Tree* in all the Park,
    With freshest Boughs, and fairest head;
I cut my Love into his gentle Bark,
    And in three days, behold, 'tis *dead*;
My very *written flames* so vi'olent be,
    They'have burnt and withere'd up the Tree.

2.

How should I live my self, whose *Heart* is found
    Deeply graven every where
With the large *History* of many a *wound*,
    Larger then thy *Trunk* can bear?
With art as strange, as *Homer* in the *Nut*,
    Love in my *Heart* has *Volumes* put.

3.

What a few words from thy rich stock did take
    The *Leaves* and *Beauties* all?
As a strong *Poyson* with one *drop* does make
    The *Nails* and *Hairs* to fall:
Love (I see now) a kind of *Witchcraft* is,
    For *Characters* could ne'r do this.

4.

Pardon ye *Birds* and *Nymphs* who lov'd this *Shade*;
    And pardon me, thou gentle *Tree*;
I thought her *name* would thee have happy made,
    And blessed *Omens* hop'd from Thee;
Notes of my *Love*, thrive here (said I) and *grow*;
    And with yee let my *Love* do so.

75.18. For] O1 *errata*, O2 *(see Textual Analysis)*; Or F1

5.

 Alas poor youth, thy love will never thrive!   25
  This blasted *Tree Predestines* it;
 Go tye the dismal *Knot* (why shouldst thou live?)
  And by the Lines thou there hast writ
 Deform'dly hanging, the *sad Picture* be
  To that unlucky *Historie*.   30

76. *Her Unbelief.*

1.

 'Tis a strange kind of *Igno'rance* this in you!
  That you your *Victories* should not spy,
  Victories gotten by your *Eye*!
 That your bright *Beams*, as those of *Comets* do,
  Should kill, but not know *How*, nor *Who*.   5

2.

 That truly you my *Idol* might appear,
  Whilst all the *People* smell and see
  The odorous flames, I offer thee,
 Thou sit'st, and dost nor see, nor smell, nor hear
  Thy constant zealous *worshipper*.   10

3.

 They see't too well who at my fires repine;
  Nay th'unconcern'd themselves do prove
  Quick-Ey'd enough to spy my Love;
 Nor does the *Cause* in *thy Face* clearlier shine,
  Then the *Effect* appears *in mine*.   15

4.

Fair Infidel! by what unjust decree
    Must I, who with such restless care
    Would make this truth to thee appear,
Must I, who preach it, and pray for it, be
    Damn'd by thy *incredulitie*?   20

5.

I by thy *Unbelief* am guiltless slain;
    Oh have but *Faith*, and then that you
    May know that *Faith* for to be true,
It shall it self by' a *Miracle* maintain,
    And *raise* me from the *Dead* again.   25

6.

Mean while my *Hopes* may seem to be o'rthrown;
    But *Lovers Hopes* are full of *Art*,
    And thus dispute, that since my heart
Though in *thy Breast*, yet is not by thee known,
    Perhaps thou may'st not know thine *Own*.   30

77. *The Gazers.*

1.

COme let's go on, where *Love* and *Youth* does call;
    I've seen *too* much, if this be *all*.
Alas, how far more *wealthy* might I be
With a contented *Ign'orant Povertie*?
    To shew such stores, and nothing grant,   5
    Is to enrage and *vex* my want.
For Love to *Dye an Infant's* lesser ill,
Then to Live long, yet *live in Child-hood* still.

76.20. be] ~, F1

2.

We'have both sate gazing onely hitherto,
    As *Man* and *Wife* in *Picture* do.
The richest crop of *Joy* is still behind,
And He who onely *Sees*, in *Love* is *Blind*.
    So at first *Pigmalion* lov'd;
    But th'*Amour* at last improv'd:
The *Statue*' it self at last a *woman* grew,
And so at last, my Dear, should you do too.

3.

Beauty to man the greatest *Torture* is,
    Unless it lead to farther bliss
Beyond the tyran'ous pleasures of the *Eye*.
It grows too *serious a Crueltie*,
    Unless it *Heal*, as well as *strike*;
    I would not, *Salamander*-like,
In scorching heats always to *Live* desire,
But like a *Martyr*, pass to *Heav'en* through *Fire*.

4.

Mark how the lusty *Sun* salutes the *Spring*,
    And gently kisses every thing.
His loving *Beams* unlock each mayden flower,
Search all the *Treasures*, all the *Sweets* devower.
    Then on the earth with *Bridegroom*-Heat,
    He does still new *Flowers* beget.
The *Sun* himself, although *all Eye* he bee,
Can find in *Love* more Pleasure then to *see*.

77.13. lov'd;] ~ . F1

The Mistress 115

78. *The Incurable.*

1.

I Try'd if *Books* would cure my *Love*, but found
    Love made them *Non-sense* all.
I'apply'd *Receipts* of *Business* to my wound,
    But stirring did the pain recall.

2.

As well might men who in a feaver fry, 5
    Mathematique doubts debate,
As well might men, who *mad* in *darkness* ly,
    Write the *Dispatches* of a *State*.

3.

I try'd *Devotion, Sermons, frequent Prayer*,
    But those did worse then *useless* prove; 10
For *Pray'rs* are turn'd to *Sin* in those who are
    Out of *Charity*, or *in Love*.

4.

I try'd in *Wine* to drown the mighty care;
    But *Wine*, alas, was *Oyl* to th' fire.
Like *Drunkards* eyes, my troubled *Fancy* there 15
    Did *double* the Desire.

5.

I try'd what *Mirth*, and *Gayety* would do,
    And mixt with pleasant *Companies*;
My *Mirth* did graceless and *insipid* grow,
    And 'bove a *Clinch* it could not rise. 20

78.7. ly,] ~∧F1

6.

Nay, God forgive me for't, at last I try'd
    'Gainst this some *new desire* to stir,
And lov'd again, but 'twas where I espy'd
    Some faint *Resemblances* of *Her.*

7.

The *Physick* made me worse with which I strove   25
    This *Mortal Ill* t'expell,
As wholesome *Med'icines* the *Disease* improve,
    There where they *work* not well.

79. *Honor.*

1.

SHE *Loves,* and she *confesses* too;
    There's then at last, no more to do.
The happy *work's* entirely done;
Enter the *Town* which thou hast *won*;
The *fruits* of *Conquest* now begin;   5
Iô Triumph! Enter in.

2.

What's this, ye *Gods,* what can it be?
Remains there still an *Enemie*?
Bold *Honor* stands up in the Gate,
And would yet *Capitulate*;   10
Have I orecome all *real foes,*
And shall this *Phantome* me oppose?

3.

Noisy Nothing! *Stalking shade*!
By what *Witchcraft* wert thou made?
Empty cause of *Solid* harms!
But I shall find out *Counter-charms*
Thy airy *Devi'lship* to remove
From this *Circle* here of *Love*.

4.

Sure I shall rid my self of *Thee*
By the *Nights* obscurity,
And obscurer *secresie*.
Unlike to every other *spright*,
Thou attempt'st not men t'affright,
Nor *appear'st* but in the *Light*.

80. *The Innocent Ill.*

1.

THough all thy gestures and discourses be
    Coyn'd and stamp't by *Modestie*,
    Though from thy *Tongue* nere slipt away
One word which *Nuns* at th'*Altar* might not say,
      Yet such a sweetness, such a grace
        In all thy *speech* appear,
      That what to th'*Eye* a beauteous *face*,
        That thy *Tongue* is to th' *Ear*.
    So cunningly it wounds the heart,
      It strikes such heat through ev'ry part,
That thou a *Tempter* worse then *Satan* art.

2.

Though in thy thoughts scarce any Tracks have bin
    So much as of *Original* Sin,
    Such charms thy *Beauty* wears as might
Desires in dying confest *Saints* excite.   15
    Thou with strange *Adulterie*
    Dost in each breast a *Brothel keep*;
    Awake all men do *lust* for thee,
    And some *enjoy* Thee when they *sleep*.
Ne're before did *Woman* live,   20
    Who to such *Multitudes* did give
The *Root* and *cause* of *Sin*, but onely *Eve*.

3.

Though in thy breast so quick a Pity bee,
    That a *Flies Death's* a *wound* to thee.
    Though savage, and rock-hearted those   25
Appear, that weep not ev'en *Romances* woes.
    Yet ne'r before was *Tyrant* known,
    Whose rage was of so large extent,
    The ills thou dost are *whole* thine own,
    Thou'rt *Principal* and *Instrument*;   30
In all the deaths that come from you,
    You do the *treble office* do
Of *Judge*, of *Tort'erer*, and of *weapon* too.

4.

Thou *lovely Instrument* of *angry Fate*,
    Which *God* did for our faults create!   35
    Thou *Pleasant, universal Ill*,
Which *sweet* as *Health*, yet like a *Plague* dost *kill*!
    Thou kind, well-*natur'ed Tyrannie*!
    Thou *chaste* committer of a *Rape*!
    Thou *voluntary Destinie*,   40
    Which no man *Can*, or *Would* escape!
So gentle, and so glad to spare,
    So wondrous good, and wondrous faire,
(We know) e'ven the *Destroying Angels* are.

80.30. *Instrument*;] F1 copies iii-iv; ~ , F1 copies i-ii, v (*see* Textual Introduction).

81. DIALOGUE,

After Enjoyment.

1.

She.   WHat have we done? what cruel passion mov'd thee,
        Thus to ruine her that lov'd Thee?
   Me thou'hast *robb'ed*, but what art thou
   Thy *Self* the *richer* now?
        Shame succeeds the short liv'd *pleasure*;   5
So soon is spent, and gone, this thy *Ill-gotten Treasure*.

2.

He.   We'have done no harm; nor was it *Theft* in *mee*,
        But noblest *Charity* in *Thee*.
   I'll the well-gotten *Pleasure*
   Safe in my *Mem'orie* Treasure;   10
        What though the *Flower* it self do wast,
The *Essence* from it drawn does long and sweeter last.

3.

She.   No: I'm undone; my *Honor* Thou hast slain,
        And nothing can restore't again.
   Art and Labour to bestow,   15
   Upon the *Carcase* of it now,
        Is but t'embalm a body *dead*,
The *Figure* may remain, the *Life* and *Beautie's* fled.

4.

He.   Never, my dear, was *Honor* yet undone,
        By *Love*, but *Indiscretion*.   20
   To th' *wise* it all things does allow;
   And cares not *What* we do; but *How*.
        Like *Tapers* shut in ancient *Urns*,
Unless it let in *ayr*, for ever *shines* and *burns*.

5.

She.   *Thou first* perhaps who didst the fault commit,   25
      Wilt make thy wicked boast of it.
  For *Men*, with *Roman pride*, above
  The *Conquest*, do the *Triumph* love:
      Nor think a perfect *Victo'ry* gain'd,
Unless they through the *streets* their *Captive* lead enchain'd.   30

6.

He.   Who e're his secret joys has open laid,
      The *Baud* to his own *Wife* is made.
  Beside what boast is left for mee,
  Whose whole wealth's a *Gift* from *Thee*?
      'Tis you the *Conqu'eror* are, 'tis you   35
Who have not onely *ta'ne*, but *bound*, and *gag'd* me too.

7.

She.   Though publique pun'ishment we escape, the *Sin*
      Will rack and *torture* us within:
  Guilt and *Sin* our bosom bears;
  And though fair yet the *Fruit* appears,   40
      That *Worm* which now the *Core* does wast,
When long t'has gnaw'd within will break the *skin* at last.

8.

He.   That *Thirsty Drink*, that *Hungry Food* I sought,
      That *wounded Balm*, is all my fault.
  And Thou in pity didst apply,   45
  The kind and onely *remedie*:
      The *Cause* absolves the *Crime*; since *Mee*
So mighty *Force* did move, so mighty *Goodness Thee*.

81.40. fair] ~ , F1

The Mistress

9.

She. *Curse* on thine *Arts*! methinks I *Hate* thee now;
       And yet I'm sure I *love Thee* too!   50
  I'm *angry*, but my *wrath* will prove,
  More *Innocent* then did thy *Love*.
       Thou hast *this day* undone me quite;
  Yet wilt undo me more, should'st thou not come *at Night*.

82. *Verses lost upon a Wager.*

1.

As soon hereafter will I *wagers* lay,
    'Gainst what an *Oracle* shall say,
Fool, that I was, to venture to denie
    A *Tongue* so us'd to *victorie*!
A *Tongue* so blest by *Nature* and by *Art*,   5
That never yet it spoke but gain'd an *Heart*:
    Though what you said, had not been *true*
    If spoke by any else but *you*.
    Your speech will govern *Destiny*,
And *Fate* will *change* rather then *you* should *Ly*.   10

2.

'Tis true if *Humane Reason* were the *Guide*,
    Reason, methinks, was on my side,
But that's a *Guide*, alas, we must resign,
    When th'*Authoritie's Divine*.
She said, she said *herself* it would be so;   15
And I, *bold unbeliever* answer'd *No*,
    Never so justly sure before
    Error the name of *Blindness* bore,
    For whatsoe're the *Question* be,
There's no man that has *eyes* would *bet* for *Me*.   20

82.11. if] If F1

3.

If *Truth* it self (as other *Angels* do
    When they descend to humane view)
In a *Material Form* would daign to shine,
    'Twould *imitate* or *borrow Thine*,
So daz'eling bright, yet so transparent clear,   25
So well proportion'd would the parts appear;
    Happy the eye which *Truth* could see
    Cloath'd in a *shape* like *Thee*,
    But happier far the eye
Which could thy *shape naked like Truth* espy!   30

4.

Yet this lost *wager* costs me nothing more
    Then what I ow'ed to thee before.
Who would not venture for that debt to *play*
    Which He were bound howere to *pay*?
If *Nature* gave me power to write in verse,   35
She gave it me thy praises to reherse.
    Thy wondrous Beauty and Thy Wit
    Has such a *Sov'eraign Right* to it,
That no Mans *Muse* for *publique vent* is free,
Till she has paid *her Customs* first to *Thee*.   40

83. *Bathing in the River.*

1.

THe *fish* around her crowded, as they do
    To the false light that treach'erous Fishers shew,
And all with as much ease might taken be,
    As she at first took me.
    For ne're did *Light* so clear   5
    Among the *waves* appear,
Though ev'ry night the *Sun* himself set there.

2.

Why to *Mute Fish* should'st thou thy self discover,
And not to me thy no less *silent Lover*?
As some from *Men* their buried *Gold* commit
  To *Ghosts* that have no use of it!
  Half their rich treasures so
  Maids bury; and for ought we know
(Poor *Ignorants*) they'r Mermaids all below.

3.

The amo'rous *Waves* would fain about her stay,
But still new am'orous *waves* drive them away,
And with swift current to those joys they haste,
  That doe as swiftly waste,
  I laught the wanton play to view,
  But 'tis, alas, at *Land* so too,
And still *old Lovers* yield the place to *new*.

4.

Kiss her, and as you part, you am'orous waves
(My happier *Rivals*, and my *fellow slaves*)
Point to your flowry banks, and to her shew
  The good your *Bounties* doe;
  Then tell her what your *Pride* doth cost,
  And, how your *use* and *beauty's* lost,
When rig'orous *Winter* binds you up with *Frost*.

5.

Tell her, her *Beauties* and her *Youth*, like *Thee*
Haste without stop to a *devouring sea*;
Where they will mixt and *undistinguisht* ly
  With all the meanest things that *dy*.
  As in the *Ocean* Thou,
  No priviledge dost know,
Above th'*impurest streams* that thither flow.

83.30. Haste] Hast F1. 32. *lineation*] *Line 32 is aligned with line 31 in F1.*

6.

Tell her, kind *flood*, when this has made her sad,
Tell her there's yet one *Rem'edy* to be had;
Shew her how thou, though long since *past*, dost find
    Thy self yet still *behind*,
      Mariage (say to her) will bring   40
    About the self-same thing,
But she, fond *Maid*, *shuts* and *seals* up the *spring*.

84. *Love given over.*

1.

IT is *enough*; enough of time, and pain
   Hast thou consum'd in vain;
   Leave, wretched *Cowley*, leave
   Thy self with *shadows* to deceave;
Think that *already lost* which thou must *never gain*.   5

2.

Three of thy lustiest and thy freshest years,
   (Tost in storms of *Hopes* and *Fears*)
   Like helpless *Ships* that bee
   Set on fire ith' midst o'the *Sea*,
Have all been *burnt in Love*, and all been *drown'd in Tears*.   10

3.

Resolve then on it, and by force or art
   Free thy unlucky *Heart*;
   Since *Fate* does disapprove
   Th'ambition of thy *Love*.
And not one *Star* in heav'n offers to take thy part.   15

4.

If ere I clear my *Heart* from this desire,
   If ere it home to'his breast retire,
   It ne'r shall wander more about,
   Though thousand beauties call'd it out:
A *Lover Burnt* like me for ever *dreads the fire*.   20

5.

The *Pox*, the *Plague*, and ev'ry *smal disease*,
   May come as oft as *ill Fate* please;
   But *Death* and *Love* are never found
   To give a *Second Wound*,
We're by those *Serpents bit*, but we're *devour'd by these*.   25

6.

Alas, what comfort is't that I am grown
   Secure of be'ing *again* orethrown?
   Since such an *Enemy* needs not fear
   Lest any else should quarter there,
Who has not onely *Sack't*, but quite *burnt down* the *Town*.   30

FINIS.

84.29. Lest] Least F1

Textual Introduction, Analysis, Collations, and Textual Notes

Editorial Principles, Sigla, Abbreviations

Editorial principles for the complete edition are outlined here. The Textual Introductions will indicate special editorial problems, should they occur, and any modifications to the general principles.

Copy Text

The copy text is the first printing, except where a manuscript or subsequent printing shows evidence that it represents the original manuscript as finally revised by the author or that the author revised the accidentals.

Reproduction of the Copy Text

The copy text is literally reprinted except for:

1. Authoritative substantive variants. Accidental features of such variants are made to conform to the copy text. Substantive changes are listed in footnotes.
2. Nonauthoritative substantive emendations. These are rarely introduced, only where the sense of a passage demands emendation. The emendations are listed in footnotes.
3. Authoritative accidental variants, as listed in the footnotes.
4. Nonauthoritative accidental emendations. These are made as sense demands and are footnoted. If (as is often the case) a later seventeenth-century edition produces the same emendation, that edition is noted in the collation.
5. Turned *b, d, p, q, n,* and *u* are accepted as *b, d, p, q, n,* and *u.* If a spelling error results, it is corrected in the text and the correction is footnoted.
6. Line numbers are added to the texts, and poems in a series or collection are numbered sequentially.

Silent Changes in the Copy Text

1. Long *s* becomes round *s*; long *f* becomes f; *VV* becomes *W.*
2. Turned letters other than *b, d, p, q, n,* and *u* are adjusted.

3. Type set in the wrong font is adjusted, and swash italics are represented by plain italics.

4. Medial apostrophes that failed to print are restored.

5. Spacing between words and before and after punctuation is normalized when no change in meaning results.

6. Titles, section titles, ornamented or oversized capital letters, the position of stanza numbers, and other such typographical details are made uniform, in the style of the present edition.

Textual Introduction, Analyses, Collations; Sigla and Abbreviations

Textual introductions contain descriptions of all possibly authoritative printings and manuscripts. Sigla for printed editions indicate the format of the printing (F = folio; Q = quarto; O = octavo; D = duodecimo) and are numbered chronologically, within a format grouping. Manuscripts are listed as "M" and are numbered in rough chronological order, insofar as dates can be determined or approximated for them. If the copy text is a printed edition, at least five copies have been collated and press variants are listed. Two or more copies of other significant earlier editions are collated, and additional copies of later editions that may contain authoritative variants have been examined for press revisions. For texts printed in seventeenth-century collections, we collate substantive variants from all editions and reprints through 1721. Full citations for the music copy texts listed under "Musical settings" can be found in the descriptions beginning on page 556.

Analyses of the descriptive textual evidence show which texts may be authoritative, how a copy text was selected, and how the present edition was determined. Collations of printings and manuscripts provide evidence for the textual analyses. The collations record all changes to the copy text, listing the authority for them, and all substantive variants of the present edition. Substantive variants in song texts appearing in musical settings are listed separately, with notes to the settings. Spelling, capitalization, punctuation, and typographical variants are listed only if they significantly affect the sense. When a variant in punctuation is listed, a wavy dash [~] is used in place of the word preceding the variant. A caret [ʌ] signifies the omission of a punctuation mark. Where a majority of printed editions and manuscripts share a reading, the identifying sigla may be replaced in the collation with a capital sigma [Σ], and departures from the majority reading are listed by individual sigla. The abbreviation "*om*" stands for "omitted." These and other editorial abbreviations are listed in the following table.

Table of Sigla and Editorial Abbreviations

CW	catchwords
D	duodecimo
ed.	the present editor[s]
F	folio
HT	head title
i	inner forme
M	manuscript
o	outer forme
O	octavo
om	omitted
Q	quarto
r	(superscript): recto
RT	running title
v	(superscript): verso
var.	variant
Σ	agreement in a majority of sources, or in all sources for which readings are not specified.
~	agreement in the word or words preceding a variant in punctuation
∧	a punctuation mark is omitted
$	gatherings

The Mistress

Textual Introduction

The first edition of *The Mistress*, O1, was published in 1647. A second octavo edition, O2, was printed in the same year and reissued, with a new title page, in 1667. The folio collection *Poems* (1656), F1, includes an expanded version of O1. These editions are described below.

O1 [within a double-ruled border] THE / MISTRESSE, / OR / SEUER-ALL COPIES / OF / LOVE-VERSES. / rule / Written by Mr A. COWLEY. / rule / ———*Hæret lateri lethalis arundo.* / rule / LONDON, / Printed for *Humphrey Moseley*, and are to be / sold at his shop at the *Princes Armes* in St *Pauls* / Church-yard. *Anno Dom.* 1647.

Collation: 8°: A–H8 [$3 signed (+ B4, D4; − A1, D3, E3)], 64 leaves, pp. [i–iv, 1] 2–115 [116–24] (misprinting 50 as 0; misprinting 39 as 3 in some copies). Bound octavo, copy v measuring 15.7 cm × 10.3 cm; watermarks: grapes (c. 24 mm top to bottom and 16 mm wide, sigs. A and B); a rectangular watermark (c. 20 mm in length), possibly a hand-and-cuff, appears in later gatherings.

Contents: A1^r title, A1^v blank, A2^r double row of ornaments above a row of harps; "To the Reader." ["A *Correct Copy of these verses / and (as I am told) writ- / ten by the Authour himselfe, / falling into my hands, I / thought fit to send them to the / Presse; cheifely because I heare / that the same is like to be don / from a more imperfect one. It is not my good / fortune to bee acquainted with the Authour / any farther then his fame (by which hee is well / knowne to all English men) and to that I am / sure I shall doe a service by this Publi- / cation: Not doubting but that, if these verses / please his Mistresse but halfe so well as they / will generally doe the rest of the world, he will / bee so well contented, as to forgive at least this / my boldnesse, which proceedes onely from my / Love of Him, who will gaine reputation, and / of my Countrey, which will receive delight from / it. I shall use no more preface, nor add one word / (besides these few lines) to the Booke; but faith- / fully and nakedly transmit it to thy view, just as it / came to mine, unlesse perhaps some* Typographi- / call *faults get into it, which I will take care shall / be as few as may be, and desire a pardon for them, / if there be any. /* Farewell."], A3^r a row of crowned roses, thistles, harps and fleurs-de-lis above a double row of ornaments, HT THE / MISTRESSE, / OR / SEUERALL COPIES / OF / LOVE-VERSES., text [poems numbered 1–76 and 84 in the present edition], H3ᵛ *"TO THE READER."* ["I*n stead of the Authors Picture in the be- / ginning, I thought fit to fixe here this / following Copy of Verses, being his owne / illustration of his Motto, and (as I conceive) the / more lively representation of him.*"], text of "The Motto.", H4 FINIˢ., H4ᵛ ERRATA. ["*The Printer made such hast (least the other im- / perfect Copie should get the start of this) / as hath occasioned these.*"] H5ʳ row of acorns above a double row of ornaments, A Table of the Heads / in this Poem., H7ᵛ rule / FINIS., H8ʳ⁻ᵛ blank.

CW] A3 I [2.I], A3ᵛ Among [5.Among], A4 The [*The*], A8ᵛ And, B1 Were [VVere], B3 2.'Tis [2.T'is], B4 The [*My*], B6 The [*The*], B8 VVisedome [Wisedome], B8ᵛ I,le [I'le], C4 Nor [2.Not], C4ᵛ The [*The*], C5 Bold [4.Bold], C6ᵛ Till ['Till], C8ᵛ THE [*The*], D1 4 If [4.If], D2 For- [Forbid], D5 4 Lust [4.Lust], D6 4.And [4.Ah], D7ᵛ Eccho [*Eccho*], D8ᵛ The, E2 Whither [VVhether], E6ᵛ Thon [Thou], E8ᵛ And, F2 T*he* [*The*], F3ᵛ Ah [2.Ah], F8 *The* [*Impossibilities*], F8ᵛ Which, G5 2.A [2.As], G8ᵛ VVith [With], H4 A [H4ᵛ begins *The*, printed approximately halfway down the page, and contains the errata; H5ʳ, containing the "Table of Heads," begins "A"], H5ᵛ *Resolved* [*Resolued*]

RT] A2ᵛ To the Reader., A3ᵛ–H4 THE MISTRESSE. var. THE MISTRESSE: [Caps used in some of the headlines are mixed from two and at times three different fonts.], H5ᵛ–H7ᵛ The Table.

Copies collated: i British Library G 11423 [-H8]; ii British Library E 1149(1) [Thomason copy]; iii Bodleian 8° W11 Art.BS(5) [rebound with other octavos published by Moseley during the later 1640s]; iv University of Glasgow BD1 g.42; v Yale, Beinecke Rare Book and MS Library Ij C839 647 [bound with *The foure Ages of England* (1648)]; vi Princeton, Robert H. Taylor collection [title page remounted and missing C7, D5]; vii British Library Ashley 518.

The book was entered to Humphrey Moseley in the Stationers' Register on 4 March 1646/7: "Master Moseley. Entred . . . under the hands of sʳ NATH: BRENT and both the wardens a book called *The Mistresse, or severall copies of Love verses*, written by Mʳ Abr. Cowley . . . vjᵈ,".

O2   The *title page*, entirely reset, reads as O1 except for an ampersand and a regularly lined (rather than superscript) *t* in "St," in the imprint: Printed for *Humphrey Moseley*, & are to be / sold at his shop at the *Princes Armes* in St *Pauls* / Church-yard. *Anno Dom.* 1647.

Collation: 8°: A–H8 [$4 signed (-H4)], 64 leaves, numbered [i–iv, 1] 2–115 [116–24] (misprinting 3 as 7; misprinting 113 as 114). Bound octavo, copy iv (in its original sheep binding) measuring 16.8 cm × 11 cm; watermark: a large, ornamented mark, possibly a shield, on a scrolled base enclosing the initial "R" (or "B"), measuring c. 120 mm × 60 mm.

Contents: As O1, except: A2 row of ornaments between two rows of acorns; A3 a row of crowned roses, thistles, harps and fleurs-de-lis above a row of ornaments and a row of acorns; H4 *FINIS*.; H4ᵛ blank [most, but not all, of the errata listed in O1 are corrected in the text of O2]; H5 row of ornaments between two rows of acorns; H7ᵛ rule / FINIS. [rule, in some copies]. *CW*] A3 I [2.I], A3ᵛ Among [5.Among], A4 The [*The*], A5 4.I [4:I], A8ᵛ And, B1ᵛ Bee [Be], B3 2.'Tis [2.Tis], B4 The [*My*], B5ᵛ Al [All], B6 The [*The*], B8 Wisdome [*Wisedome.*], B8ᵛ I'le, C1 4.All [4.Ah], C4 Nor [2.Not], C4ᵛ The [*The*], C5 Bold [4.Bold], C8ᵛ The, D2 For- [Forbid], D3ᵛ Love [Loves], D6 4.And [4.Ah], D8ᵛ The, E2 Whither [Whether], E6 2.Beauty, [2.Beauty], E8ᵛ And, F3ᵛ Ah [2.Ah], F8 The [*Impossibilities.*], F8ᵛ Which, G5 2.A [2.As], G8ᵛ With

RT] A2ᵛ To the Reader., A3ᵛ–H4 THE MISTRES. (except THE MISTRESS. on A4ᵛ, A5, A6ᵛ, A8ᵛ and TH MISTRES. on A7ᵛ and H2ᵛ), H5ᵛ–H7ᵛ The Table.

Copies collated: i Yale, Beinecke Rare Book and MS Library Ij C839 647b [rebound; missing H8]; ii British Library C12 e.10; iii Folger Library [the Grolier copy (#223), bound with ten additional leaves containing a catalogue of books printed for Humphrey Moseley]; iv (copy consulted) owned by Arthur Freeman [missing F3 and F4. Pasted inside the back cover is a list of books "Printed or sold by *William Leake*, at the sign of the Crown in *Fleet-street* between the two Temple Gates." The books listed were published during the 1650s.]; v (copy consulted) Cambridge University Library.

Sheets of this edition were reissued in 1667 with the following title page: THE / MISTRESSE, / OR / SEVERAL COPIES / OF / LOVE-VERSES. / rule / Written by Mr. *A. Cowley,* / In his Youth, and now since his / Death thought fit to be pub- / lished. / rule / —*Hœret lateri lethalis arundo.* / rule / LONDON, / Printed for *Rowland Reynolds* at the / *Sun* and *Bible* in *Postern-Street* / neer *Moore-Gate*, 1667. This title, a cancel, is framed within a double rule. The setting of the text (A2–H7ᵛ) is identical to O2; the paper bears the same watermark as O2. Copies consulted: Yale, Beinecke Rare Book and MS Library Ij C839 647D; Harvard, Houghton Library.

Humphrey Moseley, who provided O1 with a publisher's notice, "To the Reader," is probably responsible for the notes on H3ᵛ and H4ᵛ as well. The various questions suggested by these notes—in respect of the manuscript, the "other imperfect Copie," the speed of printing, and the correctness of the text—are discussed below. For an account of Moseley's publishing career, see J. C. Reed, "Humphrey Moseley, Publisher," 57–142.

The printer of O1, on the evidence of ornaments, was William Wilson. See C. W. Miller, "A London Ornament Stock, 1598–1683," 125–51. The "A" on A2ʳ of O1 is Decorative Initial A4 in Miller's list; the "I" on A3ʳ is I5;

and the "I" on H3ᵛ is I2. Miller includes an account of Wilson's career (136-38), as does R. K. Turner, "The Printers and the Beaumont and Fletcher Folio of 1647, Section 2."

Two compositors appear to have set O1. Their work is readily distinguishable in that compositor A habitually leaves a space before semicolons and question marks while compositor B does not. For instance, on A3 there are four semicolons and a question mark, and all have spaces before them. We will say that the page is the work of compositor A. On A3ᵛ there are three semicolons, none with a preceding space, so we will say that this page is compositor B's work. It may be objected that simply because the evidence of punctuation on a particular page points to one or the other compositor, it does not follow that this compositor set the entire page. There are, indeed, places where the changeover between compositors very probably did not coincide with the page-change in O1. For the present, however, and in the interest of simplicity, we will assess the print composition of the book in terms of full pages.

The straightforward evidence of punctuation suggests that compositor A set thirty-eight pages: A3ʳ, A5ʳ, A5ᵛ, A6ʳ, A6ᵛ, B1ʳ, B1ᵛ, B3ʳ, B4ʳ, B6ʳ, B6ᵛ, C1ʳ, C8ʳ, C8ᵛ, D1ʳ, D5ʳ, D5ᵛ, D6ʳ, D6ᵛ, D7ᵛ, E1ʳ, E1ᵛ, E2ʳ, E6ᵛ, E7ʳ, E8ʳ, F1ʳ, F1ᵛ, F2ʳ, F6ʳ, F6ᵛ, F7ʳ, F8ʳ, F8ᵛ, G1ʳ, G5ʳ, G7ᵛ, and G8ʳ. Compositor B can be assigned twenty-nine pages: A3ᵛ, B4ᵛ, B7ᵛ, B8ʳ, C2ᵛ, C6ʳ, C6ᵛ, D2ᵛ, D3ʳ, D8ʳ, D8ᵛ, E2ᵛ, E3ʳ, E4ʳ, E4ᵛ, E5ʳ, F2ᵛ, F3ʳ, F3ᵛ, F4ᵛ, F5ʳ, G2ʳ, G3ᵛ, G4ʳ, H1ᵛ, H2ʳ, H3ʳ, H3ᵛ, and H4ʳ.

The spellings in O1 of two common words *me* and *be* tend to reinforce the compositorial groups outlined above. On pages assigned to compositor A, *me* appears forty-three times to sixteen occurrences of *mee*; compositor B spells *me* once and *mee* forty-one times. Compositor A spells *be* thirty-two times and *bee* sixteen times; compositor B spells *be* five times to thirty-six *bee* spellings. It is too much to expect that the spelling habits of the compositors should be mutually exclusive. All the same, examination of the spelling does seem—remarkably in the case of "me"—to confirm the conclusion drawn from the punctuation and in so doing further suggests, on grounds of probability, that no third compositor was involved, at least over these sixty-seven pages.

The evidence so far shows that while a compositor often set a series of pages, in no instance is one compositor responsible for a whole forme. There is, further, nothing to suggest that the copy was cast off, or that a poem was treated as a unit and set wholly by one compositor. The text appears to have been set seriatim, rather than by formes. With this in mind, we are in a position to ascribe further pages and part-pages to the compositors on the assumption of a stint. It is also possible, using evidence of punctuation, to determine where changeovers between compositors may have occurred. The following sequence shows the probable compositor, in parenthesis, and pages ascribed. Pages where a changeover is probable are indicated. Where the evidence of punctuation and the assumption of a stint fail to offer a convincing ascription, no compositor is listed and the page signatures are given in square brackets.

(A) A3r; (B) A3v, A4r; (A) A4v, A5r, A5v, A6r, A6v; (A/B) A7r: A *last indicated in line 16*, B *first indicated in line 20*; (B) A7v, A8r, A8v; (A) B1r, B1v; [B2r, B2v]; (A) B3r, B3v, B4r; (B) B4v, B5r; (B/A) B5v: B *last indicated in line 11*, A *first indicated in line 16*; (A) B6r, B6v; (A/B) B7r: A *last indicated in line 18*, B *first indicated in line 22*; (B) B7v, B8r; (A) B8v, C1r; (A/B) C1v: A *last indicated in line 9*, B *first indicated in line 11*; (B) C2r, C2v; (B/A) C3r: B *last indicated in line 1*, A *first indicated in line 4*; (A/B) C3v: A *last indicated in line 3*, B *first indicated in line 7*; [C4r, C4v, C5r]; (B) C5v, C6r, C6v, C7r; [C7v]; (A) C8r, C8v, D1r, D1v; (B) D2r, D2v, D3r, D3v, D4r; (B/A) D4v: B *last indicated in line 12*, A *first indicated in line 14*; (A) D5r, D5v, D6r, D6v, D7r, D7v; (B) D8r, D8v; (A) E1r, E1v, E2r; (B) E2v, E3r, E3v, E4r, E4v, E5r; (B/A) E5v: B *last indicated in line 11*, A *first indicated in line 20*; (A) E6r, E6v, E7r, E7v, E8r, E8v, F1r, F1v, F2r; (B) F2v, F3r, F3v, F4r, F4v, F5r; (A) F5v, F6r, F6v, F7r, F7v, F8r, F8v, G1r, G1v; (B) G2r, G2v, G3r, G3v, G4r, G4v; (A) G5r; [G5v, G6r, G6v, G7r]; (A) G7v, G8r, G8v; (A/B) H1r: A *last indicated in line 4*, B *first indicated in line 9*; (B) H1v, H2r, H2v, H3r, H3v, H4r. Examination of the spellings in the pages identified on the assumption of a stint as wholly the work of one or other of the compositors produces the following figures: compositor A spells *be* ten times to *bee* twenty-five times; compositor B spells *be* three times to *bee* twenty-five times. Compositor A spells *me* nine times to *mee* seven times; compositor B spells *me* two times to *mee* thirty-one times. These ratios are comparable with those earlier given for pages assigned to a compositor on the straightforward evidence of punctuation.

Compositors normally added catchwords as each page was finished. This, however, may not always have been the case in the printing of O1. The irregularities in the catchwords, listed above in the bibliographical description of O1, are compounded by a number of instances wherein the catchword and the text following appear in different-sized type. On A8r, C1r, D6v, E1r, F5v, G2v, G3r, G4v, and H1v the catchword appears in medium-sized roman while the text follows in small roman. In only one of these instances (G4v) is there a change of compositors at the page break. These oversized catchwords were very possibly added after the pages had been set.

On D4r, D4v, F2r, F7r, G4r, and G5v a small or medium italic catchword is followed by large italics in the text (a title in each case). Irregular catchwords on A4r, B4r, B6r, B8r, C4v, C8v, D7v, F2r, and F8r also relate to poem titles. All but two of these show variation in font, the catchword being in roman and the title word in italic. The catchwords on B4r and F8r, however, are errors that more clearly raise questions about the authority of the order of poems in O1. On B4r, the last of three pages set by compositor A, "*The*"

Textual Introduction 137

leads to *"My"* in the following title *"My Heart discovered,"* set by compositor B. (*"The"* is the appropriate catchword for the next poem set by compositor A, *"The Vaine Love,"* appearing on B5ᵛ.) On F8ʳ, set by compositor A in the midst of the longest stint in the book, *"The"* is followed by the title *"Impossibilities."* Perhaps compositor A expected compositor B to take over on F8ᵛ with *"The Dissembler."* This title, however, does not appear until G2ʳ.

There are a few instances of recurring damaged type and recurring rules. The damaged "h" on B8ᵛ, line 6, in "the," recurs on E2ᵛ, line 9, in "Thine"; the two-line capital "T" on B1ᵛ, line 3, in " 'Tis" recurs on C5ʳ, line 1, in " 'TAke"; the second "V" in "VVomen," A5ᵛ, line 5, recurs on B5ʳ, line 2, in "Voyce." A rule identified as (i) appears on B7ᵛ and D5ʳ; rule (ii) appears on C2ᵛ, E8ᵛ and G6ᵛ; rule (iii) appears on D4ʳ and F6ᵛ. As none of the types or rules reappears within the same quire, there cannot have been any particular urgency over distribution. There is one unusual indication of a shortage of type. On D7ʳ, set by compositor A, there appears suddenly a number of wrong-font capital T's and W's. A few of the T's are to be found earlier in O1—e.g., B3ᵛ, line 7; B6ᵛ, line 19; B8ᵛ, line 3. However, the sheer number of wrong-font capital T's and W's on D7ʳ and subsequent pages set by compositor A must indicate that his case became fouled. These types are almost all found on pages set by compositor A, though a number of the T's are found later in pages set by B, presumably as a result of distribution.

Examination of the headlines in O1 shows that the printing work, in the normal fashion, began with quire A and continued through to quire H. Beginning in inner forme A3ᵛ through outer forme A8ᵛ, headlines identifiable by roman numerals i–xi appear; outer forme B shows the series xii–xix; inner forme B shows headlines xx, xxi, and then vi, vii, viii, ix, xi, x; inner forme C shows xxii, xxiii, and then i, xxiv, iii, ii, v, and iv. Repetitions of these last three series indicate that three skeleton formes were employed: skeletons 1, 2, and 3.

Quire	*Forme*	*Skeleton*
B	o	1
B	i	2
C	o	2
C	i	3
D	o	3
D	i	1
E	o	1
E	i	2
F	o	3
F	i	2
G	o	2
G	i	1

It should be noted that the heading on outer forme G1r, although it is substantially xxi, differs through the replacement of two extra-large capital E's by two of uniform size. Similarly, the headline on inner forme G4r, substantially xix, differs through the replacement of a small capital E by one of uniform size. The headlines in quire H are not located elsewhere in O1 and are not listed above.

It is not known whether William Wilson had one or two presses in 1647. The question is discussed in Miller, "A London Ornament Stock," 136 and passim, and in Turner, "The Printers and the Beaumont and Fletcher Folio," 44–45. While the employment of three skeleton formes is not necessarily inconsistent with printing on two presses, one might expect, if two presses were used concurrently over a number of quires, the need for a fourth skeleton forme to arise.

The errata list on H4v cannot have been printed at the same time as the rest of the outer forme H since the list corrects a couple of mistakes in pages of this outer forme. It is unlikely that the page was reset, for in different copies the errata is found in various positions on the page. Perhaps the errata list was printed from the stick. The errata are shown in the following table, with reference to the poem and line numbers of the present edition. Readings at these places from O2 are indicated parenthetically, and the reading from F1 is listed for comparison.

Errata in O1

Poem.line	*Uncorrected*	*Corrected*	*F1*
3.31	Pride.	Pride	Pride, (O2)
3.32	side	side. (O2)	side.
4.37	Bowes (O2)	Boughes	Bows
5.40	must (O2)	may'st	maist
10.30	see	Sees	sees (O2)
15.43	hou	thou (O2)	thou
15.43	doest	doest not do not (O2)	do'est not
15.48	force or,	force, or (O2)	*force*, or
15.49	steep	step (O2)	step
16.24	pactice	practise	practice (O2)
22.10	all in a	all in all (O2)	*all* in *all*
29.24	understanding	undeserving (O2)	*undeserving*
30.4	lest	least (O2)	least
30.11	an	a (O2)	a
31.2	a Flmes	flames	Flames (O2)
42.15	entice	entire (O2)	*entire*
51.12	That	This (O2)	*This*
52.20	sh	she (O2)	*she*
75.18	Or	For (O2)	Or
84.29	Lestany	least any	Least any (O2)

Textual Introduction 139

The index "A Table of the Heads in this Poem," H5-H7ᵛ, differs from the text in a number of ways. There are minor variations in punctuation, word-division, spelling, and typography. *"Love given over"* is listed as being on page 113, whereas it is in fact on page 112. The concluding poem "To the Reader" is omitted from "A Table," as is the subtitle *"(Suspected to Love her)"* to poem 71. The following substantive differences in titles are:

Poem	Text	A Table
3	The Given Love.	The Given Lover
7	Inconstancy.	Inconstant
9	Platonick Love.	Platonitk Lover
51	My Picture.	The Picture
68	Her Name.	The Name

In the course of printing a number of press corrections were made to O1. In the instances of changes to poems 41 and 50, it is not clear which of the readings is to be considered "correct." In poem 41, "you're" seems the correct spelling, but in holograph examples Cowley characteristically writes "yow're." Only because the correction on C7 was made after the larger number of copies had been printed do we list the sheet D "you're" readings as "corrections" in the following table. In poem 50 there appears no metrical or other reason to reduce the syllable count of "Propriety" from four to three.

Press Variants: O1

Forme	Page	Poem.line	Uncorrected [copies]	Corrected [copies]
i	C6	[page number]	3 [iv]	39 [i-iii, v-vii]
o	C7	26.13	give [i-ii, iv-v, vii]	give, [iii]
o	D8ᵛ	41.1	yow're [ii-iii, v-vii]	you're [i, iv]
o	D8ᵛ	41.3	yow're [ii-iii, v-vii]	you're [i, iv]
i	E1ᵛ	42.31	Br'other [i, iii]	Brother [ii, iv-vii]
i	E5ᵛ	48.6	Spirits [i, iii]	Sp'rits [ii, iv-vii]
i	E5ᵛ	48.8	Teare,s [i]	Teares, [ii-vii]
i	E6	48.28	unhappy [i, iii]	Vnhappy [ii, iv-vii]
i	E6	49.9	Inconstant; [i]	Inconstant, [ii-vii]
o	E6ᵛ	49.21	wast! [i, iii, vii]	wast, [ii, iv-vi]
i	E7ᵛ	50.21	Propriety [i, iii]	Prop'riety [ii, iv-vii]

The bibliographical information may now be put to use in answering a number of questions raised by Moseley's notices. Moseley, in his initial note, "To the Reader" (A2), says that he was led to understand that the manuscript he had was in the author's autograph. Though it is not possible to prove this (the publisher's manuscript could have been a highly exact transcript), there is spelling evidence in the errata and press corrections that supports the publisher's claim. In the errata marking poem 4, line 37, on A7^v, compositor B set the word "Bowes" instead of "boughes." "Bowes" is a form used earlier by Cowley (as in *The Civil War*, 3.257—*The Collected Works* 1:152). It is also the spelling that appears for poem 4 in F1, when the author (as we will see) was actively engaged in the printing process. On D8^v, before or perhaps after press correction, the "you" in "you're" is twice spelled "yow," the form preferred by Cowley in many autograph examples. That "yow" does not appear elsewhere in O1 may suggest that the compositors (A more so than B, who had earlier set "Bowes"), as well as whoever corrected the proofs, considered the spelling unusual and elected to set "you's." There is only one major textual error in O1, the omission of two lines after line 16 on C4^v (lines 23-24, at the end of stanza 4 of *"Love and Life,"* poem 23). This omission is probably due to compositorial difficulties. It is not entirely clear how C4 was set, though it seems likely to have been a collaborative effort. Stanza 4 of poem 23 shows an "unspaced" semicolon, and so may be the work of compositor B. Stanza 5 of this poem shows a "spaced" semicolon, the mark of compositor A. It is not unlikely that, in the process of changeover, the compositors failed to notice the missing lines. It is unsurprising, given the number of errors overlooked in O1, that the errata failed to produce an emendation. All other substantive errors in O1 (see collations) can be accounted for as simple misreadings of manuscript copy. To conclude this point, there is nothing in the bibliographical evidence with which to contradict Moseley's statement on the authority of his manuscript.

At the conclusion (A2^v) of his notice "To the Reader," Moseley makes a conventional promise to *"faithfully and nakedly transmit"* his autograph text *"unlesse perhaps some* Typographicall *faults get into it, which I will take care shall be as few as may be."* The surviving press corrections, though evidencing the existence of an apparently autograph copy, do not offer convincing evidence of undue attention paid to the manuscript. As noted above, the manuscript spellings of "yow're" may have been deliberately changed. On the other hand, the press correction could have gone the other way. The emendation to poem 48, lines 6 and 28, following the correction of an obvious compositor's error in line 8, show close attention to details of the manuscript. The errata, compiled after the text had been printed and ranging from the third to the final poem of *The Mistress*, suggest that the entire text was proofread. Errata in 5.40, 29.24, and 51.12 are the clearest examples that manuscript copy was consulted in this review. The printing of the errata list, however, shows signs of haste and carelessness. The instruction to correct "see" with "Sees" in poem 10, line 30, introduces a capital "S" that has no conceivable warrant. The instruction to emend "a Flmes" to "flames" in poem 31, line 2, omits the capital "F" while correcting the spelling, and the capital "L" in "Least any" (poem 84, line 29) is dropped while spelling and spacing are emended. As noted earlier, Cowley's preferred "Bowes" is cor-

Textual Introduction   141

rected to "Boughes," presumably on the authority of the printer, publisher, or proofreader. And the emendation of poem 15, line 43, carelessly reads "*add not after* doth" rather than after "doest," the signal word in the text. Finally, errors and irregularities in catchwords leading to sequent poem titles raise questions as to whether the order of the poems in manuscript is the same as the order in O1. The nine-page stint (F5ᵛ–G1ᵛ) by compositor A, with its apparent departure from the manuscript order at F8ᵛ, may have resulted from hastening the tasks of typesetting and printing.

In his notice preceeding the errata, Moseley states that the printer worked in considerable haste. Though there is no external evidence bearing on this, bibliographical evidence—including the irregularities in catchwords reiterated above—supports the publisher's claim. Haste is indicated by the fouling of compositor A's case from D7ʳ, if the case was fouled as an alternative to redistributing type of the original font. In spite of some press corrections, a considerable number of errors were left to be corrected in the errata and, if we accept that the manuscript was autograph, a considerable number more to be corrected in F1. The index appears to have been compiled quickly and carelessly. The errata list was set quickly and apparently stamped on to H4ᵛ without much care for consistent placement on the page. As noted in the bibliographical description, and then to be found in all three skeleton formes, a number of headlines combine type from two or three different fonts. An italic colon at times takes the place of the more frequent roman period. The mixture of type sizes and styles gives the visual impression of misalignment, and in some instances (G6ᵛ, H1) the ill-matched headline type has actually, and badly, slipped out of line. There are warps in the horizontal line of the poetic texts as well (F8, G7, H1ᵛ, H2, H2ᵛ, H3, for example), as though the forme had been improperly secured. Overall, the typography of O1 gives the impression of a hasty job, though not necessarily uncharacteristic of Wilson's work at this time (see Miller, "A London Ornament Stock," 137).

The claims that Moseley makes about the nature of the manuscript, the speed of printing, and perhaps *his* attention to faithfully reproduce the text all appear, on examination, to be more probably true than not. We are disposed, therefore, to accept the other claims he makes that cannot be tested. Moseley maintains twice—in "To the Reader" and in the note before the errata—that there was a threat from another edition printed from an inferior manuscript. No such edition is known, but the repeated allusion is perhaps a confirmation that the threat (at least) did exist. Though John Sparrow is correct in warning that it was a habit with publishers of the time to speak as if they possessed the author's manuscript and others, rival publishers, only inferior copies ("The Text of Cowley's *Mistress*," 3), Moseley has the reputation of being more straightforward than many of his contemporaries (see Reed, "Humphrey Moseley, Publisher," 61–72). Second, in "To the Reader"

Moseley regrets that *"it is not my good fortune to bee acquainted with the Authour any farther than his fame."* There is little reason to doubt his statement, despite Jean Loiseau's claim that Moseley denied knowing Cowley out of prudence. It would be dangerous, Loiseau argues, for the publisher to acknowledge friendship with so notorious a Royalist as Cowley (*Sa vie*, 109–10). It is not likely that the political situation in 1647 would have disposed Moseley to deny an acquaintance with Cowley, particularly in view of the fact that a large number of this publisher's authors were Royalists and Cowley was hardly the most notorious among them. Moseley himself was notorious for commissioning and printing prose prefaces, written by such friends as John Berkenhead, and swelling numbers of commendatory verses voicing distinctly Royalist points of view: witness the thirty-four commendatory poems in Moseley's edition of Beaumont and Fletcher (1647). In his address to the reader of *The Mistresse* he goes so far as to claim that this venture *"proceedes onely from my Love of Him* [Cowley], *who will gaine reputation, and of my Countrey . . ."* (A2). Loiseau's further suggestion, however, that O1 was published through the mediation of friends of the author who had remained in England, has some merit. Moseley's use of the author's holograph certainly suggests the collaboration of some friend of Cowley's. Yet there is no evidence to support the suggestion. A. H. Nethercot's argument that the manuscript may have been directly furnished by Cowley (*Abraham Cowley: The Muse's Hannibal*, 103) is likewise unsupportable. Furthermore, there is no sign that the manuscript used for O1 was prepared by the author for the press. In particular, there is none of the distinctive italicization found in Cowley's earlier and later authorized works. See, for example, the texts of *Sylva* (1636) and notes to *The Puritan and the Papist* (1643) in *The Collected Works* 1:237.

Edition O2, titled *The Mistresse* and dated 1647, has not always been properly distinguished from O1. A. R. Waller in his edition of Cowley, *Poems*: 456–58, records some of the results of a collation of five copies of *The Mistresse* dated 1647, but he believes that the variants are due to press correction. John Sparrow, in *The Mistress with other Select Poems*, 198, agrees with Waller. M. R. Perkin, in *Abraham Cowley: A Bibliography*, 32–33, misled by previous authorities, persists, despite the evidence he has collected, in regarding the variants as due to press correction. He has since, in correspondence with us, changed his mind. The basic differences between O1 and O2 are detailed in the bibliographical description above. There is absolutely no doubt that these are two editions with entirely different type settings and on different paper. Furthermore, in no copy we have examined are sheets from O1 and O2 mixed. The editions are correctly distinguished in Seymour de Ricci, *The Book Collector's Guide* (1921; reprint, New York: B. Franklin, 1970), 137, in the catalogue of the Beverly Chew sale, Anderson Galleries, New York, 8 December 1924, lots 91–92, and more recently in the Bernard Quartich Ltd. Catalogue 1027, *English Poetry Before 1701* (London), 14-15.

As stated in the imprint, O2 was published by Moseley. The ornamental capitals on signatures A2ʳ, A3ʳ, and H3ᵛ are the same as in O1 (though the decorated "I" on H3ᵛ is here printed upside down), identifying William Wilson as once again the printer. Additional bibliographical evidence, including layout of the poetic texts and shared errors in the catchwords and index, makes it manifestly clear that O2 is a reprint of O1. The priority of O1 is established by the errata. Of the twenty corrections called for in the errata list (H4ᵛ) in O1, seventeen have been made in O2 and its H4ᵛ is blank. Errata in poems 4.37 and 5.40 remain uncorrected, and the second correction to poem 15.43 produces "do not," a reading unique to O2. It is not surprising that there should have been a problem at 15.43, since the instruction in the O1 errata reads, "*add not after* doth," while it should have read, "*add not after* doest." It would appear that someone marked the major elements of the corrections in the errata list onto a copy of O1, for O2 retains other traces of the uncorrected printing in 10.30, 16.24, 31.2, and 84.29 (see the table "Errata in O1," above). In these four instances, and in the partial stop in 3.31, O2 coincidentally produces readings that appear in F1.

The priority of O1 is also proved by textual omissions noted throughout O2. For example, in poem 1, line 3, O1 (along with other sources) reads, "And I a double taske must beare" while O2 reads, "And a double taske must beare." In O1 and other sources, poem 84, line 6, reads, "Three of thy lustiest and thy freshest yeares," while O2 reads, "Three of thy lustiest and freshest yeares." In poem 15, O2 omits line 20, which appears in all other sources. These and other substantive variants between O1 and O2 are listed in the collations. Most of them are manifestly errors in O2; the others are probable errors in O2. In no case does it appear that the manuscript was consulted during the printing of O2. Aside from its numerous typographical errors, O2 varies from O1 in hundreds of accidentals. For these we can ascertain no authority.

O2, reprinting O1, appears to have been produced with no concern for emendation other than in the marked errata from O1. No press corrections are evidenced in the copies examined. O2 therefore offers undiluted proof of the shoddy printing standards of its day, in the particular example of William Wilson's shop. In its defense one can only say that it does not look as bad as it is. In matters of lineation, the layout of poetic texts, evenness of the headlines, and so on, O2 is relatively faithful to its prototype and gives the visual impression of improving O1.

As recorded above, sheets of O2 were reissued with a different title page "printed for *Rowland Reynolds*" and dated 1667. It is presumably of this reissue that Thomas Sprat complains in his "Life" of Cowley: "I am not . . . asham'd to commend Mr. *Cowley*'s Mistress. I only except one, or two expressions, which I wish I could have prevail'd with those that had the right of the other Edition, to have left out" (F2, sig. b2ᵛ). Sprat had, apparently, some negotiation with Reynolds—to no avail, however, since changing one or two expressions would have meant resetting. Plomer (*Dictionary, 1641-1667*, 153), following Hazlitt, is misleading in the claim that Reynolds "published" *The Mistresse* in 1667. Reynolds was responsible only for a new title page.

How Reynolds came by unsold copies of O2 is not known. Moseley would presumably have retained copyrights to O2, as he did to other works by Cowley, until his death (1661) and the subsequent sale of his Cowley material to Henry Herringman in 1663. Since Herringman had *The Mistress* in his purchase of F1, he may have elected not to buy O2, thereby leaving the option to Reynolds. But given the likelihood that Herringman would not have wanted a competing edition of these popular English poems, it is perhaps more probable that Moseley had sold O2 earlier. After having published F1, which contains a revised edition of O1, Moseley may have decided to sell off copies of the error-ridden, inferior edition. There is some evidence to suggest that the publisher William Leake was selling copies of O2 during the late 1650s. A notice advertising books published by Leake between 1652 and 1658 is pasted onto the original binding of at least one copy of O2 (see copies consulted in the bibliographical description).

F1 (*Poems*, 1656) was also published by Humphrey Moseley, a choice no doubt influenced by the fact that Moseley, having published O1 and O2, had rights over copy of *The Mistress*. F1 is, as "The Preface" on (a)1-(b)3ᵛ makes clear, the authorized edition for the works it contains. *The Mistress* in F1, as will be detailed below, is a reprint of O1 with a number of corrections and revisions, a few errors, and seven new poems—*"The Gazers"* (poem 77) through *"Bathing in the River"* (poem 83)—added before *"Love given over"* (poem 84). One poem from O1, there titled "To the reader," is removed to the *Miscellanies* section of F1, where it is retitled "THE MOTTO." F1 was entered to Humphrey Moseley in the Stationers' Register on 11 September 1655:

> Master Humph. Moseley. Entred . . . (under the hand of Master NORTON warden) a booke entituled *Poems, visᵗ, Miscellanies, The Mistresse or Love Verses, Pindarique Odes, and Davideis, or a sacred poem of the troubles of David*, written by Ab: Cowley . . . . vjd.
> (Eyre and Plomer, *Transcript* 2:12)

Another book, a Latin translation of the *Davideis*, was entered to Moseley at the same time: "Master Humph. Moseley . . . (under the hand of Master NORTON warden) a booke entituled *Davideis sive historia Davidis regis,*

Textual Introduction 145

Libris Quatuor, scripta p. A. Cowley . . . . vjd." This second book, so far as is known, never appeared in print. It is, however, advertised as forthcoming in one of Moseley's catalogues that is bound in with the Bodleian copy (Don. f.144) of Waller's *Poems*. The Latin translation of the first book of the *Davideis* is included in F1, and Cowley refers to it in one of his notes to the English Book 1 (note 5 on F1, sig. 4D1r). If, as is possible, its inclusion represents a change of plan either on the part of author or publisher, the change must have been occasioned by events following upon 11 September 1655.

The printer of the whole of F1, on the evidence of ornaments, was Thomas Newcomb. See C. W. Miller's "Thomas Newcomb: A Restoration Printer's Ornament Stock"; ornaments numbered 1, 9, and 14 appear with most frequency in F1. Newcomb had earlier (1650) been responsible for printing Cowley's play *The Guardian*, "mangled and imperfect" and "without my consent or knowledge," Cowley says, in his preface to F1. An interesting indication of the degree of fidelity to copy Newcomb aimed at in 1656 is given by a note before the F1 errata: *"THe Reader is desired to correct with his pen, these ensuing errors, which are material, and corrupt the sense. False pointings, false spellings, and such like venial faults (as also some mistakes in the Greek) are recommended to his judgement and candor to mend as he reads them"* (b)4r.

Signatures 2A1–2K4 of F1 contain *The Mistress*. For this sequence it is exceedingly difficult to distinguish the work of different compositors. There is a general consistency over the treatment of punctuation, spacing, and page layout. Evidence from type and rules is of little help. Damaged type recurs as in the following list, giving the type and then [in brackets] the occurrences on page, line counted from the top, and word:

B	[2B4, 39, But; 2F3v, 2, But]
h	[2B4, 4, The; 2G1, 18, that; 2K3, 4, whole]
H	[2B1v, 21, *Hand*; 2D4, 27, *Heaven*; 2I3v, 11, *Homer*]
M	[2B3v, 5, My; 2G4, 23, My]
P	[2A3v, 31, Pride; 2C4v, 8, Pity; 2F1, 13, Pox; 2I1v, 15, Pray]
T	[2F2, 5, *Taste*; 2H4v, 17, *Thoughts*]
w	[2E3, 17, womans; 2G3v, 18, t'will]
w	[2F2v, 9, wouldst; 2T1, 3, when]
W	[2C3v, 16, When; 2E3, 7, With]
W	[2A4, 36, *Women*; 2F3v, 31, *Wisdom*; 2H4, 24, *Women*; 2K4v, 24, *Wound*]
4	[as stanza number on 2A3, 2C2v, 2E3v, 2I4v]

Discounting rules in the headline, there are twelve identifiable recurring rules (where there are two rules on a page the one nearest the top is listed *1*, the other as 2): i [2B1; 2K3], ii [2B3ᵛ; 2D3; 2F1, 2], iii [2B4ᵛ, *1*; 2E2ᵛ, *2*; 2G3ᵛ, *1*; 2I4ᵛ, *1*], iv [2C1ᵛ; 2I1], v [2C3, *2*; 2E1ᵛ; H2], vi [2C3ᵛ; 2E3; 2G3ᵛ, *2*; 2K1ᵛ, *2*], vii [2C4ᵛ; 2E4ᵛ; 2H2ᵛ; 2K3ᵛ], viii [2D1, *2*; 2I3, *2*], ix [2D2; 2F2; 2H4ᵛ], x [2E4, *1*; 2H1], xi [2F1, *1*; 2I2], xii [2F3, *1*; H3ᵛ]. Two conclusions may be drawn from this evidence. First, as would be expected, recurring type and rules establish that *The Mistress* was set as a textual unit. Second, since no type or rule appears in two subsequent quires, there appears to have been no urgency over distribution.

No exceptional type shortage appears to have occurred. The use of swash forms of italic capitals—most often *A* and *M*—appears to be indiscriminate. The emphatic italicization appearing throughout F1, however, is neither indiscriminate nor characteristic of Newcomb's shop. Of the books of verse printed by Newcomb between 1650 and 1660, the only book to exhibit italicization in any way similar to that in F1 is Fanshaw's translation of *The Lusiad* (1655). Emphatic italics in this book, however, are supplemented by capitalization, and the overall effect is very different from that in F1. The system of italicization in F1 is recognizably the same as that in other of Cowley's authorized works, both earlier and later. Just as its absence in O1 suggests that the author had not prepared his manuscript for the press in 1647, the use of italics in F1 makes it clear that Cowley was responsible for preparing copy for the 1656 printing and perhaps was further responsible for directing the printer's attention to this feature of the text. As in the manuscripts of *The Civil War*, it appears in the instance of *The Mistress* that Cowley added indications for italics (probably to a copy of O1, as we will see below) as a step in preparation for printing. Other autograph manuscripts, such as the ode "Mr. Cowley's book presenting it selfe to the University Library of Oxford" prefixed to the Bodleian presentation copy of F1, do not show italics.

The only common words that exhibit noticeable variation are "be/bee" and "me/mee". No intelligible pattern of pages, however, emerges from a charting of the occurrences of these spellings. Only when the spellings constitute a change from a single *e* spelling in O1 does there appear to be some pattern. All six changes from "be" in O1 to "bee" in F1 occur in quires F, H, and I. Five of six changes from "me" in O1 to "mee" in F1 occur in quires A, B, and C. These figures, however, indicate little about compositorial practice and, as we will see, the latter set of changes could have been indicated by the author.

In addition to minor spelling differences, and to substantive revisions that will be discussed in the textual analysis, F1 varies from the earlier octavo printing in a number of accidentals that are recorded in lists at the end of this section of the textual introduction. There are differences in capitalization, apostrophes, punctuation other than apostrophes, and word division. The lists below cover the text of *The Mistress* common to both editions (that is,

O1, A3-H3, and F1, 2A2-2I4 and 2K4ᵛ). This information will be assessed in the Textual Analysis. At present, we note one feature in list 3. In a number of instances, period stops in O1 are replaced by an italic colon in F1 (16.14, 30.30, 33.26, 33.32, 56.3, 61.35, 61.36, 63.35, 64.14, 73.10). Some of these come in close proximity (poems 33 and 61) and could have been compositorial substitutions. Italic colon stops also appear in O1 (for example, poem 1, lines 26, 38, 49, 54; poem 3, line 29; poem 5, line 8; poem 20, line 18; poem 65, line 8), where they are intermixed, indiscriminately, with roman colons. These latter examples are reproduced in F1, just as indiscriminately, with either roman or (less often) italic colons—as if to suggest that the type styles were mixed in the case. The variant colons in F1, however, all occur in poems that were marked for italics in the same lines, and poem 33 is heavily revised elsewhere. It is therefore entirely possible that Cowley indicated changes in the period stops as well.

In addition to irregularities in the catchwords listed in the bibliographical description, there are a number of instances involving titles where the catchword and the sequent title appear in different type styles. As a rule (2B2ᵛ, 2B4ᵛ, 2D1, 2D1ᵛ, 2D2ᵛ, 2D3ᵛ, 2D4, 2F1ᵛ, 2F2ᵛ, 2F4, 2F4ᵛ, 2G1, 2G3, 2H1, 2H3, 2H4ᵛ, 2I1, 2I2ᵛ, 2I3, 2I3ᵛ, 2I4ᵛ, 2K1, 2K2), when the catchword includes part or all of the sequent title, it is set in a medium-sized italic and the title in large italic. However, in nine instances (2A3, 2A4, 2C2, 2C2ᵛ, 2E1ᵛ, 2E2, 2H3, 2I4 and 2K4) both catchword and title are in large italics, and in three instances (2A2ᵛ, 2E3ᵛ, and 2E4ᵛ) the catchword is in small italics while the title is (as always) in large italics. It is noteworthy that when these irregularities occur, they are all in the same half of the quire rather than in the same forme. If we assume that one compositor set sequences of these (2A2ᵛ, 2A3; 2C2, 2C2ᵛ; 2E1ᵛ, 2E2), the evidence suggests that the text was set seriatim.

Catchword irregularities in F1 are never as consequential as those in O1 (and hence O2), where differences on B4 and F8 suggest that the order of poems in the manuscript and the order in the printed octavo may differ. At issue is whether poem 11 should be followed by poem 12 or poem 14, and whether poem 62 should be followed by poem 63 or 65. The order in F1 is the same as in O1-2 in these controversial places (and elsewhere, except for seven poems added between poem 76 and, in O1, 77). This would indicate that the octavo was used to set F1, and that the O1-2 order of the poems was satisfactory to Cowley, if he concerned himself at all with sequence beyond the obvious opening and closing poems.

From 2A2ᵛ through 2K4ᵛ there are six recurrent headlines in F1. They are numbered i-vi and appear in the following order:

Recurring Headlines in F1

Forme	Sheet	:	Pages	Sheet	:	Pages
o	2A1		2A4ᵛ [iii]	2A2		2A3ᵛ [iii]
i	2A1ᵛ		2A4 [ii]	2A2ᵛ [i]		2A3 [ii]
o	2B1 [iv]		2B4ᵛ [iii]	2B2 [iv]		2B3ᵛ [iii]
i	2B1ᵛ [i]		2B4 [ii]	2B2ᵛ [i]		2B3 [ii]
o	2C1 [ii]		2C4ᵛ [i]	2C2 [ii]		2C3ᵛ [i]
i	2C1ᵛ [iii]		2C4 [iv]	2C2ᵛ [iii]		2C3 [iv]
o	2D1 [ii]		2D4ᵛ [i]	2D2 [ii]		2D3ᵛ [i]
i	2D1ᵛ [iii]		2D4 [iv]	2D2ᵛ [iii]		2D3 [iv]
o	2E1 [ii]		2E4ᵛ [i]	2E2 [ii]		2E3ᵛ [i]
i	2E1ᵛ [iii]		2E4 [iv]	2E2ᵛ [iii]		2E3 [iv]
o	2F1 [ii]		2F4ᵛ [i]	2F2 [ii]		2F3ᵛ [i]
i	2F1ᵛ [iii]		2F4 [iv]	2F2ᵛ [iii]		2F3 [iv]
o	2G1 [v]		2G4ᵛ [vi]	2G2 [ii]		2G3ᵛ [i]
i	2G1ᵛ [iii]		2G4 [iv]	2G2ᵛ [iii]		2G3 [iv]
o	2H1 [v]		2H4ᵛ [vi]	2H2 [ii]		2H3ᵛ [i]
i	2H1ᵛ [vi]		2H4 [v]	2H2ᵛ [iii]		2H3 [iv]
o	2I1 [v]		2I4ᵛ [vi]	2I2 [v]		2I3ᵛ [vi]
i	2I1ᵛ [i]		2I4 [ii]	2I2ᵛ [iii]		2I3 [iv]
o	2K1 [ii]		2K4ᵛ [i]	2K2 [iv]		2K3ᵛ [iii]
i	2K1ᵛ [vi]		2K4 [v]	2K2ᵛ [i]		2K3 [ii]

As the table indicates, three skeleton formes were used in the printing of F1, *The Mistress*. It is interesting that the third set of headlines does not make its appearance until quire 2G, where it is used for 2G1–2G4ᵛ. Given the recurrences of the skeletons, the order of printing would appear to have been straightforward, from the section title through poem 84.

The paper used in the printing of F1 allows further surmise on the order of printing for the entire contents of *Poems*. As noted in the bibliographical description, ordinary-sized copies are printed on cardinal's hat paper except for *The Mistress* and the English *Davideis*, which are printed on paper marked by an urn. In the large-paper copies, all contents are printed on paper marked with a large shield and eagle except for the English *Davideis*, which is on paper showing a smaller shield with an inner diagonal band. The difference in regular-sized paper suggests that *Davideis* and *The Mistress* were printed together, apart from the other contents. Different paper in the larger size argues that the *Davideis* was printed apart from the other contents. It is then arguable that the English *Davideis* was set and printed first, on smaller and then larger paper; next *The Mistress* was set, printed on smaller paper, and then printed on the new stock of larger paper; next the remaining contents, including the title page, preface, and ending with quire (b) with the errata, were printed on smaller and larger paper.

A small number of press corrections confirms the bibliographical commonplace that large paper copies, i and ii, were printed last. Signature 2K2 was corrected twice. Even so, there remain problems with the punctuation. The change introduced at 80.30, replacing a semicolon that was not printing clearly with a comma, is probably a compositorial error.

Press Variants: F1

Forme	Page	Poem.line	Uncorrected [copies]	Corrected [copies]
i	2E3	[catchword]	Welfare [v]	Well fare [i–iv]
o	2F1	42.2	A like [iii]	Alike [i–ii, iv–v]
o	2K2	80.12	bin. [iii–iv]	bin [i–ii, v]
o	2K2	80.16	Though [iii–v]	Thou [i–ii]
o	2K2	80.20	does [iii–v]	did [i–ii]
o	2K2	80.30	*Instrument*; [iii–iv]	*Instrument*, [i–ii, v]

Changes in Accidentals between F1 and O1

A. Capitalization. The list gives page signature in F1, poem and line number (as in the present edition), and the reading in F1. If the word is capitalized in the F1 reading, assume that it is lowercase in O1 and vice-versa.

2A2, 1.14, *Why*;   2A2ᵛ, 1.44, [thy] *Sea-*;   2A3, 2.1, *Saw*;   2A3ᵛ, 3.22, *Thing*;   2A4ᵛ, 4.27, *Nature*;   2B1, 5.3, Muse;   2B1ᵛ, 5.27, *Sun*;   2B3, 9.1, Sunny;   2B3ᵛ, 10.16, *Cloathed*;   2B3ᵛ, 11. *title, Many*;   2B4ᵛ, 13.2, soul;   2B4ᵛ, 13.11, *Cooks*;   2C1ᵛ, 14.44, *Proud*;   2C1ᵛ, 14.45, *Lover*;   2C1ᵛ, 15.31, mee;   2C1ᵛ, 15.32, *Tastes*;   2C4, 19.21, Spring-;   2C4ᵛ, 21.17, That;   2D1, 21.27, *Divine*;   2D1, 22.14, *substance*;   2D2, 24.18, Looking-;   2D2ᵛ, 25.18, man;   2D2ᵛ, 29.2, she;   2E1, 30.9, *Command*;   2E1, 30.24, *juggling*;   2E1, 31.2, Flames [*see O1, errata*];   2E2, 33.31, Times;   2F1ᵛ, 42.32, *Mad*;   2F2, 43.2, *Universal*;   2F2ᵛ, 44.1, Little;   2F4, 48.28, *Unhappy*;   2F4ᵛ, 49.7, *Where*;   2F4ᵛ, 49.22, *Smell*;   2G1ᵛ, 51.16, *Picture*;   2H4ᵛ, 67.23, *love*;   2I4, 76.28, heart;   2K4ᵛ, 84.29, Least [*see O1, errata*]

B. Apostrophes. The list does not indicate instances where the position of the apostrophe in a word is changed. The page signature, poem and line, and reading in F1 are given; it should be assumed that there is no apostrophe in O1. When an apostrophe is omitted in F1, and when a change of spelling in F1 appears to have occasioned the addition of an apostrophe, the O1 reading is shown in brackets.

2A2ᵛ, 1.38, o'retake;   2A2ᵛ, 1.48, or ['or];   2A2ᵛ, 1.50, I'll [Ile];   2A3, 2.28, the';   2A4ᵛ, 4.14, call'd;   2A4ᵛ, 4.29, call'd;   2A4ᵛ, 4.34, They're;

2B1, 4.46, depriv'd;   2B1, 5.3, do'st;   2B1, 5.4, know'st;   2B1, 5.6, dar'st;   2B1, 5.7, think'st;   2B1, 5.12, o're;   2B1ᵛ, 5.40, maist [may'st, *see O1, errata*];   2B2ᵛ, 8.23, 'Tis;   2B3ᵛ, 10.18, plac'd;   2B4, 11.20, Murther'd;   2B4, 12.27, defac'd;   2B4, 12.28, ne're;   2B4ᵛ, 13.3, *Spirit* [Spi'rit];   2B4ᵛ, 13.6, E'ven;   2B4ᵛ, 13.13, 'tis;   2B4ᵛ, 13.22, th';   2C1, 14.9, Admir'd;   2C1, 14.19, far'ed;   2C1, 14.22, *Conqu'eror*;   2C1ᵛ, 14.44, love'd;   2C1ᵛ, 14.46, *love'd*;   2C1ᵛ, 15.1, e're;   2C1ᵛ, 15.7, 'abused;   2C2, 15.43, do'est;   2C2, 15.45, *ty'est*;   2C2, 15.51, *'Imagination*;   2C3, 17.7, ne'r;   2C3ᵛ, 19.2, ne'r;   2C4, 19.13, ne'r;   2C4, 19.16, belov'd;   2C4, 19.18, eas'd;   2C4, 19.24, coyn'd;   2C4, 19.30, heav'en; 2C4, 20.4, heave'ns;   2C4ᵛ, 20.8, 'Tis;   2C4ᵛ, 20.12, *Priso'ner*;   2C4ᵛ, 20.14, *water*'s [water,s];   2C4ᵛ, 20.16, at ['at];   2C4ᵛ, 21.1, bus'ness; 2C4ᵛ, 21.21, ev'ry;   2D1, 22.1, TIs ['TIs];   2D1, 22.1, tis ['tis];   2D1, 22.4, 'Midst;   2D1, 22.5, ne'r;   2D1, 22.18, easi'ly;   2D1ᵛ, 23.8, measur'ed;   2D1ᵛ, 23.30, 'Twixt;   2D2, 24.5, ought'st;   2D2, 24.18, serv'ed; 2D2ᵛ, 25.4, *Hours* [How'ers];   2D2ᵛ, 25.18, th';   2D3, 26.14, ne'r;   2D3, 26.22, *disobey'd*;   2D3, 26.29, I'm;   2D3ᵛ, 26.35, th';   2D3ᵛ, 27.1, 'TIs;   2D3ᵛ, 27.1, 'have;   2D3ᵛ, 27.7, I'll [Ile];   2D4, 28.1, Heavens [Heav'ens];   2D4, 28.8, 'Tis;   2D4, 28.14, ne'r;   2D4, 28.17, 'Tis; 2D4ᵛ, 29.14, tow'ards;   2D4ᵛ, 30.3, *Igno'rance*;   2E1, 30.11, do'est; 2E1, 30.29, hee'll [heele];   2E1, 31.3, *Med'icine*;   2E1, 31.4, ev'en; 2E1ᵛ, 31.19, ne'r;   2E1ᵛ, 32.2, giv'en;   2E2, 33.18, I'll [Ile];   2E2, 33.19, I'll [Ile];   2E2, 33.25, 'Tis;   2E2, 33.31, Mee Times [Mee'times];   2E2, 33.33, what's;   2E2ᵛ, 34.2, pow'rs;   2E2ᵛ, 34.12, 'Tis;   2E2ᵛ, 35.1, *kill'd*; 2E2ᵛ, 35.3, that's;   2E2ᵛ, 35.3, assign'd;   2E2ᵛ, 35.6, *Met'aphor*;   2E3, 36.9, 'Tis;   2E3, 36.12, wer't;   2E3, 36.21, Whil'st;   2E3ᵛ, 37.6, cry'd; 2E3ᵛ, 37.6, hollow'd;   2E3ᵛ, 37.22, *scorcht* [scorch't];   2E4, 39.1, *Philos'opher*;   2E4ᵛ, 40.1, TIr'ed;   2E4ᵛ, 40.9, do'est;   2E4ᵛ, 40.10, do'est; 2E4ᵛ, 40.14, rav'ishing;   2F1, 41.5, 'have;   2F1, 41.6, 'have;   2F1, 41.9, I'll [Ile];   2F1ᵛ, 42.29, o're;   2F1ᵛ, 42.31, *Brother* [Br'other];   2F1ᵛ, 42.32, th';   2F1ᵛ, 42.34, *Chymicks* [Chymick's];   2F2, 43.3, *Captives* [Captiv's];   2F2, 43.5, Heav'n;   2F2, 43.21, 'twixt;   2F2, 43.22, *Heav'n*; 2F2, 43.27, *Future's*;   2F3, 45.11, ne'r;   2F4, 48.5, shut [sh'ut];   2F4ᵛ, 49.2, ev'ry;   2F4ᵛ, 49.4, compli'st;   2F4ᵛ, 49.29, *betray'd*;   2G1, 50.12, 'Tis;   2G1, 50.21, Propriety [Prop'riety, *the apostrophe does not print in some copies*];   2G2, 52.20, *happi'er*;   2G2, 52.33, *Twas* ['Twas];   2G2, 52.33, *destroy'd*;   2G3, 55.3, easi'ly;   2G3ᵛ, 56.12, 'cause;   2G3ᵛ, 57.3, Heav'en;   2G4ᵛ, 58.30, *Van'ity*;   2G4ᵛ, 59.10, e're;   2G4ᵛ, 59.18, Heav'en;   2H1, 59.28, Heav'en . . .heav'en;   2H1ᵛ, 61.12, *Cov'etous*; 2H2, 61.40, *Gar'isons*;   2H2ᵛ, 63.3, eas'ily;   2H3, 64.1, betray'd;   2H3, 64.5, dang'rous;   2H3, 64.17, ne'r;   2H3ᵛ, 65.12, understand'st;   2H3ᵛ, 65.20, Tis ['Tis];   2H4ᵛ, 67.5, ne'r;   2I1, 68.15, sev'eral;   2I1, 68.30, *Deity* [Di'ety];   2I1ᵛ, 69.15, Heav'en;   2I3, 74.6, *Twill* ['Twill];   2I3ᵛ,

Textual Introduction 151

75.18, ne'r;   2I4, 76.1, 'TIs;   2I4, 76.26, o'rthrown;   2K4ᵛ, 84.18, ne'r; 2K4ᵛ, 84.21, ev'ry

C. *Punctuation*. Changes involving commas, semicolons, colons, periods, and hyphens are recorded. F1 readings are given, followed by a bracket. Unless the O1 reading follows the bracket, it is assumed that O1 lacks punctuation. (Note that italic colons here recorded have been silently normalized to roman colons or periods in the present edition. See p. 166.)

2A2ᵛ, 1.27, sin,];   2A2ᵛ, 1.36, *Men*;] ~, O1;   2A2ᵛ, 1.36, *Beasts*,];   2A3, 2.14, *Love*,];   2A3ᵛ, 3.31, Pride,] ~. O1;   2A4, 3.35, *Gold*;] ~, O1; 2A4, 3.40, *Fellow-slave*];   2A4, 3.61, *Hymns*;] ~, O1;   2A4, 3.69, *Assise*,]; 2A4ᵛ, 4.7, *Rose-Bud*];   2A4ᵛ, 4.27, stay,];   2A4ᵛ, 4.29, away,];   2B1, 5.2, thus,];   2B1, 5.2, *you*,];   2B1ᵛ, 5.24, *Loves-Flames*];   2B1ᵛ, 5.29, trees,];   2B2, 6.18, *Spring*,];   2B2, 6.18, *Flowers*;];   2B2, 6.18, *Autumn*,]; 2B2ᵛ, 8.2, mix,];   2B2ᵛ, 8.9, I,];   2B2ᵛ, 8.11, be.];   2B2ᵛ, 8.18, *one*,]; 2B3, 9.9, dress,];   2B3, 9.11, *Center*,];   2B3, 9.12, dwell.];   2B3, 9.15, Despair,];   2B3, 9.16, Grief,];   2B3, 9.16, Fear,];   2B3, 9.17, *Persian-Tyrant*];   2B3, 9.20, Within,];   2B3, 9.21, Yours,];   2B3, 9.23, can,];   2B3ᵛ, 10.7, fair:] ~; O1;   2B3ᵛ, 11.1, Men,];   2B3ᵛ, 11.11, *East-Indies*];   2B4, 11.15, *West-Indies*];   2B4, 11.17, But,];   2B4, 12.10, descry,];   2B4, 12.16, *Mother-Mind*];   2B4, 12.19, does˯] ~, O1;   2B4, 12.20, aspire,] ~. O1;   2B4, 12.27, torn,];   2B4ᵛ, 13.8, use:] ~, O1; 2B4ᵛ, 13.10, *raw*,];   2B4ᵛ, 13.11, *Men*,];   2B4ᵛ, 13.12, desire.] ~, O1; 2B4ᵛ, 13.13, same:] ~? O1;   2B4ᵛ, 13.19, shine,];   2C1, 14.4, *Burning-Glass*];   2C1, 14.8, rich,];   2C1, 14.36, *Lovers*,];   2C1ᵛ, 15.10, brings;] ~, O1;   2C1ᵛ, 15.16, *Burning-Glass*];   2C2, 15.59, *Remembrance*,]; 2C2, 15.62, *Memorie*.] ~; O1;   2C2, 15.77, Thine;] ~, O1;   2C2ᵛ, 16.1, free,];   2C2ᵛ, 16.12, too:] ~; 01;   2C2ᵛ, 16.14, stood:] ~. O1;   2C2ᵛ, 16.15, boast,];   2C2ᵛ, 16.23, Me,] ~. O1;   2C2ᵛ, 16.24, *Tyrannie*.] ~; O1; 2C2ᵛ, 16.25, do:] ~; O1;   2C3, 17.2, brought:] ~; O1;   2C3, 17.7, friend,]; 2C3, 18.8, cry:] ~; O1;   2C3, 18.13, flame:] ~; O1;   2C3ᵛ, 18.23, sight,]; 2C3ᵛ, 18.26, *dead*,] ~; O1;   2C3ᵛ, 18.28, *Soul*;] ~! O1;   2C3ᵛ, 18.28, I,] ~; O1;   2C4, 19.15, *Guardian-Angels*];   2C4, 19.21, Spring-head]; 2C4, 19.23, lie,];   2C4, 19.34, Shee˯] ~, O1;   2C4, 20.7, *sterve*.] ~; O1; 2C4ᵛ, 20.19, bee,];   2C4ᵛ, 21.3, Ah,];   2C4ᵛ, 21.18, *Points*˯] ~, O1; 2C4ᵛ, 21.18, *Comma's*˯] ~, O1;   2D1, 21.24, *Deity*,];   2D1, 22.2, short-liv'd;   2D1, 22.10, in *all*,];   2D1, 22.18, shall˯] ~, O1;   2D1, 22.19, call;] ~, O1;   2D1ᵛ, 23.13, Me,];   2D2, 24.1, heed, thou];   2D2, 24.15, *make*,];   2D2, 24.16, *Thee*,];   2D2, 24.18, *Looking-glass*];   2D2, 24.20, *Magus*,];   2D2ᵛ, 25.2, has,] ~; O1;   2D2ᵛ, 25.4, *Minutes*,];   2D2ᵛ, 25.12, *Grey-hairs*];   2D2ᵛ, 25.13, too,];   2D3, 26.9, allay˯] ~, O1;   2D3, 26.13, give,]; 2D3ᵛ, 27.1, four,]~; O1; 2D4, 28.12, Alas,]; 2D4, 28.14, *City*ʌ]~, O1; 2D4, 28.25, there,]; 2D4ᵛ, 29.7, *Lightning*ʌ]~, O1; 2D4ᵛ, 29.8, disdainʌ]~, O1; 2D4ᵛ, 29.14, move,]; 2D4ᵛ, 29.23, grief,]; 2E1, 30.22, give,]; 2E1, 30.30, again:]~. O1; 2E1, 31.8, salute,]; 2E1, 31.14, *Conveniencie*:]; 2E1ᵛ, 31.19, descry,]; 2E1ᵛ, 32.1, say,]; 2E1ᵛ, 32.9, *Heart*,]; 2E1ᵛ, 32.14, *Hearts*:]~; O1; 2E1ᵛ, 32.16, *Allay*;]~, O1; 2E1ᵛ, 32.17, heart,]; 2E2, 33.4, Stews;]~, O1; 2E2, 33.9, earth,]; 2E2, 33.9, fixt,]; 2E2, 33.10, *Woman-kind*]; 2E2, 33.22, breath:]; 2E2, 33.25, 'tis I,]~; O1; 2E2, 33.26, descry:]~. O1; 2E2, 33.27, *Worlds*,]; 2E2, 33.32, call:]~. O1; 2E2, 33.35, come;]~. O1; 2E2ᵛ, 35.2, *Name*:] ~; O1; 2E2ᵛ, 35.3, *Name*;]~, O1; 2E2ᵛ, 35.8, by,]; 2E3, 35.15, self,]; 2E3, 35.15, flight,]; 2E3, 35.17, you,]; 2E3, 36.7, ahʌ]~, O1; 2E3, 36.11, *Wanderer*,]; 2E3ᵛ, 36.34, kind:]; 2E3ᵛ, 37.1, say,]; 2E3ᵛ, 37.9, flame,]; 2E4, 38.1, *Womankind*] Woman-kinde O1; 2E4, 38.7, *Customs*ʌ]~, O1; 2E4, 38.8, date,]; 2E4, 38.10, obstinate;]~. O1; 2E4, 38.12, *Jews*,]; 2E4, 38.13, *Gods*,]; 2E4, 38.14, *Idol-Gods*]; 2E4, 38.15, *Baal*] Bâal O1; 2E4, 38.21, out,]; 2E4, 38.23, *Deities*,]; 2E4, 39.2, away;]~. O1; 2E4ᵛ, 39.7, me,]; 2E4ᵛ, 40.3, *Nymph*,]; 2E4ᵛ, 40.5, *Nymph*ʌ]~, O1; 2E4ᵛ, 40.9, shareʌ]~, O1; 2E4ᵛ, 40.10, griefs,]; 2E4ᵛ, 40.11, *Tongue*ʌ]~, O1; 2E4ᵛ, 40.18, beget;]~, O1; 2E4ᵛ, 40.19, retire,]; 2E4ᵛ, 40.23, rebound,]; 2F1, 41.4, Fool,]; 2F1, 41.5, Youʌ] ~, O1; 2F1, 41.5, serve;]~, O1; 2F1, 41.8, bed;]~? O1; 2F1, 41.13, friends,]; 2F1, 41.15, obey;]~, O1; 2F1, 41.22, *Empress*,]; 2F1, 42.5, quite,]; 2F1ᵛ, 42.10, all.]~; O1; 2F1ᵛ, 42.19, taste;]~, O1; 2F1ᵛ, 42.29, prevail,]; 2F1ᵛ, 42.30, *North-Stars*]; 2F1ᵛ, 42.34, *Chymicks*,]; 2F2, 43.11, *First-fruits*]; 2F2, 43.15, stand,]; 2F2, 43.17, *Earnest-Money*]; 2F2, 43.20, *good*,]; 2F2, 43.20, worse,]; 2F2, 43.28, bliss;] ~, O1; 2F2, 43.31, *Hope*,]; 2F2ᵛ, 44.19, sow,]; 2F2ᵛ, 44.27, *consent*,]; 2F3, 45.12, *Head*,]; 2F3, 46.5 disdain,]; 2F3, 46.11, play,]; 2F3ᵛ, 47.3, Sight,]; 2F3ᵛ, 47.5, bee,]; 2F3ᵛ, 47.21, trace,]~—O1; 2F3ᵛ, 47.25, *Wisdom*;]; 2F4, 47.30, *unspeakable*.]; 2F4, 48.7, pure,]; 2F4, 48.7, *smoak*.]; 2F4, 48.8, *Tears*ʌ]~, O1; 2F4, 48.8, *Vapours*ʌ]~, O1; 2F4, 48.13, ow,]; 2F4, 48.24, I,]; 2F4, 48.28, *Unhappy*;]~, O1; 2F4ᵛ, 49.1, Ape,]; 2F4ᵛ, 49.8, still,]; 2F4ᵛ, 49.9, *she-Possessors*]; 2F4ᵛ, 49.11, made;]~! O1; 2F4ᵛ, 49.21, waste,]~! O1; 2F4ᵛ, 49.29, kept;]~, O1; 2G1, 50.17, return,]; 2G1, 50.21, Propriety,]; 2G1ᵛ, 51.5, draw,]~. O1; 2G1ᵛ, 51.6, saw.]; 2G1ᵛ, 51.13, well-wrought]; 2G1ᵛ, 51.13, it,]; 2G1ᵛ, 51.15, see,]; 2G1ᵛ, 51.19, *Rival-Image*]; 2G1ᵛ, 51.23, Me.]~, O1; 2G2, 52.11, *Chance-Medley*]; 2G2, 52.15, Execution;]~, O1; 2G2, 52.20, she.]~; O1; 2G2ᵛ, 53.12, *Monopolie*?]~! O1; 2G2ᵛ, 53.22, about,]; 2G2ᵛ, 54.7, round,]; 2G3, 54.13, *Love*,]; 2G3, 55.15, above,]; 2G3ᵛ, 56.3, do:]~. O1; 2G3ᵛ, 56.4, andʌ]~, O1; 2G3ᵛ, 57.1, been,]~; O1; 2G4, 57.18, hopes,]; 2H1, 59.30, *world*;]~, O1; 2H1, 60.4, *Venice-Glass*]; 2H1, 60.20, *Monarch-Love*]; 2H1ᵛ, 61.2, own,];

Textual Introduction 153

2H1ᵛ, 61.29, *Fear*,]; 2H1ᵛ, 61.35, *Formality:*] ~ . O1; 2H1ᵛ, 61.36, *Thee:*] ~ . O1; 2H2, 62.9, *Mankind*] Man-Kinde O1; 2H2ᵛ, 62.35, pretend,]; 2H2ᵛ, 62.37, calls,]; 2H2ᵛ, 63.11, *conjoyne*,]; 2H2ᵛ, 63.13, mine,]; 2H2ᵛ, 63.16, *Romance*,]; 2H3, 63.35, dye:] ~ . O1; 2H3, 64.14, *sleep:*] ~ . O1; 2H3ᵛ, 65.9, *Arrest*,]; 2H3ᵛ, 65.13, *Flame*,]; 2H3ᵛ, 65.15, be,]; 2H3ᵛ, 65.24, *Lame*,]; 2H4, 66.3, years,]; 2H4, 66.3, space,]; 2H4, 66.22, me;] ~ , O1; 2H4ᵛ, 67.6, Heart;] ~ : O1; 2H4ᵛ, 67.20, bind,] ~ ! O1; 2H4ᵛ, 67.21, Gentle,]; 2H4ᵛ, 67.27, *Qualitie*?] ~ . O1; 2I1, 68.7, been,]; 2I1, 68.30, *Deity*,]; 2I1ᵛ, 69.1, wise,]; 2I1ᵛ, 69.5, *Tears*:] ~ ; O1; 2I1ᵛ, 69.15, *Forehead*,]; 2I1ᵛ, 69.16, find,]; 2I1ᵛ, 69.19, Ah;] ~ , O1; 2I1ᵛ, 69.22, *cold*,]; 2I1ᵛ, 70.4, *Loves-Lexicon*]; 2I2, 70.21, choose,]; 2I2, 70.23, *Clothes*ˬ] ~ , O1; 2I2ᵛ, 71.9, Thee,]; 2I2ᵛ, 71.13, art,]; 2I2ᵛ, 72.3, *Physick*-potions]; 2I2ᵛ, 72.6, *kill*;] ~ , O1; 2I3, 73.1, art,]; 2I3, 73.10, *Fire:*] ~ . O1; 2I3ᵛ, 75.2, Boughs,]; 2I3ᵛ, 75.4, *dead*;] ~ ? O1; 2I4, 76.19, be,]; 2K4ᵛ, 84.27, orethrown?] ~ ; O1

D. Word division. Changes recorded do not involve hyphenation (hyphenated words are included above, in *C*). The signature in F1, the poem and line, the F1 reading, then the O1 reading are given.

2B2, 7.3, Whatever] What ever O1; 2B2, 7.5, methoughts] me thoughts O1; 2B2, 7.11, methinks] me thinks O1; 2B4, 12.5, methinks] me thinkes O1; 2B4, 12.26, Methinks] Mee thinks O1; 2C1ᵛ, 15.56, asleep] a sleepe O1; 2C3ᵛ, 19.5, methinks] mee thinkes O1; 2C4ᵛ, 21.12, methinks] me thinks O1; 2D3, 28.26, Whatever] What ever O1; 2E3ᵛ, 36.31, Well fare] Welfare O1; 2F1, 42.2, Alike] A like O1; 2F3, 46.9, apace] a pace O1; 2G2, 52.31, herself] her selfe O1; 2G3ᵛ, 56.2, hitherto] hither to O1; 2G4, 57.16, afar] a farre O1; 2I1ᵛ, 69.8, methinks] me thinks O1

Later Printed Editions

Following F1, fifteen editions of Cowley's *Works*, all including *The Mistress*, were printed between 1668 and 1721: F2-12, D1-2, and O3-4. These editions are listed in chronological order, and their authority is assessed. Entry letters and numbers from Perkin's bibliography, where expanded descriptions and reproductions of titles may be found, accompany each listing. Substantive variants from all of these editions except D1 are shown in the collations.

F2 [Perkin, B1]: THE / WORKS / OF / Mʳ Abraham Cowley. / Consisting of / *Those which were formerly* Printed: / AND / *Those which he Design'd for the Press*, / Now Published out of the Authors / ORIGINAL

COPIES. / rule / [ornament: showing a winged horse atop a snake-entwined rod; cornucopias left and right of the rod; two hands, extended from clouds, hold the rod at its base] / double rule / LONDON, / Printed by J[ohn]. M[acocke]. for *Henry Herringman*, and the Sign of the / *Blew Anchor* in the Lower Walk of the *New* / *Exchange*. 1668.

Selected contents: The Mistress, I2–T1^v. F2 will be fully described in volume 4 of *The Collected Works*, where it serves as copy text for poetry and prose printed for the first time in 1668. This posthumous folio was prepared for press by Cowley's literary executor, Thomas Sprat, and it is the direct or indirect textual authority for a number of other folio, octavo, and duodecimo editions briefly described below. F2, as detailed in the textual analysis to follow, is a reprint of F1 with emendations that are probably Sprat's.

F3 [Perkin, B2]: The WORKS of Mr Abraham Cowley . . . printed by J[ohn]. M[acocke] for Henry Herringman, 1668. This edition is recognizably different from F2 by the appearance of crossed VV's forming W's in "Works" and "Walk" in the imprint of the title page and the section title (I2) to *The Mistress*, which is represented on the same signature series as in F2. The title page of F3 has been reset, its ornament differs from that on F2, and the ornamented headpiece on I3 differs from F2. The F2 errata are corrected in the text. As the collations make clear, the text of F3 is based on F2. In every instance of substantive variation between F2 and O1-2-F1, F3 agrees with F2. Departures from F2 are mainly in the form of errors in F3 (for example, the omission of "*all*" in 8.14; the printing of "evident" for "event" in 17.13; the omission of "whole" in 81.34). Such manifest errors in F3 do not reappear in sequent printed editions other than D1. F3 is characterized by the inconsistent yet frequent respelling of "then" as "than." Leaves from F3, including the entire section *The Mistress*, appear in copies of the so-called 8th edition of 1693 (Perkin, B16). See, for instance, the Huntington copy of "1693." F3 has no independent textual authority.

F4 [Perkin, B3]: The WORKS of Mr Abraham Cowley . . . printed by J[ohn]. M[acocke]. for Henry Herringman, 1669. *The Mistress* appears in the same signature series as in F2-3. F4, though completely reset, shows the same title-page ornament as F2 and the same headline ornament in the half-title preceding the text of *The Mistress*. Errors and omissions found in F3 do not recur in F4. F4 is a resetting of F2. Some errors committed in F4 (such as the reading "name" for "flame" in 18.13, recreated in F5) reappear in F11.

F5 [Perkin, B4]: The WORKS of Mr Abraham Cowley . . . The third edition . . . printed by J[ohn]. M[acocke]. for Henry Herringman, 1672. In calling this the "third" edition, Herringman counts from F2, omitting the second edition of 1668. *The Mistress* appears in the same signature sequence as F2-4. Its section title (like others in F5) is dated 1671. Readings in 18.13, 22.6, 23.19, 49.36, 63.34, 76.1, and 79.17 (see collations) establish that F4 served as copy for F5.

F6 [Perkin, B5]: The WORKS of Mr Abraham Cowley . . . The fourth edition . . . printed by J[ohn]. M[acocke]. for Henry Herringman, 1674. The text of F6 is taken from F5. Clearest evidence of this is found in poem 24, line 35, where F6 follows F5 in the error "Add" (for "And"), and in poem 28 where omissions in F5 are repeated. Evidence of other sources for F6 is limited to the reading "flame" in 18.13, where F6 corrects the erroneous "name" found in F4-5, and perhaps the reading in 33.17 where a compositor for F5 misprints the elision "on't" as "ont" and F6, restoring the elision at least, produces "ou't." F2 may have been consulted for these corrections. A number of errors initiates in F6 (such as readings in 29.8; 55.8; 55.9; see collations) are carried through F10.

F7 [Perkin, B6]: The WORKS of Mr Abraham Cowley . . . The fifth edition . . . printed by J[ohn]. M[acocke]. for Henry Herringman, 1678. The section title for *The Mistress* (as others) is dated 1677. Errors from F6 repeated here make it clear that F7 is based primarily on F6. The publisher or printer may have consulted earlier folios (F4 or F2) for correct readings in 24.35 and 33.17; alternatively, these corrections could have been made by compositors. Some new errors committed in F7 (for example, the reading "subtle" for "supple" in 33.5; the reading "Thou" for "That" in 42.34) are carried through F10. F7 has no authority independent of the Herringman folio series.

F8 [Perkin, B7]: The WORKS of Mr Abraham Cowley . . . The sixth edition . . . printed by J[ohn]. M[acocke]. for Henry Herringman, 1680. F8 follows F7 in corrected readings in 24.35 and 33.17, and in repeating errors from F7 in 33.5 and 42.34. The publisher and/or printer, however, ventures on a haphazard program of correction in F8. The word "it" in 28.24, for example, omitted in editions F5 through F7, is restored in F8, but the omission of "there" in 28.25 (F5-10), just a line below, remains uncorrected. The error in 30.17 displayed in F5-7 is corrected in F8. Variants that affect meter are characteristic of F8; see, for example, 76.2, where "*Victories*" becomes "*Vict'ories*," and 76.8 where "odorous" becomes "od'orous." These metrical variants are sustained through F10.

F9 [Perkin, B8]: The WORKS of Mr Abraham Cowley . . . The seventh edition . . . printed by J[ohn]. M[acocke]. for Henry Herringman, 1681. Variants originating with F8 are repeated here (e.g. 75.9, 84.25, see collations), thus confirming Herringman's (by now) familiar practice of basing a new edition of the *WORKS* on the one immediately preceding it. As is also usual, new errors are committed in the new edition. In F9, for instance, note the omission of "me" in 31.23 and the less obviously erroneous *"Fruits"* in 6.18. F9 repeats the metrical variants from F8 and shows no sign of textual authority aside from the 1680 folio.

D1 [Perkin, B9]: The WORKS of Mr Abraham Cowley . . . printed by J. M. for Henry Herringman, 1681. This duodecimo edition features a newly engraved, reversed, and inferior copy of William Faithorne's engraving of Cowley that had appeared in the folios beginning with F2. For other characteristics, and Greg's opinion that D1 is a pirated edition, see *The Collected Works* 1:179–80. D1 was probably printed to take advantage of the upsurge of interest in Cowley in 1680–81, during which time Mary Clark, Charles Harper, and Jacob Tonson began their reprint series entitled *The Second Part of the WORKS*. The text of D1 is based on F3, an unfortunate choice. F3 readings in 8.14, 17.13, and 81.34, for example (see the description of F3, above), reappear in D1. This duodecimo also features an abundance of unique errors. Readings from D1 are not included in the collations.

F10 [Perkin, B12] The WORKS of Mr Abraham Cowley . . . The eighth edition . . . printed by J[ohn]. M[acocke]. for Henry Herringman, 1684. A second state of the title page adds to the imprint "and are to be sold by Charles Harper at the Flower-de-luce over against S. Dunstan's Church in Fleetstreet, and Abel Swalle at the Unicorn at the West End of St Paul's." This serves as a notice that Herringman and Harper had made arrangements to cooperate in and coordinate publishing the first and second parts of the *Works*; the two parts are frequently found bound together (see Perkin, 66). The text of F10 derives from F9 (see collations, 6.18 and 31.23). Where F10 is innovative (for instance: 38.16; 44.11; 47.14; 47.27; 53.29; 59.18; 75.1; 78.13), the variant is unique to F10 in all but one instance (59.18), and no source aside from the previous folios is known.

F11 [Perkin, B14]: The WORKS of Mr Abraham Cowley . . . printed by J[ohn]. M[acocke]. for Henry Herringman, and sold by Jos Knight and Fra. Saunders, 1688. The portrait of Cowley has been reengraved; it is here signed "W. Faithorne Sculp. 1687." The section title page for *The Mistress* is also dated 1687. As far as the text of *The Mistress* is concerned, F11 represents a break in the series of Herringman folio reprintings. The text has been reviewed, and F11 marks an end to some of the errors that had been accumulating during the twenty-year run of the *Works* series. The reading in 59.18 suggests that F10 was the immediate source for F11. There are other places

Textual Introduction 157

(such as 1.9; 3.32; 6.28) where the reading in F11 is the same as a grammatically acceptable variant introduced in one of the later folios and sustained through F10. Where F11 restores an earlier reading, the source appears to have been F4. See collations for 12.18, 13.3, 28.24, 47.19, 66.2, 68.6, 76.1, and particularly 18.13 (where F11 reverts to the erroneous "name" of F4) and 49.36 (where it is clear that the source is not F2–3). Line 14 of poem 21 is incorrectly spaced in F4 and in F11–12 but not in the intervening folios. F11 introduces variants of its own (for example, 7.27; 25.12; 69.4) and introduces a number of apostrophes indicating the possessive (such as 46.11; 53.6).

[Perkin's B16, The WORKS . . . The eighth edition . . . 1693, is not a new edition of *The Mistress*. In the copies of this folio that we have examined, the leaves containing *The Mistress* are from F3 or F2. In other respects, as far as our examination has extended, the 1693 printing is no more than a reissue of sheets from earlier folio editions except for the title and *The Cutter of Coleman Street*, which is printed on different paper from other contents and resets, in folio format, the text of the 1663 quarto edition of the play.]

F12 [Perkin, B17]: The WORKS of Mr Abraham Cowley . . . The ninth edition . . . printed for Henry Herringman; and are to be sold by Jacob Tonson, and Thomas Bennet, 1700. The Herringman folios F2–11 basically resemble one another in format. F12 has been redesigned. Layout of the poems in *The Mistress* is new, though the order is the same as in prior editions. As the collations reveal, F12 is a not very accurate reprint of F11. In some instances (51.3; 51.24) it appears that an effort has been made to improve on F11 or render it more consistent by adding apostrophes indicating the possessive. Despite some press corrections (as in 51.17, where "And hear it it breath" is corrected to "And hear it breath"), numerous minor typographical errors survive in F12. These are not recorded in the collations.

O3 [Perkin, B19]: The WORKS of Mr. Abraham Cowley, in two volumes . . . The tenth edition . . . printed for Jacob Tonson, 1707. O3, the first of the Tonson editions, was probably printed by Benjamin Motte; his name appears on some of the section titles in the companion volume 3 (for more information on the Tonson editions, see *The Collected Works* 1:181–82). The O3 text of *The Mistress*, Vol. 1, F1–N2 (pp. 65–179), is preceded by a section title (E8) and a full-page engraving showing Apollo, having slain Python, being shot by Cupid's arrow. Below the engraving is the citation *"Figat tuus omnia, Phœbe. Te meus arcus"* (Ovid, *Metamorphoses* 1.460). The engraving, signed *"B. Bernœrts 'scu,'"* is a copy taken from Octavio van Veen's *Amorum Emblemata* #21 (with poems by Richard Verstegen; Antwerp, 1608). This is a particularly early example of Balthasar Bernærts's book illustration. The textual point of departure for O3 is F12 (see, for example, 70.4; 81.36) but, like F11, an effort has been made in O3 to eliminate corruptions by recovering early readings. The error in 18.13 picked up in F11-12, for instance, is corrected in O3, as is the F12 error in 13.11. The collations generally establish that O3 could have been based on F2 or F4; the O3 reading in 18.13 is evidence that F2 is O3's alternate authority. Corruptions from F3 do not appear in O3, nor do readings common to O1-2, F1 (such as 3.4). O3 introduces numerous elisions (for example, 29.11; 53.26; 57.5) that are carried over to O4 and D2, along with apostrophes for the possessive and emphatic or decorative capitals (as 57.10).

O4 [Perkin, B21]: The WORKS of Mr. Abraham Cowley, in two volumes . . . The eleventh edition . . . printed for J. Tonson; and sold by D. Browne, J. Lawrence, J. Knapton, J. Wyat, R. Smith, W. Taylor, M. Atkins, E. Sanger, J. Pemberton, W. Mears, and J. Ward, 1710. O4, including the Apollo/Cupid engraving, follows O3 in design aspects and in the text of *The Mistress*. Layout of the poems matches O3, and erroneous readings from O3 (such as *"Possessor"* for *Professor* in 33.2) are reproduced in O4.

D2 [Perkin, B23; for two other issues, see Perkin B23a and B23b]: The WORKS of Mr. Abraham Cowley, in two volumes . . . The twelfth edition . . . printed for J. Tonson, 1721. D2 is based on O4 (see 4.35; 8.4; 31.17), but in some readings where O4 is clearly in error, D2 provides an earlier, correct reading (for example, 6.10; 25.3; 26.6; and 75.*title*). There is nothing to suggest an alternate authority other than or earlier than O3.

Two important editions of *The Mistress* were printed in the later eighteenth century: the John Bell edition [Perkin, B29], *The Poetical Works of Abraham Cowley. In four Volumes*, Edinburgh: At the Apollo Press, by the Martins, 1777 (part of *The Poets of Great Britain* series); and the "Samuel Johnson" edition [Perkin, B30], *The Works of the English Poets. With Prefaces, Biographical and Critical* . . . London: printed by H. Hugh; for C. Bathurst . . . 1779. Both of these editions were reprinted. The Bell edition has no textual authority beyond the Herringman folio series. The Johnson edition, however, adds two poems to *The Mistress*. They appear at the end, after poem 84. The first is titled "The Force of Love," with the added comment, "Preserved from an old manuscript." This manuscript has, to our knowledge, not survived. The poem consists of ten stanzas of six lines each, in couplets. The last couplet in each stanza serves as a quasi-refrain. The lines are seven-syllable tetrameters. No authorized poem by Cowley is in this song form. The only element of the poem that vaguely resembles Cowley's other writings is its use of the word *lambent*. The second addition is titled "Epigram, On The Power of Love," with the note, "This is delivered down by tradition as a production of Cowley; and was spoken at the Westminster-School election, on the following subject: *Nullis amor est medicabilis herbis.* Ovid." The four-line epigram reads:

SOL Daphne sees, and seeing her admires,
Which adds new flames to his celestial fires:
Had any remedy for Love been known,
The god of physic, sure, had cur'd his own.

These additions are not included in the present text; nor are the errors and emendations from the Bell and Johnson editions listed in the collation.

A. B. Grosart edited *The Mistress* for the Chertsey Worthies' Library, *The Complete Works in Verse and Prose of Abraham Cowley*, two volumes, 1881. *The Mistress* appears in 1:99–132. The title page that Grosart prints (p. 101) represents the imprint of O2. Next to F3, O2 is the worst possible printed copy text. Consistent with Grosart's editorial practices elsewhere in his Cowley edition, the text is silently emended time and time again. Still, signs of O2 show through—seek no further than the errors in 1.24 and 1.54. In a note to the reader (p. 100) opposite the O2 title page, Grosart justifies his selection of the 1647 octavo (without awareness of O1) on grounds that "the later editions multipy the forcible-feebleness of italics preposterously." He also notes that later editions contain additional poems and offers to include these among the *Miscellanies*. Curiously, the seven additional poems appear instead with *The Mistress*, in the same place and order as in F1 and later printed editions. Readings in these added poems reveal that Grosart recovered their texts from a copy of F2 (italics in F2 are, needless to add, omitted). Such a copy may have served, as well, the purpose of emending some of the omissions in O2.

Two editions of *The Mistress* have appeared in the twentieth century. A. R. Waller, noting some of the differences between the 1647 octavos and later editions, bases his text for *The English Writings of Abraham Cowley* (Cambridge, 1905) on "the 1668 edition," specifically, F2. John Sparrow's edition of *The Mistress, with Other Select Poems of Abraham Cowley* "pretends to a text more complete and authoritative than any produced by editors of his collected works" (199). Sparrow's main advance is in recognizing the authority of F1; he follows the Bodleian copy for his text of *The Mistress*, collating O1 and F2. His textual notes, however, represent only some of the substantive variants among these editions. The major weakness of the Nonesuch edition is that it considers very little textual evidence aside from the printed editions 1647–68 (dismissing the differences between O1 and O2, F2 and F3, as only of bibliographical interest). Despite this drawback and his highly selective textual notes, Sparrow's edition of *The Mistress* is the best so far. L. C. Martin's Oxford edition of selections from Cowley (1949) is, by comparison, regressive. Martin's texts are based on F2, although he uses O1 to restore line 22 to "The Wish."

Poems from *The Mistress* appear in many other collections. Loiseau (*Sa vie*, 662-64, 667-73) has a useful list of these, ranging from *Witts Recreations* (1650) through collections of the eighteenth, nineteenth, and the first three decades of the twentieth century. We have examined many English miscellanies and song books printed between 1640 and 1721. Those containing poems from *The Mistress* are listed and given sigla on p. 167; variant readings from them appear in the collations. Questions of authority are examined in the Textual Analysis below and in the Textual Notes.

Textual Analysis

The basic relation between the earliest editions of *The Mistress* is clear. Edition O2 reprints O1, which was set from manuscript. The text of O2 is very corrupt; in some seventy-five instances substantive error is introduced. None of these errors is found in F1, but the sequence and layout of the poetic texts common to O1 and O2 is represented in F1. A copy of O1, marked up with Cowley's revisions, along with manuscript texts of seven new poems, were the sources for F1. F2 reproduces the layout, the major errors, and—to a remarkable degree—the accidentals of F1 and is doubtless a reprint of it; see John Sparrow's conclusions in "The Text of Cowley's *Mistress*" (3). Variants between O1, F1, and F2, however, remain to be assessed and an authoritative text determined.

The basic relation between the printed editions is complicated by the factor of revision. F1, sanctioned by its author's preface, varies from O1 in substantive revisions as well as corrections (as in restoring lines 23-24 to poem 23, something only the author could have done). Many of the substantive changes—especially the rewriting of entire passages in 1.39-40, 21.5, 24.35, 33.6, 20—are to lines that show no clear errors in O1, and the changes reveal an author's rather than a corrector's hand. The substantive variants in F1, poem 1, may serve as an example. These occur in lines 9, 15, 39-40, and 54. The change in line 9 from "flow" (O1-2) to "grow" (F1) shows a sensitivity to the diction in later lines of the stanza, where the speaker's growth (line 15) is projected. In lines 15 and 54, loosely worded phrases from O1 are condensed and adjectives are added in the newly available space. The revised line 15 ironically characterizes the blind lover as "That *Happy* thing," unable to see his mistress's deformities, and in line 54 Cowley is newly able to remind us that to the cruel boy Cupid, tears of wretched lovers are "tasteful." Lines 39-40 are about Cupid's dominion over birds. "At every spring they chant thy praise; / Make me but love like them, I'le sing thee better laies" (O1) becomes "Thou all the *Spring* their Songs dost hear, / Make *me Love* too,

I'll *sing* to'thee all the *year*" (F1). The revision engages Love more directly, dramatically, and makes clear how the poet's songs will be better than the birds'. Revisions of this scope are not frequent in F1, and all occur in the first half of *The Mistress*. The last occasion, for instance, on which a line or more is rewritten is in "The Prophet," poem 33, and poem 49, on F4ᵛ is the last to show more than one revised word.

The case for authorial revisions in F1, anticipating a case for Cowley's active involvement in the printing of the first folio, is advanced by the appearance of emphatic italics in the text. It is clear from the examples above that the revised portions of the text included indications for italic type (as well as changes in punctuation and capitalization). Such italicization appears throughout F1, and it cannot be accounted for as characteristic of the printer. The italics are an extremely interesting feature of the text, similar in effect to musical notation for stress or emphasis, or a stage director's instruction to the actor on how to deliver a line. The importance attached to this feature should not be overlooked or misconstrued (as Grosart did), for Cowley apparently chose to prepare the text for italics first, introducing them throughout the series of poems, before attending to other kinds of emendation that are less consistently in evidence. Since most of F1—all but the seven new poems near the end—appears to have been set from O1, it is probable that Cowley marked up a copy of the first octavo to show where the italics should occur. As he did so it is indeed improbable, given the textual evidence of lines showing both italics and other accidental changes, that he did not make some alterations in punctuation and capitalization.

The case for Cowley's direct involvement in publishing the text of *The Mistress* may also be advanced by external evidence of his activities in 1655 and of the approximate printing date for F1. As already noted, Moseley entered the book in the Stationers' Register on 11 September 1655. The printing must have been completed by 8 April 1656, when Charles Scarborough wrote to the earl of Oxford, sending him Cowley's new book as a testimony of his friend's "incomparable merit" (Nethercot, *Abraham Cowley*, 157). The whole volume was not printed by 11 September 1655, since plans for publishing a Latin version of *Davideis*, evidenced by the Stationers' Register on this same date, were for some reason changed and the first book of the Latin was added to F1. Evidence of paper stock, however, establishes that the English four-book *Davideis* and *The Mistress* were printed together, apart from the other contents of F1; this phase of the printing could have been completed before 11 September.

Cowley was in England in 1655. When he arrived is not known, but it is well known (see Nethercot, 143) that he was arrested and imprisoned on the (justifiable) changes of spying on 12 April 1655. Sprat, in the Latin "Life" prefacing *Poemata latina* (1668, sig. a3), states that Cowley was imprisoned for a few months. Joseph Bampfield, in a letter to John Thurloe dated

22 November 1655, warns Thurloe against Cowley, saying "839 has told a friend of mine that Cowley shall apply to you, and pretend to serve your interest to secure and free himself" (*The State Papers of John Thurloe*, ed. Thomas Birch [London, 1742] 4:239). If Bampfield's information was good, it appears that Cowley was imprisoned for over six months, at the minimum.

In his English "Life" printed with F2, Sprat tells us that the passage in Cowley's "Preface" to F1 (sigs. a and b) that later caused the poet so much anxiety and embarrassment was written in prison. Charles Scarborough's 8 April 1656 letter, cited above, provides the earliest indication of the poet's release. External evidence, then, allows that Cowley's direct involvement with the production of F1 could only have been during the earlier stages of the printing—up until his arrest. Bibliographical evidence suggests that he was attentive to the printing of *The Mistress* through signature 2F.

We know that major substantive revision of the text is concentrated in the early signatures of F1. It would be reasonable to assume that authorial changes to the accidentals would be concentrated in the early signatures as well, although we have already noted that the entire text was prepared for italics. In assessing the changes in accidentals (see data on pp. 149–53), we may begin with the punctuation. Two kinds of punctuation change are unusual and unlikely to have been made by compositors: semicolons are introduced in F1 to balance clauses (1.36, 6.18, 32.16, 47.25, 48.28, 52.15, 59.30); and hyphenated compounds are formed (3.40, 4.7, 5.24, 9.17, 11.11, 11.15, 12.16, 14.4, 15.16, 19.15, 19.21, 22.2, 24.18, 25.12, 33.10, 38.14, 42.30, 43.11, 43.17, 49.9, 51.13, 51.19, 52.11, 60.4, 60.21, 70.4, 72.3). In the first of these categories, five of the changes occur before signature G and two after; in the second, twenty changes are before signature G and seven after. Altogether, F1 shows 242 changes in punctuation (excluding apostrophes); 200 of these occur in poems on signatures 2A through 2F, and forty-two on signatures 2G through 2K.

As in Cowley's autograph poetry, apostrophes are used in O1, more so in F1, to indicate elision. Of apostrophe-elisions, F1 introduces 117 changes in signatures 2A through 2F. Nearly all of these add the elision. In signatures 2G–2K there are thirty-one such changes. Capitalization for emphasis is much used in Cowley's autograph poetry, O1 and F1. There are thirty-three changes in capitalization in F1 through signature 2F, all but five of which introduce a capital in place of the lowercase letter in O1. Thereafter, in signatures 2G–2K, F1 show four changes, two of which add the capital. F1 shows twelve changes in word division before signature 2G, and four in 2G–2K. Numerical ratios in all of these categories are remarkably consistent and are also consistent with the distribution of substantive revisions in F1. Something happened during the course of setting the pages in quire 2F, or after poem 49, "Beauty," was set on signature F4^v. Relatively few changes in substantives and accidentals occur after this point. It is true that poems in signatures 2I4v–2K4 are newly added to the collection, so that the ratio of pages with texts common to O1 and F1, 2A2–2F and then 2G–2K, is 46/24 or roughly 2 to 1. Ratios in changes to accidentals, though they vary according to category, are more like 4 to 1. As noted earlier, in F1 there is little evidence in spelling of common words that shows a consistent pattern, except that five of six changes from "me" in O1 to "mee" in F1 occur in quires 2A, 2B, and 2C; the other is in quire 2H. There is no evidence to suggest that different compositors entered the scene at quire 2G, and it is highly unlikely that the compositors suddenly decided to change their habits in the ways that the textual evidence suggests. It is entirely plausible, however, that the author become disinclined to further emend the text, or that circumstances prevented him from further doing so.

Examination of the headlines in F1 establishes that three skeleton formes were used in the printing of *The Mistress*. The third set of headlines, however, does not make its appearance until quire 2G, where it is used for 2G1–2G4v. The use of a third skeleton forme would have allowed the printing to proceed more rapidly than before. It is obvious, too, that printing could proceed more rapidly if fewer changes were being introduced either as corrected pages of O1 were passed on or as the author himself may have indicated in checking proof, gathering by gathering, during the printing of F1. The fact that the few significant press corrections recorded for F1 occur in signature 2K may also suggest a faster printing. At least at this point in the run, a greater number of unexamined sheets was allowed to be printed before stop-press proofing, and the unrevised sheets were not discarded. The change in proofreading prodecure may have followed from Cowley's absence during the later part of the run; no stop-press corrections are observable in signatures 2A through 2D.

Textual and external evidence is sufficient for us to hypothesize that Cowley was actively involved with the printing of the first part of *The Mistress*, at some time before his arrest on 12 April. He could well have been correcting proof sheets, and his engagement in this process may account for the lack of surviving press corrections in F1 until the middle signatures. Thereafter the author continued to contribute to F1; Sprat says he wrote at least part of the preface in jail. But he could not have been readily available to the printer, who elected to expedite the job of printing the remainder of *The Mistress* by instructing that a third skeleton forme be employed.

Despite O1's having been set entirely from manuscript, and despite its showing only one major substantive error (as noted above, the omission of the last two lines in poem 23), the authority of F1 over O1 should be clear, at least up through sheet 2F. In the remaining quires F1 is clearly the authoritative text for poems added to the collection, numbers 77–83, which Newcomb must have set from manuscript provided by Cowley. It is also probable that Cowley changed some of the accidentals and words in the later signatures, during the course of preparing the text for italics.

The text of *The Mistress* is further emended in F2 (1668). Cowley died in 1667, and this first folio of the *Works* was prepared by Thomas Sprat, the author's literary executor. Sprat explains, in his "Life" of Cowley, the instructions in Cowley's will that he should make changes as he saw fit and publish what he thought worthy, letting nothing pass *"that might seem the least offence to Religion or good Manners"* (F2, sig. A1). As noted above, Sprat registers a complaint against the 1667 reissue of *The Mistress*, specifying "one, or two expressions" that he wished to have purged from the text. Given the substantive changes in F2, the one or two expressions involve the word *enjoyment*. In F2, the title of poem 47, "The Injoyment," is omitted, as is the subtitle "After Enjoyment" to the dialogue-poem number 81. The word *whole* appears also to have come under editorial scrutiny. The F1 reading of "Platonick Love" (poem 8), lines 2–4, is:

> When *Souls* mix, 'tis an *Happiness*;
> But not compleat till *Bodies* too do joyne,
> And both our *Wholes* into one *Whole* combine.

In F2 the lines are emended:

> When *Souls* mix, 'tis an *Happiness*,
> But not complete till Bodies too combine
> And closely as our minds together join.

So much for a pun that may have offended religion or good manners.

There are a number of other substantive changes in F2 (see collations: 3.4, 5.32, 14.16, 18.29, 18.30, 18.31, 31.1, 42.20, 48.20, 49.8, 59.4, 63.34). Of these, only the change in 3.4 (from F1's witty double-compound *"thin-sould, under-mortals"* to "vulgar sordid *Mortals*") seems perhaps to have followed from a motive to remove offensive language. Changes in 5.32 and 63.34 are trifling substitutions; in 31.1 the opening word "I" (as Sparrow correctly glosses " = Aye") is not comprehended and "Some" is substituted. Changes in 14.16, 48.20, 49.8, and 59.4 are errors in F2. The remaining changes (three in poem 18, one in poem 42) are curious gender alterations, removing the masculine pronoun "his" and substituting "its" or "her."

As John Sparrow has pointed out ("The Text of Cowley's *Mistress*," 4), F2 could be regarded as a superior text because of its more consistent treatment of accidentals. Such consistencies, however, follow from the authority of Herringman, or his printer John Macocke, or Sprat, or some combination of these persons involved in the publication. Nothing of further

Textual Analysis 165

value to the textual analysis can be obtained from the details of F2. Among the printed editions of *The Mistress*, F1 is clearly the authoritative text. The superior authority of F1, however, does not mean that it does not err, or that it does not carry over errors from O1.

Underscoring F1's derivation from a copy of O1, several errors from the 1647 printing are perpetuated in 1656. In poem 5, line 48, O1 reads "ln Sacrifice." A lowercase "l", looking somewhat like a capital "I", has mistakenly been used for the "i" in "in." F1 (sig. 2B1ᵛ) reads "In *Sacrifice*," despite the proximity of the probable error to an emendation for italics. Poem 12, line 35 (2B4ᵛ), erroneously reads "were" in O1, F1, and thence all other collated editions but for D2. In poem 46, line 6 (sig. 2F3), F1 carries over an erroneous comma from O1. In poem 75, line 18 (sig. 2I3ᵛ), all editions but O2 read "Or." The reading is grammatically satisfactory—"*Love* (I see now) a kind of *Witchcraft* is, / Or *Characters* could ne'r do this"—but it is clear from the errata printed with O1 that the original manuscript read "For" (see the errata table for O1, above). F1 is not overly scrupulous in following the O1 errata, perhaps because the hastily printed list contains its own easily recognizable errors, and this one apparently was overlooked. It is possible that Cowley reconsidered in favor of "Or." Although this passage occurs in quire 2I, where the authority of variants is less certain, the text of poem 75 was prepared for italics and an apostrophe was placed in line 18: "ne'r." "For," however, is probably the correct reading.

Some errors are created in F1. Line 22 of poem 19 is omitted; "on" is printed for "one" in 28.10; "humbly" is printed for "humble" in 29.9; and the parenthesis after the title in O1 "*The Wayting-Mayd*" (poem 71)— "(*Suspected to Love her*.)"—is omitted. This omission may well have been made by a compositor, by mistake, as no other title in O1 is followed by such a parenthesis, and it is an omission that might well have escaped the eye of a proofreader. There is another, more major omission in F1. The third stanza of "The Frailty" (poem 45, sig. 2F3, in F1) is missing. It is not clear whether this is a revision or an error. Bibliographical evidence and the contents of the missing stanza, however, argue in favor of its being a revision. First, the poem appears in the midst of quire 2F, at a point where Cowley was still in direct contact with the printer, and presumably instructing revisions. Second, "The Frailty" comes to a completely satisfactory closure after stanza 2. The third stanza (printed in the collation tables, below) relates awkwardly to the first two in tone, and its ending is one of Cowley's lesser achievements. Stanza 3 opens mechanically with an "As . . . So" construction, relating a sunrise-setting for the subject of waking remorse too sweet, too momentary and weak to counter new temptations of the flesh. The concluding lines of the stanza, ending with tears as the sign of new attraction to Beauty, do not distill the subject very well. It could have been that Cowley marked this stanza for revision and then, due to circumstances, did not complete the task.

In addition to the printed editions already discussed, all of the poems from *The Mistress* are found in Egerton MS 2326, and separate poems occur in 163 manuscript copies, some on single sheets, others in collections including from one to seventeen poems. Individual texts also appear in sixty song settings and in a number of printed miscellanies containing from one to eleven poems. Some of these textual sources can be shown to have been derived from one of the printed editions; others appear to have derived from manuscripts independent of the printed editions. In no case have readings from this latter category been introduced in the present edition, but they may have some authority. Manuscripts containing two or more poems from F1 are described in a list following the textual analysis. Single copies are described in textual notes, with the collations. Printed miscellanies are likewise treated. The texts of song settings are printed in the second part of this volume; their variants and possible authority are assessed in the notes to the settings. Unless otherwise noted, all textual sources roughly contemporary with the period 1640–1721 have been included in the collations.

We are now in a position to account for the text of *The Mistress* as it appears in this edition. It reproduces the copy text, F1, copy i, with the exception that errors carried over from O1 to F1 and errors committed in F1 have been corrected in 5.48, 12.35, 19.22, 28.10, 29.9, 30.10, 71.*subtitle*, and 75.18. F1 press corrections appearing in copy i determine the reading in the present edition except in 80.30, where we accept the "uncorrected" reading (see p. 149, above). Minor emendations have been made where F1's accidentals, in our judgment, may obscure the meaning and/or where the authority for the accidental is in some doubt. Editorial emendations are footnoted and included in the textual notes except in the case of italic colons, which appear in F1 to be a compositorial eccentricity. These are retained, though rendered consistently as roman colons, except where they occur at the end of a sentence or after a stanza number. There they are silently emended to periods in most instances. Likewise, other punctuation marks that occasionally appear in italic in F1 are silently turned to roman in this edition. Whether by the author's instruction or compositors' practice, italicized words are nearly always followed by roman punctuation in F1. This has the effect of enhancing the emphatic italics, further distinguishing them from the movement of the sentence. Misalignments in F1, where the proper position of the line is clear, are adusted and noted. Where two poems in *The Mistress* have the same title, the editors have added the roman numeral "II," in brackets, to the title of the second poem.

Though our copy text is the same as John Sparrow's, the present edition differs from his in a number of ways. Sparrow perceives more errors in F1 and shows a freer hand with editorial, substantive corrections; his *Mistress* follows F2 in spelling (for the sake of consistency with other texts that he prints from F2); in the accidentals, he corrects "trifling *errata* . . . without remark" (see *The Mistress, with Other Select Poems*, 198; there are a lot of silent emendations, not all clearly replacing errata); Sparrow's text considers neither the musical settings nor the manuscript sources, and accounts for only one of the printed miscellanies. Sparrow's is the best and the only critical edition to date, and we are grateful to have been able to consult it as a point of departure for our own.

Printed Books Containing Poems from *The Mistress*

The entries, listed in chronological order, are preceded by sigla used in the textual notes and collations. Miscellanies discussed only once and containing only one poem from *The Mistress*, are not given sigla and appear with full title in the textual notes.

S46 Richard Crashaw, *Steps To The Temple. Sacred Poems, With other Delights of the Muses.* . . . London . . . Printed by *T. W.* for *Humphrey Moseley* . . . 1646.

S48 Richard Crashaw, *Steps To The Temple, Sacred Poems. With The Delights of the Muses.* . . . London, Printed for *Humphrey Moseley* . . . 1648.

WR50 *Witt's Recreations refined Augmented . . . Recreation For Ingenious Head-peeces. Of Epigrams, 700. Epitaphs, 200. Fancies, a number. Fantasticks, abundance.* . . . London, Printed by *M. Simmons* . . . 1650. Selected contents from this edition have been collated with editions of 1654, 1663, and 1667.

C52 Richard Crashaw, *Carmen Deo Nostro, Te Decet Hymnus Sacred Poems, Collected, Corrected, Augmented, Most humbly Presented. To My Lady The Countesse of Denbigh* . . . Paris, By Peter Targa, Printer to the Archbishope of Paris . . . 1652.

MLE58 *The Mysteries of Love & Eloquence, Or, the Arts of Wooing and Complementing; As they are manag'd in the Spring Garden, Hide Park, the New Exchange, and other eminent places* . . . London, Printed for *N. Brooks* . . . 1658. The preface is signed by E[dward]. P[hillips]. Selected contents from this edition have been collated with the edition of 1685.

NAC71 *The New Academy of Complements. Compiled by L. B., Sir C. S., Sir W. D., and others, The most refined Wits of this Age.* London, Printed for Tho. Rooks . . . 1671. Selected contents have been collated with the 1698 edition.

Manuscript Collections Containing Transcriptions of Two or More Poems Published in F1, *The Mistress*, and *Miscellanies*

Manuscripts containing a single Cowley poem are described in the collations, under the appropriate title.

M1   British Library Harleian 6918. This quarto collection, 102 leaves, contains poems by Donne, Cleveland, Shirley, Herrick, Henry King, Crashaw, and others. The watermark shows a large eagle, wing feathers pointing downward, 105 mm across (similar to Heawood nos. 1298/99, dated 1644 and 1646). The name "Peter Calfe" is inscribed on the first leaf of the collection. L. C. Martin, describing M1 in his edition of *The Poems of Richard Crashaw* (lxxvi–viii), notes that Calfe is apparently the author of several poems at the end of the collection (fol. 94; part of fol. 95; and fols. 101^v–102), one of which refers to the year 1659 and all of which are in a different hand from that of the rest of the volume. If Calfe wrote the poems on the latter leaves, he was clearly not the major copyist of the collection, who also transcribed poems in Harleian 6917 (formerly bound with 6918). Martin associates the copyist of 6917 with Cambridge, during the early 1630s. M1 represents Cambridge literary circles of roughly a decade later. It offers contemporary texts of Cowley's prologue and epilogue to *The Guardian* (1642) and "Against Hope" (*The Mistress* no. 42; titled "Upon Hope" in M1), which was written in collaboration with Crashaw. Crashaw's answer-poem follows Cowley's in the manuscript.

M2   British Library Add. MSS 47111. Now listed as volume 192 of the Egmont Papers, this volume of i + 169 leaves was the commonplace book of Sir John Perceval. The book was probably compiled while he was at Madgalen College, Cambridge, 1646–49. It contains a number of poems, most unattributed, interspersed with copies of family correspondence. A transcription of "Against Hope" (*The Mistress* no. 42; titled "Hope. Nichols Trin Coll." in the manuscript) is preceded by a verse letter "On the false news of the Lord Inchiquin treason," dated "Sept. 28 [16]47" and followed by letters dated in various months of 1647. A watermark (fols. 67, 70) is a pot, c. 40 mm across, similar to Heawood no. 3553 (dated 1598) and Churchill 463 (dated 1650).

M3   Bodleian Malone 21. This miscellany, 122 leaves, contains verses transcribed in several hands. The name John Weston and the date "May 3, 1714" appear on fol. 104 in a hand different from that of any of the transcriptions. Contents, titles, and ascriptions suggest that the collection was made by an Oxford student, or students, between 1640 and 1650. The coat-of-arms watermark (fol. 42) measuring c. 40 mm across, is somewhat like

Heawood nos. 649–51 (dated 1640–50). The volume contains Cowley's prologue to *The Guardian* (fol. 38; titled "The poets peticon") and elegy "On the Death of Mr William Hervey" (fol. 24).

M4   Yale, Beinecke Rare Book and Manuscript Library, Osborn b.209. The loosely bound quarto is a commonplace book containing verse transcriptions in a variety of hands. Copies of "Against hope" and "for Hope" (*The Mistress* nos. 42 and 43) apparently date from the mid seventeenth century. Directly following these two poems is a verse transcription, in the same hand, dated 1659.

M5   Bodleian Rawl. Poet.84. According to Madan (*Summary Catalogue*, 14578), this quarto miscellany of poems and songs, some having to do with Oxford, was compiled c. 1650–70. The collection was owned by "Egigius Frampton," who signs it with the date 1659. Some of the contents may be in his hand, but there are several others as well. The watermark on fol. 34 shows a combination of three posts or pillars, c. 60 mm × 55 mm (very much like Heawood no. 3486, which is dated 1636). There are 124 leaves. A late date for the entire volume is established with the copy of a play by Charles Davenant (William's son) when he was aged thirteen. The play is dated 1670. Transcriptions of Cowley's "The Incurable" (*The Mistress* no. 78, on fol. 35^v) and "Drinking" (fol. 106) are both given the title "Song."

M6   British Library Harleian 3991. This quarto collection of "songs and poems from the time of the republic" contains 166 leaves and is written in several hands. One watermark (fol. 134) stands above an oblong frame, c. 65 mm across, enclosing the "Durand" trade name. It is comparable to Heawood 1219 (dated 1634/35). Another watermark, fol. 139 (possibly just the top part of the first mark), shows a pattern of lilies similar to Heawood 655 (dated 1677). Contents date the volume between 1655 (fol. 10^v) and 1670 (fol. 155). Included are poems by Waller and Suckling and a list of Donne's "quaintest conceits." Part of the volume is devoted to a numbered collection of thirty-two unascribed "Songs." Fourth in this collection is Cowley's anacreontic "Drinking," and song no. 30 is "The Discovery" (*The Mistress* no. 29). These transcriptions appear to derive from musical traditions of the poems.

M7   Bodleian Tanner 466. On fol. 1 of this quarto miscellany is the inscription "A collection of several Poetical extracts from Cartwright, Donne, etc.: in the hand of William Sancroft, archbishop of Canterbury." Fols. 1–39 of the collection are in the same hand—presumably that of Sancroft. Thereafter other sheets are bound in, written in various hands. The watermark on early leaves shows a dove-like bird and the initial "B," set within a circle c. 40 mm in diameter. It resembles Heawood no. 165 (c. 1670–80) as well as no. 163 (1691). Extracts from Cowley appear on fols. 8–26.

M8 Bodleian Rawl. Poet.213. This 8° copybook dated in the front cover "ANNO 1679 R[obert]. F[leming]." contains various entries in verse and prose, some by Fleming himself, and a number of personal notes. Copies of Cowley's odes 2 and 6 from *Sylva* (discussed in *The Collected Works*, vol. 1) suggest that Fleming, while copying from another author, changed some words and phrases to suit himself. Yet it is possible that variant and unique readings of Cowley's texts in M8 derive from an authoritative manuscript. If Fleming took his copies from a printed source, that source was probably one of the folio collections of the *Works* published in 1681 (or later) containing both the first and second parts—works selected by Sprat as well as the juvenilia. Fleming includes copies of poems from *The Mistress, Miscellanies,* and *Pindarique Odes*, as well as those from the early work *Sylva*.

M9 Yale, Beinecke Rare Book and Manuscript Library, Osborn f.b.107. The manuscript, an unbound, roughly stitched folio, is titled *"The THEATRE of Complements erected. Collection of Songs. composed and compiled by A Scholler of Oxford"* and "Printed for S. S. 167__". On the upper corner of the title page appears the date 1682 and the inscription "Ron Sutterly [?] His Book." It would appear that the collection of songs had been gathered together in anticipation of publication, an event that did not transpire. A number of the lyrics in the collection are given titles that appear in *The Mistress*. Some of the songs appear to be parodies of poems printed in *The Mistress*. "Song 68," on page 34 under the title "Loves Deity," is a transcription, with some unique variants, of Cowley's "The Discovery."

M10 British Library Add. MSS 34660. This folio commonplace book, written in several hands, is dated 1708 in the flyleaf. An additional flyleaf inscription and contents associate the book with the Bridgen family. Latter leaves contain family accounts and records dating to the end of the eighteenth century. Copies of two poems from Cowley's *The Mistress* are the only literary pieces in the book. The Cowley texts are written in a hand resembling that of fols. 1–34, which contain religious prose and scriptural extracts and are dated 1689.

M11 British Library Egerton 2326. The copybook, measuring c. 16 cm × 20.5 cm, contains 205 leaves with two watermarks: a coat of arms with three fleurs-de-lis (similar to the mark in M14), and a horn (somewhat similar to Heawood no. 2686, dated 1683). On fol. 2^v the book is titled "The most Ingenious & famous Abraham Cowley's Poems In Manuscript." Contents of the manuscript, written in three hands, include transcriptions of most of Cowley's *Poems* (1656) and *Verses* (1663). At the end of the volume appears

"Abrahamus Couleius Anglorum Pindarus" (signed G. D. Bucks.) and an index. The name "John Owen" is inscribed on the front flyleaf. On fol. 59ᵛ the name "Edward Elisbury" appears, in the same hand as transcriptions on fols. 3–90, 103–115, and 142–205. Transcriptions of poems in the manuscript follow the same order that appears in most printed sources, except for the Latin version of *Davideis*, Book 1, which in M11 directly follows the English text of that book rather than appearing after Book 4. Readings in this later seventeenth-century volume generally accord with those in printed texts of the *Works* (1668) and *Poemata latina* (1668), although transcriptions from *Verses lately written* accord with the 1663 edition, not the revised version of 1668. The occasional, surprising unique variants found in M11 are probably to be attributed to the copyists, primarily Edward Elisbury.

M12 British Library Add. MSS 29241. This is an 8° collection of verses on the lessons for Sundays and festivals and a miscellany of translations into Latin from Dryden, Fletcher, Cowley, and Dr. Woodford and into English from Horace and Martial. There are also some English poems, including "Upon ye fire at Whitehall" dated 1697, a Latin obituary verse to Johannis Flatmanni dated 1690, and songs dated in the 1690s.

M13 St. Paul's Cathedral 52 D 14. This bound quarto titled "Dr. Donne's Sermons" is described in George R. Potter and Evelyn M. Simpson, eds., *The Sermons of John Donne* 1:41–42. A watermark shows a pot crowned with a horned moon, c. 55 mm top to bottom, somewhat similar to Heawood nos. 3618/19 (dated 1656) and 3622/23 (dated 1634; early seventeenth century). The sermons, transcribed by K[nightley] Chetwode and dated 1625 on the hand-decorated title page, are followed on leaves 178–95 by a collection of poems and translations under the date 1696. Preceding these, on 176ᵛ, there is written, "The reason why I wrote severall of these following Verses, was not that I thought them all good, but the subjects was—what I had occasion to make use of." This note could possibly be in the hand of Catherine Butler, who inscribed the blank flyleaf preceding the *Sermons* title with another note that [the book was] "Given me by my Father, May 1693." The texts include poems and extracts from Dryden, Denham, Rochester, Katherine Phillips, Brome, Waller, Roscommon, Suckling, Davenant, and Donne, as well as Cowley. Authors and sources are listed in the margins. Transcriptions of Cowley's poems also appearing in *The Mistress* and *Miscellanies* are taken from a printed edition of the *Works*, as the marginal page numbers indicate.

M14 British Library Add. MSS 11492. The watermarks appearing on the leaves of this quarto volume—a coat of arms with three fleurs-de-lis and a smaller coat of arms with a horn—are similar to those of M11. The first of these resembles Heawood no. 656 (dated 1662) or no. 630 (dated Paris, 1684).

M14 is an exercise book bearing the title, "Essayes for attaining French," composed by Oliver Salusbury. It contains transcriptions of texts intended for translation from French to English and vice-versa. Copies of Sprat's "Life" of Cowley and poems from *The Mistress* and *Miscellanies* have been readied for the exercise, but they have not been rendered into French.

M15 Yale, Beinecke Rare Book and Manuscript Library, Osborn b.118. This late-seventeenth-century 8° copybook contains 316 numbered pages. The contents appear to be in the same hand, except perhaps for the small script written in the margins throughout the volume. The last entry in M15 is "Abrahamus Couleius Anglorum, Pindarus. . . ," signed Buckingham and dated, as of Cowley's death, 1667. The first forty pages of M15 contain copies of Cowley's poems and a number of extracts. The copyist then continues with transcriptions from Katherine Phillips and others, "Sayings of Heathens," and "Adages."

M16 Harvard, Houghton Library MS Eng 631. A large (23.4 cm × 17.6 cm) quarto of 116 (plus twenty-eight blank) leaves, written in the same hand throughout, and titled, "A collection of miscellaney poems from the greatest poets both antient and modern that I have read & here place for my own entertainment to divert malincolly thoughts & to assist my memory, that was never good at no time." The copyist is otherwise unidentified; the volume is from the library at Newburgh Priory, Yorkshire, and it contains the Belasyse family bookplate. But for Spenser, the transcriptions are from seventeenth-centuty English poets: Sandys, Herbert, Crashaw, Waller, Cowley, Cleveland, and Randolph. This selection suggests a mid seventeenth-century date for the miscellaney. The watermark shows a large, ornamented shield, c. 150 mm top to bottom, containing a fleur-de-lis.

M17 University of Chicago, Joseph Regenstein Library MS f 553. A folio volume of 366 numbered pages, plus one leaf at the beginning and three leaves, with a table of contents, at the end. The collection of poems is copied in a single hand throughout. On the front flyleaf appears the date MDCCXV:XVI. The last page of text is dated 30 July, 1717 and the last page of the table of contents reads "Finis August 6, 1717." Copies of Cowley's poems and extracts from Cowley appear in various places in M17; some are ascribed, and some are not. Most of the copies were probably taken from one of the folio editions of Cowley's *Works*, F2 or later. But the evidence of some transcriptions, such as "Inconstancy" on page 255, suggests that the copyist took some of the texts from manuscript.

M18 British Library Add. MSS 29921. This 12° copy book, 136 leaves, is signed "H. Packwood, Anno 1668" on fol. 1. Copies of poems from

Cowley's *The Mistress, Pindarique Odes*, and *Essays* are taken from the "6 Edit.1680," as the copyist acknowledges on fol. 124. There is a further note, on fol. 129, that "the Pages are ye same in Cowley's fourth Edit. A.D.1674." The Cowley transcriptions follow "Poems to ye Memory of Mr Nat.Taylor, printed for Lawrence 1702."

M19 Harvard, Houghton Library MS Eng 584. A quarto miscellany (c. 21.4 cm × 13.5 cm), apparently prepared in expectation of publication, with the carefully lettered title—MISCELLANY POEMS / By Severall Hands. / Collected by B. Cumberlege. ā° 1703.—inscribed above an ink sketch. There are two blank leaves, pages [i–x] 1–182 [1–12], and two blanks at the end. The contents include an "heroick Poem upon a Monastick Life" and other poems and translations by Cumberlege, along with transcriptions from Cowley, Tate, Dryden, and others. The watermark is not discernible.

M20 Edinburgh University Library MS Dc.3.76. A rebound quarto miscellany, verse and prose, with the watermark of the Amsterdam coat of arms—a shield with three saltires in a central vertical panel, supported by two lions under an elaborate crown (similar to Churchill nos. 39 and 70). Ownership inscriptions for George Wright (1703) and Frances Wright (1708) appear at both ends of the volume. A number of the texts included in M20 are not attributed, though most are. The copies are from late-seventeenth and early-eighteenth-century writers.

M21 Bodleian Rawl. Poet.173. The title for this folio miscellany, 1 plus 191 numbered leaves, reads "*The Muse's Magazine*, Or Poeticall Miscelanies, in two parts. The first consisting of choice translations and paraphrases selected from the Ancients, done by the best of our modern Poets, the second part consisting wholly of originall poems, selected from many of our own Poets . . . 1705." M21 was probably intended for publication. Prefatory matter, fols. 1–4^v, suggests that the manuscript might "fall into hands that would place it in public view." If the compiler is a Mr. Corbet, the inscription "John Dunton his book, for which Mr. Corbet, at the Addison's Head accepted one half guinea in full payment for it" records the immediate wages for his effort. There are a number of extracts from Cowley's *Essays* in the first part of M21. Starting with fol. 79, there appear copies of poems from *The Mistress*. Not all of these appear to have been derived from printed sources.

M22 Bodleian Rawl. Poet.90. *A collection of verses, fancyes and poems, morall and divine* is a quarto miscellany, [i] plus 180 numbered leaves, containing a number of Cowley texts. Madan (*Summary Catalogue*, 14583) lists the volume as written in the first half of the eighteenth century, though it may be earlier. The watermark shows pillars (c. 60 mm across) with grape clusters at the base of the columns. The mark resembles Heawood no. 3516 (dated 1684), no. 3519, and no. 3525 (dated 1671). The copies are in at least two hands. The Cowley transcriptions come from various sources, some probably manuscript. Copies of "Against Hope" and "For Hope" (*The Mistress* nos. 42 and 43) appear to have been taken from S46. Unusual titles and the lack of ascription for other of Cowley's poems suggest a source or sources outside the printed editions.

M23   Yale, Beinecke Rare Book and Manuscript Library, Osborn b.135. This octavo-sized, early-eighteenth-century commonplace book is inscribed "Blount, Sir Thomas Pope, bart. 1647-97. DE RE POETICA: anonymous MS collection of extracts from this work." There are extracts from other studies, too—such as Boileau's *Art of Poetry*. Cowley is cited a number of times. Extracts from "Ode. of Wit" and "Elegie upon Anacreon" precede a sketch of Cowley's life and reputation. The volume concludes with transcriptions of Cowley's poems.

M24   British Library Sloan 4456. The volume is made up of various transcriptions on differing sizes of paper and in various hands. Newspaper clippings inserted in the collection (such as *London Weekly*, Saturday, 16 September 1732) suggest an approximate date for these gathered materials. One folio sheet has been folded to make four pages, fols. 63-64, verso and recto, of the collection. Fol. 64^v is inscribed with the name "Cowley." Fols. 63-64^r contain extracts from *The Mistress, Miscellanies*, and from Sprat's "Life." The watermark on this folio sheet is a shield with the fleur-de-lis, c. 80 mm top to bottom, somewhat like Heawood no. 1753 (dated 1674).

M25   Folger Va. 308. A quarto copy book inscribed "Thomas Boydill" inside the front cover. The volume contains transcriptions of 156 poems. The contents are datable c. 1690-1730. Copies of Odes 3 and 6 from Cowley's *Sylva* (poems 19 and 22; see *The Collected Works*, vol. 1) were probably taken from either the 1681 or the 1684 folio edition of the *Works*. Copies of three poems from *The Mistress*, nos. 52, 56, and 60, were probably taken from *Witt's Recreations*: these three Cowley poems—and only these—appear in the editions of 1650, 1654, 1663, and 1667.

M26   Yale, Beinecke Rare Book and Manuscript Library, Osborn Poetry Box VI, Item 47. This single sheet, 19 cm × 29 cm, shows stitch marks along one side, indicating that it once appeared as part of a book. The sheet contains a copy of "The Discovery" and extracts from other poems appearing in *The Mistress*, all in the same hand.

M27   Yale, Beinecke Rare Book and Manuscript Library, Obsorn Poetry Box X, Item 1. Another single sheet, 14 cm × 19 cm, written in a single hand (not the same as M26), with stitch marks indicating that it was once bound in a collection. The preceding sheet may have contained additional copies from Cowley, since this one begins with the concluding twenty-six lines of "Reason" (*Miscellanies* no. 22).

Collations and Textual Notes

1. *The Request.*

Manuscripts: M11 (fol. 25^v), M8 (front cover: extract, ll. 17–20)

1. I'Have] Σ; I've D2   3. I] Σ; *om* O2   9. grow] Σ; flow O1–2   10. what ere] O1–2, F1, M11; what e're F2–6, M11; whate're F7–12, O3–4, D2   15. That *Happy* thing] Σ; When I'me that thing O1–2   20. mine] O1–2, F1; my Σ   24. springing] Σ; spring O2   25. my] Σ; mine M11   29. would] Σ; will F12, O3–4, D2   35. nobler] Σ; noble O2   39. —] Σ; At every spring they chant thy praise; O1–2   40. —] Σ; Make me but love like them, I'le sing thee better laies. O1–2; Make me Love too, I'll sing to thee all th'Year O3–4, D2   42. thy] Σ; by O2   54. one] Σ; no more one O1; no more on O2   tasteful] Σ; *om* O1–2   56. not onely] Σ; not'only O4

2. *The Thraldome.*

Manuscripts: M11 (fol. 26^v)

2. *Lightning* did] Σ; The Lightning O1–2   15. use] Σ; me F3   17. Whilst] Σ; Whist M11   20. task] Σ; aske O2   23. They pant] Σ; Thy part O2   24. Their] Σ; Thy O2

Musical settings: Purcell, *Orpheus Britannicus*, and manuscript copies as listed in notes to the settings.

3. *The Given Love.*

Manuscripts: M10 (fol. 49, unascribed), M11 (fol. 27), M24 (fol. 63, extracts: ll. 57–60, 49–56)

title] Σ; *The Given Lover* O1 (index), O2 (text and index), M11; given love M11 (index)   2. and] Σ; or M10   4. *thin-sould, under-mortals*] O1–2, F1; vulgar sordid *Mortals* Σ   12. *Learned, Wise*] Σ; wise, learned M10   19. such] Σ; *om* M10   32. to 'his] O1–2, F1–4, M11; to's F5–12, O3–4, D2, M10   36. with] Σ; wch M11   av'arice] Σ; av'rice F4–8; Avarice

O3-4, D2   40. your] Σ; you M10   42. made] Σ; make F3   *Gold*] Σ; God O2   48. They, as He,] Σ; They themselves O1-2   51. do't] Σ; do it M11   59. *Popish*] Σ; english M11   61. *Hymns*,] *ed*.; ~; F1   63. Thy] Σ; The O2   *stanza 9*] Σ; *om* M10

Musical settings: William King, *Poems*, 28; Reggio, *Songs*, 1.10.

4. *The Spring.*

Manuscripts: M11 (fol. 28)

7. *Rose-Bud*] Σ; Rose But O2   9. so] Σ; so so F12   10. so gay] *ed*.; sogay F1   15. same sight] Σ; rame in sight F12   18. every] Σ; ev'ry O3-4, D2   19. should not know] Σ; should know F12   31. followed] Σ; follow'd F8-12, O3-4, D2   34. They're] Σ; They are O2   35. *Rights*] Σ; *Right* O4, D2   39. *Flowers*] Σ; *Flower* F12

5. *Written in Juice of Lemmon.*

Manuscripts: M11 (fol. 29), M14 (fol. 121^v)

1. WHilst] Σ; Whilest F6-12   6. read] Σ; ready O2   8. thy] Σ; they O3   24. her] Σ; it M11   25. power] Σ; Pow'r O3-4, D2   28. *Plants*] Σ; *Planets* O2   32. *lineation*] *ed*.; *32 is aligned with line 31 in F1*   soon as] O1-2, F1; when a Σ   33. *Wood*] Σ; *Word* F9-12   34. buds] Σ; but O2   39. in] Σ; and M11   40. maist] Σ; must O2 (*The reading "must" in O1 is corrected to "may'st" in the Errata. This correction was missed in the printing of O2.*)   41. her] Σ; *om* O2   46. or] Σ; and O2   48. in] *ed*.; In F1 (*O1 prints a lowercase* l, *appearing somewhat like a capital* I *that the F1 compositor produces, for the* i.)

6. *Inconstancy.*

Manuscripts: M11 (fol. 30), M14 (fol. 123^v), M17 (p. 354). M13, M20, and other manuscript collections contain an unascribed extract from this poem, beginning with line 19, "The *World's* a *Scene* of *Changes* . . . ," and ending with line 28. It appears that this concluding segment of "Inconstancy" circulated independently among copyists.

title] Σ; *Inconstant* O1-2 (*index*)   9. most] Σ; more F12, O3-4, D2   10. t'another] Σ; to another M11; to t'another O4   18. *Fruit*] Σ; *Fruits* F9-12   23. doth] Σ; dos M14   25. T'imagine] Σ; To imagine M14, M17   should] Σ; will O2   28. stays] O1-2, F1-8; stay F9-12, O3-4, D2, M11, M14, M17

7. *Not Fair.*

Manuscripts: M11 (fols. 30 and 29^v)

2. th'*Idea*] Σ; the Idea O2, M11   7. count it the] Σ; count the F5; count that the F6-12   13. delusions] Σ; delusion O2   14. *Succu'bus*] O1, F1-4, M11; *Succubus* O2, F5-12, O3-4, D2   27. Be] Σ; But F11-12

8. *Platonick Love.*

Manuscripts: M11 (fols. 29ᵛ and 30), M14 (fol. 124ᵛ), M16 (poem no. 146), M24 (fol. 63, extract, ll. 1-4)

title] Σ; *Platonick Lover* O1-2 (*index*)   2. 'tis] Σ; it is M11   3. do joyne] O1-2, F1; combine Σ   4. —] O1-2, F1; And closely as our minds together join Σ; And closely as your Minds together join O4, D2   5. Heaven] Σ; Heav'n O3-4, D2   13. a] Σ; *om* M16   14. *all*] Σ; *om* F3   15. that] Σ; it M14   17. *Loves*] Σ; *Love's* O3-4, D2   21. love] Σ; prove M11   24. know't] Σ; ow't O2   28. steal] Σ; take M14

9. *The Change.*

Manuscripts: M11 (fol. 31), M14 (fol. 125ᵛ), M24 (fol. 63, extract, ll. 3-4), M26 (extract, ll. 5-6)

3. stray] Σ; stay M14   9. Flowers] Σ; Flow'rs O3-4, D2   14. my] Σ; mine M11   16. Grief, and Fear] Σ; griefs, and fears M11   17. But] Σ; for M11   19. that] Σ; what O2   20. Within] *ed.*; ~ , F1

Musical settings: Reggio, *Songs*, 1.16. R. J. S. Stevens, "Glees" (autograph score, dated 1780), British Library, Add. MSS 31810, fols. 3-4.

10. *Clad all in White.*

Other printed texts: NAC71 (p. 153, unascribed)

Manuscripts: M11 (fol. 31ᵛ), M24 (fol. 63, extract ll. 3-6)

title] Σ; NAC71 Song 108   5. Thou] Σ; For thou NAC71   wilt] Σ; would M24   18. i'th] Σ; i'th the O2   23. But they regard] Σ; But, oh they 'tend O1-2   not] Σ; no NAC71   30. *Flag*] Σ; Flags O1-2

Musical settings: William King, *Poems*, 36; Reggio, *Songs* 1.6.

11. *Leaving Me, and then loving Many.*

Manuscripts: M11 (fol. 32)

16. endless] Σ; *om* O2   19. his] Σ; has O2   20. poysons] Σ; poyson M11   falshood] Σ; falshoods O2

12. *My Heart discovered.*

Manuscripts: M11 (fol. 32)

6. brighter] Σ; brightest O2   7. the subtile] Σ; through th'radiant O1–2
8. its] *ed.* (*and* Σ); it's O1–2, F1   18. hers] Σ; her F5–10, M11   20.
its] *ed.* (*and* Σ); it's O1–2, F1   *Heaven*] Σ; *Heav'n* O3–4, D2   aspire.] *ed.*;
~, F1   26. too] Σ; *om* O2   its] *ed.* (*and* Σ); it's O1–2, F1   35. was]
ed. (*also* D2); were Σ

Musical settings: Reggio, *Songs* 1.24.

13. *Answer to the Platonicks.*

Manuscripts: M11 (fol. 33), M16 (poem no. 147)

1. love] Σ; *om* O2   3. *Spirit*] Σ; *Spi'rit* F8–10   10. they] Σ; tstey O2
11. *Men*] Σ; *Man* F12   15. *Thunderer*] Σ; *Thund'erer* F8–10; *Thund'rer*
O3–4, D2   18. 'bove] Σ; above F12   21. to] Σ; *om* O2   27. more]
Σ; most O2

14. *The vain Love.*

Manuscripts: M11 (fol. 33ᵛ)

11. of] Σ; at F12, O3–4, D2   15. Should'st thou] Σ; Should you O1–2
16. Thou'dst] Σ; You'had O1–2   most I] O1–2, F1; I most Σ   18. if] Σ;
when M11   31. I'm] Σ; I am M11   *wakened*]O1–2, F1–4, F11–12, M11;
waken'd F5–9, O3–4, D2; *weaken'd* F10   32. *Prisoners*] Σ; *Pris'oners*
F8–10   *wakened*] Σ; *waken'd* O3–4, D2   33. th'*Effects* of *Loving*] Σ;
the effects of loving M11; my Fires and Wishes O1–2   39. much 'tis] Σ;
much't is F3   41. fly] Σ; flee O1–2   42. At an] Σ; At any F12, O3;
An an O4; On an D2

15. *The Soul.*

Manuscripts: M11 (fol. 34), M16 (poem no. 148), M24 (fol. 63ᵛ, paraphrase of stanza 1 and extracts, ll. 33–34, 47–50, 77–78), M26 (extract, ll. 21–22)

2. They'have] O1–2, F1, M11; They have F2–5, F11–12, M16; They've F6–10, O3–4, D2   12. to] Σ; do M16   15. powe'rful] Σ; powerfull M16
19. Be] Σ; Are O2   20. *material's*] Σ; *Materials* F12   *O2 omits line 20*
22. *Thou*] Σ; you M11   appears] Σ; appear O3–4, D2, M26   23. I] Σ;
om M16   30. You'r] Σ; you'are M16   35. I] Σ; *om* M11, M16
40. Approach] Σ; Appear O1–2   43. do'est] Σ; do O2   45. *ty'est*] Σ;
ty'd F12   50. Thou no *Passion*] Σ; there no love ev'r M24   53. *Species*] Σ; speeches M16   56. asleep] Σ; a sleep O1   58. part;] *ed.*; ~.
F1   60. resemblance,] *ed.*; ~; F1   61. parts] Σ; Part M16   62.
Memorie;] *ed.*; ~. F1   70. she'another] O1, F1; she another Σ   73.
follow] Σ; allow M16   76. shall] Σ; may M11

Musical settings: Reggio, *Songs* 1.22.

16. *The Passions.*

Manuscripts: M11 (fol. 35ᵛ)

7. besides] Σ; beside O2   27. Be'ing] Σ; Being O3-4, D2   slaves] Σ; sloves O2

17. *Wisdom.*

Manuscripts: M11 (fol. 36), M24 (fol. 63ᵛ, paraphrased extract, ll. 8-9)

3. *Divin'ity*] Σ; *Divinity* F12   5. y'ave] Σ; you have M11   11. gift] Σ; gifts O2   13. 'event] Σ; 'evident F3

18. *The Despair.*

Manuscripts: M11 (fol. 36)

13. flame] Σ; name F4-5, 11-12   20. I] Σ; I'll M11   29. t'his] O1-2, F1; to'its Σ   30. his] O1-2, F1; her Σ   31. his] O1-2, F1; her Σ

Musical settings: James Hart, British Library, Add. MSS 19759 (fol. 41ᵛ); John Blundeville, Folger MS W.b. 515, p. 53.

19. *The Wish.*

Manuscripts: M11 (fol. 37), M16 (poem no. 149), M18 (fol. 124), M22 (fol. 57, unattributed), M23 (fol. 111ᵛ). Cowley quotes the first two lines of this poem in his essay "Of Myself" (*Works*, 1668, sig. 3T1). Similar "wish" poems, many of them derived as parodies from this text, appear in Restoration and eighteenth-century copy books. A typical, anonymous example may be found in University of Chicago MS 784 (iv), fol. 29. Walter Pope's parody of "The Wish" was set to music by John Blow (*Theater of Music* 1.110).

9. to] Σ; *om* M22   13. flee] Σ; fly M11   17. *Fountains*, when] Σ; Founts! Oh O1-2   19. when, when shall] Σ; when, shall O2   22. —] O1-2; *line om* Σ   24. and] Σ; or M16   26. *far*] Σ; *om* M16   *M16 and M22 omit stanza 5*   34. *Shee*,] *ed.*; ~ ∧ F1   37. have] Σ; *om* O2   39. hither throng to live like Mee] Σ; all come, im'itate Mee O1-2

20. *My Dyet.*

Other printed texts: NAC71 (p. 211, unattributed). This text of the poem is significantly different from all others. The second stanza is rewritten and there are many substantive variants in stanzas 1 and 3. One effect of the changes is to render most of the lines in ten syllables, rather than varying the stanzas with lines of eight syllables. If NAC71 represents the lyric to a musical setting, it could be that the setting called for uniform pentameter lines. If Cowley was responsible for the NAC71 text, however, he must have had other than metrical reasons for the changes in stanza 2.

Manuscripts: M11 (fol. 37ᵛ), M14 (fol. 126ᵛ)

title] Σ; Song 209 NAC71; The Diet M14   2. None loves you] Σ; There's none that loves thee NAC71   3. not ask] Σ; not neither ask NAC71   4. But] Σ; *om* NAC71   heave'ns] Σ; Heavens F10, NAC71   5. No *Servant*] Σ; No faithful servant NAC71   6. does] Σ; did M1, NAC71   7. I'll] Σ; I NAC71   13. *lineation*] *ed.*; *13 is aligned with line 12 in F1. Stanza 2 shows no substantive variants in any text except NAC71, which is rewritten but for line 14. The NAC71 text for lines 8–13 reads:*

> My love, fair Beauty, like thy self is pure,
> Nor could I e're a bestial love approve,
> One smile would make me willingly endure,
> It can't but keep together Life and Love.
> Being your pris'ner, and your captiv'd slave,
> So do not feast nor banquet look to have . . .

15. O'n a *sigh* of Pity] Σ; Upon your sigh for pity NAC71   16. *tear*] Σ; *Year* F11   twenty at] Σ; twenty'at O2, F8–10   17. Fifty a gentle] Σ; And fifty more a gentle NAC71   18. An . . . on . . . I'll] Σ; A . . . but . . . will NAC71   19. will added] Σ; will surely added NAC71   21. And all beyond is] Σ; They comprehend a NAC71

Musical settings: Reggio, *Songs* 2.7. *"My Dyet"* appears, without music, in *A Choice Collection Of 120 Loyal Songs* . . . (London: Printed by N.T. . . . , 1684), 226, under the title "The Dyet of COWLEY." The same song text, somewhat emended, appears in N.T.'s *A Choice Collection Of 180 Loyal Songs* (1685), 304, which was reissued as *A Collection of One Hundred and Eighty Loyal Songs* in 1694. Substantive variants found in the text printed by N.T. establish that it derives from a song tradition of the poem that is significantly different from NAC71 or from Reggio's setting (despite the fact that in Reggio's collection the poem is likewise titled "The Diet of Cowley"). The N.T. variants for 1684 and 1685 are as follows:
1. Now *by*] Now by (84); Now, now (85)   4. sake] *om* (84 & 85)   9. shall not] can't (84 & 85)   11. If't] If t (84); If I (85)   12. *Priso'ner*] Prisoner (84 & 85)   13. and] or (84); nor (85)   look] love (84 & 85)   18. An hundred years on one] An 100 one, one (84); A hundred on one (85)   19. will] *om* (84 & 85)

21. *The Thief.*

Manuscripts: M11 (fol. 38)

5. —] Σ; Even in my prayers thou hauntest me; O1–2   12. methinks] Σ;

om M11   13. does] Σ; dyes F2   14. *murthered*] Σ; *murther'd* O3-4, D2   18. every] Σ; ev'ry O3-4, D2   21. ev'ry] Σ; every F12   22. why] Σ; what O2   25. gave] Σ; give O3-4, D2

Musical settings: Reggio, *Songs,* 1.5.

22. *All-over, Love.*

Other printed texts: NAC71 (p. 209, unattributed)

Manuscripts: M11 (fol. 38), M16 (poem no. 150), M24 (fol. 63ᵛ, paraphrase ll. 8-10 and extract, ll. 16-20)

title] Σ; of Love M16; Song 203 NAC71   4. 'Midst] Σ; Mids M16   10. every] Σ; *ev'ry* O3-4, D2   11. My'*Affection*] Σ; My Affection M16   14. anothers] Σ; another M16   18. easi'ly] Σ; easily F12, M16

Musical settings: William King, *Poems,* 22; Reggio, *Songs,* 2.14.

23. *Love and Life.*

Manuscripts: M11 (fol. 38ᵛ), M14 (fol. 127ᵛ)

2. I'have] Σ; I have F10; I've O3-4, D2   3. The account] Σ; Th'Account O3-4, D2, M14   more] Σ; too M11   7. *Loves*] Σ; *Love's* O3-4, D2   11. extend themselves] Σ; extend thend themselves F12   12. take] Σ; toke O2   19. journey' he] F1-3, F8-10; journey he F4-7, F11-12, O3-4, D2, M14; course he O1-2   20. But] Σ; And O3-4, D2   treads] Σ; walkes O1-2   23-24. —] Σ; *lines om in O1-2*

24. *The Bargain.*

Manuscripts: M11 (fol. 39), M24 (fol. 63ᵛ, paraphrase of ll. 1-12, and extract, ll. 25-36)

2. Nor] Σ; Not O1-2   19. *cheapned*] Σ; *cheapen'd*] O3-4, D2   32. it for] Σ; for it O2   35. —] Σ; Add that full *Weight* too may be had F5-6; Yet lest the weight bee counted bad O1-2

Musical settings: Reggio, *Songs,* 1.16.

25. *The Long Life.*

Manuscripts: M11 (fol. 39ᵛ)

3. *Days*] Σ; *Day* O4   7. *Lucies*] Σ; *Lucy's* D2   8. *Winters*] Σ; Winter O2   11. miss] *ed.;* ~, F1   12. *Grey-hairs*] Σ; *Grey heirs* F11, O3-4, D2   13. *Patriarchs*] Σ; *Patriarch's* F12   19. Heaven] Σ; Heav'n O3-4, D2   23. Heaven] Σ; Heav'en F9; Heav'n O3-4, D2.

26. *Counsel.*

Manuscripts: M11 (fol. 40)

6. grow] Σ; strow O4   25. my] Σ; mine M11   28. part,] *ed.*; ~ . F1
29. I'm] Σ; I'am F8–10   34. *Me,*] *ed.*; ~ . F1

Musical settings: Reggio, *Songs*, 2.15; Banfield, *Comes Amoris*, 5.17.

27. *Resolved to be beloved.*

Manuscripts: M11 (fol. 40ᵛ), M14 (fol. 128ᵛ), M24 (fol. 63ᵛ, poem paraphrased)

5. fatal] Σ; welcome M14   10. find] Σ; finds M11   19. who] Σ; that M14   24. hath] O1–2, F1; has Σ

28. *The Same.*

Manuscripts: M11 (fol. 40ᵛ)

1. Heavens] Σ; Heav'ns O3–4, D2; Heaven F12   2. two;] Σ; ~ ? F11–12, O3–4, D2   6. whilst] Σ; whilest F7–11   10. one] *ed.* (*and* O1–2); on Σ   23. t'another] Σ; to another M11   24. it] Σ; *om* F5–7   25. there] Σ; *om* F5–10   27. Heaven] Σ; Heav'n O4, D2

29. *The Discovery.*

Other printed texts: NAC71 (p. 250, unascribed)

Manuscripts: M6 (fol. 139ᵛ, unascribed), M9 (p. 34, unascribed), M11 (fol. 41), M14 (fol. 129ᵛ), M16 (poem no. 151), M24 (fol. 63ᵛ, paraphrase, ll. 19–24), M26 (unascribed)

title] Σ; Song 249 NAC71; 30:Song M6; Loves Deity M9   1. BY 'Heaven] Σ; By Heav'n O3–4, D2   'tis] Σ; is M26   Shee;] Σ; ~ ? F12   3. To be] Σ; That she's M6, M9, NAC71   7. Lightning] Σ; light M16   8. sometime] O1, F1–5, F11–12, O3–4, D2, M6, M14; sometimes O2, F6–10, M9, M11, M16, M26   9. humble] *ed.* (*and* Σ); humbly F1; humbler M6   11. power] Σ; Pow'r O3–4, D2   13. so] Σ; *om* M16

Musical settings: A Song / The Words By Mʳ Cowley And Set To Mussick By Nic: Wootton (Wing C 6668); Reggio, *Songs*, 2.16.

30. *Against Fruition.*

Manuscripts: M11 (fol. 41ᵛ), M13 (fol. 181ᵛ, extract, ll. 23–32), M21 (fol. 98)

title] Σ; On Beauty M13; Mr. Cowley, on the same Subject [i.e. "Against Enjoyment"] M21   3. When] Σ; Whence F12   5. to me] Σ; for me

Collations and Textual Notes 183

F5–10   8. too] Σ; to O2   9. *freedoms*] Σ; freedome O2, M21   10. the] *ed.*; rhe F1   *Magazines*] Σ; *Mag'azines* F6–10   thine] Σ; thy M11, M21; *om* D2   14. hav'ing] Σ; having F5–10, D2   conquer'd] Σ; conquer'ed F4, F11   17. my] Σ; thy F5–7   23. first moves] Σ; first sight moves M13   25. whilst] Σ; while M21   28. himself . . . his] Σ; itself . . . its M21

31. *Love undiscovered.*

Other printed texts: NAC71 (p. 154, unascribed)

Manuscripts: M11 (fol. 42)

title] Σ; Song 109 NAC71   1. I] O1–2, F1, NAC71; Some Σ   10. The] Σ; Or NAC71   sustain:] *ed.*; ~ . F1   13. Heaven] Σ; Heav'n O3–4, D2   17. last] Σ; lost O4, D2   20. *Treasures*] Σ; treasure NAC71   21. will] Σ; should O2   23. me] Σ; *om* F9–10

Musical settings: British Library, Add. MSS 19759 (fol. 26^v: titled "The Concealment by Mr Cowley"); William King, *Poems*, 26.

32. *The given Heart.*

Other printed texts: NAC71 (p. 209, unascribed)

Manuscripts: M11 (fol. 42^v), M16 (poem no. 152)

2. giv'en] Σ; given M16   3. *Lover*] Σ; Lovers NAC71   5. If so it be] Σ; 'If so it be F12; If it be so NAC71   8. Then to *joyn*] Σ; Then joyne O2; Then joyning NAC71   9. once mine] Σ; mine once NAC71   12. Like a *Granado*] Σ; Granado-like NAC71   15. Shall] Σ; And NAC71

Musical settings: William King, *Poems*, 34; Barrett, *Thesaurus Musicus*, 1.24.

33. *The Prophet.*

Manuscripts: M11 (fol. 42^v), M16 (poem no. 153)

1. *Love*?] Σ; ~ ! F9–10   2. lineation] *ed.*; *in F1, line 2, begins beneath the* E *in line 1*   Professor] Σ; *Possessor* O3–4, D2   5. supple] Σ; subtle F7–10   6. —] Σ; Teach Sophisters and Iesuites to ly O1–2   *Jesuits*] *ed.*; Jesuit's F1   10. *Woman-kind*] Σ; Women kinde O1–2; *Women-kind* F6–10; womankind Kind M16   12. lineation] *ed.*; *aligned to the right, with line 11 in F1*   pr'ithee] Σ; neither O1–2   16. Adams] Σ; Adam's F11–12, O3–4, D2   17. on't] Σ; ont F5, ou't F6   20. —] Σ; Teares, which shall understand, and speake O1–2   22. Souls go] Soule goes O1–2 too] Σ; to F12   25. *Loves* O1–2, F1; *Love's* Σ   am; 'tis] Σ; am; it is M11   27. *Treasure*] Σ; treasures M11   32. Loves] Σ; Love's O3–4, D2   33. that] Σ; this O2   refuse] *ed.*; ~ , F1

34. *The Resolution.*

Manuscripts: M11 (fol. 43), M14 (fol. 130ᵛ), M17 (p. 264)

2. pow'rs] Σ; pow'ers F11–12; powers M14   3. grounds] Σ; ground M14
7. that] Σ; yᵉ M17

35. *Called Inconstant.*

Manuscripts: M11 (fol. 43ᵛ), M16 (poem no. 154)

2. yet] Σ; but M11   3. *Name,*] *ed.* (*and* O1); ~ ; F1   6. *Met'aphor*] Σ;
Metaphor O3–4, D2   11. fault] Σ; faults O2, M11   12. *wind*?] Σ; ~ ; F12

36. *The Welcome.*

Manuscripts: M11 (fol. 43ᵛ), M22 (fol. 122, unascribed)

title] Σ; Upon the Heart's Return M22   [*M22 contains stanza 1 only*]   3.
noble] Σ; nobler M22   4. fill'd] Σ; toucht M22   5. *Love*] Σ; Lust M22
9. part] Σ; prt F12   11. *Wanderer*] Σ; *Wand'erer* F8–10   12. Thou
wer't] Σ; Thou was't M1; You were O2   13. Hast] Σ; Hadst O2   not]
Σ; *om* O2   24. all] Σ; are F5–10   *Sand*] Σ; Land O1–2   25. chanc'd]
Σ; chance F7–10   29. *Par'adise*] Σ; *Paradise* O3–4, D2   30. kept] Σ;
shut O2   33. this] Σ; his M11   35. but] Σ; if M11

37. *The Heart fled again.*

Manuscripts: M11 (fol. 44), M22 (fol. 122, unascribed)

title] Σ; Upon the parting with yᵉ Heart again M22   [*M22 contains stanza 4 only*]   5. back] Σ; *om* O2   10. *Trojan*] Σ; Troyan O1   16. Afar]
Σ; A faire O1–2; Ah far F12   19. Ah] Σ; A M22   25. wilt] Σ; will F12
29. easi'ly] Σ; easily F11–12

Musical settings: Reggio, *Songs*, 1.39; Robert King, *A Second Booke of Songs*, 13.

38. *Womens Superstition.*

Manuscripts: M11 (fol. 44ᵛ), M17 (p. 48), M24 (fol. 63ᵛ, extract, ll. 1–2)

5. *Learn'd* may see] Σ; *Learn'd* my see F6; learned see M17   6. they'r]
Σ; they are M17   8. antick] O1–2, F1; antique Σ   14. *Idol-Gods*] Σ;
Idol Gods F5–10   nor] Σ; or M11   15. *Honour's*] Σ; Honour is M17
Bâal] *ed.*; *Baal* F1   16. *Bâal*] *ed.*; *Báal* F1   Woman-kind,] *ed.* (*and* Σ);
~ . F1; Women-kind, F10   19. *Covetous*] Σ; *Cov'etous* F8–10   20.
t'omit] Σ; to omit M11, M17

39. *The Soul* [II].

Manuscripts: M11 (fol. 45), M17 (p. 47)

title. [II] *ed.*   6. there;] *ed.*; ~. F1 (*and* Σ)   10. *Natures Law*] Σ; *Nature's Law* F12, O3-4, D2; Natures Laws M17

40. *Eccho.*

Manuscripts: M11 (fol. 45)

1. TIr'ed] Σ; Tired F8-10   the] Σ; *om* F5-10   3. come, and] Σ; come in and O2   find] Σ; *om* F12   5. who] Σ; *om* M11   22. The] Σ; *om* M11

41. *The rich Rival.*

Manuscripts: M10 (fol. 51, unascribed), M11 (fol. 45^v), M24 (fol. 63^v, paraphrase, ll. 19-24)

4. what's] Σ; what M10   7. she] Σ; we O2   13. o' your] Σ; on your M10   18. their] Σ; your M11   21. no] Σ; do O2   22. she'an] Σ; she an M10

Musical settings: Purcell, *The Theater of Music* 2.20, reprint in *The New Treasury of Musick* and in *Orpheus Britannicus* 1:81. Folger MS V.b.197 and British Library, Music Room MS RM20.h.8.

42. *Against Hope.*

Other printed texts: S46 (p. 96), S48 (p. 111), C52 (p. 128)

Manuscripts: M1 (fol. 80), M2 (fol. 68, ascribed Nicholas Trin Coll.), M4 (p. 85, unascribed), M11 (fol. 46), M16 (poem no. 155), M22 (fol. 108)

title] Σ; On Hope, *By way of Question and Answer, betweene* A. Cowley, *and* R. Crashaw S46, S48, M22; Upon Hope M1; Hope C52, M2   1. ruin'd] Σ; Ruin M16   2. Alike] Σ; A like F1 (some copies), F2-5, F11, M16   and] Σ; or C52   3. *Good* or *Ill*] Σ; Ill, and Good S46, S48, M1, M2, M22; ill or good C52   4. *Fates*] Σ; *Fate's* O3-4, D2   wound!] *ed.*; the ! is italic and inverted in F1   5. which] Σ; that S46, S48, C52, M1, M2, M22   7. stars] Σ; Fates S46, S48, M22   have] Σ; of S48   9. then] Σ; thus M4   End] Σ; ends S46, S48, M1, M2, M22   10. of] Σ; at S48   12. whilst thou shouldst but *taste, devour'st*] Σ; in stead of doing so, devour'st S46, S48, C52, M1, M22; in stead of doing so devorst M2   13. bringst us an] Σ; bring'st an M16   15. *Joys*] Σ; joy M2   we *entire*] Σ; entire we M16   18. Such] Σ; So S46, S48, M2, M22   *Custom's*] Σ; *Customs* F7-10   to] Σ; by M4   19. does] Σ; doe M2   20. his] O1-2, C52, F1, M4; its Σ   21. Fortunes] Σ; Fortune's F12, O3-4, D2   22.

an] Σ; a M2, M11, M22   23. thy] Σ; thine S46, S48, C52, M22   24. thine] Σ; thy M2, M16   25. —] Σ; Thine empty cloud the eye, it selfe deceives S46, S48, M1, M2, M22   27. gilt] Σ; guilt M1, M2   30. for] Σ; not S46, S48, M1, M2, M22   32. *merr'ier*] Σ; merry M2   33. Sire] Σ; ire O1   *Childe*] Σ; shield S46, S48, M22   34. That] Σ; Thou F7–10   blow'st] Σ; blows O2, S46, S48, M1, M2, M22   *Chymicks*] Σ; *Chymick's* D2; chymick C52   35. Leading them still] Σ; Still leading them S46, S48, C52, M1, M2, M22   36. By] Σ; With S46, S48, C52, M1, M2, M22   strange] Σ; strong O1–2, C52   37. the one does] Σ; does one M11   39. *Woman*] Σ; *Women* F8   whilst] Σ; while M1, M2

"Against Hope" was first printed, with Richard Crashaw's reply, in *Steps to the Temple*, 1646 (S46). As L. C. Martin has established, this edition was not published under the author's direction (Crashaw, *Poems*, xliv–xlvi). The text also appears in the second edition of *Steps to the Temple*, 1648 (S48). The relationship between S46 and S48 is not as clearcut as Martin makes out (see J. C. Maxwell, "Steps to the Temple: 1646 and 1648," *PQ* 29 [1950]: 216–20), but it appears, in the case of the Cowley text, that S48 derives from S46. There are two minor substantive variants (lines 7 and 10), both of which could be compositorial errors. In both S46 and S48 the stanzas of Cowley's poem are printed to alternate with those of Crashaw's reply. "Against Hope" was also printed with Cowley's own reply ("For Hope," Poem 43), in *The Mistresse*, 1647 (O1) and reprinted in the second edition of the same year (O2). "Against Hope," again with Crashaw's reply, appeared in the latter's posthumous *Carmen Deo Nostro*, 1652 (C52). The two poems are there published separately. The text of O1 was reprinted in Cowley's *Poems* 1656 (F1), with a single substantive variant (line 36). This text was reprinted in *Works* 1668 (F2), with one substantive variant (line 20) that is sustained in all printed editions of the *Works* through 1721. Independent authority is difficult to establish for variants in any of these later editions, and it is worth noting that either Herringman or his printer John Macocke regarded the variant reading in line 34, initiated in F7 and sustained through F10, as an error that they corrected in F11.

There are a number of extant manuscript texts of Poem 42. Four of these—M4, M11, M16, and M22—probably derive from printed texts. M4 reads the same as F1, its likely source, except for two unique variants, lines 9 and 18, that could easily be scribal. M11 reads with F2–6, except for a unique error in line 37 and the reading "a" for "an" in line 22, wherein it coincidentally agrees with M2 and M22. M16 appears to be the work of a less-than-careful copyist (witness the unique error in line 1, the omission in line 13, the inversion in line 15) who was probably reading from F2, 3, 4, or 5. In M22 Cowley's stanzas alternate with those of Crashaw's reply, as in S46 and S48. M22 readings agree with S46 and S48 against all other versions in the title and in lines 7 and 33. In lines 7 and 10, M22 agrees with S46 against S48. The Crashaw stanzas represented in M22 are a very accurate rendering of S46; there is only one minor variant.

Two manuscripts—M1 and M2—are almost certainly independent of the printed editions. M1 was probably copied before any of the printings. The transcription of Poem 42 is preceded by poems belonging to the decade 1633–43 (including the "Prologue and Epilogue . . . in Cambridge" to Cowley's *The Guardian*, 1642); immediately preceding "Upon Hope" is a copy of Cleveland's "The Rebellious Scott," which was written in late 1643. Poem 42, then, was copied after this date. The transcription is followed by Crashaw's "The Answer," copied as a separate poem as in M2 and C52. The collation of Crashaw's poem, below, establishes that this version of "The Answer" cannot derive from C52, or vice-versa. Nor can it derive from S46 or S48, where Cowley's and Crashaw's texts are integrated, or from M2, which has many unique readings. A date for M2 is suggested by letters in the same volume dated from 1642 to 1647. Immediately preceding Cowley's poem is a verse letter "on the false news of the Lord Inchiquin treason" (fol. 67ᵛ), bearing the latest of these dates: 28 September, 47. Cowley's poem was copied sometime after this. M2 erroneously ascribes the text to "Nicholas Trin Coll." (presumably Cowley's Westminster and Cambridge friend), an error hard to conceive had the copyist been following a printed text of the poem.

In order to determine a copy text for "Against Hope," six texts deserve close attention: S46, M47, C52, F1, M1, and M2. Except perhaps for the change of the pronoun "his" to "its" in F2, all other variant readings have no claim to independent authorial status.

The early texts M1, M2, and S46 agree in readings against O1 and F1 in lines 3, 5, 9, 20, 25, 30, 35, and 36. If M2's "devorst" is a misspelling of "devour'st," these texts also agree against O1 and F1 in line 12. The M1, M2, S46 reading in line 25—"Thine empty cloud the eye, it selfe deceives"— makes little sense; it is probably an error, following from a copyist's misreading, "Thin empty cloud, the eye itself deceives." Since M1, M2, and S46 share this probable error, they derive from a common ancestor unless one of them is the source for the others. Neither S46 nor M2 can be the common source. S46 has unique readings in the title, in line 7, and a most striking error —"shield" in line 33. M2 (aside from producing an odd construction, "cloggih" line 14, and "devorst" in line 12) has unique readings in lines 15, 19 (error), 22, 24, 32 (error), and in the ascription. M2 and S46 are clearly independent of one another. They may, however, be dependent upon M1 or a text very much like it. M1 is unique only in the title and differs from both S46 and M2 only in line 18, where it reads "Such" instead of "So." But the fact that M1 and M2 agree against S46 in two readings, lines 7 and 23, and in two spellings, lines 27 and 39, suggests that they derive from a manuscript source different from the source for S46. Since the unique readings in M2 are either errors or of a minor order, it is possible that M2 was taken from M1. Evidence against this possibility comes not from the text of Cowley's poem, but from the text of Crashaw's reply, which follows "Against Hope" in both M1 and M2. If we assume that these companion poems were copied from the same source, M1 cannot have been the source for M2. In line 48, M2 includes a word that M1, uniquely, omits, and M1 shows unique readings in the title and in line 47 (see collation for Crashaw's poem, below).

It is most likely that M1, M2, and S46 derive independently from a common ancestor. Their shared error in line 25 indicates that this common ancestor was not the author's manuscript.

Variants in lines 12, 25, 35, and 36 offer the clearest evidence for revision before the publication of O1. The reading in line 12, first appearing in O1 and then transmitted to later folio editions of Cowley's *Poems* and *Works*, is surely an improvement upon the version of line 12 rendered in M1, S46, S48, C52, M22, and M2. At the very least, the manuscript from which Humphrey Moseley set O1 was not the ancestor of M1, M2, and S46 (which Moseley also printed), since O1 corrects their erroneous version of line 25. Cowley's authorized text, F1, preserves the readings from O1, so it could be argued that O1 is closest to the author's revised manuscript. However, O1 contains an additional apparent error in line 36, which is corrected in F1: the O1 reading, "strong witchcraft," becomes "strange *witchcraft*" in F1. Although O1's "strong" makes sense, it is probably a compositor's error rather than an unrevised reading—an error easily made since Cowley spells "strange" without the final "e" (as in *The Civil War*, 1.118). Thus far, aside from having the author's explicit sanction, F1 provides the best text of "Against Hope." F1 also incorporates Cowley's characteristic, emphatic italics, which are missing from O1, O2, S46, and the early manuscripts.

C2 sometimes agrees with M1, M2, S46 (lines 5, 12, 35, 36), sometimes with O1, F1 (lines 9, 20, 25, 30, 34), and shows minor unique variants in lines 2, 3, and 34. C2 also reads "strong" in line 36, along with O1-2. Given this evidence, and underscoring the inconsequence of C2's unique readings, it would appear that the text in C2 was formed through conflation. The line 36 reading may suggest O1, rather than F1, as one source for C2. The other source, providing the M1, M2, S46 readings, could have been a manuscript resembling these texts. C52 was printed in Paris, about three years after Crashaw's death. Thomas Car, a prominent Catholic, was responsible for seeing it through the press (Crashaw, *Poems*, ed. Martin, xxxiv and xlvii). Since Cowley was in Paris during 1650-51, Car could have consulted with him on a text for "Hope." Cowley could have provided him with a copy of *The Mistresse* or suggested that Car look at a copy, or even have written a copy of the poem for him. But there is no positive evidence that Cowley and Car were acquainted, and it is more likely that Car's second source for Cowley's poem came along with other materials for the volume, as provided by Crashaw himself either directly, before he left Paris, or indirectly thereafter. The manuscript used along with O1 (or a text resembling it) to create the C2 text could well have derived from M2 or from its Cambridge-related exemplar. C52 and M2 agree in titling Cowley's poem "Hope," and readings from the S46 tradition of the poem are available in M2. It is entirely possible that Crashaw had retained a copy of Cowley's poem in its early, unrevised state; that this copy became available to Car; and that Car used it in conjunction with O1 to prepare copy for the French printer. Despite the possibility that Cowley had a hand in the production of C2 (directly or by way of an old, authorial manuscript), and thus the possibility that unique readings in C2 are authorial, there is no reason to grant C2 higher authority than F1, which was published four years later.

Finally, the case for textual authority comes down to F1 and F2. As with other poems in *The Mistress*, we prefer reading from F1, as variants in F2 could be Thomas Sprat's emendations. Thus the F1 reading in line 20 is retained here. Crashaw's reply to "Against Hope" appears in none of the editions of *The Mistress*. But since the earliest, authorial versions of "Against Hope" require Crashaw's answer as either integral to or as a companion to the text, Crashaw's poem is printed below. S46 has been taken as base text and variants from it, as they appear in S48, C52, M1, M2, and M22, are recorded. The title and stanza numbers are editorial.

For Hope

Deare Hope! Earths dowry, and Heavens debt,
The entity of things that are not yet.
Subt'lest, but surest being! Thou by whom
Our Nothing hath a definition.
    Faire cloud of fire, both shade, and light,   5
    Our life in death, our day in night.
    Fates cannot find out a capacity
        Of hurting thee.
From thee their thinne dilemma with blunt horne
Shrinkes, like the sick Moone at the wholsome morne.   10

2.

  Thou art Loves Legacie under lock
Of Faith: the steward of our growing stocke.
Our Crown-lands lye above, yet each meale brings
A seemly portion for the Sons of Kings.
  Nor will the Virgin-joyes wee wed   15
  Come lesse unbroken to our bed,
  Because that from the bridall cheeke of Blisse,
   Thou thus steal'st downe a distant kisse,
Hopes chaste kisse wrongs no more joyes maidenhead,
Then Spousall rites prejudge the marriage-bed.   20

3.

  Faire *Hope*! our earlier Heaven! by thee
Young *Time* is taster to Eternity.
The generous wine with age growes strong, not sower;
Nor need wee kill thy fruit to smell thy flower.
  Thy golden head never hangs downe,   25
  Till in the lap of Loves full noone
  It falls, and dyes: oh no, it melts away
   As doth the dawne into the day:
As lumpes of Sugar lose themselves, and twine
Their subtile essence with the soule of Wine.   30

4.

  Fortune alas above the worlds law warres:
Hope kicks the curl'd heads of conspiring starres.
Her keele cuts not the waves, where our winds stirre,
And *Fates* whole Lottery is one blanke to her.
  Her shafts, and shee fly farre above,   35
  And forrage in the fields of light, and love.
  Sweet *Hope*! kind cheat! faire fallacy! by thee
   Wee are not where, or what wee bee,
But what, and where wee would bee: thus art thou
Our absent presence, and our future now.   40

5.

>*Faith*'s Sister! Nurse of faire desire!
> Feares Antidote! a wise, and well stay'd fire
> Temper'd 'twixt cold despaire, and torrid joy:
> Queen Regent in young Loves minoritie.
>> Though the vext Chymick vainly chases   45
>> His fugitive gold through all her faces,
>> And loves more fierce, more fruitlesse fires assay
>> One face more fugitive then all they,
> True *Hope*'s a glorious Huntresse, and her chase
> The God of Nature in the field of Grace.   50

Printed texts: S46, S48, C52

Manuscripts: M1 (fol. 80ᵛ), M2 (fol. 68ᵛ, ascribed "Crashaw. Pe. house Camb."), M22 (fol. 108)

title] ed.; On Hope, By way of Question and Answer, betweene A. Cowley and R. Crashaw S46, S48, M22; The Answer M1; Answer. Crashaw Pe. house Camb. M2; M. Crashaws. Answer For Hope C52   2. things] S46, S48, M22; those M1, M2, C52   4. hath] Σ; has C52   5. —] Σ; Substantiall shade! whose sweet allay C52   6. —] Σ; Blends both the noones of night & day C52   9. thinne] Σ; lean C52   10. like] Σ; as C52   at] Σ; from C52   11. —] Σ; Rich hope! love's legacy, under lock C52   12. —] Σ; Of faith! still spending, & still growing stock! C52   13. Crown-lands] Σ; crown-land M2, C52   lye] Σ; lyes C52   14. seemly] Σ; seeminge M2   18. thus steal'st] Σ; steal'st us C52   19. kisse wrongs] Σ; stealth harmes C52   maidenhead] Σ; maydenshead M2   20. prejudge the] Σ; prejudice that M2   23. The] Σ; Thy C52   24. —] Σ; Nor does it kill thy fruit, to smell thy flowre C52   25. head] Σ; growing, head C52   26. noone] Σ; moone M2   30. subtile] S46, S48, M22; supple M1, M2, C52   31. *Fortune*] Σ; ~? C52   law] Σ; low C52   32. *Hope* kicks] Σ; Hope walks; & kickes C52   33. our] Σ; These C52   34. And *Fates*] Σ; Fortune's C52   [*C52 omits lines 35–36*]   37. or] Σ; nor C52   39. bee] Σ; *om* M22   40. absent] Σ; absence M2   42. Antidote] Σ; Antitode C52   43. Temper'd] Σ; Temper C52   cold] Σ; chill C52   47. And] Σ; Though C52   fierce, more] Σ; fierce, and M1   48. all] Σ; *om* M1   49. *Hope*'s] Σ; hope M2   Huntresse] Σ; hunter C52   50. field] Σ; feilds M1, C52

Collation suggests that S48 is a reprint of S46. There are no substantive variants between them, though there are a few (unrecorded) differences in spelling, capitals, and italics. M22 probably derives from S46, as does its transcription of Cowley's stanzas. The omission in M22, line 39, is doubtless a scribal error. Given the omission in M1, line 48, the numerous unique readings in M2, and readings in S46 title and line 2, M1, M2, and S46 would appear to have derived independently from a common ancestor. These three texts represent the earlier of two versions of Crashaw's poem; they agree in a large number of readings against C52. Variants between the M1, M2, S46 group, and C52 are clearly due to revision (cross-agreements in lines 13 and 50 are presumably fortuitous).

S46, S48, and the derivative M22 alternate the stanzas of Cowley's and Crashaw's poems as follows: Cowley 1, Crashaw 1, Cowley 2, Crashaw 2, Cowley 3, Crashaw 3, Cowley 4, Crashaw 4, Crashaw 5. Some discussion has arisen over the proper arrangement of the alternating stanzas. C. H. Miller, in "The Order of Stanzas in Cowley and Crashaw's 'On Hope,'" *Studies in Philology* 61 (1964): 64–73, argues for an alternative order. G. W. Williams, in "The Order of Stanzas in Cowley's and Crashaw's 'On Hope,'" *Studies in Bibliography* 22 (1969): 207–10, also has an alternative order in mind. But he recognizes that the poems do not always appear in an alternating-stanza format. C52 prints them separately; Cowley's "Against Hope" is a separate poem in O1 and Williams notes that the poems appear as separate units in M1 (Williams, Miller, and L. C. Martin were unaware of M2). He then surmises that the editor of S46 noticed how exactly Crashaw's stanzas 1 and 2 responded to Cowley's first two stanzas, and thence decided to alternate the stanzas—giving the last two to Crashaw, since his poem is ten lines longer than Cowley's. If the decision to alternate the stanzas was editorial, arguments as to *the* correct sequence are of little point.

Textual analysis bears out the major line of Williams's argument. Cowley's and Crashaw's poems appear separately, in the same sequence of lines, in two independent manuscripts (M1 and M2) that preserve the unrevised texts. In C52, which preserves the revised text of Crashaw's poem and a partially revised text of Cowley's, the poems are again separate. These facts, along with the knowledge that neither Crashaw nor Cowley was responsible for the printing of S46, provide sufficient reason for thinking that the authors intended two separate poems, to appear together as argument and answer. The alternating-stanza format is almost certainly editorial. It is even possible that an editor or publisher for S46 was responsible for the reading "Fates" in line 7 of Cowley's poem—thus balancing "Fates" in line 7 of Crashaw's text.

43. *For* Hope.

Manuscripts: M4 (p. 85, unascribed), M11 (fol. 46ᵛ), M16 (poem no. 156), M17 (p. 242), M22 (fol. 57ᵛ, unascribed)

title] Σ; Hope M17; Of Hope M22   [*M22 omits lines 6 and 8*]   11. *fruits*] Σ; fruit M11, M17   12. *Dawning*] Σ; Downing O2   [*M17 omits lines 13–14 and 17–24*]   17. Whilst] Σ; Whilest F8   22. *Heav'n*] Σ; *Heav'en* F11–12   26. In *Thee*] Σ; to thee M11   27. *Future's*] Σ; future M11   *Thine*] Σ; Thine Thine M16   30. canst] Σ; can. M17   [*M17 omits lines 33–36*]   34. *and*] Σ; or M16   37. flee] Σ; fly M17   [*M17 omits lines 39–40*]

44. *Loves Ingratitude.*

Manuscripts: M11 (fol. 47), M24 (extract, ll. 12 and 18)

5. wouldst] Σ; would F12   11. dost] *ed.* (*and* Σ); do st F1; doest F10   18. which] Σ; that O2   22. *flour*!] Σ; *flower*! F8–10; *flour*? F11–12; *Flow'r*; O3–4, D2

Musical settings: Blow, *The Theater of Music,* 4.66, reissued in *The New Treasury of Musick.*

45. *The Frailty.*

Other printed texts: Further Considerations about mix'd dancing: To which is added an answer to A. Cowley's Verses, Entitled, The Frailty. By a Lover of all Truth, and Vertue. London, 1704. The first two stanzas of "The Frailty" appear under the ascription "AB. C." on p. 9 of this extraordinary little volume. It is followed on p. 10 by:

THE *ANSWER*:

SAY, Speaking Brute, *why* Wilt thou *be,*
Thus Wedded *to Impuritie?*
Thou art the Cause of thine own Woe:
'Tis so, 'cause thou wilt have it so.
The Lord of Life, *Eternal* Love and Light,
Thy black fierce burning Lusts wou'd put to flight,
But that thou dost delight in thine own Misery.

2.

Vain Man! *Thou dost but strive in jest,*
If when base Lusts thy Soul Infest!
Thou think'st they can't be Vanquish'd quite;
He's sure to Conquer that will fight.
But know, *this* Fire's *not Quench'd but in a Flood*

Of thine own Tears, mix'd with thy Saviour's *Blood.*
'Tis only this can ease thy Burning Tortur'd Brest.
Oh, to the Sun of Righteousness Aspire:
That Living Flame puts out all other Fire.

The lover of all truth continues "The Answer" with some apt quotations, leading to the conclusion that the sight of women's naked breasts contributes significantly to men's burning lust and blind love. Avoidance of the sight, presumably, stands as an alternative to conversion.

Manuscripts: M11 (fol. 47^v)

In O1 and O2, "The Frailty" appears in three stanzas, thus adding:

3.

As, when the Sunne appeares,
The Morning thicknesse cleares;
So, when my thoughts let sadnesse in,
And a new Morning does begin,
If any Beauties piercing ray
Strike through my Trembling Eyes a suddaine day;
All those grave sullen Vapours melt in Teares.

The decision to omit stanza 3 was very possibly made by the author (see Textual Analysis). Grosart's edition of "The Frailty" includes this third stanza, and unnecessarily adds "away" after "Teares" in the last line; Sparrow's edition includes the stanza, following the text of O1.

46. *Coldness.*

Manuscripts: M11 (fol. 48)

9. apace] Σ; a pace O1   11. play$_\wedge$] *ed.*, ~, F1

Musical settings: Reggio, British Library Add. MSS 31440, fol. 156^v–57^r.

47. *The Injoyment.*

Other printed texts: NAC71 (p. 152, unascribed)

Manuscripts: M11 (fol. 48), M21 (fol. 96^v), M24 (fol. 63^v, extract, ll. 17–18)

title] O1–2, F1; The Enjoyment M21; Song 106 NAC71; *om* Σ   1. THen like some wealthy] Σ; Like to the wealthy NAC71; When like some wellcome M21   3. like fair] Σ; fair like M11   Albion] Σ; Abion F3   11. or] Σ; nor O1   12. thy] Σ; the M21   14. we'engendred there] Σ; we'engendered

Collations and Textual Notes   195

there F10; w'engendring were M21   15. nor] Σ; or M11   pleasures] Σ; pleasure M21   17. hands or Lips] Σ; Lips or hands M21   19. sports] Σ; sport F5-10   know] Σ; *om* M11   23. so far beneath the Sea] Σ; beneath th'Ægaean Sea O1-2   27. thou'hast] Σ; thou hast F10

Musical settings: William King, *Poems*, 6 (titled "The Enjoyment"); Reggio, *Songs*, 2.9 (untitled).

48. *Sleep.*

Manuscripts: M11 (fol. 48ᵛ)

5. *lineation*] *ed.*; *the line is set from the left margin, as line 7 in F1*   12. which in] Σ; within O1-2   17. *God*,] *ed.* (*and* Σ); ~; F1   20. same] O1-2, F1; *om* Σ   23. *Spirits*] Σ; *Spir'its* F8-10

49. *Beauty.*

Manuscripts: M11 (fol. 49), M17 (p. 288, extract, stanza 1), M24 (fol. 63ᵛ, paraphrased extract, stanza 3). British Library, Add. MSS B.105, a miscellany dating from the first half of the eighteenth century, contains an unascribed transcription of stanza 3 on fol. 98.

4. every] Σ; ev'ry O3-4, D2   5. confoundst] Σ; confounds O1-2   7. *What*] Σ; when O1-2   9. *she-Possessors*] O1-2, F1; *she-Professors* Σ   10. *Loves*] Σ; *Love's* F11-12, O3-4, D2   12. *Impostor*] Σ; Imposture O2   18. *lest*] O1-2, F1; *least* Σ   33. youths] Σ; Youth's O3-4, D2; youth M11   34. leav'st] Σ; leaves M11   35. nought] Σ; none O2   36. which hast] Σ; who has M11   wouldst] O1-2, F1-3, O3-4, D2; could F4-12, M11

50. *The Parting.*

Manuscripts: M11 (fol. 49ᵛ), M24 (fol. 63ᵛ, paraphrased extract, stanza 6)

4. there:] *ed.*; ~. F1 (*and* Σ)   16. or] Σ; and O1-2   17. mine] Σ; the O1-2   19. *descend'st*] Σ; descends O2   20. *rise* up from thence] Σ; from thence rise up M11

51. *My Picture.*

Manuscripts: M11 (fol. 50)

title] Σ; *The Picture* O1-2 (index)   1. whilst 'tis so] Σ; *om* F12   3. Suns] Σ; Sun's F12, O3-4, D2   9. *lineation*] *ed.*; *9 is aligned with line 7 in F1*   13. *Cabinet*] Σ; *Cabinent* F6   17. it] Σ; it it F12 (*some copies*)   23. *Me*,] *ed.*; ~. F1   24. *Pictures*] Σ; *Picture's* F12, O3-4, D2

Musical settings: Reggio, *Songs*, 1.30 (titled "The Picture").

196 TEXTUAL INTRODUCTION, ANALYSIS, COLLATIONS

52. *The Concealment.*

Other printed texts: WR50 (sig. S8ᵛ, unascribed), NAC71 (p. 146, unascribed)

Manuscripts: M11 (fol. 50ᵛ), M20 (fol. 54ᵛ, first stanza only), M25 (fol. 35, unascribed)

title] Σ; Silence WR50; 106. Silence M25; On his Mistriss not Loving him M20; Song 97 NAC71   3. me] Σ; thee M20   4. 'twere] Σ; 'tis M25   15. that, a] Σ; & noe M25   20. *happi'er*] Σ; *happier* O3–4, D2   25. every] Σ; ev'ry O3–4, D2   other] Σ; *om* M11, NAC71   26. an] Σ; a M11   27. last] Σ; least M25   28. Shall] Σ; Will M25   30. *envy* Mee] Σ; *envy, Me* F3

Musical settings: William King, *Poems*, 1, and *New Ayers and Dialogues* (1678, unascribed); Robert King, *A Second Booke of Songs*, 21; Purcell, British Library, MS RM 20.h.8.

53. *The Monopoly.*

Manuscripts: M11 (fol. 51)

4. *Vulcans*] Σ; *Vulcan's* F11–12, O3–4, D2   6. *Cupids*] Σ; *Cupid's* F11–12, O3–4, D2   19. into'her] Σ; into her F12   20. struck] Σ; strook O1   21. wounds] Σ; ones M11   26. powers] Σ; Pow'rs O3–4, D2   29. So'] Σ; So F10   30. the *Feathers*] Σ; their Feathers O2

Musical settings: William King, *Poems*, 48.

54. *The Distance.*

Other printed texts: NAC71 (p. 151, unascribed)

Manuscripts: M11 (fol. 51)

title] Σ; Song 104 NAC71   1. I'Have followed] Σ; I have follow'd F12; I've follow'd O3–4, D2   3. yet] Σ; *om* M11   11. a round it swiftlier] Σ; round swiftlier it O2; around it swiftlier F8–10   16. *Heart*] Σ; hearts M11   turns] Σ; turn M11

Musical settings: William King, *Poems*, 38; Reggio, *Songs*, 1.8.

55. *The Encrease.*

Manuscripts: M11 (fol. 51ᵛ)

3. easi'ly] Σ; easily F6–10   5. *Loves*] Σ; *Love's* O3–4, D2   9. should] Σ; would F6–10   16. th'hand] Σ; the hand F12   18. move] Σ; turne O2

Musical settings: Reggio, *Songs*, 1.32.

56. *Loves Visibility.*

Other printed texts: WR50 (sig. S5, unascribed)

Manuscripts: M11 (fol. 52), M21 (fol. 80), M25 (fol. 38ᵛ, no. 123, unascribed), M26 (unascribed, stanzas 3 and 4 only)

title] Σ; #123 M25; Loves Discovery WR50   1. knew] Σ; know M21   6. to teach] Σ; doth teach M25   7. have] Σ; are M21   oft so] Σ; so oft O2; often M26   9. who] Σ; that O1-2, WR50; yt M25   t'have] Σ; to have O2, F12, M25   11. arts] Σ; Art M25   or] Σ; of M21   12. it 'cause] Σ; because M21   14. left] Σ; lost M21   15. past] Σ; did passe M25   17. keep the secret wisely] Σ; wisely keep the secret M25

Musical settings: William King, *Poems*, 24; Reggio, *Songs*, 1.13.

57. *Looking on, and discoursing with his Mistress.*

Manuscripts: M11 (fol. 52)

1. been;] *ed. (and* O1); ~ , F1   4. Misers] Σ; *Miser's* F12, O3-4, D2   5. *Heavens*] Σ; *Heav'ens* F8-10; *Heaven's* F12; *Heav'n's* O3-4, D2   10. earths] Σ; Earth's O3-4, D2   show,] Σ; ~∧ F2-3   13. *lineation*] *ed.*; *13 is aligned with line 14 in F1*   14. Souls] Σ; *Soul's* O3-4, D2   17. Tapers] Σ; *Taper's* F12, O3-4, D2   18. nigh] Σ; *night* F12

Musical settings: Forcer, *Vinculum Societatis*, 1.18; [William] Hall, British Library, Add. MSS 22100 (fol. 46ᵛ).

58. *Resolved to Love.*

Other printed texts: MLE58 (p. 62; unascribed)

Manuscripts: M11 (fol. 52ᵛ)

title] Σ; Resolution to Love MLE58   5. does] Σ; do O2, MLE58   8. the] Σ; thy MLE58   11. *Wiseman*] Σ; *Wise man* F4; *wise-man* F5-10   12. so?] Σ; to. MLE58   14. eyes all watry] Σ; watry eyes to MLE58   15. cause] Σ; clause F5   *stanza number* 4.] *ed.*; *om in F1*   21. Gods] Σ; God's F11-12, O3-4, D2   22. *ign'orant*] O1-2, F1-3, O3-4, D2, MLE58; *ignorant* F4-12   23. *Action*] Σ; actions MLE58   30. *Van'ity*] Σ; *Vanity* F5-7

59. *My Fate.*

Other printed texts: NAC71 (p. 208; unascribed)

Manuscripts: M11 (fol. 53). Bodleian MS Eng. Poet. e 40 contains a copy of stanza 1, on fol. 100. It is given the title "Cowley to his Mistress" and is preceded by "A Riddle on a Needle," dated 1748/49. The manuscript appears in the fourth volume of a collection principally of epitaphs, riddles, rebuses, and verses. The unique title for poem 59 and unique readings suggest that the copyist worked from a manuscript source. Readings from Bodleian MS Eng. Poet. e 40 (abbreviated E40) are recorded here.

title] Σ; Song 202 NAC71; Cowley to his Mistress E40   1. his] Σ; it's E40   dear] *ed*.; deer F1   3. upwards] Σ; upward O2   4. Go] Σ; Or E40   *Flame*] Σ; Flames NAC71; E40   t'ascend] O1-2, F1, NAC71; ascend Σ   5. *old*] Σ; own NAC71   10. what e're] Σ; whate're F7-10, O3-4, D2   18. *Heav'en*] Σ; *Heaven* F10-12   24. *Astrol'ogy*] Σ; *Astrology* F5-10

Musical settings: William King, *Poems*, 15.

60. *The Heart-breaking*.

Other printed texts: WR50 (sig. S5ᵛ; unascribed)

Manuscripts: M11 (fol. 53), M25 (fol. 38ᵛ; unascribed)

title] Σ; Heart-Breaking WR50; 124. Heart-Breaking M25   2. *lineation*] *ed*.; *aligned beneath the* g *in* gave, F1   3. The] Σ; That M25   8. still liv'd] Σ; it liv'd M25   still it] Σ; yet it M25   12. that] Σ; the O3-4, D2   20. *Tyrant State*] O1-2, F1; *Tyrant-State* Σ

Musical settings: William King, *Poems*, 46.

61. *The Usurpation*.

Manuscripts: M11 (fol. 53ᵛ)

4. kept] Σ; *om* O2   Prisoner] Σ; *Pris'oner* F8-10   6. Fond] Σ; Proud M11   9. Thee] Σ; the F5   12. drav'est] Σ; dravest F11-12   17. *Mise'ries*] Σ; *Miseries* F11-12   *fate*] Σ; hate M11   21. a part] Σ; apart F5-7, M11   29. *Fear*,] *ed*.; ~ . F1   31. *Basilisks* breath] Σ; *Basilisks, Breath* F12; *Basilisk's* Breath O3-4, D2   38. thine] Σ; thy M11   40. *Gar'isons*] Σ; *Garrisons* D2

62. *Maidenhead*.

Other printed texts: MLE58 (p. 64; unascribed)

Manuscripts: M8 (inside front cover; unascribed extract, ll. 9-10), M11 (fol. 54), M24 (fol. 64; extracts: ll. 6-10, 23-24)

title] Σ; The Maiden-head MLE58   5. *Case*] Σ; cause MLE58   buildings] Σ; building M11   9. A thing *God* thought] Σ; Its thought by God M8   10. ruin'd] Σ; mind MLE58   12. *Africks*] Σ; *Africk's*] F11-12, O3-4, D2; *Africk* MLE 58   16. thy self] Σ; thy self thy self M11   17.

whilst] Σ; while MLE58   19. days discovering] Σ; Day's discov'ring O3-4, D2; day discovering M11   22. *Melancholily*] Σ; Melancholy O2   27. The] Σ; To MLE58   28. *Chymick*] Σ; *Chymist* D2   31. *lineation*] *ed.*; *31 is aligned with line 32 in F1*   pay] Σ; richly pay O1-2   33. more] *ed.*; ~ , F1   34. Thee] Σ; to thee MLE58   is his] Σ; to the MLE58

63. *Impossibilities.*

Manuscripts: M11 (fol. 55)

7. *Earth* and *Hell*] Σ; hell and earth M11   12. Worlds] Σ; World's F12, O3-4, D2   15. our] Σ; the O2   17. two] Σ; too O1-2, F7-10   22. *Thee*] Σ; mee O1-2   23. less-concerning] Σ; selfe-concerning O1-2   25. *Helles*] Σ; *Helle's* O3-4, D2   27. ayd] Σ; Air D2   28. *Tower*] Σ; *Tow'r* O3-4, D2   29. th'] Σ; the F12   30. *Oceans*] Σ; *Ocean's* F12, O3-4, D2   Tide] Σ; pride M11   31. eas'ly] Σ; easily F12   34. that] O1-2, F1; the Σ   me'espy] Σ; me espy F4-7, F11-12

64. *Silence.*

Manuscripts: M11 (fol. 55ᵛ)

8. for *Her*] Σ; for to *Her* F3   11. awake] Σ; away O2   20. its] *ed.* (*and* Σ); it's F1   24. *underground*] O1, F1; under-ground O2; *under ground* Σ

Musical settings: Reggio, *Songs*, 2.20.

65. *The Dissembler.*

Manuscripts: M11 (fol. 55ᵛ)

21. grow] Σ; goe M11   22. go] Σ; grow M11   24. with] Σ; without M11

Musical settings: Reggio, *Songs*, 1.29.

66. *The Inconstant.*

Manuscripts: M8 (inside front cover; unascribed extract: ll. 29-30), M11 (fol. 56), M17 (p. 255; unascribed), M20 (fol. 62), M21 (fol. 79ᵛ), Leeds University, Brotherton MS Lt 48 (fol. 43ᵛ; untitled).

Brotherton MS Lt 48 is a commonplace book (c. 1700) of prose and poetry. On fols. 20ᵛ-22 appear a biographical note on Cowley and extracts from the *Essays*. The version of poem 66 appearing on fol. 43ᵛ is attributed in the margin to "Cowley," but it is not given the title appearing in *The Mistress* and it renders only twenty lines from the full text appearing in *The Mistress*. In these regards MS Lt 48 resembles M17 and M20. These three manuscript sources for poem 66, all late-seventeenth-century or very early-eighteenth-century copies, offer transcriptions of lines 1–4, 7–10, 13–16, 19–24, 29–30, thus omitting the last two lines of stanzas 1, 2, and 3, the first four lines of stanza 5, and omitting stanzas 6 and 7 altogether. MS Lt 48, M17, and M20 also share the reading "we" in line 29—a reading that appears in no other manuscript or printed source. These manuscripts thus appear to derive from a common ancestral text that may have been independent of the printed editions. Alternatively, this shortened version of poem 66 may have been copied from one of the printed editions, circulated, and recopied. Given the errors or unique readings in the three manuscripts, we can offer that MS Lt 48 precedes M20 and M17, and that M20 and M17 derive from hypothesized manuscript X, a manuscript that closely resembles Lt 48.

Lt 48 reads "Which had no dart for me" in line 2, thereby agreeing with all early printed editions of poem 66 up to F5. It is unlikely that this reading developed independent of an authorial manuscript, one of the early printings, or a manuscript copied from an early printed text. Lt 48 agrees with M20 against all other sources in lines 13 ("stays") and line 20 ("so too"). The unique reading in Lt 48 line 7 ("of") is an obvious error that could easily have been noticed and corrected to "or," as in M20. Thus far, Lt 48 could stand as the original twenty-line version of the text. Unique readings in M20 lines 10 ("still") and 20 ("Woman") are less obviously errors. These readings in M20, along with its title and variants in line 2, establish that M20 cannot have been the model for Lt 48.

Lt 48 and M20 are closely related, but so too are M20 and M17. Both of the latter pair agree in the title "Inconstancy" and in line 2, reading "Had not a dart for me." Unique readings in M20 (lines 10 and 24) and M17 (lines 14, 23, and 24) clearly establish that neither was derived from the other. Nor, because of the title and line 2 reading, was either directly derived from Lt 48. We therefore hypothesize manuscript X, copied from Lt 48 or a text closely resembling it and introducing the title and line 2 readings shared by M20 and M17.

It is possible that the foreshortened version of poem 66 witnessed in these manuscripts was prepared for a musical setting. To our knowledge, however, no such setting survives; nor is there a setting known for the full text.

title] Σ; Inconstancy M17, M20; The Generall Lover M21; *untitled* Lt48   2. Which had no] Σ; Had not a M17, M20   for] Σ; from F5-10   3. fifties] Σ; Fifty's O3-4, D2   7. or *Shape*] Σ; of shape Lt48   *Face*] Σ; Fate O2   10. yet] Σ; still M20   *Womankind*] O1-2, F1, Lt48, O3-4, D2; *Woman-kind*] Σ   12. *lineation*] ed.; *12 is aligned with line 10 in F1*   13. slays] Σ; stays Lt48, M20   14. as the *Light*] Σ; to ye Sight M17   17. *yellow hair'd*] Σ; *Yellow-hair'd* F8-D2   20. The *Lean*, with] Σ; If lean why M21   too so] Σ; so too Lt48, M20   21. *Cupids*] O1-2, F1, M11, M17, M21, Lt48; *Cupid's* Σ   22. —] Σ; If crooked, 'tis to me his Bow

M21   23. it self] Σ; *om* M17   24. *Women*] Σ; Woman M20   26. richly-landed] Σ; richly landed F11–12   29. Him] Σ; He M17   they] Σ; we Lt48, M17, M20; you M8   31. flee] Σ; flye M21   32. *Loves*] Σ; Love's F11–12, O3–4, D2   35. this] Σ; the M21   37. at first indeed] Σ; at first instead O2; indeed at first M21   42. on Fire] Σ; Fire on D2

67. *The Constant.*

Manuscripts: M11 (fol. 57), M14 (fol. 131^v)

1. *Conqu'rour*] Σ; Conqueress M14   3. canst] Σ; cavst O2   11. an] Σ; a M14   12. I'm] Σ; I'am F8–10   nor] Σ; and O2   13. a] Σ; that M14   *Vagabound:*] *ed.*; ~. F1 (*and* Σ)   17. *Lovers*] Σ; *Lover's* O3–4, D2   24. *my Love* still] Σ; still my Love M14

68. *Her Name.*

Other printed texts: NAC71 (p. 276; unascribed)

Manuscripts: M11 (fol. 57^v)

title] Σ; The Name O1–2 (index); Song 282 NAC71   6. That] Σ; *om* F12   9. the] Σ; that NAC71   14. lineation] *ed.*; *14 is indented one letterspace from the left margin of line 13 in F1*   15. sev'eral] Σ; several F5–10   18. whisper't] Σ; whisper'd NAC71   *Angels*] Σ; *Angel's* O3–4, D2   20. *flowers*] Σ; *Flow'rs* O3–4, D2   *Meadows*] Σ; the meadows M11   23. that *They*] Σ; if they M11   29. *Astræa'* or] O1–2, F1; *Astræa* or Σ

Musical settings: William King, *Poems*, 8.

69. *Weeping.*

Manuscripts: M11 (fol. 58). A parody appears in British Library Add. MSS 28644, fol. 36. See notes to the musical setting by Purcell.

1. in] Σ; with M11   4. *sorrow*] Σ; *sorrows* F11   9. lives] Σ; lies O2   14. *Sun-shine*] Σ; *Sunshine* F7–10   24. they] Σ; thy F12

Musical settings: William Turner, British Library Add. MSS 22100 (fol. 87); Purcell, British Library MS RM 20.h.8 and other manuscripts listed in notes to the musical setting; Reggio, *Songs*, 1.15.

70. *Discretion.*

Manuscripts: M11 (fol. 58), M17 (p. 282), M21 (fol. 79)

title] Σ; Love Knows no Discretion M21   3. This] Σ; The M21   4. *Loves*] Σ; *Love's* F11–12, O3–4, D2   6. Houses] Σ; House M21   12. Are] Σ; Is M21   16. were] Σ; is M11   20. their] Σ; ye M17   23.

Mourn] Σ; More O2   24. they're] Σ; they are F5; they'are F6–10; *om* M21   bound *naked*] Σ; naked bound M21

71. *The Waiting-Maid / (Suspected to Love her).*

Manuscripts: M11 (fol. 58ᵛ)

subtitle] O1–2; *om* Σ   12. *Civil Government*] Σ; Civil-Government O4, D2   17. *Mini'string*] Σ; *Ministring* F12   18. beauty'or] Σ; Beauty or F12   19. they] Σ; thy O2

72. *Counsel* [II].

Manuscripts: M11 (fol. 59), M21 (fol. 80ᵛ)

title. [II] *ed.*

Musical settings: William King, *Poems*, 30; Reggio, *Songs*, 1.38.

73. *The Cure.*

Manuscripts: M11 (fol. 59), M21 (fol. 80ᵛ)

6. to'a] Σ; to a F7, F11–12

74. *The Separation.*

Manuscripts: M11 (fol. 59ᵛ), M26 (stanza 1 only)

2. of Mee] Σ; to me M11   6. that is] Σ; that's M26

Musical settings: Reggio, *Songs*, 1.18; Fr. Pigott, *The Banquet of Musick*, 2.10.

75. *The Tree.*

Manuscripts: M11 (fol. 59ᵛ)

title] Σ; The Three O4   1. Chose] Σ; Close O2   flour'ishingst] Σ; flourishingst F10   5. vi'olent] Σ; violent F11–12   9. many a] Σ; many'a F8–10   18. For] *ed. (also O1 errata, O2; see Textual Analysis)*; Or Σ   28. there] Σ; here M11

Musical settings: Reggio, *Songs*, 1.3.

76. *Her Unbelief.*

Manuscripts: M11 (fol. 60), M26 (extract, ll. 4–5)

1. kind] Σ; *om* M11   *Igno'rance*] Σ; *Ignorance* F4–7, F11–12   2. Victories] Σ; Vict'ories F8–10   4. That] Σ; *om* M26   5. Should] Σ; They

Collations and Textual Notes 203

M26 but] Σ; and M26   *How, nor Who*] Σ; *Haw*, nor *Who* F4; how.
M26   8. odorous] Σ; od'orous F8-10   9. nor see] O1, F1; not see Σ   19. be] *ed.*; ~, F1   21. thy] Σ; my F12   26. Mean while] Σ; Mean-while F7-10

Musical settings: Reggio, *Songs*, 1.19.

[Note: poems 77-83 were added to *The Mistress* in F1. Editions O1-2 do not appear in the collations.]

77. *The Gazers.*

Manuscripts: M11 (fol. 60^v)

8. *Child-hood*] Σ; *Childhood* O3-4, D2   13. lov'd;] *ed.*; ~. F1   15. *Statue'* it] Σ; *Statue* it F12   16. should] Σ; shall M11   22. *Salamander*-like] Σ; *Salamander* like F7, O3-4, D2   27. flower] Σ; Flow'r O3-4, D2   29. *Bridegroom*-Heat] Σ; *Bridegroom* Heat O3-4, D2

78. *The Incurable.*

Manuscripts: M5 (fol. 35^v; unascribed), M11 (fol. 61), M17 (p. 263; unascribed)

title] Σ; A Song M5   2. *Non-sense*] Σ; *Nonsense* O3-4, D2   3. *Receipts*] Σ; Receipt M17   7. ly,] *ed.*; ~∧ F1   10. those] Σ; these M5   11. who] Σ; that M11   13. drown] Σ; dround F10   17. would] Σ; could M17   20. 'bove] Σ; above F12   *Clinch*] Σ; Catch M5   could not] Σ; couldn't M17   23. lov'd] Σ; love M5   24. *Resemblances*] Σ; Resemblance M17   25. made] Σ; mov'd M5   26. t'expell] Σ; to expell M5, M17   27. *Med'icines*] Σ; *Medicines* F3

79. *Honor.*

Manuscripts: M11 (fol. 61^v), M17 (p. 280)

17. *Devi'lship*] F1-3, O3-4, D2; *Devilship* F4-10, M11, M17; *Devil-ship* F11-12   20. *Nights*] Σ; *Night's* F12, O3-4, D2   21. And] Σ; Or M17

Musical settings: Reggio, *Songs*, 1.1; Purcell, *Choice Ayres, Songs, & Dialogues*, bk. 4 (p. 42; reprinted in *Orpheus Britannicus*; titled "*A Song upon a Ground*"), and manuscripts as listed in notes to the setting.

80. *The Innocent Ill.*

Manuscripts: M11 (fol. 62)

10. ev'ery] F1; every Σ   24. *Flies*] Σ; *Flie's* D2   25. rock-hearted] Σ; rock hearted F7-10   30. *Instrument*;] F1 *copies iii-iv*; ~, F1 *copies i-*

ii, v 38. well-*natur'ed*] O1-2, F1; well-natur'ed F2-4; well natur'ed F5-10

Musical settings: Reggio, *Songs,* 1.27.

81. DIALOGUE, / *After Enjoyment.*

Manuscripts: M11 (fol. 62^v).

subtitle] F1; *om* Σ   3. thou'hast] Σ; thou hast F11-12, O3-4, D2   5. short liv'd] F1; short-liv'd Σ   6. *Ill-gotten*] Σ; *Ill gotten* F7-10   30. their] Σ; ye M11   34. whole] Σ; *om* F3   36. onely] Σ; *om* F12, O3-4   40. fair] *ed.*; ~ , F1   43. That *Thirsty Drink,* that *Hungry Food*] Σ; That *Thirsty, Drink,* that *Hungry, Food* O3-4, D2   44. wounded *Balm*] Σ; wounded, *Balm* O3-4, D2   53. *this*] Σ; to M11

82. *Verses lost upon a Wager.*

Manuscripts: M11 (fol. 63^v).

6. an] Σ; a M11   11. if] *ed.*; If F1   14. th'] Σ; the F3   15. *herself*] F1, F11-12; *her self* Σ   so;] Σ; ~ ? F3   16. answer'd] Σ; answered F5-10   32. ow'ed] Σ; owed F3   38. such a] Σ; a such F12   *Sov'eraign*] Σ; *Soveraign* F7-10   39. Mans] Σ; Man's O3-4, D2

83. *Bathing in the River.*

Manuscripts: M11 (fol. 64^v).

30. Haste] *ed. (and* Σ); Hast F1   32. lineation] *ed.*; *32 is aligned with line 31 in F1*   dy] Σ; *om* M11

Musical settings: Reggio, *Songs,* 1.14.

84. *Love given over.*

Manuscripts: M11 (fol. 65), M12 (fol. 76; Latin translation). The Latin version follows the text as it appears in F1, changing nothing of any significance except that in M12 the last three lines of poem 84 are omitted.

6. thy freshest] Σ; freshest O2   7. Tost] Σ; Post O1-2   9. o'the] Σ; o'th' F6-10   15. offers] Σ; off'ers F5-7   17. to'his] O1-2, F1; to its Σ   21. *Pox*] Σ; Poet O2   ev'ry] Σ; every F5-10   23. and] Σ; or M11   25. We're by] Σ; We'are by F8-10   but we're] Σ; but we'are F8-10   29. Lest] Σ; Least O2, F1

Critical Commentary and Explanatory Notes

References Consulted

References to Cowley's juvenilia, political satires, and *The Civil War* cite the texts as they appear in the first volume of *The Collected Works*. Citations of Cowley's later English and Latin works are from copy texts selected for further volumes in this edition. Biblical references are to the Authorized Version and references to classical texts, unless otherwise stated in the notes, are to editions of the Loeb Classical Library. The list below includes references appearing in the notes and commentary to song texts and musical settings. Since most of the seventeenth-century publications can be located through Wing's *Short-Title Catalogue* and G. K. Fortescue's *Catalogue* of the Thomason Tracts, locations of the copy used is ordinarily not specified. Certain generally accepted abbreviations, such as *OED* for *The Oxford English Dictionary*, have been used in the commentaries and notes. Short-title references are frequently employed in textual analyses, commentaries, and notes.

Modern Editions of Cowley

Grosart, A. B., ed. *The Complete Works in Verse and Prose of Abraham Cowley*. 2 vols. Edinburgh: T. & A. Constable; Chertsey Worthies' Library, 1881. Reprint, New York: AMS Press, 1987.

Martin, L. C., ed. *Abraham Cowley: Poetry and Prose* (Selections). Oxford: Clarendon Press, 1949.

Sparrow, John, ed. *The Mistress, with other Select Poems of Abraham Cowley*. London: Nonesuch Press, 1926.

———. "The Text of Cowley's *Mistress*." *Review of English Studies* 3 (1927): 22-27.

Waller, A.R., ed. *The English Writings of Abraham Cowley*. 2 vols. Cambridge: Cambridge University Press, 1905-6.

Bibliographical References

Miller, C. W. "A London Ornament Stock, 1598-1693." *Studies in Bibliography* 7 (1955): 125-51.

———. "Thomas Newcomb: A Restoration Printer's Ornament Stock." *Studies in Bibliography* 3 (1950): 155-70.

Perkin, M. R. *Abraham Cowley: A Bibliography*. Pall Mall Bibliographies. Folkestone, Eng.: William Dawson & Sons, 1977.

Reed, J. C. "Humphrey Moseley, Publisher." *Proceedings of the Oxford Bibliographical Society* 2, pt. 2 (1928): 57-142.

Turner, R. K. "The Printers and the Beaumont and Fletcher Folio of 1647, Section 2." *Studies in Bibliography* 20 (1967): 35-59.

Biographical References

Johnson, Samuel. *Lives of the English Poets*. Edited by George B. Hill. 3 vols. Oxford: Clarendon Press, 1905. "Cowley," 1:1-69.

Loiseau, Jean. *Abraham Cowley, sa vie, son oeuvre*. Paris: Henri Didier, 1931.

Nethercot, Arthur H. *Abraham Cowley: The Muse's Hannibal*. 2d ed. New York: Russell & Russell, 1967.

Phillips, Edward. *Theatrum Poetarum, or A Compleat Collection of the poets . . . .* London, 1675.

Spence, Joseph. *Observations, Anecdotes, and Characters of Books and Men*. Edited by J. M. Osborn. Oxford: Clarendon Press, 1966.

Sprat, Thomas. "An Account of the Life and Writings of Mr. Abraham Cowley." Preface to *The Works of Mr Abraham Cowley*. London, 1668 (F2).

Thurloe, John. *The State Papers of John Thurloe*. Edited by Thomas Birch. 7 vols. London, 1742. Contains a letter from Joseph Bampfield, 4:239.

Other Works

Addison, Joseph, et al. *The Spectator*, nos. 1-635, 1 March 1711-20 December 1714. London: Printed for S. Buckley and J. Tonson.

Agrippa, Cornelius. *Three Books of Occult Philosophy*. Translated by J. F. London, 1651.

Aiken, Pauline. *The Influence of the Latin Elegists on English Lyric Poetry, 1600-1650*. Orono: University of Maine Press, 1932.

Ashbee, Andrew, ed. *Records of English Court Music (1660-1714)*. 2 vols. Cornwall: T. J. Press, 1987.

Ashley, Maurice. *The Stuarts in Love*. London: Hodden and Stoughton, 1963.

Ayres, Philip. *Lyric Poems, Made in Imitation of the Italians*. London, 1687. In *Minor Poets of the Caroline Period*, edited by George Saintsbury. Vol. 2. Oxford: Clarendon Press, 1906.

Ayton, Robert. *Poems: English and Latin Poems*. Edited by Charles B. Gullans. Printed for the Scottish Text Society. Edinburgh and London: William Blackwood and Sons, 1963.

Bacon, Sir Francis. *Essays: The Essayes or Counsels, Civill and Morall*. Edited by Michael Kiernan. Cambridge: Harvard University Press, 1985.

———. *Works*. Edited by James Spedding, Robert L. Ellis, and Douglas D. Heath. 15 vols. Boston: Brown and Taggard, 1860–64.

Baron, Robert. *Apologie for Paris*. London, 1649.

———. *Pocula Castalia* (including *Eliza*). London, 1650.

Barnes, Barnabe. *Parthenophil and Parthenope* (1593). Edited by Victor A. Doyno. Carbondale and Edwardsville: Southern Illinois University Press, 1971.

Barnes, Joshua. *Anacreon*. London, 1705.

Brome, Alexander. *Poems*. Edited by Roman R. Dubinski. 2 vols. Toronto: University of Toronto Press, 1982.

Browne, Sir Thomas. *Works*. Edited by Geoffrey Keynes. 4 vols. Chicago: University of Chicago Press, 1964.

Burton, Robert. *The Anatomy of Melancholy*. Introduction by Holbrook Jackson. 3 vols. London: J. M. Dent & Sons, Everyman's Library, 1932.

Butler, Martin. *The Theatre and Crisis, 1632–42*. Cambridge: Cambridge University Press, 1984.

Butler, Samuel. *Hudibras*. Edited by John Wilders. Oxford: Clarendon Press, 1967.

———. *Prose Observations*. Edited by Hugh DeQuehen. Oxford: Clarendon Press, 1979.

Byron, George Gordon, Lord Byron. *Works*. Edited by E. H. Coleridge. 11 vols. London: John Murray. New York: Charles Scribner's Sons, 1901.

Campion, Thomas. *Works*. Edited by Walter R. Davis. Garden City, N.Y.: Doubleday, 1967.

The Card of Courtship: or, The Language of Love; Fitted to the Humours of all Degrees, Sexes, and Conditions. London: Printed for Humphrey Moseley, 1653.

Carrington, Philip. *The Early Christian Church*. 2 vols. Cambridge: Cambridge University Press, 1957.

Carew, Thomas. *Poems* [1640]. Edited by Rhodes Dunlap. Oxford: Clarendon Press, 1949.

Cartwright, William. *Plays and Poems*. Edited by G. Blakemore Evans. Madison: University of Wisconsin Press, 1951.

Cary, Patrick. *Poems*. Edited by Sister Veronica Delany. Oxford: Clarendon Press, 1978.

Cavendish, Margaret, Duchess of Newcastle. *Poems and Fancies*. London, 1653.

Chapman, George. *Poems*. Edited by Phyllis B. Bartlett. London: Oxford University Press, 1941. Reprint, New York: Russell and Russell, 1962.

Cherbury, Edward, Lord Herbert. *English and Latin Poems*. Edited by G. C. Moore Smith. Oxford: Clarendon Press, 1923.

Churchill, William. *Watermarks in Paper in Holland, England, France . . . in the XVII and XVIII Centuries and Their Interconnection*. Amsterdam: M. Hertzberg, 1935.

Clarendon, earl of (Edward Hyde). *The Life of Edward Earl of Clarendon . . . Written by Himself*. Oxford: Clarendon Press, 1827.

Cleveland, John. *Poems*. Edited by Brian Morris and Eleanor Withington. Oxford: Clarendon Press, 1967.

Constable, Henry. *Diana*. In *Poems,* edited by Joan Grundy. Liverpool: University of London Press, 1960.

Cotton, Charles. *Poems*. Edited by John Buxton. Cambridge: Harvard University Press, 1958.

Crashaw, Richard. *Poems*. Edited by L. C. Martin. Oxford: Clarendon Press, 1957.

Curtius, Ernst. *European Literature and the Latin Middle Ages*. Translated by Willard Trask. New York: Bollingen, Pantheon Books, 1953.

Daniel, Samuel. *Delia*. In *Poems and a Defense of Rhyme*, edited by Arthur C. Sprague. Cambridge: Harvard University Press, 1930.

Davenant, William. *Dramatic Works*. Memoir and notes by James Maidment and W. H. Logan. Edinburgh: William Paterson, 1872.

———. *The Shorter Poems and Songs from the Plays and Masques*. Edited by A. M. Gibbs. Oxford: Clarendon Press, 1972.

Davison, Francis. *A Poetical Rhapsody* [1602–21]. Edited by Hyder Edward Rollins. 2 vols. Cambridge: Harvard University Press, 1931.

Day, Cyrus L., and Eleanore B. Murrie. *English Song Books, 1651–1702*. Printed for the Bibliographical Society. London: Oxford University Press, 1940.

Denham, John. *Poetical Works*. Edited by T. H. Banks. 2d ed. rev., Hamden, Conn.: Archon Books, 1969.

Digby, Sir Kenelm. *Loose Fantasies*. Edited by Vittorio Gabrieli. Rome: Edizioni di Storia e Letteratura, 1968.

Disraeli, Isaac. *Curiosities of Literature.* 3 vols. Cambridge: Cambridge University Press, 1889.

Donne, John. *Letters To Severall Persons of Honour. Published by John Donne, Dr. of the Civill Law.* London, 1651.

———. *Paradoxes and Problems.* Edited by Helen Peters. Oxford: Clarendon Press, 1980.

———. *Poems.* Edited by Herbert J. C. Grierson. 2 vols. Oxford: Clarendon Press, 1912.

———. *Sermons.* Edited by George R. Potter and Evelyn M. Simpson. Berkeley: University of California Press, 1953–62.

Doughtie, Edward, ed. *Lyrics from English Airs.* Cambridge: Harvard University Press, 1970.

Drayton, Michael. *Idea's Mirror.* In *The Poems of Michael Drayton.* Edited by John Buxton. 2 vols. Cambridge: Harvard University Press, 1953.

Dryden, John. *The Essays of John Dryden.* Selected and edited by W. P. Ker. Oxford: Clarendon Press, 1926.

———. *Works.* Edited by H. T. Swedenberg, et al. 20 vols. Berkeley and Los Angeles: University of California Press, 1956–.

Dunton, John. *The Ladies Dictionary.* London, 1694.

d'Urfe, Honoré. *The History of Astrea Newly Translated out of French.* London, 1620.

Eitner, Robert. *Biographisch-Bibliographisches Quellen-Lexicon.* 11 vols. in 6. Graz: Akademische Druck-und-Verlansanstalt, 1959.

Ellrodt, Robert. *Les Poètes Métaphysiques Anglais.* 3 vols. Paris: Librarie Jose Corti, 1960.

Empson, William. *Collected Poems.* New York: Harcourt, Brace and Co., 1949.

Evelyn, John. *Diary.* Edited by E. S. de Beer. 6 vols. Oxford: Clarendon Press, 1955.

———. *Kalendarium Hortense: or, The Gard'ners Alamanac.* 1st ed. London, 1664; 2d ed. London 1666.

Eyre, G.E. Briscoe, ed., and H. R. Plomer, trans. *A Transcript of the Registers of the Worshipful Company of Stationers, from 1640–1708.* 3 vols. Reprint. New York: Peter Smith, 1950.

Fanshawe, Sir Richard. *Shorter Poems and Translations.* Edited by N. W. Bawcutt. Liverpool: Liverpool University Press, 1964.

Fellowes, E. H. *English Madrigal Verse.* 3d ed., rev. by Frederick W. Sternfield and David Green. Oxford: Clarendon Press, 1968.

Feltham, Owen. *A Brief Character of the Low-Countries Under the States.* London, 1652.

Ferguson, H. "Repeats and Final Bars in the Fitzwilliam Virginal Book." *Music and Letters* 43 (1962): 345–50.

Flatman, Thomas. *Poems.* In *Minor Poets of the Caroline Period*, edited by George Saintsbury. Vol. 3. Oxford: Clarendon Press, 1906.

Fowler, Alastair. *Triumphal Forms: Structural Patterns in Elizabethan Poetry.* Cambridge: Cambridge University Press, 1970.

The Frogs of Egypt. London, 1641.

Gay, John. *Dramatic Works.* Edited by John Fuller. 2 vols. Oxford: Clarendon Press, 1983.

———. *Poetry and Prose.* Edited by Vinton A. Dearing and Charles E. Beckwith. 2 vols. Oxford: Clarendon Press, 1974.

Gerhard, Peter. *Pirates on the West Coast of New Spain, 1575–1742.* Glendale, Calif.: Arthur Clark, 1960.

Godolphin, Sidney. *Poems.* In *Minor Poets of the Caroline Period*, edited by George Saintsbury. Vol. 2. Oxford: Clarendon Press, 1906.

Gosse, Edmund William. *Seventeenth-Century Studies: A Contribution to the History of English Poetry.* London: K. Paul, Trench & Co., 1883.

Greene, Robert. *The Royal Exchange.* London, 1590. Facsimile reprint, *The Aphorisms of Orazio Rinaldi, Robert Greene, and Lucas Gracian Dantisco.* Vol. 88 of University of California Publications in Modern Philology. Berkeley and Los Angeles: University of California Press, 1968.

Grierson, Herbert J. C. *Metaphysical Lyrics and Poems of the Seventeenth Century, Donne to Butler.* Oxford: Clarendon Press, 1921.

Habington, William. *Poems.* Edited by Kenneth Allott. Liverpool: Liverpool University Press, 1969.

Hall, John. *Poems.* In *Minor Poets of the Caroline Period*, edited by George Saintsbury. Vol. 2. Oxford: Clarendon Press, 1906.

Harington, John. *The History of Polindor and Flostella with Other Poems.* London, 1651.

Heath, Robert. *Clarastella; Together with Poems occasional, Elegies, Epigrams, Satyrs.* 1650. Facsimile reprint, Gainesville, Fla.: Scholars' Facsimiles & Reprints, 1970.

Heawood, E. *Watermarks, Mainly of the 17th and 18th Centuries.* Hilversum, Holland: Paper Publications Soc., 1950.

Herbert, George. *Works.* Edited by F.E. Hutchinson. Oxford: Clarendon Press, 1945.

Herrick, Robert. *Poetical Works.* Edited by L. C. Martin. Oxford: Clarendon Press, 1956.

Heywood, Thomas. *Pleasant Dialogues and Dramas.* London, 1637.

———. *Proverbs, Epigrams, and Miscellanies.* Edited by J. S. Farmer. London, 1896.

Hill, Richard L. *Paper Making in Britain*. London: Althone Press, 1988.

Hinman, Robert. *Abraham Cowley's World of Order*. Cambridge: Harvard University Press, 1960.

Hobbes, Thomas. *Leviathan*. Edited by C. B. Macpherson. Harmondsworth, Middlesex: Penguin Books, 1951.

Holland, Philemon, trans. *The Historie of the World, Commonly Called, The Natural Historie of C. Plinius Secundas*. London, 1601.

———. *The Romane Historie Written by T. Livius*. London, 1600.

Hookes, N[icholas]. H[ookes]. *Amanda, A Sacrifice To an Unknown Goddesse, Or, A Free-will Offering Of a loving Heart to a Sweet-Heart*. 1653. Reprint. New York: W. A. Gouch, 1923.

Howell, James. *The Familiar Letters*. Edited by Joseph Jacobs. London: David Nutt, 1890.

Hutchinson, Lucy. *Memoirs*. Edited by James Sutherland. London and New York: Oxford University Press, 1973.

Jonson, Ben. *Ben Jonson*. Edited by C. H. Herford and Percy Simpson. 11 vols. Oxford: Clarendon Press, 1925–52.

Jordan, Thomas. *Poeticall Varieties: Or, Varietie of Fancies*. London: Printed by T. C. for Humphrey Blunden, 1637.

King, Henry. *Poems*. Edited by Margaret Crum. Oxford: Clarendon Press, 1965.

The King's Musick. Edited by Henry Cart de Lafontaine. 1909. Reprint, New York: Da Capo Press, 1973.

Korshin, Paul J. *From Concord to Dissent*. Menston, Yorkshire: Scolar Press, 1973.

Laurie, Margaret, ed. *Henry Purcell: Secular Songs for Solo Voice*. Vol. 25 of *The Works of Henry Purcell*. Borough Green, Seven Oaks, Kent: Novello, 1985.

Lawler, Justin. *Celestial Pantomine*. New Haven: Yale University Press, 1979.

Leigh, Nicholas. *A Modest Means to Marriage*. London, 1568.

Leishman, J. B. *The Art of Marvell's Poetry*. 2d ed. New York: Funk & Wagnall's, Minerva Press, 1968.

Lodge, Thomas. *The Complete Works* (1883). 4 vols. Reprint, New York: Russell and Russell, 1963.

Lovelace, Richard. *Poems*. Edited by C. H. Wilkinson. Oxford: Clarendon Press, 1930.

Locke, Matthew. *Melothesia: or Certain General Rules for Playing on a Continued-Bass*. London, 1673.

Lovejoy, Arthur O. *The Great Chain of Being*. Cambridge: Harvard University Press, 1936.

Luckett, Richard. "Music" entry in *The Diary of Samuel Pepys*, edited by Robert Latham and William Matthews, 10:258–82. Berkeley and Los Angeles: University of California Press, 1970–83.

Lyly, John. *Euphues: The Anatomy of Wit*. Edited by Morris W. Croll and Harry Clemons. New York: Russell & Russell, 1964.

Madan, Falconer. *A Summary Catalogue of Western Manuscripts in the Bodleian Library at Oxford*. Oxford: Clarendon Press, 1895–1953.

Marino, Giambattista. *Poesie Varie*. Edited by Benedetto Croce. Bari: Gius, Laterza and Figli, 1913.

Marlowe, Christopher. *Doctor Faustus*. Edited by Irving Ribner. New York: Odyssey, 1966.

Marvell, Andrew. *Poems and Letters*. Edited by H. M. Margoliouth. 3d ed., 2 vols. Revised by Pierre Legouis and E. E. Duncan-Jones. Oxford: Clarendon Press, 1971.

Milton, John. *Works*. Edited by Frank A. Patterson et al. 18 vols. New York: Columbia University Press, 1931–38.

Miner, Earl. *The Cavalier Mode from Jonson to Cotton*. Princeton: Princeton University Press, 1971.

More, Henry. *Philosophical Poems* [1647]. Edited by Geoffrey Bullough. Manchester: Manchester University Press, 1931.

Naps upon Parnassus, A sleepy Muse nipt and pincht, though not awakened . . . . London: Printed by express order of the Wits, for N. Brook, 1658.

Nicholas, Sir Edward. *Papers*. Edited by Sir George F. Warner. 4 vols. [London]: Printed for the Camden Society, 1886–1920.

Nicolson, Marjorie Hope. *The Breaking of the Circle*. New York: Columbia University Press, 1962.

Oldham, John. *Poems*. Edited by Harold F. Brooks and Raman Selden. Oxford: Clarendon Press, 1987.

Osborne, Dorothy. *Letters to Sir William Temple*. Edited by Kenneth Parker. London and Harmondsworth: Penguin Books, 1987.

Parker, Geoffrey. *Spain and the Netherlands, 1559–1659*. Short Hills, N.J.: Enslow, 1979.

Parry, Graham. *The Seventeenth Century: The Intellectual and Cultural Context of English Literature, 1603–1700*. New York: Longman, 1989.

Petrarch. *Canzoniere*. Translated and edited under the title *Petrarch's Lyric Poems* by Robert M. Durling. Cambridge: Harvard University Press, 1976.

Philipott, Thomas. *Poems* (1646). Edited by L. C. Martin. Liverpool: University Press of Liverpool, 1950.

Philips, Katherine. *Poems* (1667). In *Minor Poets of the Caroline Period*, edited by George Saintsbury. Vol. 1. Oxford: Clarendon Press, 1906.

Plomer, Henry R. *A Dictionary of the Booksellers and Printers who were at work in England, Scotland, and Ireland, 1641 to 1667*. London: Blades, East & Blades, 1907.

———. *Dictionary, 1668–1725. A Dictionary of the Printers and Booksellers . . . from 1668 to 1725*. Oxford: Oxford University Press, 1922.

Plutarch. *Life of Julius Caesar*. Edited by R. H. Carr. Oxford: Clarendon Press, 1906.

Price, Curtis A. *Henry Purcell and the London Stage*. Cambridge: Cambridge University Press, 1984.

Prior, Matthew. *Literary Works*. Edited by H. Bunker Wright and Monroe K. Spears. Oxford: Clarendon Press, 1959.

Prujean, Thomas. *Aurorata*. London, 1644.

Purchas, Samuel. *Hakluytus Posthumous, or Purchas his Pilgrimes*. London, 1625. Reprinted for the Hakluyt Society. 20 vols. Glasgow: University Press, 1905–6.

Quarles, Francis. *Emblemes*. London, 1635.

Randolph, Thomas. *Poetical and Dramatic Works*. Edited by W. Carew Hazlitt. 2 vols. London: Reeves and Turner, 1875.

Richmond, Hugh M. *The School of Love*. Princeton: Princeton University Press, 1964.

Rivers, Theodore John, trans. *Laws of the Salian and Ripuarian Franks*. New York: AMS Press, 1986.

Rochester, earl of [John Wilmot]. *Complete Poems*. Edited by David M. Vieth. New Haven and London: Yale University Press, 1968.

Rose, Gloria. "Pietro Reggio—A Wandering Musician." *Music and Letters* 46 (July 1965): 207–16.

Roxburghe Ballads. Edited by W. M. Chappell and J. Woodfall Ebsworth. 8 vols. Hertford: Stephen Austin and Sons, 1871–95.

Saintsbury, George. *A History of English Prosody*. 3 vols. London and New York: Macmillan & Co., 1906–10.

———, ed. *Minor Poets of the Caroline Period*. 3 vols. Oxford: Clarendon Press, 1906.

Sherburne, Edward. *Salmacis, Lyrian & Sylvia, Forsaken Lydia, A Comment thereon, With Severall other Poems and Translations*. London, 1650.

Shirley, James. *The Lady of Pleasure*, edited by Ronald Heubert. In *The Revels Plays*. Manchester and Wolfeboro, N.H.: Manchester University Press, 1986.

———. *Poems &c.* 1646. Facsimile reprint, together with poems from the Rawlinson manuscript. Menston: Scolar Press, 1970.

Shorter, Alfred H. *Paper Making in the British Isles.* New York: Barnes and Noble, 1972.

Sidney, Sir Philip. *The Countess of Pembroke's Arcadia* ("The Old Arcadia"). Edited by Jean Robertson. Oxford: Clarendon Press, 1973.

———. *Poems.* Edited by William A. Ringler, Jr. Oxford: Clarendon Press, 1962.

Smith, John. "Song." In *The Shorter Poems of the Eighteenth Century,* selected and edited by Iolo A. Williams. London: William Heinemann, 1923.

Smith, William. *Chloris.* In *The Poems of William Smith,* edited by Lawrence A. Sasek. Baton Rouge: Louisiana State University Press, 1970.

Sole, William. "A compleat list of British songs." University of Chicago, Newberry Case MS v 8045.8. (A manuscript listing of popular British songs, giving titles, printed editions [sometimes], and comments on the kind and quality of the songs, dated in Sole's hand [fol. 1] "6 Feb. 1778."

Spenser, Edmund. *Poetical Works.* Edited by J. C. Smith and E. DeSelincourt. London and New York: Oxford University Press, 1912.

Spingarn, Joel E., ed. *Critical Essays of the Seventeenth Century.* 3 vols. Oxford: Clarendon Press, 1908–9.

Spink, Ian. *English Song, Dowland to Purcell.* New York: Charles Scribner's Sons, 1974.

Stanley, Thomas. *Poems.* Edited by G. M. Crump. Oxford: Clarendon Press, 1962.

Suckling, John. *Non-Dramatic Works.* Edited by Thomas Clayton. Oxford: Clarendon Press, 1971.

Swift, Jonathan. *Poetical Works.* Edited by Herbert Davis. London and New York: Oxford University Press, 1967.

———. *The Prose Works.* Edited by Herbert Davis. 14 vols. (vol. 8 edited with Ivan Ehrenpreis). Oxford: Blackwell, 1939–68.

Tasso, Torquato. *Le Rime.* Edited by Angelo Solerti. 4 vols. Bologne: Romagnoli-Dall 'Acqua, 1898–1902.

Tofte, Robert. *Laura. The Toyes of a Traveller, Or, The Feast of Fancie.* London, 1597.

The Travels of Peter Munday. Edited by Sir Richard Temple. Issued by the Hakluyt Society, 2d series, no. 45, vol. 3, pt. 1. Cambridge: Hakluyt Society, 1919.

Trotter, W. David. "The Poetry of Abraham Cowley." Cambridge University thesis, June 1975. Revised and published under the same title, Totowa, N.J.: Rowman and Littlefield, 1979.

Vaughan, Henry. *Works*. Edited by L. C. Martin. 2d ed. Oxford: Clarendon Press, 1957.

Waller, Edmund. *Poems*. Edited by G. Thorn Drury. 1893. Reprint. New York: Greenwood Press, 1968.

Wallerstein, Ruth. "Cowley as a Man of Letters." *Transactions of the Wisconsin Academy of Science, Arts and Letters* 27 (1932): 127-40.

Walsh, William. *A Dialogue Concerning Women, being a Defense of the sex. Written to Eugenia*. London, 1691.

Walton, Geoffrey. "The English Writings of Abraham Cowley." Master's thesis, Cambridge University, 1939.

———. *Metaphysical to Augustan: Studies in Tone and Sensibility in the Seventeenth Century*. London: Bowes & Bowes, 1955.

Walton, Izaak. *The Complete Angler*. Edited by J. Bevan. Oxford: Clarendon Press, 1983.

Warner, William. *Albion's England*. London, 1602.

Warren, Austin. *Richard Crashaw*. Ann Arbor: University of Michigan Press, 1939.

Watson, Thomas. *The Hekatompathia*. London, 1582.

Webster, John. *Complete Works*. Edited by F. L. Lucas. 4 vols. Boston and New York: Houghton Mifflin Co., 1928.

Wesley, Samuel. *Maggots*. London, 1685.

West, John E. *Cathedral Organists*. London: Novello, 1899.

Westminster Drollery. London, 1671.

Whiting, Nathaniel. *Albino and Bellama* (1637). In *Minor Poets of the Caroline Period*, edited by George Saintsbury. Vol. 3. Oxford: Clarendon Press, 1906.

Willets, Pamela. "A Neglected Source of Monody and Madrigal." *Music and Letters* 43 (1962): 329-44.

Wing, Donald. *Short-title Catalogue of Books Printed in England . . . 1641-1700*. 2 vols. 2d ed. rev. New York: Index Committee of the MLA, 1972-82.

Wither, George. *Poetry*. Edited by Frank Sidgwick. 2 vols. 1902. Reprint. New York: AMS Press, 1968.

Wits Interpreter: The English Parnassus. London, 1655, 1662, 1671.

Whythorne, Thomas. *Autobiography*. Edited by James M. Osborn. London: Oxford University Press, 1962.

Wyatt, Sir Thomas. *Collected Poems*. Edited by Joost Daalder. London: Oxford University Press, 1975.

Yates, Frances. *The Art of Memory*. London and Chicago: Routledge and Kegan Paul and the University of Chicago Press, 1966.

Zephiria. 1594. Reprint. London: Spenser Society, 1869; and New York: Burt Franklin, 1967.

Zimmerman, Franklin. *Henry Purcell, 1659–1695: An Analytical Catalogue of his Music*. New York: St. Martin's Press, 1963.

———. *Henry Purcell, 1659–1695: His Life and Times*. Philadelphia: University of Pennsylvania Press, 1983.

———. "Purcell's Handwriting" and (with Nigel Fortune) "Purcell's Autographs." In *Henry Purcell, 1659–1695: Essays on His Music*, edited by Imogen Holst. London: Oxford University Press, 1959.

The Mistress: Commentary

Echoing various earlier opinions, Leslie Stephen claims that *The Mistess* contains "the favourite love poems of the age" (*DNB*, s.v. "Cowley, Abraham"). The age, 1640–60 under the banner Cavalier, is recollected by some as licentious, by others as excessively intellectual, and by consensus as divided against itself, soul from body, mind from heart. Edward Phillips, having purloined several poems from *The Mistress*—unascribed—for his miscellany *The Mysteries of Love and Eloquence* (1658), later acknowledges the success of *The Mistress* in promoting Cowley's overall reputation as "the most applauded Poet of our Nation both of the present and past Ages" (*Theatrum Poetarum*, 1675, sig. 2A1). Thomas Sprat's apologetics in the "Life" (1668) suggest that *The Mistress* attracted an ethically unclaimed audience that needed redirection toward the "useful knowledge" available in the verses as well as their "amorous tenderness." A continuingly delinquent readership is implied by a number of critical reactions, such as Edmund Elys's *An Exclamation to All those that love the Lord Jesus in sincerity, against an apology written by an ingenious person for Mr. Cowley's lascivious and prophane verses* (London, 1670). Elys had worried over *The Mistress* for some time, having first published his suspicion that Cowley's verse promoted "Speculative Lust" in the preface to his *Divine Poems* (London, 1659; sig. A3). In pious circles, *The Mistress* was regarded as a dangerous work as late as 1697. The anonymous *A Summary Account of the Life of . . . Dr. Anth. Horneck* (London, 1697) commends this Anglican divine as follows: "You would not find him perusing *Lucretious, Spinoza, Machiavil*, or *Hobbs*, nor sporting with *Ovid, Virgil, Catullus, Tasso,* or *Cowley's Mistress*, or our modern Plays" (p. 34).

Eighteenth- and nineteenth-century critics assume the popularity and representativeness of *The Mistress*, so much so that the book becomes a touchstone for seventeenth-century love poetry. Samuel Johnson's indictment of metaphysical poetry in the *Life* of Cowley stems for his observation that "Cowley adopted . . . the metaphysick style . . . and excelled his predecessors, having as much sentiment and more musick" (*Lives* 1:22). Following Addison's objection to *discordia concors*, citing Pope, and arriving at his own facetious hyperbole, Johnson assigns *The Mistress* its modern repute and sector of literary history:

Cowley's *Mistress* has no power of seduction, she "plays round the head, but comes not to the heart." Her beauty and absence, her kindness and cruelty, her disdain and inconstancy, produce no correspondence of emotion. . . . The compositions are such as might have been written for penance by a hermit, or for hire by a philosophical rhymer who had only heard of another sex; for they turn the mind only on the writer, whom, without thinking on a woman but as the subject for his task, we sometimes esteem as learned, and sometimes despise as trifling, always admire as ingenious, and always condemn as unnatural. (*Lives* 1:42)

Johnson, catching the tone of Cowley's own remarks on *The Mistress* in the preface to F1, is in part inspired to these remarks by the "accusation of lasciviousness" advanced by censurers like Elys. But Johnson and Elys, in their differing ways and with as wide a disparity of insight as imaginable, both accept the popularity of *The Mistress* as grounds for confining it to the age it supposedly represents.

Johnson's judgment had, and continues to have, considerable impact on those who study literature at one remove from the texts. Cowley's nineteenth-century editor, Alexander Grosart, in one of his finest critical moments, defends *The Mistress* against Johnson and the "traditionary criticism" following from his dicta rather than "the outcome of personal and earnest study of the Poems" (1:li). Grosart concludes that love as Cowley expresses it *is* love as experienced in the seventeenth century "and onward," since "trifles (if you will trivialities) are fully half of love-life, as of all life," but he stops short of entertaining the other half, and later critics have not been inclined to fill in the blank. Edmund Gosse certainly does not do so in his mistaken equation of *The Mistress* and miscellanies (like *The Mysteries of Love and Eloquence*) that reprint poems from it. "*The Mistress*," Gosse states, "was fated to become one of the most admired books of the age. It was a pocket compendium of the science of being ingenious in affairs of the heart" (*Seventeenth-Century Studies*, 207).

What Gosse misses, and what Grosart fails to explain, is that whatever *The Mistress* may lose in emotional directness it gains in lambency. Desire, played through the patina of Cowley's traditional topics and tried conceits, shows itself (as at the end of poem 10, the beginning of poem 45, or throughout poem 67) with wit and warmth. Then, too, Cowley's benevolence can often be caustic—

> Though in thy thoughts scarce any Tracks have been
> So much as of *Original* Sin
> . . . .
> Thou with strange *Adulterie*
> Dost in each breast a *Brothel keep*;
> *Awake* all men do *lust* for thee,
> And some *enjoy* Thee when they *sleep*.
>   (poem 80, stanza 2)

—and his laughs are knowing laughs:

> The amo'rous *Waves* would fain about her stay,
> But still new am'orous *waves* drive them away,
> And with swift current to those joys they haste,
>   That doe as swiftly waste,
>   I laught the wanton play to view,
>   But 'tis, alas, at *Land* so too,
> And still *old Lovers* yield the place to *new*.
> (poem 83, stanza 3)

For twentieth-century critics the popularity of *The Mistress* establishes its value as an historical document that needs no longer to be appreciated but only understood. Graham Parry, for example, speculates:

The volume of new verse that seems to have enjoyed the warmest reception in these hard times was not religious but amorous: Cowley's *The Mistress* of 1647. . . . What is striking is the absence of social setting in these poems: Cowley has dispensed with the courtly or pastoral backgrounds that gave Cavalier love-poetry much of its character and appeal, writing instead of unlocalized love—and unerotic love as well—in a way that was immediately successful. Perhaps because Cowley freed love from being the property of the Cavaliers and made it over to intelligent men of any party, he was admired beyond the understanding of all later generations; maybe his cool reasonable approach to love had the appeal of a new fashion after an era of courtly wooing; for whatever cause, Cowley was the coming man.
(*The Seventeenth Century*, 87)

In this interesting inversion of the formula "poetry defines its age," Parry's thought is mostly engaged in ways that the age may have defined and promoted poetry.

None of the foregoing assessments of the popularity and representativeness of *The Mistress* is sustained by evidence other than the poems themselves and the accumulating opinions of earlier readers. At the onset of this editorial project we were prepared to challenge the commonplace reputation of the book. But materials made newly available or newly accessible in the present edition—records of manuscript copies, reprints of all or parts of *The Mistress*, musical settings of the poems—turn out to confirm what readers had been saying, though for differing reasons, all along. The sheer mass of surviving copies shows Cowley second only to Donne as the seventeenth-century reader's and singer's choice for love lyrics. The documentary evidence, then, may serve to illustrate the ways in which Cowley's love poems became popular and to some extent among whom they became popular.

Reprints of the entire collection show it to have been desirable and marketable throughout the period 1647–1721, with peak interest in 1647 (two editions), 1656 (its appearance with the folio *Poems*), 1668–69 (one reissue and three editions with the posthumous *Works*), and 1680–81 (three editions with the *Works*). The full text also appears in British Library MS. Egerton 2326 (M11), titled "The most Ingenious & famous Abraham Cowley's Poems In Manuscript." It was probably copied in the early 1680s, taken primarily but not exclusively from the printed collection F2, by Edward Elisbury (though there are two other hands, one of which is professional).

Other manuscripts, song versions, and the texts of poems appearing in printed miscellanies can be useful in documenting the dissemination and reception of particular poems. One example will have to serve here to illustrate the uses of this kind of information (for identification of sigla and further description, see the Textual Introduction). Poem 29, "The Discovery," exists in all of the printed editions, in M11, and in nine additional states. These are: M6 (as no. 30 in a section of unascribed and untitled songs written in the time of the republic); M9 (as Song 68, titled "Loves Deity," in a manuscript collection that may have been intended for publication in the 1670s, under the title *The Theatre of Complements*); M14 (as an entry in the copybook of Oliver Salusbury, one of his "exercises for attaining French"); M16 (in a miscellany described by its copyist as "from the greatest poets both antient and modern that I have read & here place for my own entertainment to divert malincolly thoughts & to assist my memory, that was never good at no time"); M24 (as one of a number of extracts paraphrased so that an edifying message stands clear); M26 (a single sheet with the full text of poem 29 and extracts from other *Mistress* poems); Halliwell-Phillips broadside no. 1929 (as text for a musical setting, titled "A Song, The Words By Mr. Cowley, And Set to Mussick by Nic: Wootton" and composed before 1700); Pietro Reggio's *Songs* (as a song text, ascribed and titled "The Discovery"); NAC71 (as the unascribed "Song 249" in this printed miscellany, collected by "the most refined wits of the age," including William Davenant, and containing "all the newset songs in use"; published in 1671 and again in 1698).

A collation of variants shows that some of these states are related. M6, M9, and NAC71 are by no means identical texts, but they share a distinctive reading in line 3, all are unascribed, all are designated as songs, and they disagree only in minor ways. Collectively, they represent a rendering of Cowley's poem as a song text. It is likely, given the variations among the three, that the words were somewhat loosely adapted to extant music (the tune is not identified), and it is possible that the song was known as "Love's Deity." NAC71 makes the claim that this was a popular song "in use" in 1671 and revised in 1698.

The song texts set by Wootton and Reggio are not related to one another nor to the M6, M9, NAC71 group (see collations in the musical notes). In both of these examples the music was written for the words and Cowley's authorship is clearly indicated. In contrast with M6, M9, and NAC71, both of these settings can be considered "art" songs—original scores by professional musicians treating a literary text by a highly respected poet.

A similar distinction can be made among manuscript copies not intended for singing. The copyists of M14, M16, and M24 regard Cowley's literary text as something to be used, applied to a moral or practical end. The M24 copyist paraphrases Cowley's fourth stanza so as to discern the morality "I would not find my relief to your disadvantage." Oliver Salusbury, in M14, must have regarded "The Discovery" as an example of good idiomatic English worthy the challenge of translation into French. Unfortunately—at least as far as Salusbury's learning French—he did not complete the exercise, so we cannot tell how he may have understood the poem. Errors and omissions in M16 leave no doubt that its melancholy copyist needed to improve his or her memory. These more or less diligent applications of the text stand in contrast to its reception by copyists like Elisbury, the predominant hand in M11, who reveals in his ascription of the text and fidelity to F1 and F2 wording that he wanted to produce a manuscript memorial to Cowley's art. Elisbury had enough money to employ a professional scribe for part of the copying.

The text of "The Discovery" was received with a variety of expectations. Some read and preserved it because of the reputation of its author; others took it, unascribed, as a good song; still others, who may have known the poem to be Cowley's, cared less for its status than their own and used the text to promote their skills or understanding. We will return to this example to see how well the authorized text of "The Discovery" stands the test of differing expectations. For the moment, it is in order to recognize that Cowley had audiences rather than a monolithic audience, and the overall evidence of surviving states establishes that Cowley's poems were read, copied, excerpted, translated, paraphrased, memorized, or sung for at least three-quarters of a century. The claim that *The Mistress* represents the popular taste of an age, or may be defined by the cultural climate of a generation, needs to be reconsidered, or the definition of an "age" considerably broadened.

The more narrow claim that most of the poems in *The Mistress* were written at a time not far removed from their initial publication is advanced by both of Cowley's twentieth-century biographers—Loiseau (*Sa vie*, 110) and Nethercot (*Abraham Cowley*, 90–111, passim). Others have followed with the more specific assumption that Cowley wrote the love poems in Paris (cf. Parry, *The Seventeenth Century*, 90), where he served as secretary to Henry Jermyn, and was thus in the service of the queen for several years before the publication of *The Mistress* and onwards to 1655. The first clear evidence of his presence in France is a letter in his hand dated 7 February 1645. Cowley would then have been twenty-six years old.

External evidence provides an approximate date for only one of the eighty-four poems in *The Mistress*. In his essay "Of My self," Cowley states that "The Wish" (poem 19) was written when he lived in "the Court of one of the best Princesses in the World." This remark does not strictly limit the place of composition, however, since Henrietta Maria held court at Oxford until her departure on 3 April 1644, and in 1643 as well as part of 1644 Cowley was at Oxford, writing *The Civil War* among other activities. Cowley's resignation from partisan political poetry is apparent in the unfinished state of the war epic and his evident decision not to publish any part of it. The optimism with which he began this project in the summer of 1643, founded on early Royalist military successes and projecting a swift, complete Royalist victory, could survive the realities of war no further than Newbury and the death of Falkland.

The dating of one other poem, "Against Hope," can be entertained in light of the fact that it was first published in *Steps to the Temple* (1646), paired with Richard Crashaw's "For Hope." Cowley and Crashaw became friends at Cambridge, a likely setting for the poems, which thus could date from 1636, when Cowley arrived, until spring of 1643, when he left for Oxford. If the likelihood is accepted, Johnson's *Life* is vindicated in one small detail. Johnson, generally unapproving of "amorous ditties" and happy to regard them as products of "the solitude of a college" (*Lives* 1:6–7), implies that *The Mistress* was written while Cowley was studying at Cambridge. But Crashaw and Cowley could have been together at Oxford in 1643–44 (see Martin, ed., *Poems*, xxxii), and they certainly met again in Paris in 1645–46. Geoffrey Walton has suggested ("The English Writings of Abraham Cowley," 38) that the later dates and places are just as plausible for "Against Hope." One of the manuscript versions of "Against Hope" not known to Johnson or Walton (M1) appears to have been copied before any of the printings, probably nearer 1643 than 1646 (see the Textual Notes, above, p. 187). On the evidence of this manuscript copy, which is immediately followed by a transcription of Crashaw's answer-poem, "Against Hope" could well be a wartime composition written shortly before Cowley left Cambridge in 1643, or shortly thereafter at Oxford.

Seventeenth-century sources all claim that *The Mistress* was written in Cowley's youth. The earliest such report appears in a poem by Jo. Leigh, "To the Stationer (Mr. Moseley) on his Printing Mr Cartwright's Poems," appearing among the commendatory verses in the 1651 edition of Cartwright's poems and plays (sigs. *[1]–[1]v). Responding to the success of *The Mistress* and the hopes that Moseley would publish more of Cowley's poems, Leigh writes:

> Give us what Cowley's later years brought forth,
> His *Mistresse* shews he was a *Wit* by birth.

These lines are also interesting in that they suggest Leigh's knowledge of other works by Cowley—perhaps the *Davideis*—circulating in manuscript.

Commentary 225

Dorothy Osborne writes, in a letter of June 1654 (*Letters*, 169-70), of having seen parts of the *Davideis* in manuscript.

Next, Thomas Sprat says of the poems in *The Mistress*: "it may be alledg'd that they were compos'd, when he was very young" (F2, sig. b2r). Though he says this in the midst of an apology for *The Mistress*, parts of which he no doubt had altered in keeping with Cowley's will, Sprat is in general a most reliable source of biographical information. Finally, Edward Phillips writes in *Theatrum Poetarum* (sig. 2A1) that Cowley's *Mistress* represents "the amorous profusions of his youthful Muse." Leigh, Sprat, and Phillips offer no further evidence in support of their assertions, but it would seem that their opinions were independently formed, and their collective assessment cannot be ignored.

Internal evidence is not very helpful for the purposes of dating. Unlike Cowley's satires, where topical allusions are deliberately specific, the lyric poems are seldom topical. Occasional allusions to such matters as writing in invisible ink (poem 5), Spanish and Dutch colonial conflicts (poem 16), or Greenland discoveries (poem 50) could as likely derive from earlier books and poems as from specific events. Explanatory notes following this commentary include evidence that might suggest an approximate date for particular poems. Verbal parallels with Cowley's earlier poems suggest that poems 16, 17, and 18 could be early compositions, written before the first Civil War. Poems 60 and 61 both appear to be connected with Thomas Hobbes, whom Cowley would have seen with some regularity in Paris during 1645-46. "Resolved to Love" (poem 58) is one of several poems that refers to the "business" of love in terms similarly used in Cowley's essay "Of My self" to describe his service with the exiled court. It may seem reasonable to assume that poems 77-83, added to the collection for the 1656 folio edition, were written after the publication of O1-2 and thus composed in Paris, but aside from from poem 78 and perhaps the fact that the only very obviously French word in *The Mistress* appears in "The Gazers" (poem 77, line 14: "th' *Amour*"), this group exhibits no characteristics remarkably different from those published in O1-2, and parts of poem 82 could represent an original version of poem 12 (see Explanatory Notes).

One may conclude that the poems in *The Mistress* were composed over a decade, 1636-46; some derive from and reflect the latter years of the Caroline peace and others the early years of the Civil War and exile. Some of the poems were written in England, many others no doubt in France, where a manuscript establishing the priority of poem 1, the final position of poem 84, and many other features of the authorized text was put together but not fully prepared for printing. Emphatic italics, for instance, were not indicated. Stylistic and thematic consistency in the volume may reflect a continuity of Royalist and court aesthetics, values sustained or even amplified during the exile. Moseley's decision to publish *The Mistresse* in 1647, complicitous with Cowley or not, must have had to do with the politics of promoting these values.

The year 1647 was a time of negotiation, following the end of the first sustained phase of the Civil War. There was prospect of peace by way of a compromise settlement that would restore the monarchy and sustain the principles of Parliament. The king, returned to England by the Scots and technically a prisoner in his own country, was greeted with displays ranging from sympathy to enthusiastic support. If Moseley and his associates saw in *The Mistresse* a profitable appeal to such sentiment, or if they were so prescient as to recognize its potential in melding Royalist values with perceptions of the common reader, they could hardly have been disappointed in the results of the venture. The first edition sold out, and a second edition had to be hastily set and printed.

The initial success of *The Mistress* had been prepared, not least by Moseley himself, by earlier wartime publications of amorous verses. In 1645 and 1646 Moseley published Edmund Waller's *Poems*, John Suckling's *Fragmenta Aurea*, and James Shirley's *Poems &c.*, three volumes closely related to *The Mistress*. In "The Given Love" (poem 3), Cowley announces of his mistress: "I'll fix thy title next in fame / To *Sacharissas* well-sung name," and Cowley's "Sleep" (poem 48, see Notes), especially in lines 1–7, is connected with Waller. Suckling's "Against Fruition" is matched in *The Mistress*, as are elements of the "Sonnets," "Love's World," the paired poems on absence, and others. *The Mistress* also shows verbal, thematic, and topical parallels with Shirley; see notes to poems 1, 3, 19, 23, 34, 40, and 75 for examples. Other wartime publishers were responsible for Thomas Prujean's *Aurorata* to Cœlia (1644), Thomas Philipott's *Poems* to Julia and others (1646), and Henry Vaughan's *Poems* to Amoret (1646).

All of these books are more earthbound than *The Mistress* in that they mix love lyrics with other more topical genres, and their relation to events of the day is thereby more accessible. Shirley's *Poems &c.*, as a case in point, is also prefaced with dedicatory poems by such as Thomas Stanley and Tom May that lament "Love's pale decaying Torch" in "these sad times that Civil swords did rage" (sigs. A4, A5). Shirley's own intentions are made most clear in "On a black Ribband" (52–53), where the emblem of Odelia's wreath of hair is subordinated to the poet's honor and pride in wearing the black ribbon, sign of the "Order of the black Arme-let," emblem of loyalty to Charles I. The confederacy of the Black Ribband was presumably instigated by Thomas Stanley, whose translated romances *Aurora* and *The Prince* and verse narrative *Oronta* Moseley published in the same year as *The Mistress*.

Like the romance, the love lyric of the 1640s was recognized as a Royalist genre. Is appeal lay in its familiarity, its idiomatic association with national culture and identity. Lyrics in all of the books listed above echo the topics and sentiments of the 1630s (given summary treatment in collections like

Thomas Jordan's *Poeticall Varieties*, 1637), which are themselves echoes of the topics, sentiments, and lyric forms to be found in places like Francis Davison's *A Poetical Rhapsody* (1602, 1608, 1611, 1621). The homogeneity of the genre links Elizabethan, Jacobean, and Caroline monarchies; wartime proponents frequently point this out by alluding to their ancestors in the national literature. Cambridge medical student Thomas Prujean, for example, aspires only to be a star in Sir Philip Sidney's firmament (preface to *Aurorata*, 1644); Suckling's "Session of Poets" shadows the pretensions of the new wits with the presumptions of old Ben Jonson and his tribe, whose shades likewise appear in the first of Vaughan's *Poems* (1646).

The design of *The Mistress*, its hail and farewell to love, and the topics of the poems are familiar in light of the Petrarchan Renaissance tradition. "Against Fruition," the promenade poem "The Spring," "Weeping," "The Tree," "The Soul," "The Passions," "Eccho," "My Picture," "Maidenhead," poems debating platonic love, poems on the lover's rival, even Cowley's poem on the suspicion that he loves his mistress's waiting-maid, are all on set topics and clearly reveal the author's appreciation of their literary heritage. The Explanatory Notes document the topics; in collecting material for them a Scriblerian impulse is almost unavoidable, and perhaps desirable since it can recapture one way in which *The Mistress* was originally read. To read Cowley's love poems for their novelty is to invite such disappointment as occurs in Dr. Johnson's appraisal of "Bathing in the River." Johnson reproduces the first stanza (omitting typographic features and elisions)—

> The fish around her crouded, as they do
> To the false light that treacherous fishers shew,
> And all with as much ease as might taken be,
>   As she at first took me:
>   For ne'er did light so clear
>   Among the waves appear,
> Though every night the sun himself set there.

—in order to conclude that the fiction is entirely unnatural, as though the poet "sought only for novelty" (*Lives* 1:28–29). It is arguable that "Bathing in the River" is the least novel poem in *The Mistress*. Ovid sets the situation with the story of Actæon, and from then other poets take up the topic, responding to the question of what happens when a man spies a lady bathing. Cowley knew what Donne attempted to accomplish in "The Baite," and he was no doubt amused by Thomas Randolph's distracted, scholarly meditation upon seeing six maids bathing in a river. Who might they be? There are not six Dianas; these are three too many to be the Graces and three too few to be the Muses. . . . If Cowley had not read Lovelace's "Lucasta at the Bath," he, like any Anglo-Petrarchist, could have predicted the basis of its paradox that Lucasta's chaste, cold breast could heat the stream she bathes in. Following Cowley, John Harington's claustrophobic thought of being locked in a literary tradition is relieved in the following title: "The Author's first Dream of Flostella, not seen Bathing, but as he rode on Hunting" (*The History of Polindor and Flostella* [London, 1651], 80).

In the "Preface" to *Poems* (1656), Cowley aligns himself not with the Order of the Black Ribband but of poets in general, all of whom must pass through the trial of love verses "like some *Mahumetan Monks*, that are bound by their Order, once at least, in their life, to make a *Pilgrimage* to *Meca*" (one can see now where Dr. Johnson derived his hermit). Cowley's elaborate simile shows the range of his liberty and the humor of his servitude. As the slave of his profession, he is in the same preposterous situation as the lover who, try as he might, can find no release from the mistress and the passion that oppress him. His only relief is in speaking out—or as in the prefatory remark, speaking way out, lofting verbal grenados that he knows are duds. Like the confederates of the Black Ribband, his loyalty is to a lost cause; unlike them, he knows it.

Time and again in the course of *The Mistress* Cowley invokes the figure of the slave or servant to characterize his speaker. He is an oarsman in love's galley, a prisoner paraded through the streets in chains, a town beseiged, a fortress sacked, and, in "The Dissembler," a victim of his own fiction or self-perception. He is low born; his mistress is not. He is poor; his rival is rich. It is too tempting to omit that he is the queen's amenuensis, toiling hour by hour turning language into cipher code. Circumstances of all kinds confine him, shadows of his mistress are everywhere, and the chain that binds him is no less than his mortality masquerading as affection, caught and made known by the social order. Cowley witnesses his bondage with a smile, in terms that reflect the range of his understanding:

> Close, narrow *Chain*, yet soft and kind,
> As that which *Spi'rits* above to *good* does bind!
> Gentle, and sweet *Necessitie*,
> Which does not *force*, but *guide* our *Libertie*!
> ("The Constant," ll. 19–22)

Cowley brings to love poetry a thorough awareness of its tradition and thereby an unusual sensibility that the classifications of modern criticism have obscured. Most persistent is the classification "metaphysical" and the placement of Cowley in the school of Donne. Cowley's direct debt to Donne, perhaps most influentially stated by Dryden in "The Original and Progress of Satire" (*Essays of John Dryden* 2:19), is beyond dispute and noteworthy in the case of poems such as "Platonick Love" and "My Diet," where Cowley's emulation is clear. The virtual conjunction of Cowley and Donne, however, is a highly misleading ascription of Cowley's literary inspiration.

Donne's poems serve sometimes as his matter, not his muse. Furthermore, similarities with Donne often follow from a common classical source; Cowley's "The Inconstant," for instance, resembles Donne's "The Indifferent" because both imitate Ovid (*Amores* 2.4).

Clarendon was first to relate that Cowley modestly ascribed his success to "the example and learning of Ben Jonson" (Clarendon, *Life* 1:34). While Jonson's influence is evident in *The Guardian* and in Cowley's translations from the classics (see *Collected Works* 1:314), it is not conspicuous in *The Mistress*. Cowley shares with Jonson a dramatist's skill in rendering the speaking voice, but the kind of drama Cowley engages in *The Mistress* is lyrical. On this note, let us return to the example of poem 29 and the expectations of its audiences.

"The Discovery" gains coherence and effect through the speaker's voice and the way the persona is situated in relation to the reader. Like many others in *The Mistress*, this poem is a dramatic soliloquy; it begins with false, Donnelike bravado: "By 'Heaven I'll tell her boldly that 'tis Shee; / Why should she asham'd or angry bee, / To be belov'd by Mee?" There follow twenty-one lines of conceited talk wherein the man attempts to convince himself to "tell her" by rehearsing arguments not against her objection (she has said and says nothing) but against his own sense of unworthiness. His confidence unravels, ironically, with every successful argument, and the "discovery" of the title becomes the inverse of the opening claim, revealed not to his mistress but only to us, the audience of readers. The joke is on him; the poet knows it and lets us know it.

The pace of Cowley's talk is carefully modulated, quickening in each stanza where the lines shorten from ten to eight to six syllables, and slowing with each pentameter pseudoconclusion. The lines are metrical, musical, but decorated with aural gestures; the speaker's *fortes* are signaled by italics that theatrically exaggerate the designated words and foster the illusion that someone is acting a part. The voice is a stage voice, or a salon voice whereby a level of artificiality is maintained even among intimates, crafted by the assumption that everything that he says, even the most personal doubts, will be overheard. Soliloquies always are. In a world that denies privacy, the world of the stage, of the Louvre-bound Caroline court, as well as the world promised to published poems and realized as soon as a reader engages the text, all speech (even silent speech) is a performance.

It is no wonder that Cowley's texts appealed to musical composers like Reggio, Blow, and Purcell, who were interested in developing the expressive, recitative style. The voice that Cowley creates is entirely suited: declamatory, witty, touched up with dynamic gestures, yet at the same time adhering to principles of the lyric and sensitive to the sound as well as the meaning of words. The regular stanza development of "The Discovery," shorn of decorative touches as it was in manuscript transmission, also meets the demands of simpler, strophic adaptation, as was probably the vehicle for its M6, M9, and NAC71 manifestations. It is also true that dramatic speech and song texts alike, if their expression is not relatively straightforward, require expansion by way of repetition and recapitulation. If the point is not heard the first time, it will be on the second or third variation.

As observed earlier, "The Discovery" also appealed to readers seeking to develop their own skills or understanding, and to readers interested in collecting and preserving works of art. The text stands the test of these differing expectations. It certainly exhibits the wit and elegance requisite to the Restoration collector, and the opening stanza reveals a nice Virgilian echo (*Aeneid* 2.351-52) in "The Gods may give their Altars o're" (though the M11 copyist shows no sign of having caught it). The demands of the Sloane MS copyist, however, that the text produce in Sprat's words some "useful knowledge," are also met.

Cowley's persona is given dimension as the poet orchestrates his remarks. If we attend the voice that links the stanzas of witty talk together, the character of the soliloquist emerges; he lets us know what the mistress should not know—that he is an unhappy man; that he is a mere spectator to the brilliant subject he attends; that he is low while she is high; and that in being the mirror-opposite of his mistress, he too can only create, or be alone. Cowley touches ground sufficiently for the Sloane copyist to hear and write out his synopsis: 'I would not seek my relief at your expense' (cf. l. 16).

If the clever talk leaves us temporarily with only its chiming ironies—the undeserving deserves; the worthless is worthy; confidence lacks conviction; the discovery is a concealment—we ought to be able to sort out that in the eyes of Love's Deity the worthless can become worthy, since he acknowledges the status and charity of the goddess and lacks presumptions of equality. If we hear this much, we are prepared for what *is* addressed to the woman in "Against Fruition," the poem following "The Discovery." The speaker wants her to remain a deity, not just something like one. So, in the posture of a subservient and fabricator, he advises her in the witty, dramatic language she enjoys to keep her distance, not to yield nor tyrannize too much. That way, if she really is a goddess or if the fiction is sustained, his arguments about the worth of the worthless will not fall from the status of truth to the worldly level of simple irony. "Thou in my *Fancy* dost much higher stand, / Then *Women* can be place'd by *Natures* hand," he cautions, and the poem ends with a sharp but kindly recognition, that awareness of the dangers of fruition alone maintains the "spirit and sweetness" of love. Without that curb, the fiction and the fear, love becomes a tyrant or a drone.

The usefulness of such perceptions is of course relative, but readers seeking to comprehend the ways of love found, and will continue to find, much good sense in *The Mistress*. The point, though, is that compared to Donne and compared to earlier Caroline court poets, Cowley makes the search easy.

Donne was and, despite much glossing, still is a hard poet; *The Mistress*, aside from a few obscure passages, is accessible. Cowley, speculating and expostulating upon the tight conceits so admired by earlier seventeenth-century coteries (and by earlier twentieth-century critics who wanted their poetry to be difficult), offers up the treasures of the national literature to a far wider audience than had either read them or understood them before.

Cowley's immediate followers, however, as Sprat's apology suggests, were not attracted to *The Mistress* for its good sense, useful or otherwise. The word-thief Robert Baron, the nostalgic idealist turned jester Robert Heath, satiric Nicholas Hookes, amorous angler Charles Cotton, the University Wits who produced *Naps upon Parnassus*, and the maggot-witted Samuel Wesley all point to Cowley as a fount of inspiration. What they seize upon from *The Mistress*—aside from recyclable topics, titles, phrases and lines—is the self-awareness within all its posturing. Cowley characteristically arrives at his recognitions after much contrivance, and the recognitions expose contrivance for what it is. In *The Mistress* there is a humorous, tenuous balance of artifice and candor: a balance easily tipped by parody.

Of his immediate followers, Charles Cotton is closest to Cowley in temperament and best maintains the tone of *The Mistress*. Cotton's answer to Cowley's "Beauty" establishes a parodic dialogue between the writers, but Cotton's pursuits of Chloris and Cœlia tend more toward expository paraphrase than witty response. Cotton takes good lines from *The Mistress*—lines 7-9 from "Loves Visibility," for example—

> Men without *Love* have oft so cunning grown,
> That something like it they have showne,
> But none who had it ever seem'd t'have *none*.

—and dilutes them: "In all past Ages, as this one, / This love-sick Age wee live in now; / Now hee, and shee, from high to low / Or lovers are, or would seeme soe . . . Hee is a Traytor to love's Throne, / That has no love, or seems t'have none" ("Love's Triumph," *Poems*, 184). If Cowley unlocked Cupid's cabinet, making accessible Love's conceits, Cotton pours out the contents. Baron, Heath, and Hookes pillage them.

"The Author's Motto," parodying Cowley's "Motto" as printed in O1-2 and prefacing *Pocula Castalia* (London, 1650), is the first sign of Robert Baron's activities in recasting *The Mistress*. Though Baron expresses his ambition to cast the "perfumed corruption" of his verse beside the laurels of Carew and Suckling, many of his poems to and about Eliza derive from Cowley, as the phrase-theft in the first line of the first poem signals: "When her faint Metaphore, Heavens radiant eye" (see *The Mistress*, poem 7, line 4). Baron's "Sonnet, the Protestation" is a pastiche of Cowley's poems 15, 33, and 59 whereby he intends to explode already hyperbolic expressions, turning expansive humor into dregs of bitter jest. "Pardon," Baron begs, "I blaspheme in jest" (*Pocula*, 97).

Robert Heath's *Clarastella* was published by Moseley in 1650 and, anticipating Harington's *Flostella* by one year, echoes Sidney in the title to mark the literary tradition he will parody and waste. The book displays at the beginning a sense of naive play, setting wide-eyed lyrics—

> Here's musick to the sight:
> She looks and sings with such Majestick grace,
> That when I Clarastella hear,
> She more than woman seems . . .
> (*Clarastella*, 17)

—off against titles that situate and make trivial the idealized mistress, tumbling her to earth: "To Clarastella affrighted at the sight of a Cats fiery eies in the dark, which caused her to shreik"; "Bleeding at the nose at Clarastella's approach"; "On a Fleabite espied on her fair hand." As the volume concludes, Heath shifts to a more openly lewd humor—"*Madam*! I vow I never knew / One creature of your sex till you / Find fault with what was long in men. / O do not geld by Phansie then!" (59)—now accepting as the content of his poems what is implicit in the juxtapositions of text and title earlier on. Should there be doubt as to the reason for Heath's changing tone, the occasional poems appended to *Clarastella* clear it to a degree. These include elegies to men killed in the Civil Wars and the remarkable exercise in "limping" rhyme "On the Creeple souldiers marching in Oxford in the Lord Thr. Cottington's Companie," its shocking content delivered in a bravado style:

> Stay Gentlemen! and you shal see a very rare sight;
> Souldiers who though they want arms, yet wil fight:
> Nay some of them have never a leg but onely *Will*
> Their Governour, and yet they'l stand to it stil.
> . . . .
> Oh the courage of a drunken and valiant man!
> For each wil be going when he cannot stand!
> Then room for Criples! here comes a companie,
> Such as before I think you ne'r did see . . .

They appear, one trussed and pinioned like a pigeon, another with half a leg strapped up like a goose, some crawling like snails or crab-lice. "Most of these fighters, I would have you to know, / Were our brave Edgehil Mermidons awhile ago" (*Occasional Poems*, 23-24). Such men fought for the dream of Clarastella; Heath's farewell to love (10) is set in terms of a soldier's "wise retreat."

Amanda. A Sacrifice to an Unknown Goddesse, or A Free-will Offering of a Loving Heart to a Sweet Heart (London, 1653), written by "*N. H.* of *Trinity*-Colledge in Cambridge," moves away from postwar despairing comedy toward the ridiculous, away from the court and into the college, and away from whatever remote potency Venus, Cupid, and their train held for Cowley toward Philip Ayers and the valentine. The academy is invoked in an onslaught of dedicatory poems and, apart from a single poem—"The Authour to the Ladies"—the talk is very much among the boys. Amanda is a "toy," an infinitely fascinating, changing image, something to be shared; she provokes witty and often straightfaced discussion on such collegially varied matters as platonic court-love and how to account for hung-over fantasies of being trampled by cupids. "Amanda's beauty" (11) is seen through the print-wearied eyes of a reader of Grotius's commentary on *Canticles*; Amanda's question about why there has been so much rain, nothing to be dismissed profoundly, is answered in the spirit of Catullus's 'Acme and Septimius' (which Cowley also adapted, perhaps when he was at Cambridge) that Heaven, having looked too much on Amanda, sneezed. The inspiration for much of this verse is not the pertinence or even the whimsy of the classics, but rather a desire to confront the pretense of the past by parody—sometimes droll, sometimes supercilious, sometimes more simply adolescent. One gets this kind of thinking: if Amanda is beautiful, she will be loved by Jove; if Jove loves her, he will turn her into a cow; since she, then, is a cow, *N.H.* will be her milkmaid (*Amanda*, 74; and see notes to poem 9, below).

In the later 1650s, following the publication of F1 with the annotated Pindaric odes, Cowley's youthful admirers found opportunity to expand the range of their satire. *Naps upon Parnassus, A sleepy Muse nipt and pincht, though not awakened . . . Printed by express order of the Wits* (London, 1658), an amusing testimony to the lack of inspiration in the guise of rapt admiration for obscurity, is a collegiate parody of involuted, "analytical" poetry. It was succeeded by such productions as Samuel Wesley's *Maggots*. Wesley (ordained by Thomas Sprat and father of John Wesley) published his poetic issues of a maggot-muse anonymously, in 1685. His endeavor extends the humor of the college wits to cover activities of the Royal Society and may be said to conclude a chapter on the parody of Cowley's poetry if not to open one on the heritage of Methodism.

Wesley was not the first to pursue the link between *The Mistress*, academic raillery, and the Royal Society. Henry Stubbe's *A Censure upon certain passages contained in the History of the Royal Society, as being destructive to the established religion and Church of England* (Oxford, 1670) is a diatribe largely directed at Thomas Sprat's *History*, but it ends with scornful comments on Sprat's editorial treatment of Cowley's *Works*. Sprat, according to Stubbe, ought to have purged *The Mistress* of "the application of *Sacred Wit* to vulgar discourse, and the manner of *Holy Raillery* deduced from Scripture" (62–63). Stubbe quotes stanzas from poems 25 and 27 to make his point. Sprat, a cleric of wider sympathies whose editorial modification centered on purging *The Mistress* of the word *enjoyment*, apparently never paused to think that anyone's religious susceptibilities would be offended by Cowley's religious allusions, most of which are to the Old Testament (cf. notes to poem 2) and cumulatively suggest that love is the occupation of the unenlightened.

Samuel Wesley, seeking to mock pedantry by setting a record for pedantic observations, leeches mainly from the notes appended to the *Davideis* and *Pindarics*, but he is inspired to parody generally by Cowley's awareness and display of literary tradition in *The Mistress* and by the college wits who exploited it. *Parodia*, the form of literary imitation that begins with a close paraphrase and continues with lines that turn away from the sense of the original, is a common practice among Renaissance writers. Often, as in Henry Vaughan's imitations of George Herbert or Cowley's of Donne, the practice has nothing necessarily to do with burlesque or mockery, which more modern use of the term suggests. Sir William Temple, however, in his essay "Of Poetry" (1690), which surveys the whole century, perceives a vein of "ridicule." He sees it as originating in Rabelais and passing through Cervantes, Tassoni, Scarron, Sir John Mennes, Butler, Charles Cotton, and, as he adds, "with greater height of *Burlesque* in the *English* than, I think, in any other Language" (see Spingarn, *Critical Essays* 3:102). From Temple's list it would appear that, despite the English propensity towards burlesque, "ridicule" was largely a feature of the Restoration; certainly it is with works like *Hudibras, Scarronides*, and *The Rehearsal* that ridicule moves to the center of things. Though there are connections between Cowley's political and satirical writing of the early 1640s and Butler's mock-epic and rumors that he had a part in the writing of *The Rehearsal* (Nethercot, *Abraham Cowley*, 230), Cowley had little direct association with these later developments, for little in Cowley's work is inspired by ridicule—although Dr. Johnson justly observes that "the lines from Jersey are a very curious and pleasing specimen of the familiar descending to the burlesque" (*Lives* 1:38). But *The Mistress* does appear to be alive to, and made vital by, a sense of its own ridiculousness. No doubt other contemporary or earlier love poetry was similarly inspired. But no other seventeenth-century poet develops this brand of self-consciousness with such persistence and energy as Cowley, and those who followed him—those mentioned above and others such as Patrick Cary, Philip Ayers, and Swift—certainly recognized and exploited it. *The Mistress* has therefore suffered, or perhaps enjoyed, much distortion.

Cowley had his share of more straightforward imitators. Andrew Marvell derived a number of phrases and figures from *The Mistress* (see notes to poems 14, 15, 20, 54, 63, 75). So too did poets like Brome and Flatman. It is clear, however, that *The Mistress* proved particularly susceptible to parody, and the decade following its publication reveals a transformation in the character of love poetry that is to a significant extent sponsored by readings of Cowley's book. This move was well under way by 1651, when Thomas Dring published Edward Sherburne's *Salmacis . . . With Severall other Poems* (London 1651) and Moseley published Thomas Stanley's *Poems*—academic volumes by Black Ribband compatriots wherein love verse is largely an exercise in translation. The antiplatonics and academy satirists took over the production of new love verse, while the old either surfaced in the form of literary retrospectives (as in the plays and poems of William Cartwright, which Moseley published in 1651, and, if you will, Herrick's *Hesperides*) or entered a wider stream of distribution by way of miscellanies, including a variety of "Wit Restored" volumes as the years neared 1660. Moseley had a hand in such ventures. See for instance his *The Card of Courtship: Or, the Language Of Love; Fitted to the Humours of all Degrees, Sexes, and Conditions*, published in 1653 with poetry mostly predating 1640.

Cowley had nothing directly to do with miscellany reprints of poems from *The Mistress* but, as in the example of NAC71, these printings often represent texts from song traditions of the poems, and Cowley may have written some of the poems in *The Mistress* as songs. While it is not possible to say so with certainty, the likelihood is encouraged by the fact that forty of the poems, roughly half of the book, survive in musical settings. Circumstance brought Cowley and the musician William King together at Oxford in 1643-44 (and, periodically, after 1655). King set fourteen poems from *The Mistress* and published them as a memorial to Cowley in 1668. Some or all of these could have been worked out in collaboration with Cowley (see Composers, p. 313). The case for a particular poem as song text is also arguable where there is early manuscript or printed evidence of texts, called songs or in collections of songs, showing variants that regularize the meter (as strophic settings would require) and/or substantive changes that could have resulted from aural transmission. We have already noted a song tradition for "The Discovery." There are two song versions of "My Dyet" (poem 20), widely divergent from the printed poem, independent of one another and of Pietro Reggio's professional setting of the text. The collation tables indicate similar evidence for other poems. Poem 18 sounds like a song, and the later composers Blundeville and Hart may have elected to set this particular poem because they knew it as a song text. Evidence of surviving musical scores shows that the same poems are set over and over again, while others are never set, which suggests that certain of *The Mistress* poems became known as songs. It is demonstrable that some of the compositions dated later in the seventeenth century derive song texts from earlier surviving compositions; in other cases, later settings appear to follow from earlier muscial treatments that do not survive except in the traces of textual variants. The collations of the song texts with the literary text F1, however, also show a number of instances where it is probable that a composer took the text of a poem from F1 or one of the editions of Cowley's *Works*.

Whether Cowley conceived his poems as songs or not, musical setting became an important medium for their transmission in the later seventeenth century. Of the fourteen composers known to have set poems from *The Mistress* during the seventeenth century, nine (John Barrett, John Blow, John Blundeville, William Hall, James Hart, Robert King, Francis Pigott, Henry Purcell, and William Turner) were associated with either the Chapel Royal or the King's Music, or both. One can assume, then, that some of the compositions were intended for court occasions, but most of these men also wrote music for use in the public theater, and Robert King had his own consort and music hall for public performances. Among the other five composers, Francis Forcer wrote primarily for the theater and Pietro Reggio was well known for performing his works in private households. Performances of poems from *The Mistress* thus reached a varied courtly and urban audience. Publications of lyrics and settings in Playford's and Carr's songbooks widened the potential cast of performers and prospective audiences even further, though by this stage of its dissemination the name of the book, of the author, and titles of poems were most often omitted. The songs, freed from association with the Caroline peace or the wars that followed, freed from association with the nation's most revered poet and from any presumption of literary art, were on their own. According to William Sole's *A compleat list of British songs* (1778), some of the songs remained popular through the eighteenth century. "The Change" (poem 9), which had found its way in paraphrase to the opera house stage in Handel's *Acis and Galatea*, was reset in 1780 as a glee for group singing—a transformation representing one kind of terminus in the historical popularity of *The Mistress*. There need not be another, should this edition succeed in attracting new readers and performers of Cowley's love lyrics.

Explanatory Notes

Poem 1. "The Request."
   4. *First to woo him*. His inability to love has precedent in Ovid *Amores* 1.1, a popular resource for Renaissance poets. Ben Jonson has to petition Cupid in *A Celebration of Charis*, poem 2, "How he saw her," ll. 5-10. Cupid's absence or inactivity is also the subject of Jonson's "Why I Write Not of Love," the first poem in *The Forest*. Cf. Thomas Randolph, "Complaint Against Cupid," (*Works* 2:531), and Thomas Stanley, "Expostulation with Love in Despair" (*Poems*, 249). The subject of this poem is treated from a different point of view in Fulke Greville's popular song "Away with these selfe-loving lads, / whom *Cupids* arrow never glads" (*Cœlica*, sonnet 51; first printed in John Dowland's *First Booke of Songes or Ayres* in 1597. See Doughtie, *Lyrics*, 82).
   7. *Ile think Thee else no God to be*. A standard threat. Cf. Francis Davison, "Madrigal I. To Cupid": "Love, if a God thou art . . . if a God thou would'st accounted be. . ." (*A Poetical Rhapsody* [1602], ed. Rollins, 1:65), and James Shirley, "Cupid *ungodded*," in *Poems &c*, 73.
   8. In Cowley's "Elegie upon Anacreon, Who was choaked by a Grape-Stone" (*Poems* [1656], 39) the speaker, Cupid, corroborates this idea.
   9. *all beauties grow*. Cf. Campion, "There is a garden in her face. . ." (*Works*, 178: from *The Fourth Booke of Ayres*).
   10-16. The "deformed mistress" genre, its rules laid out by Ovid (*Remedia Amoris* 325-30) and perpetrated by Sidney (in ironic praise of mistress Mopsa, *Old Arcadia*) and others, is designed to liberate love's victims. It is here absorbed and displaced by the speaker's elaboration on the subjectivity of love. Cf. Suckling's "Of thee (kind boy) I ask no red and white" (*Works*, 48, Sonnet 2, ll. 17-18); Thomas Stanley's "The Deposition" (*Works*, 31, ll. 1-2); and Alexander Brome's Song 1, "Plain Dealing" (*Poems* 1:69).
   21-24. For a similar antiperistaltic phenomenon, see Cowley's "Elegie upon Anacreon . . . ," ll. 37-40 (*Poems* [1656], 40). In "To her having got a great Cold," Robert Heath's thoughts are occupied, nearly to the exclusion of his mistress, with a new technology: the way "fire Ice is / Made by Antiperistasis." This explains why his mistress is cold. See *Clarastella*, 12.

25-32. *Lukewarmness I account a sin. Revelation* 3:15-16: "I know thy works, that thou art neither cold nor hot: I would thou were cold or hot. So then because thou art lukewarm, and neither cold nor hot, I will spue thee out of my mouth." Cf. Cowley's portrait of the Puritan preacher, designing his lecture to fire the sisters of his congregation, *The Puritans Lecture*, ll. 25-26: "The *Wauld O Lawd* he cries / *Lukewarmenesse*: And this melts the Womens eyes" (*Collected Works* 1:94). The extremeties of love are, in Ovid, depicted as Cupid's sharp and golden arrow, which causes love to burn, and Love's dull, lead-tipped arrow that freezes the heart (*Metamorphoses* 1.465-75). These extremeties become the erotic borders of Petrarch's *Canzoniere* (cf. the poet's lament: "Non è . . . chi li agghiacci et scaldi, / né chi gl'empia di speme et di duol colmi. / Fuor di man di colui che punge et molce, / che già fece di me sì lungo strazio, / mi trovo in libertate amara. . ." no. 363, ll. 6-11). Tasso's "Rime amorose estravaganti," poem 80, is headed: "Persuade la sua donna ad essere o in tutto crudele or in tutta pia" (*Rime*, ed. Solteri, 2:355). The erotic presentment, or presentiment, is refined by Renaissance usage. Jonson's "The Dreame" thus begins: "Or Scorne, or pittie on me take, / I must the true Relation make" (*Underwood*, poem 13), and Sidney Godolphin writes, "Or love me less, or love me more" (*Minor Poets*, ed. Saintsbury, 2:238). Closer to Cowley's full statement in these lines is Thomas Carew's "Give me more love, or more disdaine; / The Torrid, or the frozen Zone, / Bring equall ease unto my paine; / The temperate affords me none" ("Mediocritie in love rejected," *Poems*, 12). Following Carew and Cowley, see Heath's "Or love me not at all, or love me more" (*Clarastella*, 57), and Dryden's "To . . . Dr. Charleton": "*Columbus* was the first that shook his [Aristotle's] throne; / And found a *Temp'erate* in a *Torrid* zone" (*Works* 1:43, ll. 9-10).

"Come . . . prove" in Cowley's l. 29 echoes another rich literary heritage, extending from Catullus's "Vivamus, mea Lesbia, atque amemus" (*Poems* 5.1) through a variety of translations, adaptations, and echoes—Marlowe, Donne, Campion, Jonson, Carew—to Richard Crashaw's translation, "Come and let us live my Dear," wherein the words are returned to Catullus (but not in time; the phrase lives on to become "Come live with me and be my whore" in *Westminster Drollery* [London, 1671], 16). It is worth noting here that Addison elects "The Request," among other of Cowley's *Mistress* poems, for parodistic summary in his discussion of "mixed wit" (*The Spectator*, no. 62, 11 *May* 1711).

"The Request," as the first poem in *The Mistress*, signals a literary heritage; as Cowley comments, with questionable sincerity, in his preface to the folio *Poems* of 1656: "*Poets* are scarce thought *Free-men* of their *Company*, without paying some duties, and obliging themselves to be true to *Love*" (sig. [a] 4v).

33-43. The conquest of animals, birds, and fish is common to Renaissance poetic and iconographic depictions of Cupid's triumph following upon Petrarch's *Triumphus Cupidinis* (wherein, as in Ovid, such creatures are metamorphosed lovers).

34. *Bores*. Grosart felt it desirable to gloss *Bores* as "boars" (*Complete Works* 1:238).

43. *armour . . . Scales*. A pun may be intended, "scales" being an admissible term for "armour." This would be an early example of the substitution (see *OED*, s.v. "scale," 7 and 12).

44. *Sea-born Mother*. Venus.

52. *thy skillful Ovid*. In reference to Ovid's *Remedia Amoris*, which opens, like "The Request," with an address to Cupid. Pauline Aiken cites this line, among others, as evidence that for the love poems, Ovid was Cowley's "Roman master" (*The Influence of the Latin Elegists on English Lyric Poetry*, 37). Addison (*Spectator*, no. 62; see note to l. 25ff., above) sees much in common between Ovid and Cowley, along with Martial and all "the *Italians*, even in their epic Poetry." All are prone to "mixed wit," which promotes epigrammatic mixtures or resemblances of ideas and of "mere words" —puns being the lowest form of it.

Poem 2. "The Thraldom."
Title. As ll. 7–8 and 25 suggest, the "thraldom" alludes to Israel's bondage in Egypt. The Egyptian analogy was frequently employed in the seventeenth century, especially in its capacity to figure millenarian aspirations of the Puritans. Cf. *The Frogs of Egypt*, where bishops and monopolers become the first and second plagues. See Cowley's own application in the Pindaric ode "The Plagues of Egypt" (*Poems* [1656], 3H2^v, 54).

1. "Veni, vidi, vici." According to Plutarch, this was said by Julius Caesar in giving an account of his victory over Parnaces, son of Mithridates who had aided Pompey, at Zela in Asia Minor (47 BC; *Life of Caesar*, ed. Carr, 93). Suetonius, however, says that the inscription was displayed after Caesar's Pontic triumph. Both Plutarch and Seutonius treat the words as referring to the speed of Caesar's victory (*De vita Caesarum* 1.37). Cf. poem 63, ll. 4–5.

In Shakespeare's *Love's Labour's Lost* 4.1.70–86, Armado employs Caesar's words in the context of a love letter, and in *As You Like It* 5.2, Oliver and Celia's mutual undoing is narrated in terms of "Caesar's thrasonical brag." Robert Burton, discoursing on beauty as a cause of love-melancholy, writes, "Ut vidi, ut perii!" [I saw, I was undone] (*Anatomy*, 3.2.2.2; 3:76).

2. *Lightning did through my bones and marrow run*. Compare Catullus "ut multo mihi maior acriorque / ignis mollibus ardet in medullis" [as (I swear) more strongly and fiercely burns in me the flame deep in my melting marrow], *Carmina* 45, ll. 15–16. Cowley's translation of this poem, under the

title "Ode. Acme and Septimius out of Catullus," was first published posthumously in *Works* (1668), and it became a popular song in a setting by John Blow. Cowley's use of lines 15-16 here suggests that his translation was done before 1647.

7-8. *destroying . . . Plague.* Cf. the plagues in Egypt, Exodus 7:14-11:10.

8. *hasty Death.* In Revelation 9, hasty death comes with the plagues brought on when the sixth angel blows his trumpet.

10. *Legion.* Mark 5:9. "Legion" is the name given by the evil spirit[s] inhabiting the "poor wretch" who wanders about tombs and cuts himself with stones. When he sees Jesus, the man worships him, crying out "Jesus . . . torment me not." Cf. poem 66, ll. 5-6.

11-12. In Revelation 9, the plague of locusts (evoking the Egyptian plague in Exodus) brought on by the fifth angel makes "men seek death . . . [but] death shall flee from them."

22-24. *Galleys . . . sighs.* Cf. Petrarch *Canzoniere* 189, for the nautical figure and "un vento umido eterno / di sospir." The term *Galleys* may suggest Wyatt as Cowley's point of reference.

25. *Egyptian Tyrant.* He appears in Exodus 1:11-14.

28. *Quarries of a stony Heart.* Cowley's literary quarries would extend back to Dante's *Rime petrose*.

31. *the Mine.* The idea that "loves delights / Are treasures hid in caves and mines" (Fulke Grevile, *Cælica*, sonnet 5, first published in Dowland's *First Booke of Songs or Ayres*, 1597) is a popular conceit in amorous lyrics. Doughtie (*Lyrics*, 456) notes that the figure recalls the saying of Democritus "that the truth of nature lies hid in certain deep mines and caves," as cited by Bacon, *de Augm. scient.* 3.3. Cf. Sidney, *Astrophel and Stella*, 2.3-4: "But known worth did in mine of time proceed, / Till, by degrees, it [love] had full conquest got." And cf. Donne, "Loves exchange," ll. 34-35, and "Loves Alchymie," l. 1: "Some that have deeper digg'd loves Myne then I. . . ." The possibility of an egocentric pun is not to be ignored. See, for comparison, "Mine/*Mines*" in "Leaving Me, and then loving Many," poem 11, ll. 15-16, and Shakespeare's "The Phoenix and the Turtle," l. 36: "Either was the others mine."

Poem 3. "The Given Love."

1-2. Cf. Thomas Carew, "A Rapture," l. 1: "I will enjoy thee now my *Celia*, come . . ." (*Poems*, 49).

3. *those exceptions.* Among the "under-mortals" voicing such opinions would be Ben Jonson's Charis who, in the ninth lyric of *A Celebration*, tells what kind of man would please her: "I would have him, if I could, / Noble; or of greater blood: / Titles, I confesse, doe take me . . ." (*Ben Jonson* 8:140, ll. 3-5).

4. *thin-sould, under-mortals.* The phrase was rewritten, probably by Sprat, to "vulgur sordid *Mortals*" for publication in F2 and subsequent editions of *The Mistress.* See Textual Collation, p. 175.

5. *my Fate's too mean and low.* In *Davideis* 3, David sings "Though so *Exalted* she / And I so *Lowly* be" (*Poems* [1656], 4N3^r, 101). It is this "dull cause" that Diomede advances with Criseyde, to the detriment of Troilus (Chaucer, *Troilus and Criseyde* 5.871ff.), and which echoes in later romance literature. Cowley frequently voices this perception of class. In one of his earliest poems a young knight, "his state but small," loves Constantia, "in birth and Parentage as high / As in her fortune great," and faces a rich rival, Guiscardo, who owns land and houses "which Gold and *Parian* stone adorne" (*Constantia and Philetus*, ll. 71, 31-32, 535; *Collected Works* 1:21ff.). Cf. Robert Heath's "To one blaming my high-minded Love" (*Clarasella*, 13), asserting the privilege of love over obstacles of class.

21-22. *flatter or oppose the King, / Turn Puritan.* Cowley's *The Puritan and the Papist* shows the Puritans flattering and opposing at the same time (see *Collected Works* 1:109, ll. 199-202). The Puritan/Papist allusions in "The Given Love" (see l. 59 for the Papist comparison) suggests an early date of composition for the poem, perhaps 1642 or earlier, when such lines would have had considerably more topical currency than in 1647.

32. *The Rib.* The metonymy may seem to vitiate the speaker's chances. Prelapsarian semantics, however, apply. Man reigns in Paradise, and "the Rib" refers to "Joynture." See poem 41, l. 12 and note.

33. *the man.* Cf. Cowley's Anacreontic "Gold": "A *curse* on her, and on the Man, / Who this traffick first began!" (*Poems* [1656], sig. F2, p. 35, ll. 9-10). Pauline Aiken (*Influence*, 38) compares Tibullus 1.4.59-60: "at tua, qui venerem docuisti vendere primus, / quisquis es, infelix urgeat ossa lapis" [whosoever thou art that first didst teach the sale of love, may an unhallowed stone weigh heavily on thy bones]. William Walsh (*A Dialogue*, 22-23) adds dozens of parallels such as Horace, Ovid, Marino, Guarini, Ronsard, and so forth. Cf. Hookes, *Amanda*, 12: "His love to Amanda."

41-42. *Poets . . . of old.* For the story of Zeus and Danae, see Horace *Odes* 3.16 and Ovid *Metamorphoses* 6.112. Zeus, seducer, turned into gold that showered down upon Danae. Therefore, he was what he gave (see l. 48).

51. *The Spaniard.* By the 1640s Spanish colonial investments in the Indies were far less worthy of this allusion than had been the case under Phillip II.

59. *Popish thought.* See l. 22 and the note above for a Puritan comparison.

66. *Sacharissa.* The name (deriving from the Latin for "sugar") refers to Lady Dorothy Sidney, whom Edmund Waller courted, at least in his poems (published in 1645), from 1635-38. Nethercot (*Abraham Cowley*, 100) makes the point that Waller's *Poems* were well known in manuscript before their

publication and that Cowley's reference may be regarded in the sense of a rivalry. Cowley may have met Waller in England (perhaps by way of Lucius Cary). He certainly encountered Waller in Paris, between Waller's removal to France in 1646 and return to England in 1652 (Waller, *Poems*, lix-xi). There are several later connections between the two poets. They both wrote poems on *Gondibert*, poems on the Restoration, and poems on the queen's repairing Somerset House (1664). They were both fellows of the Royal Society, both belonged to the Society for the Restoration of the Language (Nethercot, *Abraham Cowley*, 258), and both have been implicated in *The Rehearsal* (ibid., 230). Such affinities, over such a time, argue against the idea of a rivalry. For Buckingham's dramatic version of the contest between mistress's names, see *The Rehearsal* (London, 1672) 4.2.

69. *the last great Assise*. The first "great Assize" (judgment) during the reign of Henry II established that legal proceedings be substituted for trial by combat. The last judgment, in these lines, turns out to be a beauty contest. Cf. James Shirley, "That, that is she; O straight, surprize / And bring her unto Loves Assize" ("Loves Hue and Cry," *Poems &c.*, 8).

Poem 4. "The Spring." Hugh M. Richmond offers a description of the "promenade poem" in *The School of Love*, 162-68.

1-2. Displays of the obsequious elements, considered fallaciously or otherwise, were a permanent source of amusement for Cowley's contemporaries. Cf. Cleveland's "Upon Phillis walking in a mourning before sun rising" (*Poems*, 14) or Waller's "At Penshurst." J. B. Leishman considers that Ralph Strode's version of Tasso's "Ritorno di Madonna in tempo di neve," titled "On Chloris walking in the Snow" and printed in Porter's *Madrigals and Airs* (1632), was probably responsible for exciting British poets to the prospect of witty elaboration on this hyperbolic pastoral convention (*The Art of Marvell's Poetry*, 80). Cowley's treatment, a gentle parody, has much in common with Suckling's side of the dialogue with Carew, "Upon my Lady Carlisles walking in Hampton Court Garden" (Suckling, *Non-Dramatic Works*, 30).

17-18. A biblical allusion (e.g., Genesis 1, 3:8) is offered. Cf. Henry Vaughan, "Religion," ll. 4-5: "I see in each shade that there growes / An Angell talking with a man" (*Works*, 404, alluding to 1 Kings 19:5). Cf. poem 5, l. 1 and note. L. C. Martin compares Pope, *Pastorals*, "Summer," ll. 73-74: "Where'er you walk, cool gales shall fan the glade, / Trees, where you sit, shall croud into a shade." In ll. 59-62, Pope introduces the "Descending Gods" who haunt the forest shade.

23-24. The story of Apollo's pursuit of Daphne and her transformation into a laurel (Ovid, *Metamorphoses* 1.468ff.), one of Petrarch's mythic touchstones in the *Canzoniere*, is a common topic in the seventeenth century:

e.g., Marino's "La transformazione di Dafne" (*Poesie Varie*, 175); Waller's "The story of Phoebus and Daphne, applied" (*Poems* 52); Marvell's "The Garden," ll. 29-30: "*Apollo* hunted *Daphne* so, / Only that She might Laurel grow" (*Poems*, 48).

25-30. Cowley had earlier elaborated on Horace, Ode 1.12.7-8, representing the parade of trees following Orpheus, in his Ode 1. *On the prayse of Poetry*, published in the second edition of *Poetical Blossomes*, 1636 (see *Collected Works* 1:83 and note, 314).

47-48. Grierson includes poem 4 (along with poem 9, "The Change") in *Metaphysical Lyrics and Poems*. Against the concluding lines of "The Spring" he considers Donne's "To the Countesse of Bedford" ("Madame, You have refin'd"), ll. 13-16: "to this place / You are the season (Madame) you the day, / 'Tis but a grave of spices, 'till your face / Exhale them, and a thick close bud display."

Poem 5. "Written in Juice of Lemmon." The conceit of this poem may very possibly, as Geoffrey Walton suggests, have its origin in the secretive aspects of Cowley's secretarial duties in Paris (*Metaphysical to Augustan*, 61). Letters in lemon juice or sympathetic ink occasionally survive among the correspondence of the Civil War period (e.g., Sir Edward Nicholas, *Papers*, ed. George F. Warner, 1:73). Such firsthand experience was hardly necessary, however, since secret writing in invisible inks was a familiar literary topic. John Carey directs us to Ovid's advice, in *Ars Amatoria* 3:627-28: "Tuta quoque est fallitque oculos e lacte recenti / Littera: carbonis pulvere tange, leges" [A letter too is safe and escapes the eye, when written in "new milk": touch it with coal-dust and you will read]. G. P. Goold glosses the passage with references from Pliny and Ausonius on the "herba lactaria" used by the ancients as invisible ink (see the revised Loeb edition of *Ars Amatoria*, 162). Ovid adds, in 3:629-30, that writing with a stalk of wet flax works the same way as the milk plant.

Ben Jonson exploits the notion that lemon juice is a basic constituent of diplomatic intrigue in *Epigrams*, 92, ll. 25-29 (*Ben Jonson* 8:59):

> They all get Porta, for the sundry ways
>   To write in cipher, and the several keys
> To ope the character. They've found the sleight
>   With juice of lemons, onions, piss, to write,
> To break up seals, and close 'em.

The element of secrecy in these matters is dispelled during the 1650s and the Restoration. For instance, the editions of *Wits Interpreter: The English Parnassus* (1655, 1662, 1671) treat special inks and codes with increasing detail;

they include instructions for letters that cannot be read unless dissolved in water, on letters that must be held up to the heat and light of a candle, and (1671) instructions for writing in codes.

Lemon juice writing as a form of literary obscurity is entertained in *Naps upon Parnassus*, a parodic miscellany by Oxford wits, mainly perhaps by "T. F. lately F. N. C. Oxon" (sigs. B2, B3). Cowley's *Mistress* is specifically mentioned (sig. B5) and his Pindarics are admiringly parodied (sig. E2, "A Pindaric Ode: on the ingenious poet Mr. Cowley"). See note to l. 39, below.

2. *you*. The poem is addressed to the writing paper.

33. *a new-born Wood*. This may be comparable to the sonnet and romance convention of carving or hanging poems on trees, e.g., *As You Like It* 3.2.5-6: "These trees shall be my books / And in their Barks my thoughts I'll character." Wood was not proposed as a fiber source for paper until the early eighteenth century (Hill, *Paper Making in Britain*, 143-55). Henry Vaughan alludes to the seventeenth-century process of making paper from linen in "The Book" (ll. 5-8, *Works*, 540).

39. *sense in this, and Mysterie*. Among the many cryptically ascribed dedicatory poems in *Naps upon Parnassus*, all praising the author's achievements in obscurity, is "Upon the Author's Mystery of Babylon," which reads:

> I cannot say thou writ'st instead of *Ink*
> With *juice* of *Lemons*, that's too *sharp* a drink,
> And *quick*; but yet as that *conceals what's writ*,
>   *Writes* well enough, but then
>   *Blots out* as fast agen;
>   And so by riddling play
>   Brings *Night* in midst of *Day*,
>   And none must hope to *see*
>   What's *written*, though there it be,
> Just so thou *jugglest*, speak'st good *sense* and *wit*,
> Yet so *obscure* in every part of it
>   As that it disappears
>   From all our *eyes* and *ears* . . .
>
>   (sig. C2)

Here, lemon juice is associated with sharp, quick wit.

Poem 6. "Inconstancy."

1. *Five years . . . Story*. If "Story" is history, this poem puts poem 84 (the last in F1; the penultimate one in O1-2) out of chronological sequence. "Love given over," in l. 6, allows love's story a three-year duration.

4. In "Womans constancy" Donne challenges the woman who would claim that, as time passes, "We are not just those persons, which we were"

(l. 5, *Poems*, 9). By the end of the poem, however, the speaker turns to admit that "by to morrow, I may thinke so too." Jonson's "Another: in Defence of Their Inconstancy: A Song" has the women speak, defending the argument that it is not "inconstancy to change" (*Underwood*, poem no. 6, l. 13). Cowley's "Inconstancy" portrays the women's argument in the voice of the male speaker.

5. *No Flesh is now the same.* Among the various natural forms of inconstancy common to Renaissance poetry is the periodic restoration (often regarded as septennial) of the body. Cf. Donne, "Obsequies to the Lord Harrington, brother to the Lady Lucy": "As bodies change, and as I do not weare / Those Spirits, humours, blood I did last yeare . . ." (ll. 45-46, *Poetical Works*, 1:272). Cowley treats the physical restoration as cinquennial, though he may mean no more than is stated in l. 22: "Our *Substances* themselves do fleet, and fade."

11. *Members.* A sexual connotation is here obscured by the plural.

19. *The World's a Scene of Changes.* Lucretius *De rerum natura* is the basic source for the principle of universal mutation (cf. 5.833-35: "porro aliut succrescit et e contemptibus exit / sic igitur mundi naturam totius aetas / mutat et ex alio terram status excipit alter"). Cowley's line, however, is close to Ovid's "nihil est toto, quod perstet, in orbe / cuncta fluut, omnisque vagans formatur imago" (*Metamorphoses* 15.177-78).

20. [*to be*] *Constant, in Nature were Inconstancie.* Cf. d'Urfe, *Astrea . . . Newly Translated*, sig. B^v: "there is nothing constant, but inconstancy onely durable in her changes." Cf. poem 66, ll. 29-30.

19-28. This section of "Inconstancy" appears independently in commonplace book copies (see Textual Notes).

Poem 7. "Not Fair." The subjective premise of this poem is the same as may be found in poem 1, "The Request," ll. 9-16, and in other poems of the period. See for example Thomas Stanley, "The Deposition": "Though when I lov'd thee thou wert fair, / Thou art no longer so" (*Poems*, 31), and Alexander Brome, who follows Cowley with "Only because I think she's fair, she's fair" (*Poems* 1:90). Cowley's misogynous turn at l. 9 inverts the complaint of Ovid *Amores* 3.3.1-2: "Esse deos, i crede—fidem iurata fefellit, / et facies illi, quae fuit ante, manet!" [Go, believe there are gods—she swore and has failed her oath, and still her face is fair, as it was before!]. There are affinities of tone in Lovelace's sonnet "When I by thy faire shape did sweare" (*Poems*, 44), in Shakespeare (e.g., sonnet 40), and particularly Thomas Jordan (cf. "A Gentleman's deploration . . ." and "A Paradox . . ." in *Poeticall Varieties*, 4 and 11).

2. *th' Idea.* There may be an allusion to Drayton's sonnet sequence *Idea's Mirror*.

4. *a faint Metaphor of Thee.* Cf. Robert Baron, "these are but faint Metaphors of her . . ." (*Apologie for Paris*, 36).

14-16. *Succu'bus . . . cleft Foot.* The knight's bedtime visitor in *The Faerie Queene*, 1.1, stanzas 47-49 (along with Duessa's feet, revealed in canto 8) may have been somewhere in Cowley's mind (cf. title to poem 10, and note). See also James Shirley's *The Lady of Pleasure*, 4.1, ll. 63, 79-83: "Has she no cloven foot? . . . This doth more / Confirm she is a devil, and I am / Within his own dominions. I must on, / Or else be torn a-pieces; I have heard / These succubi must not be crossed" (ed. Ronald Heubert, *The Revels Plays*.)

Poem 8. "Platonick Love." It is well known that of all the commonplaces of seventeenth-century poetry, the subject of platonic love (and antiplatonic reactions) was the preoccupation of the court of the 1630s and prewar 1640s. Loiseau comments on *The Mistress* in this context, and there are any number of possible sources and literary analogues for "Platonic Love." Cowley would appear to be especially indebted, in stanzas 1 and 4, to John Donne's "The Extasie," as Loiseau (*Sa vie*, 380-81), Sparrow (*Mistress*, xvi), and others have pointed out. Donne is most clearly echoed in stanza 4.

1. *Indeed I must confess*, and the lines following. Cf. Sir Robert Ayton, "Upon Platonic Love: To Mistress Cicely Crofts, Maid of Honor," ll. 21-24: "But I must needs confess I doe not finde / The motions of my minde / Soe purifyed as yet, but at there best / My body claims in them some interest" (*Poems*, 196). Thomas Clayton notes that Ayton's poem was written after Walter Montagu's platonic/pastoral play *The Shepherd's Paradise*, 8 January 1632/33, and is in effect an antiplatonic reaction to it (Sucking, *Poems*, 99).

11. *one even in that difference.* Stanzas 1 and 4 frame the central stanzas on the uniting of genders vs. narcissism. Alastair Fowler, comparing this poem with Donne's "The Extasie," comments on the symmetries of the poems, particularly the conjunction of sexes that forms their structural centers. In "Platonick Love," "one" appears in the center of each central stanza—i.e., at ll. 11 and 18 (*Triumphal Forms*, 73n). For the sexual implications of "perfect Love," cf. Propertius's explicit "in amore . . . masculus et totum femina coniugium" [in love, masculine and feminine are joined in one whole], *Elegies* 2.15, 27-28. Caroline poets frequently cast the hermaphrodite as an embodiment of this idea.

18. *one.* See l. 11, above.

22-23. Cf. Donne, "The Extasie," ll. 49-60.

26-28. The descent from spirit to flesh in the concluding stanza is entirely expected. The further descent, by way of similie, into erotic melodrama may come as a surprise. The situation of two male friends and one woman, however, is a favorite of Cowley's (cf. Philetus, Philocrates, and Constantia;

David, Jonathan, and Michol). Here he is probably dramatizing the conclusion of Donne's "The Extasie," where "some lover" has the chance to look at both the speaker and his mistress.

Poem 9. "The Change." The conceit of this poem has a Petrarchan provenance, to be marked where "Amor vien nel bel viso di costei" (*Canzoniere* 13, 1.2). The general development of Cowley's poem is available in Robert Tofte's *Laura*, no. xii (sig. A8ᵛ):

> The Beautie that in Paradice doth grow
> Lively appears in my sweet Goddesse face,
> . . . .
> But in her daintie (yet too cruell) Brest
> More crueltie and hardnes doth abound,
> Than doth in painfull Purgatorie rest:
> So that (at once) she's faire and cruell found,
> When in her face and breast, (ah grief to tell)
> Bright Heaven she showes, and craftie hides dark hell.

Cowley may have been more immediately affected by *Astrophel and Stella*, no. 11 (see ll. 5-6, below). Among Cowley's contemporaries to draw on the same figure is Henry More, whose "Cupid's Complaint" reads "And frantick phansie, in my Mistris eye / Should I a thousand fluttering *Cupids* find / Bathing their busie wings?" (*Philosophical Poems*, 302). Edmund Gosse considers the probable association of More and Cowley in *Seventeenth-Century Studies*, 208. Following Cowley is Nicholas Hookes, whose *Amanda* displays more cupids than any other *Mistress*-inspired volume. One nightmarish swarm appears in "To Amanda drinking to him" (24): "My flesh turns all to *Cupids*; here, and there / How *I* engender *Cupids* ev'ry where! / Still I teem *Cupid's*; *Cupids* chaste and pure, / I shall be eaten up with *Cupids* sure; / On my chap't heart I feel them creep about, / Like *Emmets* at their crannies in and out. . . ." John Gay draws upon "The Change" in the air "Love in her Eyes sits playing," set to music by Handel (*Acis and Galatea*, c. 1718). See Gay, *Dramatic Works*, ed. Fuller, 1:270 and 452n.

George Saintsbury considers the opening stanza of "The Change" as "perhaps the finest measure of all" in *The Mistress* (*A History of English Prosody*, 2:292).

title. L. C. Martin notes that "change" is meant "in the obsolete sense of exchange" (Cowley, *Poetry and Prose*, 117). Cf. Donne's "Loves Exchange" and *Much Ado About Nothing* 2.1.287-90: "As you are mine, I am yours. I give away myself for you, and dote upon the exchange."

2. Cf. Edmund Waller, "A thousand Cupids in those curls do sit" ("To the Servant of a Fair Lady," *Poems*, 55).

3-4. Cf. Jonson, in "An Elegie" (*Underwood*, poem no. 19, ll. 9-10; *Poetry* 8:170-71):

> And lastly by your lips, the banke of kisses,
>   Where men at once may plant, and gather kisses.

5-6. Cf. Sidney, *Astrophel and Stella*, no. 11, where Love is:

> Playing and shining in each outward part:
> But, foole, seekst not to get into her hart.

7. *Within Love's foes*. Grierson notes, "Professor Moore Smith conjectures 'Fort' for 'Foes.' . . . It seems to me a certain correction." But he prints "foes," following F2, in *Metaphysical Lyrics and Poems*. See his editorial note, 227. Sparrow disputes the Moore Smith emendation in his note to "The Change," *Mistress*, 204, and prints "foes."

17. *the Persian-Tyrant*. The harem-keeper's acting in secrecy, or invisibly, appears to be Cowley's invention. For the Persian tyrant's life of luxury, see Horace *Odes* 3.9.4. Burton associates the Persian ruler with lust in *Anatomy*, 3.3.2.3.

24. The exchange of hearts implies an exchange of genders. Cf. poem 8, stanza 2. Justus Lawler relates this passage to the obscure pronouncement of Jeremiah 31:22, "The Lord hath created a new thing in the earth, A woman shall compass a man," as well as to the conclusion of Donne's "Aire and Angels" (*Celestial Pantomime*, 147-51). Nicholas Hookes takes the change to a ridiculous, Ovidian extreme: "A female shape my loving soul should take, / So would I be a Milkmaid for thy sake; / My lips should milk thee. . ." ("Amanda's Beautie preferr'd," *Amanda*, 74).

Poem 10. "Clad all in White." A. H. Bullen read this poem, unascribed, in *The New Academy of Complements* (1671); finding it so remarkable in context of the miscellany, he included it in his *Speculum Amantis* as an anonymous poem. See J. B. Leishman for this and other remarks on poem 10 (*The Art of Marvell's Poetry*, 92-100). Leishman's main point is that "Cowley has successfully synthesized a great variety of more objectively descriptive manners and traditions in a way that is truly original, or (it amounts to the same thing) which produces an impression of true originality" (93). Swift's "Clad all in Brown" is a parody of Poem 10.

The main classical precedent is Ovid *Amores* 1.5. The particular direction of Cowley's treatment is influenced by Propertius *Elegies* 1.2 and 2.15 (ll. 11-16, praising nakedness). Donne follows Ovid in Elegy 19, and further echoes may be heard in Carew's "A Rapture," Randolph's "A Pastoral Courtship," Cartwright's "Song of Dalliance," and in the popular ballad

"The Hasty Bridegroom," where the man calls his sweet love to put off her gown, for he "had rather be dealing in white" (*Roxburghe Ballads* 7:458-59). Robert Burton has things to say on the attraction of veiled nakedness as well as on the passion inspired by seeing a woman "all in white" (*Anatomy*, 3.2.2.3; pp. 92 and 97). See also Lovelace's "Bella bona roba" and poems in a subcategory indicated by titles such as John Harington's "Flostella's Hand in Glove" (*The History of Polindor and Flostella*, 89) and "The Wooer, sending his Mistress a pair of white-fringed gloves" (*The Card of Courtship*, 30). Among paintings in the prewar royal collection depicting the "Fairest thing that shines below" would have been Titian's "Diana and Actaeon" and "Venus [?] with an Organ Player."

That this Ovidian fantasy had fully engaged the imagination of seventeenth-century writers is nowhere better demonstrated than in Sir Kenelm Digby's *Private Memoirs* or "Loose Fantasies." Herein "Theagenes" (Digby) finds "Stelliana" (Venetia Stanley) asleep. When he tries to slip between the sheets without waking her, she rolls about to reveal her naked legs and thighs: "white pillars . . . like warm alabaster, whose extreme perfection of colour would have dispersed and dazzled the admiring beholder's sight, but that a natural ruddiness did shine through the skin, as sun-beams do through crystal or water, and ascertained him that it was flesh that he gazed upon, which yet he durst not touch for fear of melting it, so like snow it looked" (*Loose Fantasies*, ed. Gabrieli, p. 115. Also printed in the appendix "Castrations from the *Private Memoirs*," in E. W. Bligh, *Sir Kenelm Digby and His Venetia* [London: Sampson Low, 1932], 294).

title. Cf. Spenser, *Faerie Queene* 1.1.45: "Her all in white he clad." See also *Zephiria*, Canzon. 36, ll. 17-18: "Thy face being vayld, this pennance I award, / Clad in white sheet thou stand in Paules Churchyard."

1. Leishman (see headnote, above) compares Davison's "My love in her attire doth shew her Wit," *Poetical Rhapsody*, as a point of departure for the first stanza.

Fairest thing. Cowley makes the pretense that the "fairest thing" is a visiting ghost. Cf. Donne, "An Anatomie of the World. The first Anniversary," ll. 70-71, 74: "Her Ghost doth walke; that is, a glimmering light, / A faint weake love of vertue, and of good. . . . The twilight of her memory doth stay." Cf. poem 82, ll. 21-24, and note on Angels' "clothes."

9. *clouds . . . like Suns*. Cf. Thomas Jordan, "To Leda his Coy Bride" (*Poeticall Varieties*, p. 8, sig. C2):

> What is this cloud
> That keepes the day light from us, and's allow'd
> More priviledge then I? (Though it be white)
> Tis not the white I aime at (by this light)
> It shall goe off . . .

11-12. *Lillies in a glass.* Cf. Ovid *Metamorphoses* 4.354-55: "in liquidis translucet aquis, ut eburnea si quis / signa tegat claro vel candida lilia vitro" [flashes with gleaming body through the transparent flood, as if one should encase ivory figures or white lilies in translucent glass]. See also Martial *Epigrams* 4.22.5-6 and 8.68.7-8. Of all the English adaptations, Herrick's "The Lilly in a Christal" comes first to mind, though it is not the first; see Sylvester's translation of Du Bartas, Second Week, Fourth Day, as Leishman notes. See also Herrick's "To Anthea lying in bed," "To Electra," and "Clothes do but cheat and cousen us" (which derives from Martial *Epigrams* 11.104). Cowley takes up the figure again in poem 12, "My Heart discovered," ll. 1-8.

19-20. *robes the Saints.* Revelation 6:11; 7:9-14.

29-30. *Peace and yielding.* The whiteness need not symbolize truce or submission. The figure invoked by the author of *Zephiria* (see title note, above) is one of contrition. On the penitential wearing of white, see Ashley, *The Stuarts in Love*, 56.

Poem 11. "Leaving Me, and then loving Many."
3-6. Whoring after other gods subsequent to the pronouncement of the first commandment (Exodus 20) and post-Reformation religious disunity are paralleled to characterize the "fair *Apostate*" addressed in l. 7. For Cowley's use of O.T. parallels, cf. poem 2, "The Thraldome."

10. *The Universal Monarch of her All.* Carew had called Donne "The universal monarch of wit" ("An Elegy Upon the Death of Doctor Donne," l. 96).

11-16. *mine, her fair East-Indies were . . . her rich West-Indies . . . Where Mines of gold.* Cf. Donne, "The Sunne Rising," l. 17: "both the'India's of spice and Myne." Grierson notes that "the use of the word *mine* specifically for mines of gold, silver, or precious stone is, I believe, peculiar to Donne" (Donne, *Poems* 2:13-14). Cowley, in his expansion of Donne's line, has rendered both the possessive pronoun and the gold mine. Cf. poem 2, l. 31 and note, and poem 27, ll. 13-16.

17. *the Pellæan Conqueror.* Alexander the Great, born at Pella, capital of the Macedonian kingdom. Cf. poem 30, l. 13.

Poem 12. "My heart discovered." The conceit in poem 10 is expanded here, along lines suggested by the autopsy in Donne's "The Dampe," stanza 1. Cowley's ll. 1-6 are comparable to Crashaw's "Wishes To his (supposed) Mistress," ll. 10-12:

> Till that Divine
> Idæa, take a shrine
> Of Chrystall flesh, through which to shine.
>   (*Poems*, 195)

John Smith's "Song" ("I saw Lucinda's bosom bare") is an adaptation of poem 12 (published 1713; see *Shorter Poems of the Eighteenth Century*, ed. Iolo A. Williams, 52).

1-2. Cf. Chapman, *Hero and Leander*, "The third Sestiad," ll. 117-18 (". . . all her body was / Cleer and transparent as the purest glass") and cf. poem 10, ll. 7-8. Cowley adapts the expression again in poem 82, l. 25. Ruth Wallerstein, considering this one of Cowley's most delightful poems, recollects Donne's description of Elizabeth Drury: "her pure, and eloquent blood / Spoke in her cheekes, and so distinctly wrought, / That one might almost say, her body thought" ("Of the Progresse of the Soule," ll. 244-46). Wallerstein continues: "the theme is not as in Donne the yearning of personal feeling, or imagination trying to transcend fact. It is objective reflection, half pathetic, half comic, and the temper in which it views its subjects might well be called that of social comedy" ("Cowley as Man of Letters," 136-37).

3-4. *Cristal . . . soft*. See Browne, *Pseudodoxia Epidemica*, 2.1, "Of Crystall," where "the most pure and limpid juice" of earth becomes a stone or crystall (*Works* 2:86). Cf. Claudian *Carminum Minorum* 33-39 on crystal still containing a drop of water, unfrozen, inside. In no. 37 Claudian marvels, "quod fluit et lapis est" [it is a stone, yet fluid].

5-6. *through her flesh*. Cowley adapts this figure in his Pindaric ode "*To Dr.* Scarbrough," stanza 4 (ll. 75-76), where Scarbrough's diagnostic skill is celebrated as a consequence of his ability to see through the "*living Chrystal Man,*" discovering the internal workings of the body. Cowley's note to this passage suggests a source, or a macrocosmic analogue, in Claudian's epigram "In sphaeram Archimedis" (*Carminum Minorum*, no. 51): "The like Sphere of Glass one of the Kings of *Persia* is said to have had, and sitting in the middle of it, as upon the Earth, to have seen round about him all the Revolutions and Motions of the heavenly Bodies" (*Poems* [1656], 3F3ᵛ, p. 38).

31. *Alcione*. Ovid *Metamorphoses* 11 and cf. Cowley's *Poetical Blossomes*, poem 18 (*Collected Works* 1:316n).

Poem 13. "Answer to the Platonicks." See notes to poem 8 for analogues and cf. Cleveland's "The Antiplatonick" and Cartwright's "No Platonic Love."

1. *Angels love*. Some commentators allowed a not-entirely metaphysical love for angels. Cf. Raphael's blush, *Paradise Lost*, bk. 8, ll. 618-19.

11. *Love Cooks*. For such culinary imagery, see Margaret Cavendish, Duchess of Newcastle, *Poems and Fancies*, e.g., "*Natures* Cook": "Some *Meates shee* rosts with *Feavers, burning hot,* / And some *shee* boiles with *Dropsies* in a *Pot* . . ." (ll. 3-4, p. 127). Cf. Suckling's figure in "Love's World," ll. 33-36.

13. *ancient fame.* Jove's activities are the subject of Ovid's *Metamorphoses*, especially books 1 and 2.

15-16. According to Hesiod, Zeus swallowed his first wife, Metis, to prevent the imminent birth of Athene. After having married Hera, he fathered Athene himself, out of his head. *Theogony* 880ff.

18. *pleasure, 'bove his state.* Ovid's central point in *Metamorphoses* 2 appears in ll. 846-47: "non bene conveniunt nec in una sede morantur / maiestas et amor" [majesty and love do not go well together].

22. *Lambent flames.* For the context, cf. poem 50, ll. 1-4. Cowley uses *lambent* frequently, and the term becomes self-characterizing. It is encountered first in the Latin text from which Cowley translated poem 20, "On the uncertainty of Fortune," in *Poetical Blossomes*, and Cowley first uses it in *The Civil War*, 1.78 (*Collected Works* 1:317nn, 393nn). See also *Davideis* 3: "How *Lambent Fires* become so wondrous tame" (*Poems* [1656], 4M2, p. 91 and note 40), and the Pindaric ode "Destinie" (*Poems* [1656], 3E4, p. 31): "The *Star* that did my *Being* frame, / Was but a *Lambent Flame*, / And some small *Light* it did dispence, / But neither *Heat* nor *Influence*." *Lambent* appears in Virgil *Aeneid* 2.682-84, which Cowley cites in n. 40 to *Davideis* 3—

> ecce levis summo de vertice visus Iuli
> fundere lumen apex, tactuque innoxia molis
> lambere flamma comas et circum tempora pasci.

[lo! from above the head of Iulus a light tongue of flame seemed to shed a gleam and, harmless in its touch, lick his soft locks and pasture round his temples.]

—and again in *Aeneid* 10.559-60: "alitbus linquere feris aut gurgite mersum / unda feret piscesque impasti volnera lambent" [to the birds of prey you will be left, or sunk beneath the flood, the wave will bear you on, and hungry fish shall lick your wound].

23-25. *The Sun . . . With nuptial warmth.* A commonplace. Cf. poem 50, stanza 6. Piscator offers some interesting local conjecture about sun-bred species in Izaak Walton, *The Complete Angler*, chaps. 8 and 10.

29-30. *Pygmalion . . . the hot youth of Troy.* Pygmalion (*Metamorphoses* 10), in loving a statue, was more lustful than Paris. Bacon comments on Pygmalion's "frenzy" as an emblem of the first distemper of learning, when men study images and not things (*Works* 3:284).

Poem 14. "The vain Love."

subtitle. This is the only poem to sustain a subtitle through the various editions of *The Mistress*. Poem 71 loses its subtitle "(*Suspected to Love her*)" after printings in O1 and O2. The subtitle to poem 81, "*After Enjoyment*," appears only in its first printing, F1, and the title of poem 47, "The Injoyment," is deleted in editions following F1. It is possible that the deletions to poems 81 and 47 were made in the interest of good taste by Sprat, following terms of Cowley's will. There is no similar explanation, however, for the deletion in poem 71 or for the fact that the subtitle remains here. Ovid's *Amores* 1.2 may have been Cowley's model for poem 14; see especially the lover as slave in his victor's triumph, noted below.

2. *Cold to kindle Mee.* See poem 1, stanza 3, and note to ll. 21-24, where the paradox is expanded. Cf. Henry King, "Sonnet. The Double Rock," and Suckling, "The Miracle," for contemporary versions of the Petrarchan figure. Cf. Philip Ayers, "Love's New Philosophy": "Cold Cynthia to my zeal yields no return / Though ice her heart, she makes my heart to burn" (*Lyric Poems*, in Saintsbury 2:301), where the concept becomes an epithet or motto, suitable for explaining a picture.

4. *a Burning-Glass of Ice.* Cf. poem 12, ll. 2-4, and note. Since, according to vulgar opinion, crystal was formed from frozen water, it is not fatally preposterous that crystal should be worked into a magnifying lens.

4-6. Cf. John Hall, "A Burning Glass," ll. 9-14 (*Poems*, in Saintsbury 2:192):

> Witches may cheat us of his [the sun's] light awhile,
> But this can him even of himself beguile:
> In heaven he staggers to both tropics, here
> He keeps fix'd residence all times of th'year.
> Here's a perpetual solstice, here he lies,
> Not in a bed of water, but of ice.

See also Suckling, "Love's Burning-glass."

8. *sunny Dyamond.* Cf. Claudian *Carminum Minorum*, "De crystallo cui aqua inerat," no. 35: "Solibus indomitum glacies Alpina rigorem / sumebat nimio iam pretiosa gelu / nec potuit toto mentiri corpore gemmam" [Alpine ice was becoming so hard that the sun could not melt it, and this excess of cold was like to make it precious as diamond].

19-25. *a slave / In Triumph lead.* Cf. Ovid *Amores* 1.2.24-30 and poem 81, ll. 25-30.

41-43. There is an echo in Andrew Marvell's "The Definition of Love," ll. 1-4 (*Poems*, 36):

> My Love is of a birth as rare
> As 'tis for object strange and high:
> It was begotten by despair
> Upon Impossibility.

Poem 15. "The Soul." Though in the form of a lover's petition, the poem is an anatomy of the soul. Each of the stanzas consists of a single sentence, the first progressing through the five senses, the second enumerating the passions, and the third engaging the understanding, imagination, and will. The twenty-eight-line stanza 2 is mirrored in the four seven-line stanzas of poem 16, "The Passions." Poem 15 is related by title to poem 39.

1-2. The formula for these lines derives from Donne, cf. "The goodmorrow," ll. 6-7: "If ever any beauty I did see, / Which I desir'd, and got, 'twas but a dream of thee." Robert Baron's "The Protestation," a pastiche including lines from poems 33 and 59 as well as this one, paraphrases Cowley: "If any object to mine eye / Seems fair, but what in thee is found; / If my dull ear hears melody / Besides thy voice in any sound . . ." (*Pocula Castalia*, 103).

13-16. *a Burning-Glass*. See poem 14 and note to ll. 7-10.

17-19. Cf. Marvell, "A Dialogue, Between The Resolved Soul, and Created Pleasure," ll. 51-54—

> All this fair, and soft, and sweet
> Which scatteringly doth shine,
> Shall within one Beauty meet,
> And she be only thine.

—and note, *Poems* 1:11 and pp. 242-243. Margoliouth sees Marvell imitating Cowley here and elsewhere in the "Dialogue," and he emends a printer's error in l. 51, "coft" to "soft," with the supporting evidence of Cowley's l. 18.

51-54. Cf. Browne, *Religio Medici*, 2.2: "I hold moreover that there is a Phytognomy, or Physiognomy, not only of men, but of Plants and Vegetables; and in every one of them, some outward figures which hang as signes or bushes of their inward formes. The finger of God hath set an inscription upon all his workes, not graphicall or composed of Letters, but of their severall formes. . . . The pattern or example of every thing is the perfectest in that kind, whereof wee still come short. . . ." (72-73).

56. *The lower Soul*. Reason, or "Understanding" as in l. 63 "Imagination" is the "higher" soul. Cowley's assessment of reason, imagination, and memory appears unaffected by Hobbes (cf. *Leviathan*, 1.2).

62. For the anatomy of the mistress as a mnemonic device, a way of locating the virtues by corporeal similitudes, see Frances Yates on Petrarchan memory systems, *The Art of Memory*, 101-4; 313-14. Cf. Donne's elegy "The Anagram" for a perverse example, beginning "Thy *Flavia* . . . Hath all things, whereby others beautious bee . . ." (*Poems*, 80).

Poem 16. "The Passions."

1. This line is an inversion of poem 15, stanza 2, where the passions are pledged to the defense and honor of the mistress. Thus the poems are paired. Both may be early compositions, c. 1642. See note to ll. 26-30, below.

11-14. *Baal, Astarte, Accaron, Molock, the Calf of Bethel*. The reference is mainly to the religious crisis of the ninth century (1 Kings 17 to 2 Kings 23), although the Lord has called for the destruction of idols at other times (e.g., Judges 6:25), as Cowley implies by the "Sometimes" in l. 9. The idol of the calf, its image associated with the Canaanite deity Baal, was erected at the Bethel shrine by Jeroboam (1 Kings 12:28-31). Astarte, or Ashtoreth, is notable as one of Solomon's harem of idols (1 Kings 11:5). Accaron is a place name and the epithet for Beelzebub, as Cowley explains in a note to his Pindaric ode "The Plagues of Egypt": "*The God* of *Flies, Belzebub*, a *Deity* worshipped at *Accaron*" (*Poems* [1656] sig. 3K, p. 67). See also *The Civil War*, 2.507-18, and notes in *The Collected Works*, 1:423. Josiah's campaign against cult shrines, including Moloch's, comes to a conclusion in 2 Kings 23, wherein the cult center at Bethel is destroyed. Cf. poem 38, ll. 15-16.

15-17. The figure is drawn from Isaiah 5:1-3.

19. *vinegere*. Alluding to the vinegar given to the crucified Jesus (Mark 15:36; Matthew 27:48; Luke 23:36; John 19:29).

20-21. Cupid's metamorphosis of nectar is an inversion of Jesus' turning water into "nectar." For the Gods' activities, cf. poem 13, ll. 17-18.

26-28. *Indians . . . Call in the States of Holland*. The broad allusion is to Dutch/Spanish rivalry for colonies in the Americas and in the East during the earlier seventeenth century. Cowley may intend a specific reference to the Araucanian Indians of Valdivia, Chile, who formed a brief alliance with the Dutch West India Company expedition, headed by Hendrick Brouwer, in the summer of 1642. The Dutch built a fort at Valdivia and stayed on for about a year, until it became clear that the Indians were disinclined to serve them in the design to liberate Chile from the Spaniards. From the Araucanian point of view, alliance with the States of Holland may have amounted to no more than a "change of Ills." See Peter Gerhard, *Pirates on the West Coast of New Spain*, 131, and Geoffrey Parker, *Spain and The Netherlands*, 78-79. If the specific, topical allusion is intended, since the lines make no reference to the conclusion of the Chilean event we may assume that Cowley wrote the poem near the time of the Dutch/Indian alliance, in 1642.

Poem 17. "Wisdom." This cryptic poem mixes Jacobean iconography (the king figured as Solomon) with a Caroline emphasis on pleasure and love. The allegorical figures and compressed plot of ll. 9-20 sound like a synopsis or reminiscence of a court masque—a little like Davenant's *The Temple of Love* (1635), which engages the relationship between proper pleasure and true wisdom, or *Salmacida Spolia* (1640), wherein Henrietta Maria appears as a kind of "Southern Queen." The direct address of the speaker (see l. 7), the Puritan-Papist reference in l. 4, and the diction of ll. 5 and 18 relate this poem to Cowley's epistolary satire *The Puritans Lecture* and to *The Puritan and the Papist*, 1642-43. Martin Butler notes that "descriptions of masques were commonly sent into the country," as were manuscript transcripts of plays (*The Theatre and Crisis*, 105-6). It is possible that a description or transcript was sent to Cowley at Cambridge.

5. *With tedious Repetitions*. Cf. *The Puritans Lecture*, ll. 19-21: " 'Twas the most teadious Soule, the dullest he / That ever came to Doctrines twenty three, / And nineteene uses" (*Collected Works* 1:94).

7. *friend*. The poem is addressed to a vain, repetitious, and (presumably) falsely moralistic male "friend."

9-10. *The wisest King . . . Wisdom*. The allusion is to Solomon. Also, perhaps, Charles I. In the *Wisdom of Solomon*, wisdom is personified as a woman.

14. *the Southern Queen*. The Queen of Sheba (1 Kings 10:1-13). Also, perhaps, Henrietta Maria, who has roamed "far from her own Countrey" (l. 17). For an extended assessment of the Queen of Sheba's intent in journeying to Solomon, see William Walsh, *A Dialogue concerning Women*, sig. D, p. 33, and sig. H3ᵛ, p. 102. Cowley writes at greater length on the encounter between Solomon and Sheba in "The Garden," stanza 7—verses sent to John Evelyn on 16 August 1666—where Solomon represents art and urban riches while Sheba, proclaimed "wiser far than He," values nature and gardens.

15. *a good old Wife*. She, unlike the "Southern Queen," is interested in "*Saving Lives*" (l. 20) with herbal remedies. Cf. the "herbwives" who appear in *The Puritans Lecture*, l. 172 (*Collected Works* 1:99).

18. *scall'd heads*. Cf. *The Puritans Lecture*, l. 36: "Nay their scaldheaded children they come too" (*Collected Works* 1:95).

Poem 18. "The Despair." This lament is similar to lyric moments in Cowley's early Ovidian narrative poems, where the young poet likes to dramatize and stylize expressions of grief. The alternating six- and ten-syllable lines and the "echo" repetitions of stanzas 1 and 2 bring Spenser's "Epithalamion" and "Prothalamion" to mind, along with "The Eccho" and such lines as "*Doe not these teares, these speaking teares, despise: / And dolorous sighes*" from *Constantia and Philetus* (*Collected Works* 1:26, 37), which are inspired by Spenser's *Complaints* and *Astrophel*. As Spenser writes in "The Teares of the Muses" (l. 541): "A dolefull case desires a dolefull song." The particular doleful song that provided Cowley a point of departure may have been Marino's "Eco" (*Poesie Varie*, 154-59). This poem appears to have been in circulation during the early 1640s. Thomas Stanley translated it twice, the 1647 version reading:

> *In a dark and shady Grove*
> *(The sad witness of his love)*
> *Poor* Siringo, *vainly who*

> *Did* Licoris *long pursue,*
> *Here his weary steps restraind,*
> *And so sweetly he complaind,*
> *That the waters and the air*
> *Wept, and sigh'd his plaints to hear.*
> (Stanley, *Poems*, 179)

See also poem 40, "Eccho," headnote and note to l. 6.

"The Despair" is the most aurally oriented poem in *The Mistress*. It sounds as though it had been written for musical expression. If it was, the original setting has not survived. The settings by John Blundeville and James Hart printed on pp. 354 and 356 of this edition were made after Cowley's death.

1-5. The formula for lament may also reflect Donne's hyperboles; cf. "Twicknam garden."

22. *A dull ill-acted Comedy.* Cf. "Prologue to the Guardian" (*Miscellanies, Poems*, sig. C4, p. 15, ll. 19-20): "a thing that's *play'd* / Ere't is a *Play*, and *Acted* ere 'tis *Made*."

24. *the Suns busie and imperti'nent Light.* Cf. Donne, "The Sunne Rising," l. 1: "Busie old foole, unruly Sunne."

31. *row his Galley.* Cf. poem 2, l. 22.

Poem 19. "The Wish." This poem is an elaboration on the Horation theme of "A Vote" (*Sylva* [1636], *Collected Works* 1:70), as "*The Garden*" (letter and poem to Evelyn, 1666) is an elaboration on poem 19. In his essay "Of My self," Cowley transcribes the first two lines of poem 19, referring to it as a renewal of his "old School-boys Wish," written in Paris between 1645 and the publication of *The Mistress* in 1647. He precedes the quotation with a modified transcription of the last three stanzas of "A Vote," the "Schoolboys Wish," where his retirement theme is first sketched: "Bookes should, not businesse, intertayne the light, / And sleepe, as undisturb'd as death the night. / My house a cottage more / Then pallace, and should fitting bee / For all my use, no luxurie. / My garden painted ore / With natures hand, not arts. . . ." The retirement theme is extended in Cowley's *Plantarum* and under other titles in the *Essays*. See, particularly, "*The Garden*", the first stanza of which is a reworking of "The Wish," stanza 2. There are five extant manuscript copies of poem 19, along with numerous paraphrases and parodies. See Textual Notes, and for further example, Philip Ayres's adaptation "In Praise of a Country Life" (Saintsbury 2:332).

3. *Honey.* The term could mean loved one, with sexual connotations. See *OED*, s.v. "Honey," 5.

5-8. Patrick Cary's "The Country Life: To a French Tune" appears to derive from these lines. Cary begins: "Fondlings! Keepe to th'Citty / Yee shall have my pitty . . ." (*Poems*, 23, ll. 1-2).

10-16. Cf. *Essays*, "*The Garden*," in the prose epistle and stanza 1. Cf.

James Shirley, ("The Garden," *Poems &c*, 69, ll. 9-12): "Give me a little plot of ground. . . ." Shirley's garden is moated by tears against any woman's encroachment.

19-20. John Evelyn paraphrases these lines in the Epistle Dedicatory (to Cowley) of *Kalendarium Hortense: or, The Gard'ners Alamanc*, perhaps after he had received Cowley's letter with "The Garden" (which is printed in later editions of the *Kalendarium*). Evelyn's epistle reads: "whilst you still continue in the *possession* of your *Self*, and of that *repose* which few men understand, in exchange for those *pretty miseries* you have essay'd: O the sweet *Evenings* and *Mornings*, and all the *Day* besides which are yours,

> . . . while Cowley's made
> The happy Tennant of the Shade!

And the *Sun* in his *Garden*, gives him all he desires, and all that he would enjoy: the purity of visible Objects, and of true *Nature* before she was vitiated by Imposture or Luxury!" The general theme had not escaped Evelyn in earlier years. See *The State of France* (London, 1652, sig. B6): "Happie that man who lives content / with his own *Home* and *Continent*."

19-28. *Fields . . . flood . . . Eccho*. The terms echo poem 18, stanzas 1 and 2.

36. *desarts Solitude*. See poem 20, note to l. 21.

Poem 20. "My Dyet." There is a rich and varied song tradition for this poem (see Textual Notes). Its literary genesis may be Donne's "Loves Diet." Loiseau (*Sa vie*, 381) asserts that "My Dyet" paraphrases "Love's Diet"; Sparrow (*The Mistress*, xvi) considers Cowley's poem an "actual imitation" of Donne. The chronological priority between the two texts (Donne's was published in 1633) is clear, and it is also clear that Cowley writes a poem to be paired with Donne's. But Cowley's is less a reply to "Loves Diet" than a text to which Donne's poem can be seen as a rebuttal. Unlike other *Mistress* poems engaged with poetic replies (e.g., "The Thief" and "The Antithiefe"; "Against Hope" and "For Hope"), Cowley here produces the positive "Diet" against which Donne's poem can assert its antidote. Given their differing stanza forms, the pro/con relationship between Cowley's and Donne's poems would not appear to have been transmitted by way of the same musical setting.

8. *luxurious*. The term could mean both what it does now—given to material extravagance—and something close to the "*Lusty*" of l. 9. See *OED*, 3a and 3b.

15. *a sigh*. Cf. Donne's "And if sometimes by stealth he [love] got / A she sigh from my mistresse heart, / And thought to feast on that, I let

him see / 'Twas neither very sound, nor meant to mee'' ("Loves Diet," ll. 9-12).

16. *One tear.* Cf. Donne's "If he [love] suck'd hers [tears], I let him know / 'Twas not a teare, which hee had gott. . . ." ("Loves Diet," ll. 15-16).

15-21. Margoliouth (Marvell, *Poems* 1:222), and Martin (*Poetry and Prose*, 117) note that Marvell imitates these lines in "To his Coy Mistress," ll. 13-20. Had Marvell been reading *The Mistress* sequentially, the first term of the phrase "desarts Solitude" (poem 19, l. 36) and "vast Æternity" (poem 20, l. 21) could be seen as the conflation producing "Desarts of vast Eternity" ("To his Coy Mistress," l. 24).

Poem 21. "The Thief." In Bodleian MS Top. Oxon. e.202, fol. 77 there is an answer-poem titled "The Anti-thiefe," ascribed to Gowin Knight, M.A. and fellow of Merton College. As a "for love" poem, it begins "Happy thou makest my days with true delights."

5-7. Cf. poem 78, ll. 9-12.

13-14. For the inverse, his ghost stalking the "murdresse," see Donne, "The Apparition." Philip Ayres's *Emblem*, no. 20, "Ever Present," shows the poet in bed, in his study, with his mistress's ghost standing with one foot on the bedstep. The text reads:

> Her name is at my tongue, whene'er I speak;
> Her shape's before my eyes where'er I stir;
> Both day and night, as if her ghost did walk,
> And not she me, but I had murder'd her.

15-18. Cf. poem 5, ll. 31-42, for another example of paleographical reproduction.

Poem 22. "All-over, Love."

title. There may be a pun intended, implying that love's defeat and triumph are simultaneous.

16-17. *disperse / My Atoms.* Cf. Donne, "An Anatomie of the World: The first Anniversary," ll. 211-12: "they see that this / Is crumbled out againe to his Atomies"; and cf. Donne's sermons on the resurrection, e.g., *Death's Duel*: "I must dye againe in an *Incineration* of this *flesh*, and in a dispersion of that dust. . . ." (*Sermons*, 10, p. 229).

18-19. Cowley's Pindaric ode "The Resurrection" reads, "Then shall the scatter'ed *Atomes* crowding come / Back to their *Antient Home.* . . . And where th'*attending Soul* naked, and shivering stands, / Meet, salute, and joyn their hands" (*Poems*, sigs. 3D2-3, pp. 21-22, ll. 37-38, 44-45).

20. The stamping of coins is an irresistible catalyst for seventeenth-century poets. Cf. Donne, "A Valediction: of weeping," ll. 3-4.

Poem 23. "Love and Life." Here Cowley exercises his Donne vocabulary, starting from a paradox in "The Computation" and piecing together an extended, Ptolemaic conceit in stanzas 3-5.
    1-2. Cf. Donne, "The Computation," ll. 1-2: "For the first twenty yeares, since yesterday, / I scarce belieev'd, thou could'st be gone away."
    3-4. *Love runs much more fast.* Time's relativity is associated with romantic love in *As You Like It* 3.2.306ff. Burton associates it with love melancholy in the *Anatomy*, 3.2.3 (3:140): "And when he is gone, he thinks every minute an hour, every hour as long as a day, ten days a whole year, till he see her again. *'Tempora si numeres, bene quae numeramus amantes'* [Ovid: If thou canst count the moments which we lovers count]." cf. Marvell, "To his Coy Mistress," ll. 45-46.
    6. *Methusalem.* Who lived 969 years. Genesis 5:21-27.
    7-8. In "To Odelia" (*Poems &c.*, 5) James Shirley poses the question, "Is't fit / Time measure Lov, or our Affection it?" Cowley in effect negates the question.

Poem 24. "The Bargain." See poem 3, ll. 33-48 and notes, with reference to Cowley's Anacretontic "Gold." For arguments against marrying for money, hear the vociferous Bellama in Nathaniel Whiting's *Albino and Bellama* who, when courted by the wealthy Don Fuco, "faults, and vows that gold / Shall never force her love to have and hold" (in Saintsbury, 3:442, ll. 143-44 and ff. to 198).
    1. Cf. Donne, "The Prohibition," l. 1: "Take heed of loving mee."
    12. *in thy Mines.* Cf. poem 2, l. 31 and note.
    20. [*Simon*] *Magus.* Acts 8:9-24; the sorcerer at Samaria who offered money to Peter and John to obtain the power of the Holy Ghost. Hence the term *simony* (l. 22). As for the Magus's boldness, his claim to be a god, his association with a prostitute named Helen whom he was heaven-sent to liberate, and other legends that won him the title "father of gnostic heresies," see Philip Carrington, *The Early Christian Church*, 1:55ff. and 245ff.

Poem 25. "The Long Life." Alastair Fowler's assessment of this poem includes his argument that it derives from Spenser's "Epithalamion" (*Triumphal Forms*, 13-15).
    3-4. *Hours . . . as Days . . . Minutes, Hours are grown.* A reworking of the terms of poem 23.
    7-8. *Lucies . . . St. Barnabie.* Saint Lucy's day, 13 December (c. the winter solstice), was popularly regarded as the shortest day and longest night.

Saint Barnabas's day, 11 June, was the longest day and shortest night. The subjective truth for Cowley's speaker is the inverse.

13. *old Patriarchs*. Cf. poem 23, l. 6: "The great *Methusalem* of *Love*."

Poem 26. "Counsel."
17. *Loves Hell*. Cf. poem 9, ll. 11-12; poem 21, ll. 26-28.
20. *thy Diswasions me perswade*. The argument here and the character of the speaker conspiring in his own defeat bear comparison to Shakespeare's sonnet 35. Cf. l. 7: "Myself corrupting, salving thy amiss. . . ."
25-26. *Thy Tongue comes in . . . Against thine Eyes*. The language of the eyes as it may be played against what is said is one of Ovid's favorite subjects. Cf. *Amores* 2.5. For Donne's adaptation, cf. "Breake of day," ll. 7-12.
35. The figure of the wounded captive (see l. 2), now part of Love's triumph, is from Ovid *Amores* 1.2.29-30: "ipse ego, praeda recens, factum modo vulnus habebo / et nova captiva vincula mente feram" [Myself, a recent spoil, shall be there with wound all freshly dealt, and bear my new bonds with unresisting heart]. For the woman's argument, cf. poem 81, stanza 5.

Poem 27. "Resolved to be beloved."
1. *'Tis true*. As Donne opens "Breake of day." The stanza continues, by way of numerical escalation, as a parody of another Donne claim. Cowley's count "three or four" in l. 1 outdoes Donne's "two, or three" ("Song": "Goe, and catche a falling starre," l. 27). The fantastical hundreds of lovers suggests comparison with the Anacreontic "The Account" (*Poems* [1656], F^v, p. 34).
4. Cf. Brome, song 3, "The Resolve," ll. 11-12. Brome's "song" is a kind of synopsis, generalizing where Cowley is specific, of poem 27.
8. *Honey*. This reference to the new Canaan is biblical, but cf. poem 19, "The Wish," ll. 3-4 for sexual connotations of "honey."
9. *The Needle*. Cf. poem 59, l. 1. Compare, also, Carew, "To her in absence," ll. 5-8, "My heart doth, like the needle, touch'd with love, / Still fix'd on you, point which way I would move; / You are the bright pole-star . . . " (*Poems*, 23), and Francis Quarles, *Emblemes*, bk. 5.4.9-10: "Like to the Artick needle . . . At length he slacks his motion, and doth rest / His trembling point at his bright Pole's beloved brest."
13. *my Vessel torn and shipwrackt*. Cf. Drayton, *Ideas Mirrour*, "Armour," no. 34, where "my poore soule, the Barke of sorrow" is headed for shipwreck on "those fayre Ilands of thy lookes" (*Works* 1:115). See Ernest Curtius, *European Literature and the Latin Middle Ages*, 128-30, for a survey of the tradition of the ship of love. A good example, associating

phallic ships (pinaces) with the Indies, comes from Falstaff in *The Merry Wives of Windsor* 1.3.71-80: "They shall be my East and West Indies, and I will trade to them both. Go, bear thou this letter to Mistress Page; and thou this to Mistress Ford . . . bear you these letters tightly; Sail like my pinnace to these golden shores."

24. *Manna, hath the Taste of all in it.* According to Dr. Johnson (*Lives* 1:23), this is a "Rabbinical opinion." Exodus 16:14, 31, suggests that manna was less inclusive a diet. The taste of it was like "wafers made with honey." See Isaac Disraeli, *Curiosities of Literature* 1:190-91: "This manna had . . . the quality to accommodate itself to the palate [and] . . . St. Austin repeats this explanation of the rabbins, that the faithful found in this manna the tast of their favorite food!"

Poem 28. "The Same" [i.e., "Resolved to be beloved"].

10-11. *To hunt so long one nimble prey, till we / Too weary.* These lines have affinities with Wyatt's adaptation from Petrarch, "Whoso list to hunt, I know where is an hind, / But . . . The vain travail hath wearied me. . . ."

15-18. Cf. "Inconstancy," poem 6, l. 20 and note. And cf. poem 66, "The Inconstant," ll. 29-30.

21. *perpetual, fruitless Round.* Bacon habitually uses the circle as a symbol of scholastic falsehood and stagnation. See Marjorie Hope Nicolson, *The Breaking of the Circle,* 8-10.

24-25. There is a blunt sexuality underlying the figure. When Cowley confronts "hardness and pride," he "rebounds" (l. 23) to "another side." The "other side" does not necessarily mean the opposite of love, or hatred; the rebounding may be better understood as a transformation of sexual impulse to metaphoric expression. On the contrary, and less frequently, given the conceitedness of so many poems in *The Mistress,* when his love hits one who is soft and yielding it becomes transfixed.

Poem 29. "The Discovery."

4. *The Gods may give their Altars o're.* Adapted from Virgil *Aeneid* 2.351-52: "excessere omnes adytis arisque relictis / di, quibus imperium hoc steterat" [the gods of this empire have gone, deserting shrine and altar]. The lines come from Aeneas's heroic but suicidal exhortation before he rushes into the burning city of Troy. Cf. poem 84, l. 30.

9. *Furzes.* Evergreen shrubs, also known as French furzes. *OED* cites Cowley's use of the term.

10. *She being so high, and I so low.* Cf. poem 3, l. 5 and note.

19. *If there be man.* Cf. poem 41, "The rich Rival."

22. *cheat.* That is, advance the false claim that he and "She [who] like a

Deity is growne" (l. 17) are equal. In making such a claim, the rival lover becomes a false god, stealing divinity from the mistress like the "Thief" that he is labeled in l. 24.

Poem 30. "Against Fruition." Once the platonic lover has yielded to the blandishments of the antiplatonic, the next rung down love's ladder may be represented by the argument of this anti-antiplatonic poem. Cowley's classical precedents include Marital *Epigrams* 1.57: "nolo nimis facilem difficilemque nimis. / illud quod medium est atque inter uturmque probamus: / nec volo quod cruciat nec volo quod satiat" [I dislike one too yielding, and one too coy. The middle type I approve. I like not that which racks me, nor that which cloys] and Ausonius *Epigrams* 56.1: "Hanc volo, quae non vult; illam, quae vult, ego nolo" [I will have her who won't have me; she who will, I don't want]. The topic gained the impetus of wider readership, if not entrance in English verse, with Jonson's translation of a fragment presumed to be by Petronius, published as the third to last poem in *The Underwood* in 1640. Drummond, however, had heard Jonson read the verse (1618), and records the event in *Conversations*, item 5. Though Drummond believed Jonson's "epigram of Petronius" to be a translation of the Roman author, scholars have disclaimed it as a false attribution in Linocerius's edition (Paris, 1585; see *Ben Jonson* 11:109). Jonson's poem is directly responsible for John Oldham's "A Fragment of Petronius Paraphrased" (*Poems*, 215) and indirectly for other adaptations. Hugh M. Richmond has a synopsis of the English tradition (*The School of Love*, 244-48). Major examples include Suckling's "Against Fruition [I]," answered by Waller and Henry Bold; "Against Fruition [II]," answered by Bold (see Suckling, *Non-dramatic Works*, 37-39, 181-84; Waller's reply to [I] is printed [in 1647] as a "pro" argument, along with the "con" stanzas from Suckling); Cartwright's "A Song of Dalliance" ("Give a grant, and then forbear it; / Offer something, and forswear it, . . . Easie riches is no treasure; / She that's willing, spoils the pleasure," ll. 19-20, 27-28, *Plays and Poems*, 468); Henry King's "Paradox: That Fruition destroys Love" (*Poems*, 182); and Lovelace's "To Chloris: Love in the First Age." The idea that love survives only if repulsed is advanced in Brome's Song 11, "The Contrary," which begins as a lyrical adaptation of Cowley's poem 30 but argues only for a prolonged pursuit: "Do not be won too soon I prithee, / But let me woe, whilst thou dost fly me" (ll. 9-10; cf. Suckling, "Upon A.M."). Orinda's "Against Pleasure" (Katherine Philips, *Poems*, and Bodleian MS Rawl. Poet. 173, fol. 98) manages to achieve Cowley's tone and makes explicit that pleasure's "next successor is Despair, / And its attendant Shame" (ll. 27-28). Sparrow (*The Mistress*, xx) maintains that Cowley's theme is "shame succeeds the short lived pleasure." Cf. poem 81, l. 5.

4. *For a learn'd Age is always least devout.* Cf. Suckling, "Against Fruition [I]," l. 2: "Knowing too much long since lost Paradise."
13. *Pellæan Prince.* Alexander the Great. Cowley recalls Juvenal *Satire* 10.168: "Unus Pellae iuveni non sufficit orbis" [one globe is too little for the Pellaean youth]. Cf. poem 11, l. 17.
17. Cf. Katherine Philips, "Against Pleasure," ll. 11-12: "In being than in fancy less, / And we expect more than possess."
18. *Women can be place'd by Nature's hand.* Of the many observations on women's nature, Samuel Butler's is worth citing in this context. "The Femals of Human Creatures are always ready to generate, and the Males seldome Contrary to all other Animals, whose Males are allways ready and femals seldom" (*Prose Observations*, 183 / BL Add. MS 32625, fol. 217r). Donne (*Paradoxes and Problems*, paradox 10, p. 21) elicits "tanquam non liceat, nulla puella negat" [As if it were not permitted, no girl says no] from Martial *Epigrams* 4.71. Dr. Johnson reads lines 17-18 as merely saying "a mistress beloved is fairer in idea than in reality" (*Lives* 1:31).
31. *His spirit and sweetness dangers keep alone.* There must be a story behind this.

Poem 31. "Love undiscovered."
3. Burton quotes Johannes Secundus on the point that a kiss can restore life to the dying man (*Anatomy*, 3.2.2.2; 3:75).
8. *salute.* From *salus* (health). The "salute" characteristically called for in this context is a kiss, at least by way of salutation. See *OED*, s.v. "Salute," 1.1.2.
12. *a Fate too low.* Cf. poem 3, l. 5 and note.
13-14. Swift cites these lines in "A Letter Concerning the Sacramental Test" (*Prose Works* 2:114): "I remember that there is in some of Mr. Cowley's Love Verses, a Strain that I thought extraordinary at Fifteen, and have often since imagined it to be spoken by *Ireland*." Swift either means that he was fifteen when he first read these verses, or that he considered Cowley to have been fifteen when he wrote them. If it is the latter, Swift may be following Sprat's allegation, printed in the *Life* (1668 and subsequent editions of Cowley's *Works*), that the love verses were composed when the author was very young.
Conveniencie. The *OED* lists the term as archaic, even in the seventeenth century.
24. Nethercot (*Abraham Cowley*, 106) sees a debt to Drayton. Cf. "Idea," sonnet 61 (*Works* 2:341, ll. 9-14):

> Now at the last gaspe, of Loves latest Breath,
> When his Pulse fayling, Passion speechless lies,

> When Faith is kneeling by his bed of Death,
> And Innocence is closeing up his Eyes,
>   Now if thow would'st, when all have given him over,
>   From Death to Life, thou might'st him yet recover.

Cowley's stanza is imitated by Charles Cotton in "Ode Valedictory" (*Poems*, 149-50, ll. 25-32):

> But, if thou wilt I dye, and that
> By, worse than thousand deaths, thy hate;
> When I am dead, if thou but pay
> My Tomb a Teare, and sighinge say,
> Thou do'st my Timeless Fall deplore,
> Wishing th'hadst knowne my trust before;
> My dearest Dear, thou makest me then,
> Or Sleepe in peace, or Live againe.

A further adaptation may be found in Dryden's "Roundelay" (*Works* 4:424), wherein Chloe grants the saving kiss just before the wretched lover, Amyntas, dies.

Poem 32. "The given Heart." Explosive developments in stanza 3 reveal the naive address of the first stanza and the rhetorical question in stanza 2 is disingenuous, leading with the false aim of probity. This gives the poem the kind of satiric edge that is characteristic of Cowley's *The Puritan and the Papist*. There are other resemblances to his earlier political poems. See note to l. 12.

   5-8. Sparrow (*The Mistress*, xvi) makes a comparison with the last stanza (ll. 23-33) of Donne's "Loves Infiniteness."

   12. *Like a Granado shot into a Magazin.* Cf. *The Civil War*, 2.598 (*Collected Works* 1:144 and note, 424-25).

   16. *Allay . . . Metal.* The metallurgic conceit is popular during the earlier seventeenth century. Cf. Donne, "The Extasie," l. 56: "Nor are drosse to us, but allay."

Poem 33. "The Prophet." This poem has been given recent audience in that the first lines are excitedly read by one of the boys in Peter Weir's film *The Dead Poets Society* (1989), filmed at St. Andrew's School in Delaware. The lines originate with a poet much longer dead than Cowley.

   1-2. Ovid writes, at the beginning of *Ars Amatoria* 1.7-8, 17: "Me Venus artificem tenero praefecit Amori; / Tiphys et Automedon dicar Amoris ego . . . Aeacidae Chiron, ego sum praeceptor Amoris" [Venus set me as master over tender Love; I shall be called the Tiphys and Automedon of Love . . . Chiron taught Aeacides, I am Love's teacher]. Automedon was

Achilles's chariot driver; Tiphys was navigator of Jason's ship, the *Argo*; Aeacides is Achilles, so called by his grandfather's name, who was taught by the centaur Chiron.

Charles Cotton follows Cowley in "A Valedictorian," ll. 5–8: "I goe th'exact'st professor of / Desire, in its diviner sence, / That ever in the Scoole of Love / Did yet commence" (*Poems*, 200).

3–12. Cf. Donne, "The Will," e.g. ll. 12–13: "Mine ingenuity and opennesse, / To Jesuites . . ." The spirit of the post-Ovidian mock will and testament is much in evidence in Cowley's "Preface" to the *Poems* of 1656, where he cites Donne's "The Will," l. 51: "And I think *Doctor Donnes Sun Dyal in a grave* is not more useless and ridiculous then *Poetry* would be in that *retirement*" (*Poems* [1656], a3ᵛ).

3. *craft to Scots, and thrift to Jews*. In "The Protestation," Robert Baron contrives "Scots forget craft, and Avarice Jews . . ." (*Pocula Castalia*, 103). See poem 15, note to ll. 1–2.

13. *The God of Love, if such a thing there be*. Cf. poem 1, "The Request," ll. 6–8.

25. *Love's Columbus*. Cf. Donne, "Elegie" 19, ll. 27–30, and cf. Cleveland's "Fuscara; or The Bee Errant," ll. 57–58: "The bold *Columbus* still designes / To find her undiscovered mynes" (*Poems*, 58).

Poem 34. "The Resolution." Seventeenth-century love poetry rests on a greater distinction between the sexes than may be commonly realized. See Lucy Hutchinson's *Memoirs* for the insistence, here from a woman's point of view, on the relative insignificance of females. For example: "One day there was a greate deale of company mett att Mr. Coleman's, the gentleman's house where he tabled, to heare the musick, and a certeine song was sung which had bene lately sett . . . 'twas believ'd that a woman in the neighbourhood had made it. . . . Mr. Hutchinson, fancying something of rationallity in the sonnett beyond the customary reach of a she witt . . . could scarcely believe it was a woman's" (31–32).

6. *Samson*. A barbed example, since Samson was caught by female wiles.

9–12. *French Laws . . . Salique Law*. *Pactus legis salicae* no. 59 says that no portion of the land belonging to Salian Franks could be inherited by a woman. This proviso regarding Salic lands in no way applied to the succession of the French crown. The so-called Salic Law invoked in 1316 to exclude the daughters of Louis X and later Philip V from the throne of France never existed. Thereafter, the Salic Law only rested upon precedent. This subject may have been of some currency in the exiled court of Henrietta Maria, whose conceivable succession fell under Salic Law. See *Laws of the Salian and Ripuarian Franks*, trans. Theodore John Rivers. Cowley uses the term "Salique Lawes" in *The Civil War*, 1.38, referring to the beginning of the

Hundred Years' War when the French supporters of Philip VI opposed Edward III's claim to the throne, derived from his mother, with arguments based on Salic Law. See notes to this term in *Collected Works* 1.391-92 for legendary sources of the law.

In "A Letter to the Lady D. S. sent with a New Comedy," James Shirley writes that he cannot allow "A Salique law in Poetry, to bar / Ladies th'inheritance of wit" (*Poems &c*, 39).

Poem 35. "Called Inconstant." Cf. Thomas Stanley, "Changed, Yet Constant," ll. 1-3 (*Poems*, 7): "Wrong me no more / In thy complaint, / Blamed for inconstancy...."

7-10. *shore . . . Waves*. Cf. poem 47, ll. 1-6, and poem 83, ll. 15-21.

13-14. *drunk . . . The things turn round to you*. One of Cowley's favorite perceptions. Cf. "Ode: Sitting and Drinking in the Chair, made out of the Reliques of Sir Francis Drake's Ship," ll. 7-8: ". . . by my head I know, / We round the World are sailing now" (*Verses* [1668], A4^v, p. 8), and the ode "Here's to thee Dick" in *Miscellanies* (*Poems* [1656], C^v, p. 10), l. 26: "Let the *Glass walk*, till all things too *go round*."

18. *Men in motion think the Trees move too*. Cf. poem 23, ll. 3-4 and note, on the subjective perception of time.

Poem 36. "The Welcome." In Bodleian MS Rawl. Poet. 90 (M22, see Textual Notes), stanza 1 appears, in somewhat more religious guise, under the title "Upon the Hearts Return."

This poem is thematically related to poem 37, and both poems are written in the same verse form.

2. *Prodigal's come home*. Luke 15:11-32. During his reckless sojourn, the prodigal son had been reduced to the role of swinekeeper (l. 6).

19-21. *Dog-star . . . Northern Bear*. The Petrarchan fire and ice of love are here related in a metaphor of the constellations. Sirius is the Dog-star of the southern constellation Canis Major. It is associated with lust and scorching heat (cf. Virgil, *Georgics* 4.425) or lust despite such heat (see Thomas Lodge, "second Sonnet," *Rosalynd*, in *Works* 1:130-31). Cowley's "*Dog-star . . .* Rages with immoderate *heat*" follows E. K.'s gloss to *The Shepheards Calendar*, "July," ll. 21-22, nearly verbatim: "the Dogge starre . . . reigneth, with immoderate heate." Ursa Major, the Northern Bear (the Big Dipper or, more topically for Cowley, "Charles' Wain"), is associated with coldness, being a northern constellation, and with pride in Ovid's story of the nymph Callisto, Zeus, and their son, Arcas. Zeus transforms Callisto into a she-bear and then mother and son become the constellation and the star Arcturus. Juno complains that they are proud usurpers of her heavens. *Metamorphoses* 1.400ff.

23. *where these are temp'rate known.* Modifying his metaphor, Cowley identifies the temperate zone, distinguished from the torrid and the frigid, with barren deserts.

25-28. *well-govern'd . . . Like China.* The idea that China was well governed probably derives from *The Travels of Sir John Mandeville,* where city and state planning is particularly praised. William Warner's *Albion's England* (bks. 11 and 12) links the travels of Mandeville with affairs of the heart. The Great Wall of China was one device for keeping invaders on the frontiers. It is described in Samuel Purchas's *Hakluytus Posthumous, or Purchas his Pilgrimes* (12:103-4), just following comments on China's laws barring strangers except for ambassadors or slaves. Chapter 7.6—"Of Strangers"— relates the rebuffs of the Jesuit Father Ricci and stresses the laws permitting neither "egresse to the native, nor ingresse to Aliens" (464-69). The pervasive xenophobia, elements of protocol, and the linguistic and logistic barriers encountered by foreign traders are reported by Peter Munday, who was a member of the royally sanctioned British free-trade expedition led by Captain John Weddell in 1636. See *The Travels of Peter Munday,* no. 45, vol. 3, pt. 1, p. 175ff., for Munday's comments on the point where access was forbidden on the river approach to Canton.

30. *an Angel.* Genesis 3:24.

Poem 37. "The Heart fled again." This is an answer to poem 36, on the prodigal heart's return. Both poems are composed in the same stanza form, both are highly allusive, both feature a constellation metaphor. Both are partially transcribed in M22 (see Textual Notes), where stanza 4 of poem 37 appears under the title "Upon the parting with ye Heart again."

7. *Tyrian Dame.* Dido. See the quotation from Virgil *Aeneid* 4.73 on the title page for *The Mistress*: *"Haeret lateri lethalis arundo."* Virgil compares Dido with a hind, struck by a shepherd's arrow and fleeing through the forests of Crete, in pain and fright, unaware of the deadly arrow she carries with her. The scene invoked in poem 37, ll. 7-12, is from *Aeneid* 4.584-705, which ends "in ventos vita recessit" [life passed away into the winds].

Here, as in ll. 13-17, Cowley identifies his speaker with the abandoned female, Dido and Ariadne, and the fled heart with the male, Aeneas and Theseus. Cf. poem 44, ll. 7-8 and note.

13-17. *Ariadne . . . Theseus . . . Bacchus.* The event is from Ovid *Metamorphoses* 8.169-80, where Theseus abandons Ariadne at the island of Dia (Naxos). Bacchus comes to her, out of sympathy, and hurls her crown into the heavens, where it becomes a constellation.

24. *by none slain.* Cain, with whom the wandering heart is now compared, could not be killed: Genesis 1, 4:12-16.

27. *My Head.* I.e., the "rational soul," associated with the head. Burton

states, "This reasonable soul, which Austin calls a spiritual substance moving itself, is defined by philosophers to be 'the first substantial act of a natural human, organical body, by which a man lives, perceives, and understands, freely doing all things, and with election.' Out of which definition we may gather that this rational soul includes the powers, and performs the duties, of the two other [vegetal and sensitive] which are contained in it" (*Anatomy*, 1.1.2.9; 1:164-65). See the headnote to "Womens Superstition," poem 38, for another version of the autonomous head.

29-30. Cleveland has some humorously grotesque and sympathetic observations on desperate self-sufficiency in "Upon an Hermaphodite," ll. 21-42 (*Poems*, 10-11).

Poem 38. "Womens Superstition." For poets, ritualistic sacrifice of males has much to do with the story of Orpheus, whose misogyny may have been promoted by the death of Eurydice and whose fate, as Milton relates it, was that his disembodied head "down the stream was sent, / Down the swift *Hebrus* to the *Lesbian* shore" (*Lycidas*, ll. 62-63). For post-Orphic rites of sexual sacrifice, see Samuel Daniel, *Delia*, sonnet 8, and the whole of William Habington's *Castara*, pt. 1 (London, 1634). See poem 37, l. 27 and note.

3. *Contexture*. A term common in the seventeenth century. It could mean the connected structure of a literary composition. See *OED*, s.v. "Contexture," 5b.

11. *Loves Prophets*. Cf. poem 33, ll. 31-36, where Cowley promotes himself as "Loves last and greatest *Prophet*" and anticipates "the *Prophets fate*," martyrdom.

15-16. *Ashtaroth . . . Thundering Bâal*. Cf. poem 16, ll. 11-14 and note. Ashtaroth, "she who enriches," is also called Astarte as in poem 16; she becomes Aphrodite, of Cyprian origin, to the Greeks. She was goddess of fertility and reproduction among the Canaanites and Phoenicians. Bâal, "lord" or "master," appears in different combinations (like Bâal-zebub, "lord of the flies"). Cowley asserts that pride is the "Bâal" of women. Katherine Philips has much to say on this, both critically of other women and humorously of men's complaints. Cf. "Injuria Amicitiae," "Against Love," and "An Answer" (*Poems*, in Saintsbury, 1:539, 538, 594). See Richmond, *The School of Love*, 162, on the tradition of attributing to women the powers of "their *Mothers Gods*."

24. *Hearts . . . sacrifice*. Cf. Philip Ayres, *Emblems*, no. 22, *'Tis honorable to be Love's Martyr*. Austin Warren gives a wonderful description of the emblem collections *Schola Cordis* and *Cardiomorphoseos* in *Richard Crashaw*, 72-74. Graphic representations of the sacrificed heart appear in the engraved title to *Castara* (1640) and, more elaborately, in the engraving for

Nicholas Hookes's *Amanda,* where four cupids hold an altar (or a casket) that is inscribed *"to an* Unknowne Goddesse." A fifth cupid ignites a human heart atop the construction.

Poem 39. "The Soul [II]."
title. Poem 15 is the first to be given this title. Both are in three parts, corresponding to the traditional tripartite division of the soul (see Burton, *Anatomy,* 1.1.2.5-11).
1. *dull Philos'opher.* Presumably a Baconian, who has disjoined the study of "Natures Law" (l. 10) from the laws of religion (l. 12). See *The Advancement of Learning,* e.g., bk. 2.7,3: "Physique inquireth and handleth the *material* and *efficient causes*; and . . . Metaphysique handleth the *formal* and *final causes"* (*Works,* ed. Spedding, Ellis, and Heath).
6. *a Form Servient.* The relocated soul is a subordinate form, doing service to "another." *OED* cites Cowley's use of "servient."
11-12. Compare these lines, along with l. 1, to George Herbert's "The Agonie," stanza 1 (*Works,* 37):

> Philosophers have measur'd mountains
> Fathom'd the depths of seas, of states, and kings,
> Walk'd with a staffe to heav'n, and traced fountains:
> But there are two vast, spacious things,
> The which to measure it doth more behove:
> Yet few there are that sound them; Sinne and Love.

Poem 40. "Eccho." English poets developed two kinds of "echo" poem. One is a lyric reflection on aspects of the Narcissus and Echo story (Ovid *Metamorphoses* 3), and the other, which may contain elements of the first, is the formal use of echoing phrases. Cowley wrote both kinds (see notes to poem 18, "The Despair"). Early examples of these kinds are Thomas Watson's poem 25 in *The Hekatompathia* and Sidney's "The Second Eclogue" echo poem from *The Countess of Pembroke's Arcadia* (160-62). Barnabe Barnes shows the adaptability of echoing phrases in *Parthenophil and Parthenope* (sonnet 89, ode 2, canzon 2, and sestine 4), and formal possibilities may have reached their zenith in William Smith's *Chloris,* sonnet 22, where echo phrases to end-words in the lines of the sonnet can be read vertically, down the page, as a coherent sentence. Lord Herbert of Cherbury adapts the structure and theme of the echo to secular and sacred contemplations in the paired poems "Echo to a Rock" and "Echo in a Church" (*Poems,* 46-47). See also Thomas Stanley's versions of "The Eccho" by Marino (*Poems,* 179). For a more expansive summary of the echo tradition, including examples of Erasmus's delight in punning, see F. L. Lucas's annotation to Webster's *Duchess of Malfi,* 5.3.21 (*Complete Works* 2:195-96).

6. *In hollow, solitary Caves. Metamorphoses* 3.394: "Solis ex illo vivit in antris."

13. *Thy flame, whilst living, or a flower.* For *flame*, see *OED*, s.v. "Flame," 6b, where Cowley's use here is the first cited for "the object of one's love." Cowley's meaning is perhaps implicit in Ovid *Metamorphoses* 3.370-74. When Echo sees Narcissus, she is inflamed with love; as she follows him, she is burned by a "nearer flame," as sulphur-tipped torches can quickly ignite one another. For "Flower," *Metamorphoses* 3.509-10 tells that Narcissus' body became a flower, yellow at the center with white petals.

18-23. *things by opposition / The gainers grow.* Robert Hinman writes, "When two opposed and equal qualities meet, one would expect them to cancel each other out. However, according to the theory of antiperistasis, one quality could actually preserve, develop, even intensify its opposite. . . . Because of antiperistasis, Cowley believed, contrary forces supported and reinforced each other." Of poem 40, ll. 18-21, Hinman continues: "That is, warm and fluid sunbeams, striking cold and hard earth or cold and hard burning glass, are driven back upon themselves. They do not cool, as a result of this reflection, but gain heat. The image transmitted by tenuous light is doubled when the light reaches the unyielding solidity of the mirror. The airborne motion that Galileo had shown sound to be encounters a motionless object and is duplicated or amplified. For a description of sound based on Galileo's *First Dialogue on Motion*, see Kenelm Digby, *Of Bodies* (London, 1658), chap. 28, p. 301" (*Abraham Cowley's World of Order*, 42-43 and 345n.). Cf. poem 1, ll. 21-24 and note.

22-24. *my barren Love . . . Producing neither Image, Fire, nor Sound.* Cf. James Shirley, *Narcissus, or the Self-Lover* (bound with *Poems &c.*), stanza 113, p. 19: "Since his owne Image doth procure the fire, / And nothing left in nature to repair / His vext affections. . . ."

Poem 41. "The rich Rival." The rich rival is a perennial figure in dramatic and romance literature, beginning perhaps with Ovid *Amores* 3.8, and one that attracted Cowley from the start. He figures as the spiritually debased Guiscardo in *Constantia and Philetus* (published in *Poetical Blossomes*, 1633) and many times thereafter. For allusions in *The Mistress*, see poem 3, l. 5 and note; poem 24; poem 29, ll. 19-24; poem 31, l. 12. Cf. Suckling's "To His Rival," published in *Fragmenta Aurea*, 1646 (*Works*, 41).

Rumor that the rival is also a figure in Cowley's life appears to have begun with remarks by Joshua Barnes (see his *Anacreon*, xxxii). Johnson passes them on: "Of Cowley we are told by Barnes, who had means enough of information, that, whatever he may talk of his own inflammability and the variety of characters by which his heart was divided, he in reality was in love but once, and then never had resolution to tell his passion" (*Lives* 1:6 and n. 8). Part of this may derive from Cowley's own comment in the essay "Of

Greatness": ". . . if I were ever to fall in love again (which is a great Passion, and therefore, I hope, I have done with it) it would be, I think, with Prettiness, rather than with Majestical Beauty" (F2, 4Q^r, p. 121). Pope elaborated the matter by identifying Cowley's one love (and hence his "rival") with the wife of Sprat's brother. Owing to this failure in love, "Cowley, in the latter part of his life, showed a sort of aversion for women, and would leave the room when they came in" (see Spence's *Anecdotes*, nos. 447 and 448, and c.f. poem 62, ll. 20–21 and note). Nethercot advances and then appears to retract the argument that there was such a rival in Cowley's life.

In "The Bargain" [poem 24] comes the introduction of the first real complication, one which might have some basis in actuality. A wealthy competitor enters the field, and entices the lady with his money. Again he appears, in "The rich Rival." And that some such event did actually occur, Cowley's ode addressed many years later to Lord Broghill, Earl of Orrery, would seem to prove; for it contains these lines:

> I wrote and wrote, but still I wrote in vain,
> For after all my expense of wit and pain,
> A rich, unwriting hand carried the prize away.

. . . If Cowley had any basis of actuality for these poems, it was a very slight one. According to Sprat's Latin life, he played with, or counterfeited, love-adventures (*"De amoribus lusit"*) with the ease and ingenuity of Ovid and Catullus, and his own modesty. (Nethercot, *Abraham Cowley*, 102)

1. Geoffrey Walton remarks: "The opening stanza of 'The rich Rival' has, I think, [Cowley's] finest use of speech rhythms" (*The English Writings of Abraham Cowley*, 72).

12. *Joynture.* The legal definition is a provision of property and/or money for the woman in a marriage, in the event of her widowhood. See *OED*, s.v. "Jointure," 4a. Cf. poem 3, ll. 29–32, and poem 70, l. 5.

17–18. *Blood.* In view of theories of sexual reproduction at the time, which were exceedingly sanguine, these lines may be more forceful than they now appear. See, for example, Donne's "The Flea," ll. 4–7.

Poem 42. "Against Hope." This poem first appears in Richard Crashaw's *Steps to the Temple*, where its stanzas alternate with those of Crashaw's poem on hope. In *Carmen Deo Nostro*, it appears separately but next to Crashaw's "For Hope." An edited text of Crashaw's poem, for which we make no claim to be definitive, appears on p. 189 of this edition. Crashaw's poem, as would be expected, is referenced in Cowley's "Against Hope"; it is also alluded to in Cowley's poem 43, his own answer, printed to accompany "Against Hope" in *The Mistress*, 1647 and subsequent editions. See the Textual Notes for variants between "Against Hope" in the Crashaw editions and poem 43 as we print it.

The Cowley/Crashaw collaboration produces a combination of two poetic kinds. One is the lyric description of an abstract idea, as one finds in Herbert's "Prayer [I]," Henry Vaughan's "Son-dayes" and "The Night," Henry King's "The Forlorne Hope," and Cowley, again, in poem 49 "Beauty." These poems are lists, strings of epigrammatic phrases and clauses, all of which contribute to the definition of a subject that has been announced in the title. Robert Ellrodt has a note on possible classical precedents, particularly in the form of printed collections of Latin epigrams (see *Les Poètes Métaphysiques Anglais* 3:283). An early precedent for Cowley's subject is the 1601/02 version of Samuel Daniel's *Delia*, sonnet 20: "Come Tyme the anchor-hold of my desire, / My last Resort whereto my hopes appeale . . ." (*Poems*, 176). Cf. also Thomas Wythorne's "Of hope" (*Autobiography*, 225), which represents a standard Renaissance treatment of the topic. The second kind of poem presents one rhetorical position, as in a debate, and is answered by an adjacent poem (or in alternating answer-stanzas) expressing the opposite point of view. Cowley has shown his inclination towards this sort of pairing in *The Mistress*, poems 15 and 16, 36 and 37. See also Denham's "Friendship and Single Life Against Love and Marriage," (*Works*, 96), and Davenant/Suckling (or possibly Suckling/Suckling) in "For Absence" and "Against Absence." Later versions include poems for and against sleep in *Cleveland Revived* (London, 1662) and Thomas Flatman's "For Thoughts" and "Against Thoughts" (*Poems*, in Saintsbury 3:321-25). Rochester writes a burlesque of Cowley's poem 42 in his "On Nothing" (*Complete Poems*, 118).

4. *Horns of Fates Dilemma*. Each of the alternatives of a dilemma. *OED*, s.v. "Horn," 5.26, cites this line as the first use of the phrase, following Udall's definition of the Latin *argumentum cornutum*, which is Crawshaw's point of departure for "their thinne dilemma with blunt horne," l. 9, "For Hope," (see p. 189).

5-6. *Vain shadow*. Cf. Henry King, "The Forlorne Hope," ll. 9-10: "They that in hunting Shadowes pleasure take, / May benefitt of thy [hope's] illusion take" (*Poems*, 168-69), and Robert Ayton, ("Sonnet: on Hope," ll. 1-2, in *English and Latin Poems*, 160): "You hopes . . . shaddowes which Cephisus sonne did chase. . . ."

9. *If things then from their End we happy call*. Cf. Browne, *Hydriotaphia*, chap. 4: "It is the heaviest stone that melancholy can throw at a man, to tell him he is at the end of his nature; or that there is no further state to come, unto which this seemes progressionall, and otherwise made in vaine . . . the happinesse of inferiour Creatures . . . being framed below the circumference of these hopes, or cogitation of better being, the wisedom of God hath necessitated their Contentment" (*Works* 1:163-64).

30. *Ignes fatui*. Fool's fire; a phosphorescent, mobile light, used figuratively to mean a deceptive guide.

31. *Brother of Fear*. See Spenser, the masque of Cupid (*The Faerie Queene* 3.12, stanzas 12-13), where Hope, a gaily clad woman, is paired with Feare. Hope follows Desire (3.12, stanza 9) and precedes Repentaunce (3.12, stanza 24). Cowley would seem to be recollecting this source, embellishing it with his own geneology rather than consciously imitating.

Poem 43. "For Hope." The headnote to poem 42 includes observations on this poem, which Cowley introduced in place of the original companion to "Against Hope," Richard Crashaw's "For Hope." The idea of inheritance permeates Cowley's poem and may derive from Crashaw's "For Hope": e.g., l. 1, "Earths dowry"; l. 11, "Love's Legacie." Cf. also Robert Ayton, "Sonnet: On Hope" (*Poems*, 160). It is helpful to see this aspect of the poem in relation to poem 41, "The rich Rival."

It is puzzling to consider that while Crashaw included Cowley's poem in *Steps to the Temple*, Cowley declined to include Crashaw's in F1. Lines 47-50 of Cowley's elegy "On the Death of Mr. Crashaw," published in *Miscellanies*, 1656 (F1, sig. E3-E3ᵛ, pp. 29-30), may offer a clue to Cowley's motives as far as the manuscript for O1 is concerned: "Pardon, my *Mother Church*, if I consent / That *Angels* led him when from thee he went, / For even in *Error* sure no *Danger* is / When joyn'd with so much *Piety* as *His*." Cowley could not have included the text of his well-known Catholic-convert friend, should he (or Moseley or both) have aimed to keep *The Mistress* politically uncontroversial. It is difficult to imagine that the same motive may have extended to the publication of F1, despite the politics of its "Preface," since Cowley's beautiful elegy to Crashaw is printed in the section of *Poems* just before *The Mistress*.

1-2. *Universal Cure*. Cf. Philip Ayres, *Lyric Poems*, 80: "Hope. Out of Italian from Fra. Abbati." The second chorus reads: "*This* Universall Remedy, / To hope and live."

5-6. *Manna . . . To every Taste a several Meat*. Cf. poem 27, l. 24 and note.

8. *alienate*. To transfer to the ownership of another. *OED*, s.v. "Alienate," 2.

21. *Brother of Faith*. Paralleling the beginning of stanza 4, l. 31, of "Against Hope." Cf. Crashaw, "For Hope," l. 41, "*Faith's* Sister."

35-36. *Fruition more deceitful is*. Cf. "Against Fruition," poem 30, and cf. Crashaw, "For Hope," ll. 25-28.

Poem 44. "Loves Ingratitude." Cowley's thoughts throughout "Loves Ingratitude," and particularly in stanza 3, appear to be turning upon poem no. 33 from the *Anacreontea*. This text was especially popular among Cowley's contemporaries. Herrick translates it as "The Cheat of Cupid: Or, The ungentle guest" (*Works*, 26); in Stanley it is titled "Loves Night Walk" (*Poems*, 75); in Robert Heath's *Clarastella* it is "Loves entertainment." On a cold, wet night, Love comes knocking at the poet's door. The poet lets the boy in, not knowing who he is, and makes him warm and dry. Then, Love tests his bow and shoots the unsuspecting host.

7-8. *breast . . . suck*. The speaker is characterized as Love's nurse. Cf. poem 37, l. 7 and note, and other gender reversals in Cowley. See also Cowley's translation, *Anacreontique* no. 4, "The Duel," l. 26: "Since in my *Breast* the Foe I bear."

9-12. *I nourisht Thee / With Idle thoughts and Poetrie*. In Cowley's "Elegie upon Anacreon," following the *Anacreontiques* and the last poem in *Miscellanies*, Cupid confesses how poetry nourishes love and makes him stronger than he could otherwise be. Cf. poem 55, l. 11, and poem 65, "The Dissembler," where the poet becomes what he had earlier, idly, written about: "The *Play* at last *a Truth* does grow." And cf. Cowley's *Anacreontique* no. 4, "The Duel," ll. 14-17:

> But when I thought all danger past,
> His *Quiver* empti'd quite at last,
> Instead of *Arrow*, or of *Dart*,
> He shot *Himself* into my Heart.

16-18. *Snake . . . stings*. Cupid is implicitly compared to, and assaulted by, a winged snake that stings (a bee) in *Anacreontea* no. 35. Cf. *The Mistress*, poem 60, l. 6 ("The mighty *Serpent Love*") and poem 61, l. 30.

27-30. *by my own unforc'd consent, / The Traytor . . . is so settled in the Throne*. Cowley uses this figure frequently. Cf. poem 60, l. 20, and poem 61, "The Usurpation." If these lines were written as an oblique reference to the war (as they must have been read) they are hardly tactful, especially prior to 1647.

30. *Rebellion*. Cf. Cowley's *Anacreontique* no. 4, "The Duel," l. 2: "I will not now *Loves Rebel* prove."

Poem 45. "The Frailty." John Sparrow marks the first stanza of "The Frailty" as Cowley's supreme achievement in *The Mistress* (*The Mistress*, xx). The editions of 1647 include a third stanza, printed with the Textual Notes on p. 194 of this edition. It was probably Cowley's decision to omit these lines in the authorized *Poems* of 1656.

9. *my Chain*. Cf. poem 18, ll. 28-30, where the chain is that of love's slave (who also must row in his mistress's galley, as in poem 2, l. 22). The figure occurs in Ovid *Amores* 1.7.1: "Adde manus in vincla meas—meruere catenas" [Put the shackle on my hands—they have deserved the chain], but

Cowley means more by it than Ovid does. In poem 59, l. 7, it is "the fast-link'd *Chain* of everlasting *Fate*." The chain is most elaborately developed in poem 67, stanza 3, as the internal, neurological links binding ordinary feelings and their "ideas." It is described as a bond of "Gentle, and sweet Necessity" maintained by "*Spirits* above." See notes to poem 67.

12. *chiefest Christian Head*. The allusion is probably to David, whom Cowley saw as the beginning of the Messianic line (cf. *Davideis* 2, p. 55, from note 40ff., and p. 63, note 97ff. (*Poems* [1656]): ". . . from thy blest seed shall spring / The promis'd *Shilo*, the great *Mystick King*." For David's struggles with erotic love, see 2 Samuel 11:1-12:25.

Poem 46. "Coldness." The central conceit derives from the idea of water's metamorphosis to ice, and then to crystal. Cf. poem 12 and notes; poem 14, l. 8 and note. Thomas Philipott rivals Cowley in "To a Gentlewoman viewing her selfe in her glasse," wherein the speaker, in order to approach and view his mistress, undergoes a threefold metamorphosis. His liquid eyes melt, in tears, to a spring that the "cold, but charitable North" congeals into "a Chrystall Masse, / Of which was form'd this Looking-glasse." L. C. Martin notes "Neither Cowley nor Cleveland has . . . anything more ingeniously trivial" (Philipott, *Poems*, 25).

3-4. Cf. poem 83, l. 28, for another use of the comparison.

18. *Crystal*. Claudian, *Carminum Minorum* no. 36, "De Crystallo," speaks of crystal (formed of ice) that even the July heat of Sirius the dog star cannot melt."

Poem 47. "The Injoyment." This poem is found in Bodleian MS Rawl. Poet. 173, fol. 96^v, where it is followed by Etherege's "The imperfect enjoyment" and then "Against enjoyment" by Mr. [Thomas] Yalden, a poet whose contemplations in verse, like Francis Willis's, are nearly always occupied by the words of Cowley's poems.

Cowley's poem 47 is comparable, in a general sense, to Donne's "The Extasie" and other derivations on the emotional parabola experienced in coitus. In Cowley, the alternation of line lengths (syllabically, 10, 8, 10, 10, 8, 10 to the stanza break; then resuming 10, and so on) provides a pulse and forward-seeking movement. Stanzas 1 and 2 represent the pleasures of foreplay; the central stanza represents the ecstasy or climax; stanzas 4 and 5 recede to secrecy and silence.

title. "The Injoyment" is given in O1-2 and F1. It appears as "The Enjoyment" in M21 (see Textual Notes). Thereafter the poem is printed without a title. The deletion is probably Sprat's.

1-6. This stanza derives in part from figures developed in Sidney's *Old Arcadia*, bk. 3 (ed. J. Robertson, 241), Daniel, *Delia*, sonnet 44 (*Poems*, 32), and Carew, "A Rapture," l. 44 (*Poems*, 49). From Sidney there is an anatomical reference reading, "Lift up their stately swelling banks / That Albion cliffs in whiteness pass." From Daniel: "Florish faire *Albion*, glory of the North, / *Neptunes* darling helde betweene his armes." From Carew: ". . . the bubbling stream shall court the shore."

13-14. *like Doves*. The heat of doves was considered therapeutic, and their fidelity is a commonplace. Cf. Pliny *Naturalis Historia* 10.52.

18. Cf. Donne's verse letter "To Sʳ *Henry* Wotton," l. 1: "Sir, more then kisses, letters mingle Soules" (*Poems* 1:180).

21-23. *Alpheus . . . Sicanian Fountain*. A classical curiosity of continuing fascination for English poets (see Milton's "Lycidas" and Shelley's "Arethusa"). The story of the Arcadian river Alpheus's love and pursuit of the nymph Arethusa is noted in Ovid *Amores* 3.6.29-30, and the story is told in *Metamorphoses* 5.572-641. "Sicanian" means Sicilian (see *OED*, which cites Cowley's erudite l. 22). Arethusa, having been pursued by Alpheus underwater from Hellenic Arcadia, emerged as a fountain in Sicily. Cf. poem 64, ll. 19-24.

Poem 48. "Sleep." Cowley's "Sleep" is closely associated with Waller's "The Apology of Sleep, for not approaching the lady who can do anything but sleep when she pleaseth" (*Poems*, 80). Waller's poem, spoken by Sleep, can be read as an answer to Cowley—though it is more obviously a response to Waller's own "Of the Lady [Sacharissa] who can Sleep when she pleases" (*Poems*, 49).

1. *drousie God*. Underlying Cowley's somewhat philosophic exposition of sleep is Spenser, *The Faerie Queene* 1.1.40: "Morpheus . . . drowned deepe / In drowsie fit."

1-7. The first stanza is reduced to a synopsis in Waller's "The Apology of Sleep," ll. 21-25: "I, that of fumes and humid vapours made, / Ascending, do the seat of sense invade, / No cloud in so serene a mansion find, / To overcast her ever-shining mind. . . ."

10. *The fate of Egypt*. Cf. Waller, "The Apology of Sleep," l. 26: ". . . flowing Nilus want of rain supplies."

15. *as Nights to Colours do*. Cf. Lord Herbert of Cherbury, in his poems on the color black—e.g., "Thou Black, wherein all colours are compos'd, / And unto which they all at last return" ("Another Sonnet to Black it self," ll. 1-2, *Poems*, 39).

Poem 49. "Beauty." Beauty is a popular topic for definition-poems (see poem 42, headnote). Cf. "What is beauty . . ." in Thomas Greaves's *Songes of sundrie kindes* (1604; in *Lyrics*, ed. Doughtie, 188) and John Hall's "Of Beauty" (in Saintsbury 2:205). Poem 49, however, proceeds as a demonstration of arguments against beauty. Following Cowley, see Nicholas Hookes's first poem in *Amanda* (1653) and Charles Cotton's "Pindarick

Ode: Beauty," written in answer to Cowley (*Poems*, 170). Buxton, commenting on Cowley's poem in a note to Cotton's (276), suggests by way of comparisons to Tasso, "Sopra la Bellezza," and Donne's elegy 2, "The Anagram," that Cowley's poem belongs to the Renaissance tradition of the paradox. Cowley's position in poem 49 bears comparison to Donne in "An Anatomie of the World. The first Anniversary," ll. 249-372, on the death of Beauty.

1. *Ape*. Charles Cotton has Love as an ape in "Love's Triumph," l. 49 (*Poems*, 186).

3. *brown . . . white*. The lover to whom color of skin does not matter is, notably, Donne. See "The Indifferent," l. 1: "I can love both faire and browne . . ." and cf. poem 66, "The Inconstant."

12-13. *False Coyn . . . Mettal ill*. Cf. Carew, "To T. H., a Lady Resembling My Mistress," ll. 16-18: "To lead, or brass, or some such bad / Metal, a prince's stamp may add / That value which it never had" (*Poems*, 26).

19. —] Charles Cotton, in his usual manner, makes this into "Beauty, thou active, passive good!" See headnote.

21-22. *Thou Tulip, who thy stock in paint dost waste*. Cowley's is an early version of this point of view. Cf. Marvell, "The Mower against Gardens," ll. 12-14: ". . . Flow'rs themselves were taught to paint. / The Tulip, white, did for complexion seek; / And learn'd to interline its cheek."

Poem 50. "The Parting." This and poem 51, "My Picture," are about the mistress leaving him. "The Parting" is, throughout, an elaborate simile. The basis for comparison to the speaker's situation may be found in any number of earlier seventeenth-century reports on the exploration of Greenland. Those to be found in Purchas's *Hakluytus Posthumous* contain all of the specific details, as noted below. Cf. poem 13, ll. 20-22, for the opening figure. Following Cowley, cf. Robert Baron's "The Temper": "Cease Winter crown'd with Cristall ice / To frigidate my ELIZA. / Her Heart's the Court of *Dian* nice, / Who makes it Greenland . . ." (*Pocula Castalia*, 92).

3. *sad half year*. During which the sun was, by popular opinion, not to be seen in Greenland. Purchas's text of the third navigation of William Barents (or Bernards), 1596-97, written by Gerart de Veer, tells of a six-month stay, iced-in from October to April, but includes the detail that the sun "miraculously" reappeared after three months (it was lost from 4 November 1596 until 24 January 1597). See *Hakluytus Posthumous* 3.5.2 (13:88ff.).

12. *beyond eighty*. Addison (*Spectator*, no. 62, 11 May 1711) is particularly astonished by this expression. "When she is absent he is beyond eighty, that is, thirty Degrees nearer the Pole [assuming the 'warm degree' of l. 10 to be either England or France] than when she is with him." Reports printed in Purchas's *Hakluytus Posthumous* make it generally clear that Greenland had been explored from its southernmost part, c. 76 degrees, 30 minutes,

northwards to c. 80 degrees. Beyond that was uncharted territory. Cf. Robert Fotherby's "Description of Greenland," 3.2.2 (ibid. 13:33).

16. *Bears or Foxes.* The subtitle to Gerart de Veer's report of the Barents expedition's six ice-bound months reads, "Their cold, comfortlesse, darke and dreadfull Winter: The Sunnes absence, Moones light . . . Of Beares, Foxes, and many, many wonders" (13:88). Other reports frequently mention the "creatures" of Greenland as bears, foxes, and deer, along with sundry sorts of wild fowl.

17. *gay Planet.* The sun, as made clear in l. 22.

21. *Propriety.* Quality of character. *OED*, s.v. "Propriety," 4.

24. *let Me and my Sun beget a Man.* Cf. Shakespeare, sonnet 7, ll. 13-14 —"So thou, thyself outgoing in thy noon, / Unlook'd on diest unless thou get a son"—and cf. poem 13, ll. 23-25.

Poem 51. "My Picture." Pictures, ordinarily miniatures, were exchanged in life as well as literature. See, for instance, Dorothy Osborne's letter (no. 27, June 1653) to William Temple, promising to have a little picture drawn for him from a larger portrait. She mentions John Hoskins and Samuel Cooper as miniaturists of choice (Osborne, *Letters*, 95-97). Walton's conclusion to the "Life of Dr. John Donne" centers on the contrast between a picture taken in youth and the picture in age. This is the main theme of English Renaissance "picture" poems, as, for example, Samuel Daniel's *Delia*, sonnet 34 (*Poems*, 27):

> When winter snowes upon thy golden heares,
> And frost of age hath nipt thy flowers neere,
> When darke shall seeme thy day that never cleares,
> And all lyes withred that was held so deere.
> Then take this piucture which I heere present thee,
> Limned with a Pensill not all unworthy;
> Heere see the giftes that God and nature lent thee.

Jonson, with some self-depreciating humor, comments on the inverse situation—the effects of an old man's picture on a younger amorous prospect (*Underwood*, no. 9; "My Picture left in Scotland"). Such picture poems should be distinguished from "advice to the painter" poems that center on the artist's ability to control or alter what "God and nature lent"—for example, James Shirley, "To the Painter, preparing to draw *M. M. H.* (*Poems*, 12), and later ones by Waller and Marvell.

1. *Here, take my Likeness.* Donne's elegy 5, "His Picture," begins, "Here, take my Picture." Cowley is writing a parody. Donne's speaker departs on an adventure, the rigors of which may reduce him to a "sack of bones"; Cowley's speaker will become "pale, lean, and old" overnight because his mistress is leaving him.

8. *shadow*. Picture. Cf. Charles Cotton, "Ode: To Chloris from France," ll. 6-9: "In darke, and Melancholly Groves, / When prettie birds discourse their Loves, / I dayly worshippe on my knee / Thy shaddow, all I have of thee" (*Poems*, 154).

12. *substance . . . shadow*. Cf. Thomas Randolph, "Upon his Picture," ll. 15-16: "Behold what frailty we in man may see, / Whose shadow is less given to change than he" (*Poetical and Dramatic Works* 2:578), and Robert Heath, "On Clarastella's Picture . . ." (*Clarastella*, 14, l. 1): "Fair shadow of a fairer substance!"

13. *Cabinet*. A case for the safekeeping of jewels (or small pictures). *OED*, s.v. "Cabinet," 1. 5.

16. *The new-sould Picture gaze on Thee*. Cf. "thin-sould" in Cowley's unemended version of poem 3, l. 4 and note. The idea of the picture coming to life derives from Ovid's story of Pygmalion (*Metamorphoses* 10). Cotton points to the source while following Cowley in his "The Picture," ll. 13-24 (*Poems*, 143):

> Perhaps you fear m'Idolatry
> Would make the Image prove
> A woman fit for Love;
> Or give it such a soul, as shone
> Through fond Pygmalions living bone . . .

The example of Marital, however, ought also be considered. Cf. *Epigrams* 1.109.21-23: "Issam denique pone cum tabella; / aut utramque putabis esse veram, / aut utramque putabis esse pictam" [In fine, set Issa alongside her picture; you will either think that each is genuine, or that each is painted]. Cf. poem 65, headnote, and poem 77, ll. 13-16.

Poem 52. "The Concealment." This poem was heard in at least three song settings during the later seventeenth century (see Textual Notes and scores on pp. 437, 440, and 449). On the theme of concealment, cf. poem 31, "Love undiscovered"; poem 32, "The given Heart"; poem 56, "Loves Visibility."

11. *Chance-Medley*. *OED*: a casualty, the cause of which is chance, mixed with intent.

26. *Sacrifice . . . without an Heart*. Cf. poem 38, l. 24 and note.

Poem 53. "The Monopoly."

2-5. *æternal burnings . . . Ætna . . . Vulcan*. Burton, gathering phrases from Ausonius, Terence, Seneca, and Theocritus, writes: "For love is a perpetual flux, *angor animi* [mental anguish] . . . and a lover's heart is Cupid's quiver, a consuming fire (*accede ad hanc, ignem*, etc.), an inextinguishable fire.

> *Alitur et crescit malum,*
> *Et ardet intus, qualis Ætnaeo vapor*
> *Exundat antro.*

[As Aetna rageth, so doth love, and more than AEtna or any material fire.]

> *Nam amor saepe Liparaeo*
> *Vulcano ardentiorem flamman incendere solet.*

[Vulcan's flames are but smoke to this.]

(*Anatomy*, 3.2.3; 3:149; see notes, 460, on his sources)

6. *Cupids Forge*. Cf. Drayton, *Idea*, no. 40 (*Works* 2:330): "My Heart the Anvile, where my Thoughts doe beate, / My Words the Hammers, fashioning my desire, / My Brest the Forge, including all the heate. . . ."

14-16. Donne, in "Love's Usury," strikes a Faustian bargain with Love: "For every hour that thou wilt spare mee now, / I will allow, / Usurious God of Love, twenty to thee . . ." (*Poems* 1:13; ll. 1-3). Cowley outdoes this, giving over everything for the sake of revenge.

24-27. *Civil to none but Woman-kind*! / *Vain God*! This is very much in the spirit of Ovid *Amores* 3.3, e.g., 23-24: ". . . aut, siquis deus est, teneras amat ille puellas / et nimium solas omnia posse iubet . . ." [or, if there is a god, he is in love with women and too quick to ordain that they alone may do all things]. Ovid continues that men are not treated this way; Love punishes them for their offenses. Pauline Aiken cites Ovid's ll. 12 and 42, on the gods' human characteristics and indulgences, as sources for Cowley's l. 25: "*Vain God*! who *women* dost thy self *adore*!" (*The Influence of the Latin Elegists*, 38).

Poem 54. "The Distance."

3. In poem 7 of *The Forrest*, "That Women are but Mens shaddowes," Jonson writes: "Follow a shaddow, it still flies you; / Seeme to flye it, it will pursue . . ." (ll. 1-2; *Works* 8:104). Following Cowley, cf. Charles Cotton, "Les Amours" (*Poems*, 195): "Shee, that I pursue, still flies me."

9-10. *in vain I strive / The wheel of Fate faster to drive*. Cf. Marvell, "The Definition of Love" (*Poems*, 37, ll. 13-14): "For Fate with jealous Eye does see / Two perfect Loves; nor lets them close."

Poem 55. "The Encrease." Cowley works with love's arithmetic elsewhere; see particularly, *Anacreontique* no. 6, "The Account."

1. Cf. Donne, "Loves growth," ll. 5-6: "Me thinkes I lyed all winter, when I swore, / My love was infinite, if spring make it more."

4. *the top of Numbers*. Love's "score" is presented in various of Catullus'

poems. In poem 5 ["Vivamus, mea Lesbia . . ."] , ll. 7-9, we hear: "da mi basia mille, deinde centum, / dein mille altera, dein secunda centrum, / deinde usque altera mille, deinde centrum . . ." [give me a thousand kisses, then a hundred, then another thousand, then a second hundred, then another thousand, then a hundred . . .]. See Jonson's version in *The Forrest*, poem 6, "To the Same" (i.e., "To Celia"): "Kisse me sweet . . . Kisse, and score up wealthy summers on my lips . . ." (*Works* 8:103).

11. *mine own Fancy now drives on my Love.* Cf. poem 44, ll. 9-12 and note.

12. *shadows.* Images or pictures. Cf. poem 51, "My Picture."

14. *By Cyphers.* Recall that Cowley showed his devotion to Jermyn and the queen by writing letters in cipher code.

Poem 56. "Loves Visibility." In his Cambridge University thesis (June 1975), W. David Trotter writes that "in this poem ["Loves Visibility"] and elsewhere, Cowley's attitude towards love is unquestionably neurotic, preoccupied with concealment" (67). Trotter's published version, *The Poetry of Abraham Cowley*, omits this particular observation but advances the psychoanalytic assessment in another direction (see 47). Concealment is unquestionably one of Cowley's predominant subjects—see poem 31, "Love undiscovered"; poem 52, "The Concealment"; poem 64, "Silence"; and elsewhere. In these instances the writing (then printing) of the poem, ironically and playfully, vitiates secrecy. Cowley's ultimate "concealment" comes in his overtly erotic poem 47, "The Injoyment," ll. 29-30:

> For there's no danger I should tell
> The Joys, which are to Me *unspeakable.*

9. *But none who had it ever seem'd t'have none.* The hapless policy of concealment engages the form of poem 56, throughout, by way of self-contained triplet stanzas. The central line, 9, is doubly policed, by end-rhyme and by the punning repetition "none . . . *none.*" In "Loves Triumph," ll. 11-12 (*Poems*, 184), Charles Cotton, eviscerating Cowley's point, writes: "Hee is a Traytor to love's Throne, / That has no love, or seems t'ave none."

16. *if . . . the Face betray not it.* Cf. Cowley's *Anacreontique* 2, "Drinking," ll. 9-11: "The busie *Sun* (and one would guess / By's drunken fiery face no less) / Drinks up the *Sea.* . . ."

Poem 57. "Looking on, and discoursing with his Mistress."

3-7. *To look on Heav'en with mighty Gulfs between.* The "Gulfs" are biblical, from the story of Dives and Lazarus (Luke 16:19-31). The story plays upon one of Cowley's favorite situations, the confrontation between a rich man and a beggar. Dives, dead and in hell, lifts up his eyes and sees

Lazarus, the former beggar, far away in the bosom of Abraham. The rich man begs Abraham to send Lazarus, "that he may dip the tip of his finger in water, and cool my tongue; for I am tormented in this flame." In the ensuing collqluy, Abraham remarks "between us and you there is a great gulf fixed" (16:26).

This parable had earlier been adapted to the Petrarchan situation with which Cowley begins poem 57 (ll. 1-2). Cf. Henry Constable, *Diana*, 6, sonnet 2, l. 1: "To live in hell and heaven to behold . . ." (*Poems*, 203). John Oldham follows Cowley's phrasing in "The Parting," ll. 9-10: "So Heav'n was by that damned *Caitiff* seen, / He saw't, but with a mighty Gulf between" (*Poems*, 234). William Empson, in "This Last Pain" (*Collected Poems*, 33, ll. 1-2), writes:

> This last pain for the damned the Fathers found:
> "They knew the bliss with which they were not crowned."

11. *My Lowness, and her high Desert*. Cf. poem 3, l. 5 and note.

Poem 58. "Resolved to Love."
1. *the Grave and Wise*. Bacon relates the conventional wisdom in "Of Love" (*Essays*, 31-33), e.g., ll. 42-43: ". . . whosoever esteemeth too much of Amorous Affection, quitteth both *Riches*, and *Wisedome*."

24. *My Love's my Business*. Cf. Nicholas Hookes, "My businesse ever is to wait on thee" (*Amanda*, 21). "Business" and love are traditionally opposed, as in Bacon's "Of Love," ll. 10-11: ". . . great Spirits, and great Businesse, doe keepe out this weake Passion." Cf. poem 78, l. 3, on "business" as an attempted cure for love. In the essay "Of My self," Cowley accounts his time spent in Paris not as a period of loving or fulfilling service to the exiled court and queen but as a time when "Business . . . both Militant and Triumphant" supplanted his natural inclinations and "the Original Design of [his] Life" (F2, sigs. S4ᵛ-T, pp. 143 [misnumbered, should be 144]-145).

25. *These are but Trifles*. Donne writes: "It is a good definition of ill love, that St. *Chrysostom* gives, that it is Animae *vacantis passio*, a passion of an empty soul, of an idle mind . . . fill a man with business, and he hath no room for such love" (*Sermons* 4:121). Bacon, "Of Love," ll. 48-51, continues: "They doe best, who, if they cannot but admit *Love*, yet make it keepe Quarter: And sever it wholly, from their serious Affaires, and Actions of life."

29-30. *The wisest King who . . . Pronounc'd all Van'ity*. Though Solomon is usually accorded the epithet "wisest," David is meant here, who "from his sacred brest" Cowley thought to have pronounced "verily every man at his best state is altogether vanity" (Psalms 39:5).

Poem 59. "My Fate."

1. For magnetism as a kind or symbol of erotic attraction, see Claudian *Carminum Minorum* 29, "Magnes." Thomas Randolph translates this as "The Magnet" (*Works* 2:543). Browne, in *Pseudodoxia Epidemica*, bk. 2, chap. 2, entertains magnetism in more scientific but no less syncretic terms: "The Magnetical Vigour of the Earth" resides in "effluviums" that either "flye by striated Atoms . . . or glide by streams attracted from either Pole and Hemisphere of the Earth unto the Equator, as Sir Kenelm Digby excellently declareth" (*Works* 2:90). For the figure of the compass and its fixation on the polar north, cf. poem 27, ll. 9-12 and note. Robert Baron follows Cowley in "The Protestation": "The Needle its dear North shall shun . . ." (*Pocula Castalia*, 103). See Cowley's poem 15, ll. 1-2 and note.

5. *their old Motions*. Cf. poem 54, "The Distance," and poem 55, "The Encrease," ll. 19-21, on the natural motion of love. Cowley here relates love's "motion" with the natural phenomena of magnetism, gravity, and the upward movement of fire. Burton (*Anatomy* 3.2.1.1) extends the range of example to include motions of plants. That these are examples of love, see the underlying argument in Lucretius and Bacon, "Cupid, or the Atom" (*Wisdom of the Ancients*).

7. *fast-link'd Chain*. Cf. poem 45, l. 9 and note, and poem 67, ll. 19-27.

13. *the Stoicks*. Cowley's reference, as he clarifies in l. 17, is to the Stoic doctrine that the universe continues, endlessly, in cycles that end and begin in divine fire.

15. *Prædestinators*. Those who believe in or maintain the doctrine of predestination. *OED* cites this line, though not as the first use of the term.

Poem 60. "The Heart-breaking." Poems 60 and 61 portray love's monarchic and tyrannic power in Hobbesian terms. It is possible that Cowley, who writes a knowledgeable Pindaric ode on Hobbes (F1, sig. 3E1ᵛ, p. 26), wrote these poems for Hobbes's amusement, wittily expressing Hobbes's arguments as metaphors and similes. See Nethercot, *Abraham Cowley*, 95-96, on Cowley's association with Hobbes, and Paul J. Korshin, *From Concord to Dissent* (22), for another point of view on the relationship between the two men.

4. *Poyson put into a Venice-Glass*. This, according to Grosart, is "a long lived vulgar error" (*Complete Works* 1:238). James Howell reports it in a letter from Venice, 1 June 1621: "The Art of Glass-making here is very highly valued; for whosoever be of that Profession are Gentlemen *ipso facto*, and it is not without reason, it being a rare kind of Knowledge and *Chymistry* to transmute Dust and Sand (for they are the only main Ingredients) to such a diaphanous pellucid dainty Body as you see a Crystal-Glass is, which hath this Property above Gold or Silver, or any other Mineral, to admit no Poison" (*Familiar Letters*, 1.29.67). Byron uses the concept fancifully in

The Two Foscari: "*Doge*: 'Tis said that our Venetian crystal has / Such pure antipathy to poisons as / To burst, if aught of venom touches it" (5.1.194–96; *Works* 5:192).

6. *Serpent Love*. Love is "a poisoned serpent" in Raleigh's "Farewell false Love" (printed in William Byrd's *Psalmes, Sonets, & songs* [1588], in *English Madrigal Verse*, ed. E. H. Fellowes, 49). Cf. Donne, "Twicknam garden," l. 9: ". . . I have the serpent brought" (*Works* 1:28). Cf. poem 44, "Loves ingratitude," l. 16 and note.

7–8. *Cut . . . in pieces small*. Cf. Donne, "The Broken Heart," ll. 23–31: ". . . Love, alas / At one first blow did shiver it as glass. / Yet nothing can to nothing fall . . . Therefore I thinke my breast hath all / Those peeces still, though they be not unite; / And now as broken glasses show / A hundred lesser faces, so / My ragges of heart can like, wish, and adore . . ." (*Works* 1:49).

13–16. The military simile engages a Hobbesian perception, seeing that people are more combative and destructive in smaller groups, when the discipline of a singular military unit has been relaxed and fragmented.

19–20. Cf. poem 44, ll. 27–30 and note. The idea of Monarch becoming a Tyrant is resumed immediately in poem 61, "The Usurpation."

Poem 61. "The Usurpation." See headnote to poem 60 for associations with Thomas Hobbes in poems 60 and 61.

2–3. *I was mine own, and free / Till I had giv'n myself*. Hobbes's second Law of Nature is "that a man be willing, when others are so too, as farreforth, as for Peace, and defense of himselfe he shall think it necessary, to lay down this right to all things . . . To *lay downe* a mans *Right* to any thing, is to *devest* himselfe of the *Liberty* . . ." (*Leviathan* 1, chap. 14, p. 190). Both Hobbes and Cowley follow I Samuel in considering a peoples' decision to submit to a monarch—a text that Cowley had been working on at Cambridge, before commencement of the first Civil War. See Cowley's reworking of I Samuel 8, Samuel's famous warning against kings, as printed in the *Davideis* 4 (*Poems* [1656], sig. 4Q4ᵛ): "You're sure the first (said he) / Of *freeborn* men that begg'd for *Slaverie*."

5–6. *insolent . . . Tyrant*. Hobbes writes: "For they that are discontented under *Monarchy*, call it *Tyranny*; and they that are displeased with *Aristocracy* call it *Oligarchy*" (*Leviathan* 2, chap. 19, p. 240).

8. *Elective Monarchy*. Hobbes discusses the category of "Elective Kingdomes, where Kings have the Soveraigne Power put into their hands for a time" and do not name their successors, in *Leviathan* 2, chap. 19. To Hobbes, such "Soveraignes" are really not "Soverainges, but Ministers of them that have the Soveraigne Power," the electors (245–47). Cf. Disraeli's "Secret History of an Elective Monarchy" (*Curiosities of Literature* 3:255).

15–16. *To be both Emp'rour, and Pope too*. Hobbes's *Leviathan* 3, chap.

42, is in part a refutation of Cardinal Bellarmine's *De Summo Pontifice*, wherein papal authority is extended and the pope becomes a "Universal Monarch" (579). The temporal powers of the pope are the subject of 598-609.

31. *like the crowned Basilisks breath*. On the basilisk's crown, its hissing that drives away all other serpents, and its fatal breath, see Pliny *Naturalis Historae* 8.33 and 19.19. By the simile engaging deadly powers of hissing or breathing, Cowley suggests the lethal power of slander, as Spenser does in the figure of the Blatant Beast. According to Browne, it was more commonly held that the basilisk, which in "elder times was a proper kind of Serpent . . . poisoneth by the eye, and by priority of vision" (*Pseudodoxia Epidemica* 3.7; *Works* 2:174).

Poem 62. "Maidenhead." Formally, "Maidenhead" masks as a definition poem, like "Beauty" (poem 49). Rhetorically it belongs to the tradition of arguments against maidenhood, or virginity. A prose version of the argument may be found in Erasmus's colloquy "Proci et puellae," translated in Nicholas Leigh's *A Modest Means to Marriage* and done into English verse in Thomas Heywood's *Pleasant Dialogues and Dramas*. Another version of the argument, closer to Cowley in some of the figures of speech, may be found in Lyly's *Euphues: The Anatomy of Wit*: Euphues's denunciation of Lucilla and his "Cooling Card for Philautus and All Fond Lovers" (83-86 and 91-107). Donne's *Paradoxes and Problems*, paradox 12, "That Virginity is a Vertue" (listed among the *Dubia* in the edition by Helen Peters, 55), relates that "Some perchance will say that Virginity is in us by *Nature*, and therefore no *vertue*." In paradox 10, "That it is possible to find some vertue in some women" (21), Donne allows the chance for a 'good virgin'— "I am not of that sear'd impudency that I dare defend women, or pronounce them good: yet when we see phisitians allow some vertu in every poyson, alas why should we except women?"—yet invokes Marital (*Epigrams* 4.71.4) to suggest the impossibility of finding her: "Tanquam non liceat, nulla puella negat" [As if it were not permitted, no girl says no]. A memorable dramatic argument against virginity comes from Parolles in *All's Well That Ends Well* 1.1.123-64.

1. *sex that's worst*. The standard report, but counterarguments may be found, such as those of Agrippa on the superiority of women. His Latin treatise on the subject was translated as *Female Pre-eminence: or The Dignity and Excellency of that Sex, above the Male* (London, 1670).

12. *parched plains of Africks sand*. Cf. the temperamental geographics of poem 36, l. 23.

15-16. *bring / Monsters and Serpents forth*. For sun-bred species (in this instance self-induced images), cf. poem 13, ll. 23-25, and poem 50, l. 24.

20-21. *that thou shouldst be / Such tedious and unpleasant Company*.

Joseph Spence records a comment told him by Pope: "Cowley, in the later part of his life, showed a sort of aversion for women, and would leave the room when they came in. 'Twas probably from a disappointment in love" (*Observations, Anecdotes, and Characters of Books and Men*, no. 447).

23. *slippery*. Cf. Lyly, *Euphues*, 83, where the distraught Euphues describes Lucilla as slippery, like an eel. For the proverbial saying, see Thomas Heywood, *Proverbs*, 24. Following Cowley, Philip Ayres writes "Virgins are like the silver finny race, / Of slippery kind . . ." ("Love a Ticklish Game," ll. 1-2, from *Emblems*, in Saintsbury 2:356).

32. *With good unsought exper'iments by the way*. Referring to the *Chymick*, or alchemist (l. 28), who fails to discover the philosopher's stone. Cf. Donne: "I am now, like an Alchymist, delighted with discoveries by the way, though I attain not my end" (*Letters to Severall Persons of Honour*, 172). See also Donne's "Loves Alchymie," ll. 7-12. Disraeli notes the relation between Cowley and Donne and adds a further connection: "Fontenelle remarks 'It is proper, however, to apply one's self to these inquiries; because we find, as we proceed, many valuable discoveries of which we were before ignorant.' The same thought Cowley has applied, in an address to his mistress. [D'Israeli quotes "Maidenhead," ll. 25-32: all of stanza 4.] The same thought is in Donne" (*Curiosities of Literature*, "The Six Follies of Science," 1:122). Bacon inveighs against pursuit of such follies. The idea of an unsuccessful or impossible quest yielding something unsought, and of value, has a precedent in Petrarch: "Ma si com uom talor che piange et parte / vede cosa che li occhi e'l cor alletta" [sometimes a man who departs weeping sees things that gladden his eyes and heart]; *Rime*, poem 325, ll. 39-40.

Poem 63. "Impossibilities."

4-5. *Cæsar . . . little Asian foes*. This is puzzling, since after his triumphs in Rome, Caesar's last battle was in Spain, against the sons of Pompey. The reference is probably to the quick battle at Pontus, against Pharnaces (son of Mithridates the Great), which took place after Caesar's defeat of Pompey at Pharsalia and would constitute his victory over lesser Asian foes. See Plutarch *Caesar* 50; Suetonius *De Vita Caesarum*, 1. 35. Cowley alludes to the same event in poem 2, l. 1.

11-15. Cf. Marvell, "The Definition of Love," ll. 29-32.

16. *some bold Romance*. This may be the first use of "romance" to indicate a work of prose fiction, or novel. *OED*, s.v. "Romance," 2.5, cites Cowley's "that weep not ev'en *Romances* woes" (poem 80, "The Innocent Ill," l. 26) as a personification and then lists Dorothy Osborne's letter 54 as the first identification of "romance" with "novel." Dorothy Osborne writes: ". . . can there bee a more Romance story then ours would make if the conclusion should prove happy" (*Letters*, no. 54 [14 January 1654], 164). Other letters to William Temple refer to their love relationship as "our Story,"

which Dorothy Osborne tests against French "romances." See letter 40 (1653), for example, on her judgments (and his, too) on characters in George [or Madeline] de Scudery's *Artamene; ou, Le Grand Cyrus*. Her identification of such texts as "romances" is clearly anticipated by Cowley's use of the term in "Impossibilities," l. 16.

25. *the Amo'rous Youth's ore Helles Sea*. Leander, who swims the Hellespont to Hero. A similar use of the Leander story appears in Daniel's *Delia*, sonnet 38 (*Poems*, 29): "Faire and lovely maide, looke from the shore, / See thy *Leander* striving in these waves . . . Once let the Ocean of my cares finde shore, / That thou be pleas'd, and I may sigh no more."

30-31. *Such Seas betwixt us*. Poem 50, "The Parting," presents a similar situation.

34-35. *that Taper . . . thy Light*. Cf. poem 57, l. 17, for "Taper."

Poem 64. "Silence." The topic of concealment is dealt with in poem 31, "Love undiscovered"; poem 52, "The Concealment"; poem 56, "Loves Visibility."

1. *Curse on this Tongue*. Cf. poem 56, l. 18, for the tongue betraying the heart.

19-24. Cf. poem 47, ll. 21-23 and note, on the story of Alpheus and Arethusa.

Poem 65. "The Dissembler." The way in which fiction becomes fact, in its reflexiveness, is a topic in poem 44, ll. 9-12 (see note), poem 55, l. 11, and elsewhere. The story of Pygmalion (Ovid *Metamorphoses* 10) is a prototype; see poem 51, l. 13 and note, and poem 77, l. 13. That fiction and fact are always intermixing is Celadon's candid message in d'Urfe's *Astrea*: "They say true, contraries cannot be at one time in one place; yet Love and dissembled love are ordinarily in my actions" (sig. C2, p. 11). Cowley's comments on *The Mistress* in the "Preface" to *Poems* (1656) would have us understand that the entire volume is a dissembling.

> *Poets* are scarce thought *Free-men* of their *Company*, without paying some duties, and obliging themselves to be true to *Love*. Sooner or later they must all pass through that *Tryal*, like some *Mahumetan Monks*, that are bound by their Order, once at least, in their life, to make a *Pilgrimage to Mecca*,
> *In furias ignemque ruunt; Amor omnibus idem*
> [They all rush into the fires of passion; all feel the same Love.
>   Virgil *Georgics* 3.244]

The degree to which the fictionalizing becomes real, or reflects a reality, is also indicated in the "Preface":

... it is not the *Picture* of the *Poet*, but of *things* and *persons* imagined by him. . . . Neither would I here be misunderstood, as if I affected so much gravity, as to be ashamed to be thought really in *Love*. On the contrary, I cannot have a good opinion of any man who is not at least capable of being so. (*Poems* [1656], (a)4ᵛ–(b)ʳ)

Edward Sherburne's "The Surprise" (*Salmacis*, 106 [misnumbered as p. 98]) is comparable to poem 65 in phrase and concept.

4–6. *fooling with the Devil . . . a real Spright*. As in Marlowe's *Doctor Faustus* 3.3, where the clown (Robin) and Dick, having tricked a vintner, invoke the devil. When Mephistophilis actually appears, they cry, "We called you but in jest" (3.3.39). See also the Benvolio/Frederick episodes in act 4.

16. *sad fame of Prophesie*. Cf. the boast of poem 33, "The Prophet," ll. 31–32.

17–18. *Truth gives a dull Propriety to my stile, / And all the Metaphors does spoil*. On the propriety of extravagant metaphors, see poem 19, "The Wish," ll. 25–26.

24. *counterfeiting Lame*. Following Cowley, Philip Ayres writes: "Art I see can ne'er avail / Him that plays the counterfeit; / For I find, now time is past, / Jest to Earnest turn'd at last" ("'Tis dangerous jesting with Love: A Song," in Saintsbury 2:293, ll. 21–24).

29. *Phalaris*. The cruel tyrant in Sicily, who had a bull in which his prisoners were killed. The maker of this lethal device was its first victim. Cowley may be following Propertius *Elegies* 2.25.11–12: "Nonne fuit satius duro servire tyranno / et gemmere in tauro, saeve Perille, tuo?" [Were it not better to be a cruel tyrant's slave and groan within thy bull, savage Perillus?].

Poem 66. "The Inconstant." This is one of many seventeenth-century poems derived from Ovid *Amores* 2.4; Ovid's theme is stated in ll. 9–10: "non est certa meos quae forma invitet amores— / centum sunt causae, cur ego semper amem" [no fixed beauty calls up my passion—there are a hundred causes to keep me always in love]. What follows in Ovid is adapted and displayed in "The Inconstant," stanzas 2, 3, and 4. See also Donne, "The Indifferent"; George Wither, "Shall I wasting in despair"; Herrick, "No Loathsomeness in Love," "Love lightly pleased," and "Love dislikes nothing"; Alexander Brome, "Song 2: The Indifferent." Stanley's "Love's Heretic" (*Poems*, 32) derives the Ovidian topic by way of Marino's "Amore inconstante." Another variation on this Ovidian theme is found in Cowley's "The Chronicle" (*Miscellanies*, 1656), and in Thomas Jordan's "A Gentleman in love with twenty Mistresses" (*Poeticall Varieties*, 1).

6. *Legion*. From Mark 5:9. See poem 2, l. 10 and note.

14–16. *If Fair . . . If Black*. Cf. poem 49, "Beauty," l. 3. And compare Lovelace, "The Scrutinie. Song. Set by Mr. Thomas Charles" (*Poems*, 26), ll. 13-15: "But I must search the black and faire / Like skilfull Minerallists that sound / For Treasure in un-plow'd-up ground."

29-30. *Constant . . . Always All*. Cf. poem 6, "Inconstancy," ll. 19-21 and notes.

33-36. *Bee*. A popular figure for the lover. Cf. Jonson, "Begging another . . . ", ll. 5-6 (*The Underwood*, 2, 7; *Works* 8:139); Lovelace, "The Scrutinie," ll. 16-20; and following Cowley, Alexander Brome, "The Libertine," ll. 14-26 (*Poems*, 78-79). The more Carew's bee spends, the more it has. The bee's flight transpires in "A Rapture," ll. 55-80, beginning:

> Then, as the empty Bee, that lately bore
> Into the common treasure, all her store,
> Flyes 'bout the painted field with nimble wing,
> Deflowring the fresh virgins of the Spring,
> So will I rifle all the sweets, that dwell
> In my delicious Paradise, and swell
> My bagge with honey . . .
>
> (*Poems*, 50)

42. *by every Spark in set on Fire*. See Jonson, *The Underwood*, 36. "A Song," ll. 9-10: "A Sparke to set whole worlds a-fire, / Who more they burne, they more desire . . . " (*Works* 8:189).

Poem 67. "The Constant." "The Constant" is related by title to poem 66.
4. *one Quarter*. Cf. poem 60, 13-16 and note.
6-8. *my vanquisht Heart . . . 'Tis Garison'd*. For the military figure, cf. poem 44, ll. 27-30; poem 60, ll. 19-20; and poem 61, ll. 9-16 and 37-40.
19. *Chain*. Cf. poem 45, l. 9, and poem 59, l. 7. The figure of the mistress as conqueror and her lover as enslaved, imprisoned, or chained (cf. poem 2, l. 19 and elsewhere) is amplified here. The "chain," by the simile in l. 20, is related to the old cosmic order wherein all elements of the lower world are ordered and linked to a higher "good" by the operation of "*Spi'rits above*," or love. Cf. Spenser, "An Hymne in Honour of Love" (l. 89 reads, "Together linkt with adamantine chaines"), and Arthur O. Lovejoy, *The Great Chain of Being*, chap. 4. Cowley serves the monarch-mistress, literally the queen, by the "sweet *Necessity*" of this chain.

Poem 68. "Her Name." The name of the mistress is concealed throughout. Cf. Donne, "The Curse": "Who ever guesses, thinks, or dreames he knowes / Who is my mistris, wither by this curse . . ." (ll. 1-2, *Poems* 1:41); Habington, "To a friend inquiring her name, whom he loved" (*Poems*, 22); Carew, "Song: To One that desired to know my mistress."
1. *Jewish Reverence*. Like the Jews, who would not speak the name of their fierce deity and rendered it unpronounceable.
13-14. Cowley echoes Spenser's "Epithalamion," but only as a forecast

of marriage. Another echo, appropriate to the present tense, is heard in the refrains to stanzas 1 and 2 of "The Despair," poem 18. See also poem 19, "The Wish," ll. 17-20.

25. *I will not dare to make a Name.* Any pseudonym, like Astræa or Cælia, would be a profanation, a false "stamp" (l. 24). Cowley's comments in this stanza are comparable to those found in Cornelius Agrippa's *Occult Philosophy*, chap. 70, "Of the virtue of proper names": "Hence Magicians say that proper names of things are certain rayes . . . keeping the power of things, as the essence of the thing signified" (*Three Books of Occult Philosophy*, 153).

As Cowley says in the first line, he has more than Jewish reverence. The Jews allowed the consonants YHWH. Cf. poem 3, "The Given Love," stanza 9, where the mistress's "title" will be fixed next to Sacharissa's.

Poem 69. "Weeping." Dr. Johnson remarks in his *Life of Cowley* (26) that "the tears of lovers are always of great poetical account." Earlier treatments of the topic tend to be self-portraits, like Drayton's (*Ideas Mirrour*, amour 14) and Donne's "A Valediction: of weeping" or "Twicknam garden." Most seventeenth-century versions feature the lady weeping. Cf. Herbert, "Marie Magdalene"; Cartwright, "The Teares" and "On one weepeing"; Crashaw, "The Weeper"; Lovelace, "Lucasta *Weeping*" and "Lucasta paying her Obsequies"; John Hall, "Julia Weeping"; and Marvell, "Mourning." This topic was extremely popular in songs. See Ferrabosco, nos. 23 and 24 in Nicholas Younge's *Musica Transalpina* (1588: "I saw my Lady weeping . . . ," translating Alessandro Lionardi's "Viai pianger Madonna . . ."), and the king of lyrical tears, John Dowland: e.g., "I saw my Lady weepe" in *The Second Booke of Songs or Ayres* (1600). See Doughtie, *Lyrics*, 100 and 474-75. Cowley's poem has some affinities with Stanley's "A Ladie weeping" (translated from Montalvan's play *El Señor don Juan de Austria*, [1638]; see *Poems*, 47 and 387n.). Charles Cotton's "Takeinge leave of Chloris," stanza 2 beginning "See, see, she weeps!" (*Poems*, 147), is a synopsis of Cowley's "Weeping."

1-2. *See . . . Drops Tears.* Cf. Lovelace, "Lucasta paying her Obsequies," ll. 1-2 (*Poems*, 77): "See! what an undisturbed teare / Shee weepes. . . . "

9. *The Baby, which lives there.* Margoliouth suggests a comparison with Marvell, "Mourning," ll. 2-3: "What mean these Infants which of late / Spring from the Starrs of *Chlora's Eyes*?" (*Poems* 1:31 and 223n). The figure, as others have noted, derives from a Latin pun on *pupula*, pupil of the eye, and *pupa/pupuo*, child. Cf. Heath, "To a Lady wearing a Lookingglass at her girdle," l. 31: "When th'am'rous youth looks Babies in your eyes" (*Clarastella*, 50).

15. *that pure Hill of snow.* Cf. Crashaw, "The Weeper," ll. 4-5: "Snowy hills, / Still spending, never spent."

20. *Limbeck.* Alembic; often used figuratively. *OED*, s.v. "Limbeck," b,

lists Tofte, *Alba* (1598): "What my sad eye Distils from Lymbeck of a bleeding Hart."

22-23. *so wondrous cold, / As scarce the Asses hoof can hold.* Frozen, as sheer ice, so that the ass can scarcely find a foothold. Cowley's "The Motto," appended in lieu of the author's portrait in the 1647 editions of *The Mistress*, helps to explain this strange line. Cowley portrays himself as "the *Muses Hannibal*" in ll. 17-24:

> Unpast *Alpes* stop me, but I'll cut through all,
>   And march, the *Muses Hannibal*.
> Hence all the *flattering vanities* that lay
>   *Nets* of *Roses* in the way,
> Hence the desire of *Honors*, or *Estate*;
>   And all, that is not above *Fate*.
> Hence *Love* himself, that *Tyrant* of my days,
>   Which intercepts my coming praise.
>   (*Miscellanies*, in *Poems* [1656] sig. B1-B1ᵛ)

The frozen Alps stand for social vanities, including love, summed in the frigid mistress of poem 69 and others in the collection. Hannibal's crossing the Alps, as told by Livy in *Ab urbe condita*, book 21, held considerable fascination for Cowley. He invokes the story again in the second stanza of the Pindaric ode "To Dr. Scarborough" and annotates Livy's notorious passage about Hannibal breaking through the rocks by treating them with fire and vinegar (*Works* [1656, 3F3ᵛ). As the story goes, when Hannibal faced the precipitous descent on the Italian side, men and beasts of burden had to make their way over treacherously slippery ice just beneath the surface of melting snow:

Taetra ibi luctatio erat via lubrica non recipiente vestigium et in prono citius pedes fallente. . . . Iumenta tamen etiam secabant interdum infimam ingredientia nivem, et prolapsa iactandis gravius in conitendo ungulis penitus perfringebant, ut pleraque velut pedica capta haererent in dura et alte concreta glacie.

[Then came a terrible struggle on the slippery surface, for it afforded them no foothold. . . . The baggage animals, as they went over the snow, would sometimes cut into the lowest crust, and pitching forward, striking out with their hoofs, as they struggled to rise, break through it, so that numbers of them were caught, as if entrapped, in the hard, deep-frozen snow]. *Ab urbe condita* 21.36.7-8.

Just following, in 21.37.1-4, the fires and vinegar are mentioned. Philemon Holland's translation of this passage appeared in *The Natural Historie of C. Plinius Secunda*, 1601. See also Cowley's Pindaric "The Extasie," stanza 10: "The *Snow* and *Frosts* which in it lay / A while the sacred *footsteps* bore, / The *Wheels* and *Horses Hoofs* hizz'd as they past them ore" (*Poems* [1656], 3G2). For a less imaginative (and less cryptic) version of the figure, see Thomas Philipott, "On Julia, throwing snow-balls at him": ". . . where I did but rest / My hand upon the Alps of her white brest, / The snow that lay dispers'd o're that chast seat, / Straight curb'd the uproare of my former heat" (*Poems*, 3).

The turn in "Weeping," stanza 4, is comparable to John Hall's assessment of "Julia Weeping": "Fairest, when thy eyes did pour / A Crystal shower, / I was persuaded that some stone / Had liquid grown . . . Why weep'st thou? 'cause thou cannot be / More hard to me? / So Lionesses pity . . ." (ll. 1-4, 7-9; in Saintsbury 2:197). Following Cowley, see Charles Cotton's "Takeinge leave of Chloris," ll. 10-18.

Poem 70. "Discretion." "Discretion" and the following three poems 71-73 —"The Waiting-Maid," "Counsel [II]," and "The Cure"—are all related by stanza form. They are written as dramatic addresses in the manner of poem 41, "The rich Rival," which is echoed in poem 70. The argument against discretion appears again in poem 79, stanza 2.

5-6. *Joynture . . . Land*. Cf. poem 41, "The rich Rival," l. 5, 9 and note.

11-12. *Friends and Interest*. Cf. "The rich Rival," ll. 13-14.

15-16. *One who in Love were wise*. Cf. poem 17, "Wisdom," ll. 10-12.

24. *bound naked to the Stake*. For a visual representation, see Philip Ayres, *Emblems of Love*, 22: "'Tis Honourable to be Love's Martyr" (in Saintsbury 2, plate facing 356).

Poem 71. "The Waiting-Maid. (Suspected to Love her)." See headnote to poem 70, on the relationship of poems 70-73. Ovid advises: "Sed prius ancillam captandae nosse puellae / Cura sit: accessus molliet illa tuos" [Be sure to know the handmaid of the woman you would win; she will make your approach easy (*Ars Amatoria* 1.351-52)]. Dramatizations of this advice appear in Ovid's *Amores*, e.g., 1.11; 2.7; and 2.8. Burton adds, "many a gentleman runs upon his wife's maids" (*Anatomy*, 3.2.2.4; 3:103). David Trotter has an assessment of the Ovidian influence on this poem in *The Poetry of Abraham Cowley*, 52-55, wherein he notes Johnson's selection of stanza 4 as exemplary of a telling wit combined with easy urbanity.

title. The subtitle, "Suspected to Love her," appears only in the 1647 octavo editions. Its omission in *Poems* 1656 (and thus in subsequent editions based on the 1656 text), appears to have been accidental. See note to the title of poem 14.

9-12. *Tyrannie . . . Civil Government*. Cf. poem 61, "The Usurpation," stanzas 1 and 2. Alastair Fowler sees the speaker's sophistical denial as perhaps a deceit. Fowler remarks, on ll. 11-12: "But in what sense would the lady's government be more civil if she did not augment her beauty's power?

It is only that fewer cosmetic additions would poison less a dart 'too apt before to kill'? Or are the hours of toilet spent maliciously in another sense, by keeping the maid from her lover?" (*Triumphal Forms*, 76).

14. *a barb'arous skill*. A barberous pun.

16. *Too apt before to kill*. Cf. Ovid *Amores* 1.14.27–30.

21. *Thou art my Goddess, my Saint, Shee*. Cf. Waller's lines to his "fellow-servant," Sacharissa's attendant Mistris Braughton: "Of that stern goddess. You, her priest, declare / What offerings may propitiate the fair . . ." ("To the Servant of a Fair lady," *Poems*, 55, ll. 25–26).

Poem 72. "Counsel [II]." See headnote to poem 70 on the relationship of poems 70–73. Poems 72 and 73 are particularly close in another way, as they are both spoken to the "Doctor." If they were to be joined together, the resulting single poem would be formally identical to poem 71: four stanzas 8*a*6*b*8*a*6*b*, and a fifth stanza with two additional lines 8*a*6*b*8*a*8*b*8*c*10*c*. It is conceivable that the combined five stanzas of poems 72 and 73 were written as a single poem that was divided when printed in 1647. If so, however, Cowley declined the opportunity to rejoin the texts in 1656.

title. [II] is editorial. Poem 26 is the first to be titled "Counsel."

3. *who would Physick-potions give*. Cf. poem 78, "The Incurable," ll. 25–26.

7–8. *the adverse wind / Does make them greater*. Cf. poem 78, ll. 13–16.

Poem 73. "The Cure." See the headnote to poem 72.

1–3. *roughest art . . . Cut, burn, and torture*. Pauline Aiken (*The Influence of the Latin Elegists*, 38) suggests comparison with Propertius *Elegies* 1.1.25–27: "aut vos, qui sero lapsum revocatis, amici, / quaerite non sani pectoris auxilia. / fortiter et ferrum saevos patiemur et ignes . . ." [Or else, my friends, do what would recall me all too late from the downward slope, seek all the remedies for a diseased heart. I will bravely bear the cruel fire and knife].

Doctors are called to anatomize the lover's corpse in Donne's "The Dampe." Burton offers some homeopathic counsel similar to Cowley's "cure a fire with a fever" in the *Anatomy*, 3.2.5.2: "Heathen philosophers drive out one love with another, as they do a peg, or a pin with a pin," and in 3.2.5.5:

> The last refuge and surest remedy, to be put in practice in the utmost place, when no other means will take effect, is to let them go together, and enjoy one another . . .
>
> *Julia*, sola potes nostras extinguere flammas,
>   Non nive, non glacie, sed potes igne pari.
> Julia alone can quench my desire,
> With neither ice nor snow, but with like fire.

Poem 74. "The Separation." On the evidence of M26 (see Textual Notes), stanza 1 circulated independently. Cf. poem 50, "The Parting," for another valediction.

1. *Ask me not what my Love shall do or bee.* Here is an inversion of Donne's "A Valediction: forbidding mourning," where the poet says exactly what he will do, and be, as well as what she will do and be: "Such wilt thou be to mee . . . Thy firmnes makes my circle just. . . ."

9. *For 'tis the Body of my Love.* Cf. poem 39, "The Soul [II]," ll. 13-18.

Poem 75. "The Tree." Ovid's *Heroides* 5 and Longus's *Daphnis and Chloe* set points of departure for the habit of carving love graffiti in the bark of trees. Following Longus, carving goes on in d'Urfe's *Astraea*. This becomes the subject of comedy in *As You Like It* 3.2. Hudibras later promises to do it with love knots and decorated letters (Butler, *Hudibras* 2.1.565-66). See poem 5, "Written in Juice of Lemmon," l. 33 and note. "The Tree," however, is more closely associated with Ovid's *Heroides* 5, where Paris has carved fatally prophetic love-verses to the unhappy Oenone.

Cowley's poem is comparable to Waller's poems titled "At Penshurst" and "The Fall." It is of some biographical interest that Katherine Philips wrote a poem entitled "Upon the Graving of her Name upon a Tree in Barn-Elms Walks" (in Saintsbury 1:546). Philips was a friend of Cowley's and Barn-Elms was one of the sites of Cowley's retirement.

1. *flour'ishingst Tree in all the Park.* Cf. poem 4, "The Spring," ll. 17-24, on trees that flourish despite (or because of) the mistress's absence. Herein Cowley notes the relation between tree and woman by an allusion to the Apollo/Daphne story. He also alludes to Old Testament episodes about god or his angels residing in groves and gardens. Cowley's more cultivated "park" is shaded with biblical language in ll. 23-24, below.

3-4. *I cut my Love into his gentle Bark.* On the wounding of trees, cf. Marvell, "The Garden," ll. 19-23 (*Poems* 1:48):

> Fond Lovers, cruel as their Flame,
> Cut in these Trees their Mistress name.
> Little, Alas, they know, or heed,
> How far these Beauties Hers exceed!
> Fair Trees! where s'eer your barkes I wound . . .

11. *Homer in the Nut.* Pliny notes the curiosity: "Cicero hath recorded, that the whole Poeme of *Homer* called Ilias, was written in a piece of parchment, which was able to be couched within a nut shel" (trans. Philemon Holland, *The Historie of the World* 1.7.21). The marvel is repeated with some frequency; cf. Thomas May(?), "Upon Aglaura," ll. 17-18 (in Thomas Clayton's edition of Suckling's *Non-Dramatic Works*, 203), and Cleveland's pamphlet "The Character of a London diurnal" (London, 1647; sig. A2).

17. *Witchcraft*. Cf. Burton, *Anatomy*, 3.2.2.2 (3:85-86): "Heliodorus, *lib*. 3, proves at large that love is witchcraft. . . ." James Shirley, "To his Mistris upon the Bayes withered" (*Poems*, 23, ll. 45-46), offers a less arcane explanation: "'Tis thy unkindness that doth kill / The leaves, which fade like me. . . ."

18. *For*. The copy text of 1656 and subsequent printings read "Or." O1 (errata) and O2 read "For," and bibliographical evidence supports this as the authorial reading (see Textual Notes). There is a substantive difference, and "Or" may be preferred by some readers. "Or" allows the inscribed "characters" to be active agents of Love, transmitting the "Poyson." This is in keeping with Cowley's appreciation of verbal "witchcraft" in "This Dissembler." "For" exculpates the written characters, making them passive agents.

23. *thrive here (said I) and grow*. Cf. Genesis 1, 2:9, 1:22: "And out of the ground made the Lord God to grow every tree that is pleasant to the sight, and good for food; the tree of life also in the midst of the garden, and the tree of knowledge of good and evil . . ."; "And God blessed them, saying, Be fruitful, and multiply. . . ." Cowley introduces a biblical tone in this line, giving momentum to the idea of the "fall" that transpires in stanza 5.

25. *Alas poor youth*. In poem 52, "The Concealment," ll. 31-33, there is a change of narrative voice as the mistress is imagined addressing the dead lover: *"Twas onely Love destroy'd the gentle Youth."* Here, Cowley offers less a change in narrative voice than a sense that the poet speaks to himself, from a suicidal perspective (like that of Despair in Spenser's *Faerie Queene* 1.9.44-47, who offers: "Then doe no further goe . . . Death is the end of woes: die soone . . .").

27. *Go tye the dismal Knot*. Ironically close to "love-knot" (see headnote, in reference to Butler on figures carved in trees). Waller's "At Penshurst" ("While in the park I sing") is far less dramatic in conclusion. Apollo, who narrates the resolution, only advises, "On yon aged tree / Hang up thy lute" (ll. 37-38, *Poems*, 64).

Poem 76. "Her Unbelief." Stanzas 1-3 are comparable to poem 56, "Loves Visibility."

6. *my Idol*. The idea that loving a woman is a form of idolatry pervades *The Mistress* as it does earlier sonnet cycles, starting with Petrarch's. In Cowley's poem 16, stanza 2, the poet writes of destroying heathen idols. In poem 21, ll. 6-7, his "wild idolatry" reascends. Poem 29, l. 17, relates that his mistress "like a *Deity* is grown."

8. *The odorous flames, I offer thee*. The lover in heat is known to others by smell. Any olfactory observer of adolescents will recognize the truth of this.

14-15. *the Cause in thy Face*. Cf. poem 59, "My Fate," ll. 21-22.

16. *Fair Infidel*. His idol turns infidel. Cf. poem 38, "Womens Supersti-

tion," ll. 13-14, on women turning to worship "vain *Idol-Gods* that have no *Sense* nor Mind."

25. *raise me from the Dead again*. Aside from the obvious biblical allusion, cf. poem 31, "Love undiscovered," stanza 3.

Poem 77. "The Gazers." This is the first of seven poems added to those in O1-2 for publication in F1, *Poems*, 1656. The additional poems, here numbered 77 through 83, were placed in this sequence between "Her Unbelief" and the final poem to *The Mistress* in O1-2 and F1, "Love given over." The seven new poems offer little internal evidence to establish that they were written after the publication of O1-2. It is just as plausible to maintain that they are earlier compositions that for some reason were not part of the manuscript collection that fell into the hands of Humphrey Moseley in 1647.

title. The title is explained in ll. 9-10 by the "*Man* and *Wife* in *Picture*."

9-10. Cowley first uses the comparison in *The Guardian*, 4.7: Aurelia, shuddering at a prospective marriage, compains: "We should sit all day together like pictures of man and wife, with our faces towards one another, and never speak."

James Shirley, in "Love for Enjoying," ll. 25-27, develops the more Donne-like idea as "Why do we coward-gazing stand, / Like Armies in the Netherland, / Contracting fear at eithers sight?" (*Poems*, 27). Cf. Donne, "The Extasie," ll. 11-14: "And pictures in our eyes to get / Was all our propagation. / As 'twixt two equall Armies, Fate / Suspends uncertaine victorie . . ." (*Poeticall Works* 1:51).

13-16. *Pigmalion*. Cf. poem 65, headnote, and poem 51, l. 13 and note.

14. *th'Amour*. Here is the single instance of Cowley's using a very obviously French word in *The Mistress*.

17. *Beauty to man the greatest Torture is*. For the stamp on the other side of the coin, cf. Thomas Jordan, "Achrostick to his Mistresse," l. 8: "*Beauty* makes your *gazers* eloquent" (*Poeticall Varieties*, 21).

22. *Salamander-like*. Browne, *Pseudodoxia Epidemica*, 3.14, states: "that a Salamander is able to live in flames, to endure and put out fire, is an assertion, not only of great antiquity, but confirmed by frequent, and not contemptible testimony." He adds that asbestos was called salamander's wool (*Works* 2:202-4). For the comparison between lover and salamander, see Robert Greene, *The Royal Exchange* (1590)—"The poets seeing lovers schorchant with affection, likeneth them to salamanders"—and Cleveland, "The Antiplatonick," ll. 7-8: "Y'are Salamanders of a cold desire, / That live untouch't amid the hottest fire" (*Poems*, 54).

25-26. *the lusty Sun . . . kisses every thing*. The Sun's sexual engagements are usually limited to heliotropes. Cf. Carew, "Boldness in Love," ll. 1-8, and Cleveland, "Upon Phillis walking in a morning before Sun-rising," ll. 27-30.

Poem 78. "The Incurable." See headnote to poem 77 on the issue of dating. Cf. poem 31, ll. 1-4; poem 73, "The Cure" (for the remedy that works); and Philip Ayres's derivation "Ever Present," number 20 in *Emblems of Love* (in Saintsbury 2:359). The remedies in Cowley's inventory here may be amplified by a reading of Burton, *Anatomy*, 3.2.5.1 and the following subsections.

    3. *Receipts of Business*. Cf. poem 58, ll. 1, 24, 25, and notes.

    20. *a Clinch*. Grosart glosses this "clench, supposed unanswerable reply" (*Works* 1:239). Cowley probably means the term as a play on words or pun or quibble (*OED*, s.v. "Clench," 4; "Clinch," 6). Herein lies the expression "to rise above a clinch."

Poem 79. "Honor." In the later seventeenth century this poem was probably better known than any other from *The Mistress*. It was performed in Pietro Reggio's setting before 1680 and thereafter became even more popular in the setting by Henry Purcell. See Textual Notes, p. 203; the settings on pp. 537 and 543; and music notes, p. 635. Cf. Rochester, "Womans Honor" (*Poems*, 14).

    9-12. *Bold Honor . . . this Phantome*. Cf. Carew, "A Rapture," ll. 3-4, 12: "The giant, Honour, that keeps cowards out, / Is but a masquer . . . He is but form, and only frights in show."

    20. *By the Nights obscurity*. Cf. poem 49, "Beauty," ll. 10-19, on Beauty enjoyed at night.

Poem 80. "The Innocent Ill." See headnote to poem 77 on the issue of dating. "The Innocent Ill," generally comparable to poem 7, "Not Fair," is a variation on the antiplatonic topic differently developed in poems 8 and 13. The case is made in poem 80 by way of a string of increasingly terse paradoxes. The first requires an entire stanza. By stanza 4, the paradoxes come at the rate of one or two in a line. Crashaw, as in his "A Hymn of the Nativity" and "The Weeper," is the master of this style; Cowley is undoubtedly working from Crashaw's example here.

    5. *Yet such a sweetness, such a grace*. There is a Jonsonian ring to this line. Cf. the song "Still to be neat," from *The Silent Woman* 1.1: "Though arts hid causes are not found, / All is not sweet, all is not sound. / Give me a looke, give me a face, / That makes simplicitie a grace."

    11. *thou a Tempter worse than Satan art*. Thus the initial paradox is fully expressed. Cf. Donne, *Problem* 7, "Why hath the common opinion afforded woemen Soules?", ll. 26-27: "wee have given woemen soules, onely to make them capable of damnation" (*Paradoxes and Problems*, 28-29).

    18-19. The lines represent Cowley's glib wit at its best. Compare his argument that hope sponsors fantasies of fulfillment, so that none, when wed, can possibly be virgin: "The *Joys* which we *entire* should wed, / Come *deflowr'd Virgins* to our bed" (poem 42, "Against Hope," ll. 15-16).

24. *a Flies Death's a wound to thee.* Cf. Carew, "A Fly that Flew into My Mistress's Eye," which is a variation on Donne's "The Flea." The subject held particular appeal to Lovelace. Cf. "A Fly caught in a Cobweb," "A Fly about a Glasse of Burnt Claret," and "Against the Love of Great Ones," ll. 62-65.

30. *Principal and Instrument.* The terms are meant in their legal sense.

32-33. *treble office.* The lines echo Donne's "three sinnes in killing three" ("The Flea," l. 18), perhaps by way of Carew's "Funeral flame, tomb, obsequy" ("A Fly that Flew into My Mistress's Eye," l. 20).

39. *chaste committer of a Rape.* Cf. Donne, holy sonnet 14, l. 14: "Nor ever chast, except you ravish mee."

44. *the Destroying Angels.* Cf. poem 2, l. 7 and note.

Poem 81. "DIALOGUE, After Enjoyment." See headnote to poem 77 on the issue of dating. A classical precedent for the amorous dialogue, distinguished from other dialogue forms, is Horace's *Odes* 3.9, spoken between Horace and Lydia. There are many permutations, such as the introduction of an arbiter and a chorus in Jonson's "A Song" (*Underwood*, poem 36). Cf. Habington's dialogues between Araphill and Castara (*Poems*, 25 and 69); Sidney Godolphin's "A Dialogue between a Lover and his Mistress" (in Saintsbury 2:260); Thomas Randolph's "A Dialogue" between Thirsis and Lalage (*Works* 2:583); and the four dialogue poems in Thomas Jordan's *Poeticall Varieties* (12, 17, 28, and 33). Jordan features Castadorus and Arabella in bed; Icarus and the surprised Phillida; Fidelius and his silent mistress, Flora (necessarily using the "echo" form); and Adversus vs. the Lady Contra. Dialogues between pastoral lovers, such as Carew's "A Pastoral Dialogue" (*Poems*, 45) and many others, establish a link between the urbane, Horatian dialogue and pastoral eclogues.

Alastair Fowler sees thematic ambiguity in this poem's delicately formed spatial arrangement. "The girl, who feels conquered while seeming victorious to her lover, is given the central speech [stanza 5]—but uses it to regret what she thinks of as submission. As for her conqueror, he follows after the defeated triumphator, bound, in the position of a captive spared. We are left . . . uncertain how to apportion victory and defeat" (*Triumphal Forms*, 75). Fowler's reading must have included "A Dialogue betwixt Adversus and his Mistresse the Lady Contra," wherein Thomas Jordan's Lady Contra says: "Is this your stories end? is your game don? / Where be your losing winners? who hath won?" (*Poeticall Varieties*, 29).

The "turn" at the end of poem 81 follows Horace *Odes* 3.9. Cf. the conclusion of Thomas Randolph's "A Pastoral Courtship," where Phyllis's "smoth'red smile" and subsequent weeping turns the speaker, up to now presumably the victor, into Phyllis's anxiety-ridden follower (*Works* 2:611).

subtitle. Omitted in editions after F1. See notes to poem 14.

5-6. *Shame succeeds the short liv'd pleasure*. A standard argument in the "against fruition" poem. See headnote to poem 30.

23-24. *Tapers shut in ancient Urns*. Cf. Donne, "Ecclogue. 1613. December 26 . . . Epithalamion," ll. 215-16: "Now, as in Tullias tombe, one lampe burnt cleare, / Unchang'd for fifteene hundred yeare" (*Works* 1:140). Grierson notes the "ridiculous story" associated with the tomb of Tullia, who he understands to be Cicero's daughter. When the tomb was opened, some fifteen hundred years after her death, the woman's body instantly turned to ashes and a lamp that had burned in her tomb for centuries suddenly went out. Browne entertains the curiosity in *Pseudodoxia Epidemica* 3.21, where he is considering whether air is required as a "nutriment" to maintain fires: ". . . that which substantially maintaineth the fire, is the combustible matter in the kindled body. . . . Why some lamps included in those bodies have burned many hundred years, as that discovered in the Sepulchre of Tullia, the sister of Cicero, and that of Olibius many years after, near Padua, because whatever was their matter, either a preparation of gold, or Naptha, the duration proceeded from the purity of their oyl which yielded no fuliginous exhalations to suffocate the fire; For if air had nourished the flame, it had not continued many minutes, for it would have been spent and wasted by the fire" (*Works* 2:229-30). In *Hydriotaphia*, chap. 2, Browne writes of the lamps found in Roman urns, placed therein along with coins, bottles of liquor, "and other appurtences of affectionate superstition . . . as sacred unto the *Manes* [shades of the dead], passionate expressions of their surviving friends." In chap. 5, the Roman lamps are found comparable to the "light in ashes" of the Jews, who placed a lighted wax candle in a pot of ashes, in the sepulchre (Browne, *Works* 1:143, 149). Needless to say, none of these lamps was found to be still burning. Cf. Carew, "Song. Eternitie of love protested," ll. 15-16 (*Poems*, 24), and Davenant, *Gondibert*, 3.7, lines 9-12.

27-30. *Roman pride . . . they through the streets their Captive lead enchain'd*. Cf. poem 14, "The vain Love," ll. 19-25, and poem 63, "Impossibilities," ll. 1-5 for other uses of the figure. See poem 26, l. 35 and note for Ovid's precedent. Cowley frequently uses chains in a more figurative sense.

Poem 82. "Verses lost upon a Wager."

25. *So daz'eling bright, yet so transparent clear*. This is a reworking of, or perhaps the original version of poem 12, ll. 1-2. See also poem 10, ll. 7-8.

21-24. *Angels . . . When they descend to humane view*. Cf. Donne, "Aire and Angels," l. 23: "Then as an Angell. . . ." For the kind of body assumed by angels, Grierson cites Saint Thomas Aquinas *Summa Theologiae* 1.51.2, who offers the conclusion "Et sic Angeli assumunt corpore ex aere." Grierson gives further testimony from Plotinus, Apuleius, Dante, Tasso, Fairfax, Nashe (from *Pierce Penniless*), and Milton. See Donne, *Poems* 2:21-22.

29-30. *thy shape naked like Truth*. Cf. poem 10, "Clad all in White," ll. 3-4. The comparison is a longstanding commonplace. Cf. John Dunton's defense of nakedness in *The Ladies Dictionary*, 314-18.

39. *publique vent*. Public expression or utterance, as *OED*, s.v. "Vent," *sb* 1.3b—but punning on the sense of 1.4b: to put coins into circulation.

Poem 83. "Bathing in the River." See headnote to poem 77 on the issue of dating. One classical source for poems on women bathing is the story of Actaeon and Diana (Ovid *Metamorphoses* 2). Thomas Randolph alludes to it in the whimsical "On Six Maids bathing themselves in a River" (*Works* 2:643). Another popular Nereid-lover story was Ovid's (also Theocritus's) Acis, Galatea, and Polyphemus the cyclops (*Metamorphoses* 13). This may have been the point of departure for Gongora's "Oh claro honor del liquido elemento," translated by Fanshawe as "A River" (*Shorter Poems*, 34), a text comparable to Carew's "To My Mistress Sitting by a River's Side: An Eddy" (*Poems*, 14). See also Lovelace's more localized "Lucasta, taking the waters at Tunbridge," and "Lucasta at Bath" (*Poems*, 53 and 132). The subject was so frequently treated that J[ohn] H[arington] felt compelled to make the subtle distinction in his title "The Author's first Dream of Flostella, not seen Bathing, but as he rode on Hunting" (*The History of Polindor and Flostella*, 80).

1-4. *The fish around her crowded*. See the figure in ll. 1-4 of Spenser's *Amoretti*, 52, and its development as the suitor-fish "take pleasure in her cruell play." Cf. Donne, "The Baite," ll. 9-11: "When thou wilt swimme in that live bath, / Each fish, which every channell hath, / Will amorously to thee swimme, / Gladder to catch thee, then thou him." The display of obsequious plants (cf. poem 4) here becomes a display of devoutly obsequious fish who can easily be taken since they are willing sacrifices to the mistress. There are many treatments of this. Cf. Waller, "Upon a Lady's Fishing With an Angle," ll. 17-20: "See how they crowd and thronging wait / Greedy to catch the proffered bait . . ." (*Poems*, 244).

2. *the false light that treach'erous Fishers shew*. Cf. Walton, *Complete Angler* (wherein a version of Donne's "The Baite" is printed), chap. 2, on fishing ethics.

10-11. *Gold commit / To Ghosts that have no use of it*. Cf. poem 81, ll. 23-24 and note on vain burial practices. Browne explains that the coins found in funeral urns helped the archaeologists date their discoveries.

15-16. *The amo'rous Waves . . . new am'orous waves*. Cf. poem 35, "Called Inconstant," ll. 7-10 for the same figure in a different context. See also poem 47, "The Injoyment," stanzas 1 and 2. The metamorphosis of pursuing and ensuing lovers to hours, and then to waves, appears in one of Ovid's finest passages, *Metamorphoses* 15.181-84.

> . . . sed ut unda inpellitur unda urgueturque eadem veniens urguetque priorem, tempora sic fugiunt pariter pariterque sequuntur et nova sunt sempter . . .
>
> [. . . like water, wave on wave, pursued, pursuing, forever fugitive, forever new] Rolfe Humphries's translation.

22, 29, 36. *Kiss her . . . Tell her . . . Tell her*. The progression of phrases is reminiscent of Petrarch's *Rime* 208: "Basciale 'l piede o la man bella et biance; / dille (e 'l basciar sie 'n vece di parole): 'Lo spirto e pronto, ma la carne e stanca'" [Kiss her foot or her lovely white hand; tell her (let your kiss be heard as words): The spirit is ready, but the flesh is weak].

28. *rig'orous Winter binds you up with Frost*. Cf. poem 46, "Coldness," ll. 3-4, for a different use of the figure: "So in *warm Seasons Love* does loosely flow, / *Frost* onely can it hold."

42. *she . . . shuts and seals up the spring*. Alluding to the Song of Solomon 4:12: "A garden inclosed is my sister, my spouse; a spring shut up, a fountain sealed."

Poem 84. "Love given over." This serves as the final poem in O1-2, as well as F1 and subsequent editions. "The Motto," concluding the volumes O1 and O2, is not printed as part of *The Mistress* but as a substitute for the author's portrait.

6. *Three of thy lustiest and thy freshest years*. See poem 6, "Inconstancy," l. 1 and note.

8-10. *helpless Ships. . . burnt in Love . . . drown'd in Tears*. Cf. Donne's epigram "A burnt ship": "So all were lost, which in the ship were found, / They in the sea being burnt, they in the burnt ship drown'd" (*Poems* 1:75).

17. *home to 'his breast retire*. Cf. poem 36, "The Welcome."

30. *not onely Sack't, but quite burnt down the Town*. Cf. poem 29, l. 4 and note, on Virgil's hero, facing the burning city of Troy.

The Musical Settings

Editorial Principles

Settings in this edition are close to diplomatic transcriptions, with a minimum of editorial emendations and with a limited number of editorial figured-bass symbols to assist performers. Principles for editing the musical settings and song texts are generally consistent with those for editing the literary text of *The Mistress*. Our aim is to represent the copy text in a clearly legible form, with emendations of errors and corruptions that may appear in the original copy. This entails the reproduction of some features that appear archaic if judged by modern standards. For instance, accidentals repeated within a bar at times appear redundant, against the convention of sustaining an accidental on any given note throughout the bar. Multiple or redundant accidentals, where they appear in copy texts, are reproduced in this edition. Accidentals in the figured-bass are printed to the left of the numbers, as they are normally in the copy texts. Editorial practices listed below account for all instances where the substance or appearance of the copy texts has been changed.

Copy Text

For most settings, the copy text is the first printing or the sole surviving manuscript known to us. For settings with multiple manuscript and/or printed sources, the copy text is the one showing strongest evidence of representing the composer's original manuscript and the composer's intentions regarding accidentals and ornamentation.

Reproduction of the Copy Text

Copy texts for the musical settings include autograph manuscripts, manuscript copies, hand-engraved printed settings, settings printed from woodblocks, and typeset printings. There is little consistency in calligraphic and typographic conventions among these various mediums. There are also frequent inconsistencies within a medium or within a single setting. In order to achieve an economical and relatively consistent form for reprinting, the following features have been standardized and introduced as silent emendations of the copy texts.

1. Clef signs for treble and bass are made uniform in the style of the present edition.

2. Time signatures for common time and *alla breve* are made uniform as C and ¢.

3. Key signatures are represented by uniform sharp and flat signs shown on lines or spaces of both staffs.

4. Rests are represented by uniform modern symbols and are presented economically. For example, a series of two quarter rests is represented by a half rest.

5. Notes carried across a bar line are represented on both sides of the line with a tie between, as is most characteristic in the copy texts. Two other seventeenth-century conventions—drawing a note on top of the bar line; placing the tied note to the left and a dot to the right of the bar line—are thus represented by the standard tie.

6. Square notes become round notes.

7. Straight braces are introduced in the notation in place of wavy braces and, wherever appropriate, in place of a series of flags. The various flag configurations in the copy texts are normalized and represented by a standard flag.

8. Bar lines, notes within a bar, along with words of the song text within the bar, are vertically aligned. Where the textual underlay is incompatible with notes in the vocal score and there is no obvious error in the vocal score, syllables in the song text have been elided to provide compatibility. Such infrequent instances are recorded in the notes.

9. Performance-related signs such as the fermata, trill, and repeat are standardized and represented as follows: the fermata as a dot hooded by a curved line; the trill as "*tr*"; the repeat as the "D.S." sign. First and second endings are normalized and identified by number. If such normalization involves any substantive change in notation, the matter is explained in the Textual Notes.

10. Custodes, appearing at the end of a line on the manuscript or printed page to indicate the pitch of the first note on the following line, are not represented in this edition. If a change in the key and/or time signature occurs at the beginning of a system in the present edition, the change is forecasted at the end of the preceding system.

11. Ties that are solely accidents of the printed or manuscript page, where the measure is interrupted at the right margin and completed at the left of the next system, are omitted. The note appears as the total value of the two segments.

12. Song titles and the typography of the song texts are made uniform in the style of this edition.

13. The composer, the copy text, and the literary text are identified under the title of each setting.

14. Bar numbers are shown in boxes at the beginning of each system after the first.

Editorial Principles

The following editorial emendations in the scores are indicated by way of brackets:

1. Authoritative substantive variants are bracketed and explained in the Textual Notes.
2. Nonauthorial substantive emendations are rarely introduced, only where the copy text clearly shows an error. These emendations are explained in the Textual Notes.
3. Accidentals in the scores at times appear in brackets:
    (a) as a sign that a note which has been changed in the previous measure is now back to its natural state;
    (b) as an editorial correction (these are explained in the Notes);
    (c) or, in places where the natural sign in the present text replaces the old system of using the sharp to cancel a flat and a flat to cancel a sharp.
4. Where normalization of a time signature involves the significant alteration of a sign, as is often the case in designations of triple time, the time signature is bracketed and the original sign is noted.

The figured bass is treated according to the following principles and practices:

1. All figures appearing in the copy texts are represented below the bass score, in the typographic style of this edition, with accidentals to the left of numbers. Inverted figures are silently righted.
2. Authoritative variants to the figured bass are introduced as bracketed figures and are included in the Notes.
3. Nonauthoritative emendations to the figures are introduced only in cases where the copy text is probably in error. These instances are explained in the Notes.
4. Many of the basses show a scarcity of figures though the melodic and bass lines together show the need for chord changes, especially where inversions of triads and seventh chords are implied. There are also a number of examples of an accidental in the vocal line that is not indicated in the bass, especially relating to the third of a chord. The third inversion of the seventh chord is often used and is not identified in the figured bass. Likewise the first inversion triad that follows a third inversion triad is usually not represented. Many 4-3 suspensions within cadence figures are missing. To account for these inconsistencies, this edition, in one respect, departs from the singular intention of representing a corrected copy text. Where the copy text lacks bass figures, these are supplied by the editor in instances where they may be helpful to a reader interested in harmonic structure or a performer interested in suggestions for realizing the bass. All bracketed figures that are not included in the Textual Notes appear in the text under the aegis of this courtesy.

308   THE MUSICAL SETTINGS

Editorial considerations and practices bearing particularly on Pietro Reggio's settings (*Songs*, 1680) are summarized below. These have to do with the figured bass, signatures for triple time, and stylized features appearing in the engraved scores. It should be noted that the great majority of Reggio's settings reflect features of the transition between modal scales and major/minor scales. His key signatures do not signal the tonality of the piece so much as accidentals in the score and the figures in the bass line do.

1. With the exception of Reggio's ground-bass "Honour," the settings in *Songs* show the figured bass. Numerical and accidental figures are drawn within the bass score, sometimes above the score, and—infrequently—below it (those appearing as penned additions are listed in the collations, pp. 561-62). The figures are usually clear, but when they appear within the score, crowded with the notation, combinations of accidental and numerical figures are at times ambiguous. It is not always clear if an accidental sharp or flat pertains to the third above the bass note or to the numerical figure. The graphic alignment of a ♯/6, for example, could indicate a sharped sixth or a sharped third plus a sixth. In instances of such ambiguity, this text portrays the most probable configuration and notes the alternative.

All numerical figures appearing in *Songs*, copy iv, are represented in this text. Accidentals used in *Songs* to indicate the pitch of the third degree above the bass note are here represented by the sharp, the flat, or a bracketed natural. Only the sharp and flat appear in *Songs*, and they serve multiple functions. For instance, the flat figure may literally represent a flatted third for the accompaniment. This usage is clearest when the vocal score itself shows the flatted third (e.g., "The Thief," bar 35, note 1). At other times, since his vocabulary for the figured bass includes no natural sign, Reggio uses the flat figure to signal a natural third in the accompaniment (e.g., "The Thief," bars 1, 6, 7, 18, 20). Instances where the pitch is to be rendered natural after having been altered, where Reggio seeks to cancel an accidental in the key signature, or where a note in the modal scale implicit in the composition is to be changed, are nearly always indicated by a flat figure in *Songs*. Such instances, recognizable when a literal interpretation of the accidental produces pitches wholly incompatible with the harmonies implied in the bass and treble scores, are represented here by a bracketed natural. The bracketed natural appears for no other reason in the figured bass of the present edition of Reggio's settings. This headnote therefore serves to explain all occurrences, and the matter is not treated in the Notes to individual musical settings.

2. For triple time in settings showing the equivalent of three quarter notes to a bar, the copy text for Reggio's songs uses the signature 3/4 (e.g., "Clad All in White," bar 1), C 3/4 (e.g., "The Injoyment,"), 3 (e.g., "The Heart fled again," bar 1), or ₵ 3 (e.g., "Honour," bar 1). The 3s are sometimes

elongated; the C's appear in differing sizes and configurations. Some of this latter variety is likely the result of different copyists and/or engravers, but distinctions in meter may be suggested by the four variant signatures. Three-quarter-note triple time is normalized to 3/4 in this edition; those places where "C 3/4," "3" and "C 3" occur in the copy text are indicated by a bracketed 3/4 and the original signature is shown in the Textual Notes.

3. Reggio's *Songs*, printed from hand-engraved plates, displays a number of stylized calligraphic features in the song text and in the musical setting. These include embellished letters, clef signs, notes, multiple bar lines and "Finis" at the end of a setting, and verbal designations of stanzas ("The First Part," "The Second Part," and so on) drawn above the vocal score. More than one engraver was employed for *Songs*, and such stylized features are not consistently designed. They are not represented in this edition. Two engravers, whose work may be represented by "The Given Love" (*Songs* 1:10) and "Councel [II]" (*Songs* 1:38) consistently draw double dots alongside double-bar divisions, at times where a "D.S." is shown at the same place. A third engraver, whose work may be represented by "The Diet of Cowley" (*Songs* 2:7), represents double bars with no dots. This feature, or its absence, would appear to follow from the engraver's practice. Compare the example of Francis Tregian, whose double dots may well be ornamental, calligraphic features (H. Ferguson, "Repeats and Final Bars in the Fitzwilliam Virginal Book," 345-50). Alternatively, Reggio may have intended that all sections so distinguished be repeated—in which case his intent is inconsistently observed by the engravers and pen corrections do not remedy the inconsistency. In this edition the double dots are regarded as calligraphic idiosyncrasies and omitted in the settings. Their occurrences in the copy text are indicated in the Notes.

4. Closure in *Songs* appears also to have been affected by engravers' practice. Where there is room in the score, the final bar of a song is most often extended by a calligraphic flourish (e.g., "Honour," *Songs* 1:3) or a tie doubling the final note value (e.g., "The Distance," *Songs* 1:9). Elsewhere, especially where the engraver must squeeze bars into a shorter space to finish a setting on a single plate (e.g., "Clad All in White," *Songs* 1:7), there is either no closural extension or, if some small space permits, the flourish is preferred to a doubled end-note. In this edition, such closural bars are normalized as the ordinary value of the final note is represented. The notes indicate where the copy text extends the final bar.

This final headnote refers to editorial treatment of the Purcell settings. "(The Concealment)," for which we follow RM20, is the only Purcell copy text to show forefalls and backfalls. These appear only in the first part of the setting—bars 5, 7, 10, and 25/26. Since the manuscript is only partially ornamented, the decorated notes are out of character with the rest of the setting. Furthermore, the backfalls and forefalls appear anomalous in context of the other Purcell copy texts used for this edition. The editor has elected to print "(The Concealment)" without the decorations. This matter is further discussed in notes to "(The Concealment)." Two anomalous trills appearing in the RM20 copy of "The Rich Rivall" (bars 33 and 45) are likewise not represented in this edition.

Abbreviations

In addition to the abbreviations listed for the Notes to the literary texts (p. 131), the following appear in Notes to the musical settings.

t. sig	time signature
k. sig.	key signature
fig.	numbers and/or accidentals in the figured bass
|	bar line
||	double bar line
. . .	Dots appearing beneath letters in title page descriptions indicate the appearance of red ink in the original.

The Composers

Where the *New Grove Dictionary*, the *Biographical Dictionary of Old English Music*, or the *Dictionary of National Biography* cites the composer, these references are indicated [*NGD, BD, DNB*] and information offered here is centered on details that relate to song settings of Cowley's texts and to other composers who set texts from *The Mistress*.

Michael Banfield [Banfeild] (fl. 1694). We have discovered nothing about this composer other than the setting of Cowley's "Counsel" attributed to him in the fifth book of *Comes Amoris* (1694). Banfield's setting is an adaptation of Pietro Reggio's treatment of the same song text, printed in *Songs* (1680) and reissued in 1692.

John Barrett (c. 1676–1719). See *NGD, BD*. Barrett was a child chorister in the Chapel Royal under John Blow, about whom he wrote: "[all that] I hold, is only held from you" (*Amphion Anglicus*, sig. a2^v, p. iv). Barrett's exit as child of the Chapel Royal is documented by a livery allowance dated 8 December 1691 (*The King's Musick*, 407). He then served as organist for St. Mary at Hill and music master to the boys at Christ's Hospital. Barrett is notable as a composer of theater music, both vocal and instrumental, for productions during the first two decades of the eighteenth century. Several of his songs appear in Gay's *Beggar's Opera* (1728).

John Blow (1649–1708). See *NGD, BD, DNB*. Blow's biography and musical accomplishments are well known. His composition of secular music, highlighted by the masque for the entertainment of King Charles II, *Venus and Adonis*, is centered in the 1680s; songs appear in printed collections of John and Henry Playford. Blow was contemporary with John Blundeville and William Turner in the Chapel Royal, and he encountered James Hart and William Hall no later than 1671, when Hall took on a position as musician of the Chapel and Hart began performing as a singer. Blow was the teacher of Henry Purcell, Francis Pigott, and John Barrett. Beginning in 1680, Robert King was at least a working acquaintance of Blow's; both participated in activities of the king's private music.

John Blundeville [Blundivile] (fl. 1670s–). *The King's Musick* (178–79) and *Records of English Court Music* (1:63) note a 17 May 1665 warrant authorizing master Henry Cooke the amount of £30 to provide for John Blundeville, late child of the Chapel Royal. John Blow is designated "late child" in the same warrant, and Cooke is granted £30 for him as well. An unspecified amount is also granted for Blow's and Blundeville's clothing. The third late child noted in the warrant in Pelham Humfrey; his grant is £40, with no clothing allowance. One may presume that Blundeville's voice changed, thus accounting for his release, though Zimmerman suggests that the plague of 1665 may have been cause to release boys from active duties (Franklin Zimmerman, *Purcell: His Life and Times*, 17). Blundeville's compositions do not appear in print. Manuscript copies are in British Library Add. MSS 29397 (c. 1682–90) and, notably, Folger W.b.515 (c. 1680), where fourteen settings attributed to Blundeville appear along with compositions by Locke, Blow, Humfrey, Hall, Banister, Turner, with an early setting of Cowley's "Honor" by Henry Purcell. Eitner (*Biographisch-Bibliographisches*, 73) records that "John Blundevill" is listed in an unnamed catalogue on Ely Cathedral as "Layclerk," at Ely, in 1669.

Francis Forcer (c. 1650–1704). See *NGD*. Forcer is noted for contributing songs to shows by Behn, Shadwell, and Otway during the latter years of the 1670s. His songs appear in the second book of John Playford's *Choice Ayres and Songs* (1679), the second and third books of Henry Playford's *The Theatre of Music* (1685, 1686), the third, fourth, and fifth books of Henry Playford's *The Banquet of Musick* (1689–91), and elsewhere.

William Hall (d. 1700). See *NGD, BD*. "Mr. Hall" is listed as a Chapel musician-in-waiting (violin) as of 4 November 1671 (*The King's Musick*, 237), hence his affiliation with Blow, Hart, Turner, and the younger Henry Purcell. Association with these men continues through the latter years of the seventeenth century as they performed with the King's Music in various productions including the 1674 Whitehall masque *Calisto*, royal progresses, and the coronation of William and Mary in April 1689. By this year Francis Pigott had become a child of the Chapel. Robert King had become an associate by 1680, though Hall may have known him earlier, since both published airs for string trio in *Tripla Concordia* (1676). Hall was primarily a performer. Just two vocal settings attributed to him survive in manuscript, one of these being Cowley's "Looking on, and discoursing with his Mistress." Compositions by Blow, Turner, and Purcell appear in the same collection as Hall's Cowley setting. This manuscript miscellany, British Library Add. MSS 22100, is dated 1681/2.

James Hart (1647–1718). See *NGD, BD*. On 4 November 1671, Hart is listed as a gentleman of the Chapel in attendance at Windsor, along with Henry Cooke, Pelham Humfrey, William Turner, and the organist John Blow (*The King's Musick*, 236). Hart performed as a bass singer, composed songs for the theater, and contributed numerous songs to Playford publications from the 1670s to the 1690s. The setting of Cowley's "The Despair" attributed to him, however, was not published. Ian Spink gives Hart relatively high marks as a composer. See *English Song*, 160–61, 172–73.

Robert King (d. 1728). See *NGD, BD*. Robert King's 1680 appointment as violinist to the Private Music of Charles II marks his association with Blow, Turner, Hall, Hart, Purcell, and others connected with the King's Music. He was made composer-in-ordinary to William and Mary in 1689 and then granted a royal license to set up a consort of music. King's Consort, for which the director controlled all details from concert schedules to admission prices, presented public concerts in the Covent Garden area. In 1700 King added the selling of music that had been published in Europe to his activities as performer, composer, and concert promoter. Before this, however, he had published his own two books of songs, the second of which (1695) contains his Cowley settings. King, a jack-of-many-trades in the music profession, contributed songs for the theater, and a large number of his songs found their way into Playford publications during the 1680s and early 1690s. Robert King continued to perform with the royal band until his death.

William King (1624–80). See *NGD, BD*. William King is remembered mainly for the music printed in *Poems of Mr. Cowley and Others*, which he published in 1668, shortly after Cowley's death. It is probable that King knew Cowley and that the book of songs was meant as a tribute to the poet. According to *BD* and *NGD*, William King arrived at Oxford as one of the musicians gathering round the court of Charles I. The court had removed to Oxford, before the first Civil War, in 1642. Cowley arrived at Oxford in 1643, having been evicted from Cambridge. King apparently stayed on at Oxford through the wars. He was at Magdalen College as of 18 October 1648, graduating 5 June 1649, and he was chaplain at that college from 1652–54. After that he was a fellow of All Souls, and in 1664 he became organist of New College. He could have met Cowley during the early 1640s or later on. Cowley left Oxford in 1644 or 1645 to attend Henry Jermyn and Queen Henrietta at Paris, but he was in and about Oxford during the later 1650s, receiving a medical degree in 1657. William King's father, George, who had been organist at Winchester Cathedral, is represented by a composition in *Poems*. A setting by "E.Y." is also published in the collection. *Poems* thus appears to be an intimate, personal publication.

Francis Pigott (c. 1665–1704). See *NGD, BD* (s.v. "Child, William"). Watkins Shaw's sketch in the *NGD* gives Pigott's approximate birth date without comment. *Records of English Court Music* (1:183) lists "Fran: Piggett" as a child of the Chapel as of 8 April 1679. He is designated "late Child of the Chapel" on 28 November 1683, but Dr. John Blow, Master of the Children of the Chapel, is warranted £30 for Pigott's continued maintenance on 5 March 1684. He began his career as an organist soon thereafter. By 1685 he had become organist at St. John's, Oxford, and he is listed as organist extraordinary of the Chapel Royal in 1695. During his early Chapel years, Pigott would have had acquaintance with Hall, Hart, Turner, and probably Purcell, in addition to his teacher John Blow. Pigott was a composer of songs and keyboard music. The setting of Cowley's "The Separation" is one of his few attributions in the multivolume *Banquet of Musick* (1688-92).

In his commentary to *The Diary of Samuel Pepys* (10:327), Richard Luckett distinguishes Francis Pigott the organist from an acquaintance of Pepys' by the same name who participated in after-dinner singing with Pepys (15 September and 1 December 1667) and who was a member of the Musick Society meeting in the Old Jury, London. The relation between the earlier Musick Society member and the later organist/composer, if there is any beyond the coincidence of their names, is not known.

Henry Purcell (1659-95). See *NGD, BD, DNB*, and Zimmerman's *Henry Purcell: His Life and Times*. Purcell began his musical career as a boy chorister in the Chapel Royal, where he remained until 1673—hence his association with many of the song writers in this listing. Purcell's serious interests in composition, taking shape in the early 1680s, were significantly influenced by Cowley's texts. Ian Spink designates this formative stage (roughly 1682-87) as Purcell's "Cowley period" (*English Song*, 209 and 215). By Zimmerman's count, sixteen Purcell settings of Cowley poems are extant. It is particularly noteworthy that Purcell's interest in Cowley corresponds with his development of affective or dramatic declamatory songs. This is the predominant literary style of *The Mistress*, and of all the poets Purcell worked from or with, he had none better than Cowley.

Pietro ("Pedro") Reggio (1632-85). See *NGD*. Additional biographical details are available in Gloria Rose's essay "Pietro Reggio—A Wandering Musician" and Richard Luckett's notes to *The Diary of Samuel Pepys*, 10:350. Reggio was baptized in Genoa. He later was employed as singer and lutenist by Queen Christiana at Stockholm (1652-53) and subsequently worked in Europe. He had arrived in London by 1664. It is thus possible that Reggio met Cowley in the London area sometime before the poet's death in 1667. Pepys, with his characteristic ambivalence about musical professionals, notes that he heard "one slovenly and ugly fellow, Seignor Pedro, who sings Italian songs to the Theorbo most neatly" (22 July 1664; *Diary* 5:217). Reggio apparently made his living in London as a performer and tutor. His reputation as a composer rests importantly on the volume *Songs* published in 1680, a collection chiefly of Cowley settings that recognizes and to a degree anticipates an increased interest in Cowley's poetry at this time (*The Puritans Lecture* reappeared in 1675, 1678, and 1680; a new edition of collected early poems appeared in 1681 following three editions—the sixth and seventh in folio, the first in duodecimo—of the collected later *Works* in 1680 and 1681; *The Puritan and the Papist* was reissued in 1682). The "Preface" to *Songs* indicates Reggio's association with Oxford and with the music master John Jenkins. Ian Spink regards Reggio as the most influential of the immigrant Italian musicians on English composers of the Restoration era (*English Song*, 205). His settings of "Arise Ye Subterranean Winds" (for Shadwell's adaptation of *The Tempest*, 1674) and Cowley's "Honor" and "Weeping" are bases for Purcell's "deliberate improvements," in Zimmerman's estimation. The issue of Reggio's being a native Italian and hence relatively insensitive to the English language, raised by John Playford in his preface (2 November 1680) to the third book of *Choice Ayres and Songs*, is discussed by Zimmerman (*Purcell: His Life and Times*, 73). Counteropinions are offered by Thomas Shadwell (*Songs*, fol. 3^v) and Thomas Flatman (*Songs*, fol. 4^v), among others. One should also consider that Playford was asserting his nationalism in a year of popish-plot intrigues, and that as a publisher Playford was Reggio's commercial rival. Reggio died in London, 23 July 1685; the Burial Register of St. Giles in the Fields records that "Peter King" was interred there a day later.

William Turner (1651–1740). See *NGD, BD*. After serving as chorister at Christ Church, Oxford, and then the Chapel Royal, Turner was appointed a gentleman of the Chapel, singing countertenor (as of 14 April 1674). His connection with the Chapel continued for the rest of his long life. Turner's association with William King, at Oxford, and even with Cowley, is a possibility. He was trained by Captain Cooke and continued in the service of John Blow who, along with Blundeville and Humfrey, was about his age. Turner's association with Hall, Hart, and indirectly with Reggio, may be marked by his singing in Shadwell's *Tempest* (1674). He also sang in *Calisto*. Turner's association with Purcell would have begun when the younger Purcell joined the Chapel (before 1673). According to British Library Add. MSS 31447, fol. 94, Turner was one of the original singers for Purcell's welcome song "Sound the Trumpet" (1687). Pigott, Barrett, and Robert King would have been among his circle of associates. As a composer, Turner is mainly known for his sacred music, but his surviving secular compositions number over fifty.

Nicholas Wootton (d. 16 April 1700). According to John E. West (*Cathedral Organists*, s.v. "Canterbury"), Nicholas Wootton was admitted organist and lay-clerk at Canterbury Cathedral on 1 December 1692. Despite a summons to answer objections against him (April 1698) and alleged "misdemeanours" that apparently resulted in his dismissal from this musician's post, he was buried in the north aisle of the cathedral. Some of Wootton's compositions appear in Thomas Tudway's collection of services and anthems (British Library Harley MSS 7337-42). Robert Eitner notes that some of his compositions are held in the archives of Rochester Cathedral (*Biographisch-Bibliographisches Quellen-Lexicon* 2:301).

The Musical Settings of Poems from *The Mistress*

318   THE MUSICAL SETTINGS

The Thraldom, the Words by Mr. Cowley.

Settings of Poems from *The Mistress* 319

Settings of Poems from *The Mistress* 321

Settings of Poems from *The Mistress*

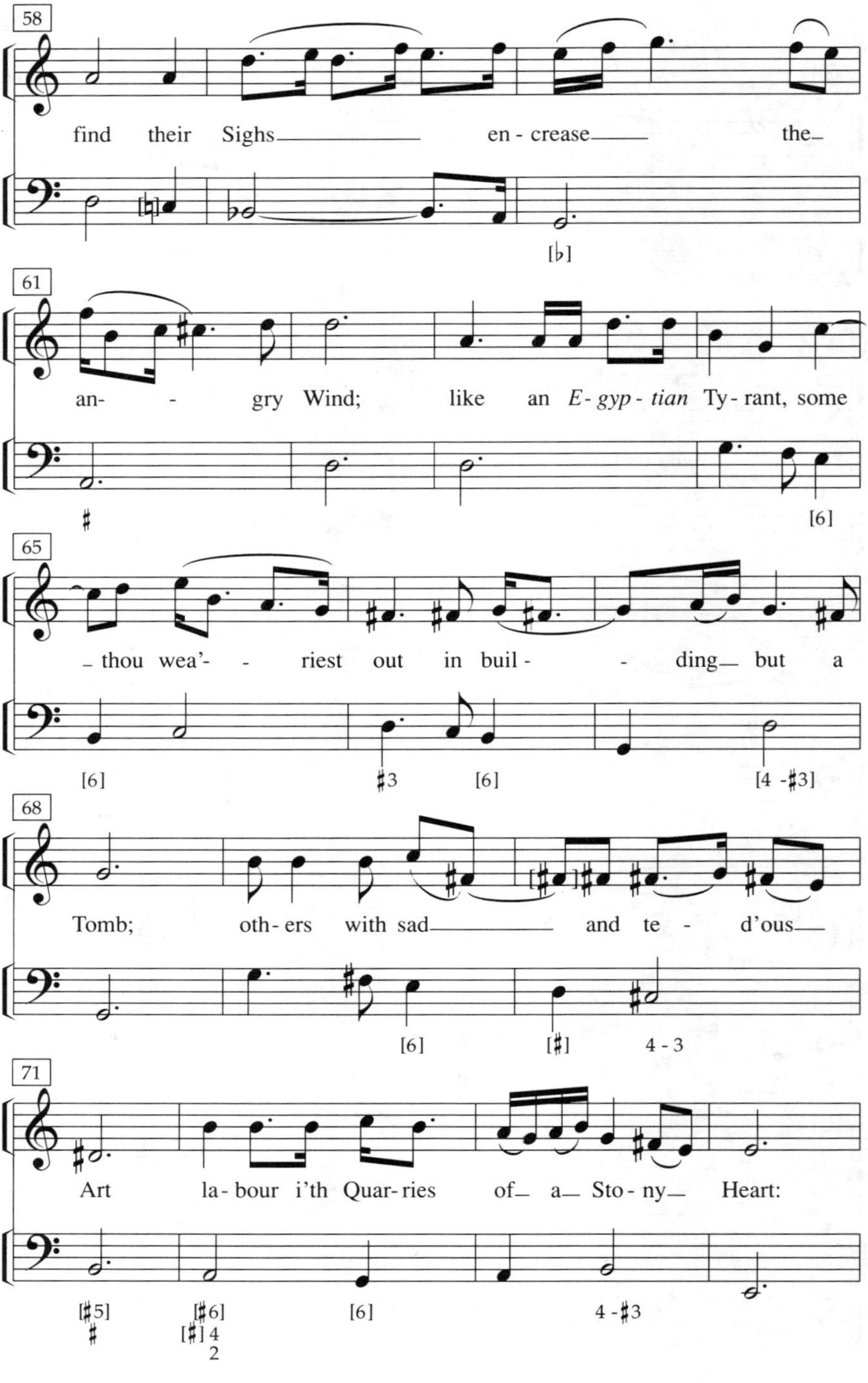
58
find their Sighs en - crease the
[♭]
61
an- - gry Wind; like an *E- gyp - tian* Ty- rant, some
♯ [6]
65
thou wea'- - riest out in buil - - ding but a
[6] ♯3 [6] [4 -♯3]
68
Tomb; oth- ers with sad and te - d'ous
[6] [♯] 4 - 3
71
Art la- bour i'th Quar- ries of a Sto - ny Heart:
[♯5] ♯ [♯6] [♯] 4 2 [6] 4 -♯3

Settings of Poems from *The Mistress* 325

The given LOVE.

Settings of Poems from *The Mistress*

The Given love.

Settings of Poems from *The Mistress* 329

330   THE MUSICAL SETTINGS

Settings of Poems from *The Mistress*   333

334 THE MUSICAL SETTINGS

The Change.

Songs (1680), I, p.16.
F1 poem 9.

Pietro Reggio

Settings of Poems from *The Mistress* 335

Clad In WHITE.

Poems (1668), p. 36.
Fl poem 10.

William King

Settings of Poems from *The Mistress*   337

Clad all in white.

Settings of Poems from *The Mistress*

Settings of Poems from *The Mistress*

Settings of Poems from *The Mistress*

My heart discovered.

346

Settings of Poems from *The Mistress*

Settings of Poems from *The Mistress*

The Soul.

Songs (1680), I, p. 22.
F1 poem 15.

Pietro Reggio

Settings of Poems from *The Mistress*

[*The Despair.*]

Folger *ms* W.b.515, p. 53.
F1 poem 18.

John Blundevile

Settings of Poems from *The Mistress* 355

356   THE MUSICAL SETTINGS

[*The Despair.*]

BL *ms* Add 19759, f. 41v.   James Hart
F1 poem 18.

Settings of Poems from *The Mistress* 357

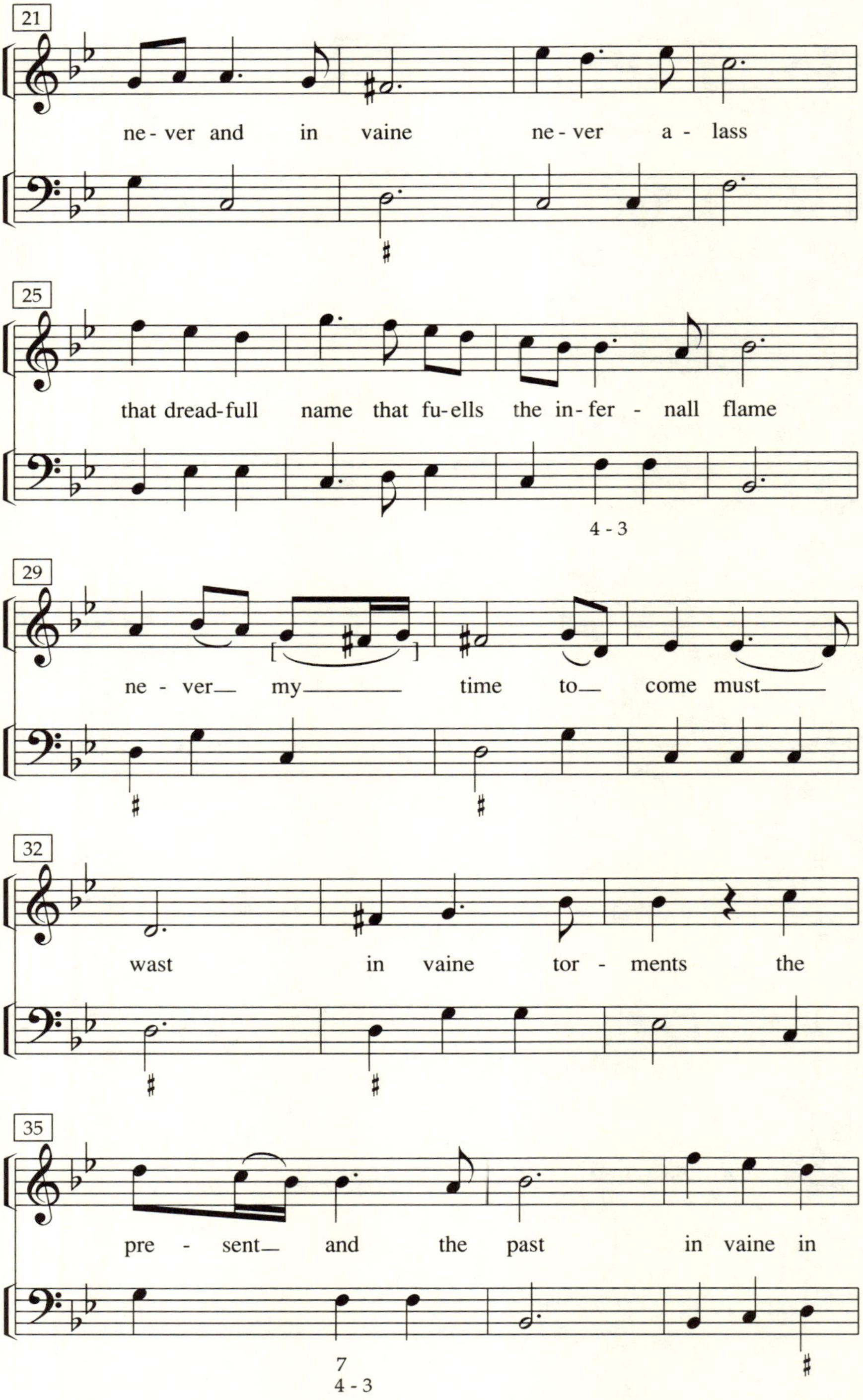
21
ne- ver and in vaine ne- ver a - lass
♯
25
that dread-full name that fu-ells the in- fer - nall flame
4 - 3
29
ne - ver my time to come must
♯ ♯
32
wast in vaine tor - ments the
♯ ♯
35
pre - sent and the past in vaine in
7
4 - 3
♯

Settings of Poems from *The Mistress*

360　　　　　　　　　THE MUSICAL SETTINGS

Settings of Poems from *The Mistress*   361

Settings of Poems from *The Mistress*

The Diet of Cowley.

Songs (1680), II, p. 7.
F1 poem 20.

Pietro Reggio

Settings of Poems from *The Mistress*

Settings of Poems from *The Mistress* 367

The Thief.

Songs (1680), I, p. 5.
F1 poem 21.

Pietro Reggio

Settings of Poems from *The Mistress*

Settings of Poems from *The Mistress*

All-over LOVE.

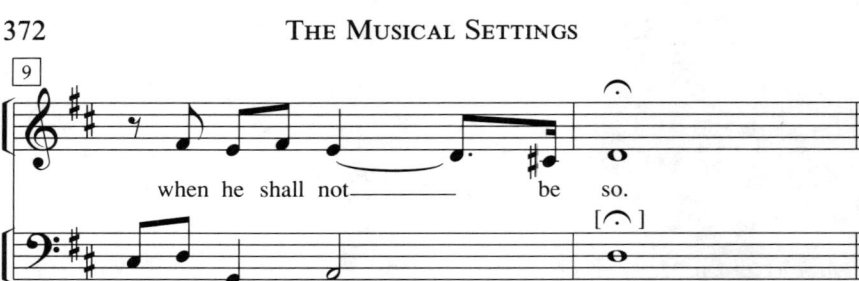

Settings of Poems from *The Mistress*

All-over Love.

Songs (1680), II, p. 14.
F1 poem 22.

Pietro Reggio

Settings of Poems from *The Mistress*

376   THE MUSICAL SETTINGS

The Bargain.

Settings of Poems from *The Mistress*   377

Settings of Poems from *The Mistress*

Counsel.

Settings of Poems from *The Mistress*

Settings of Poems from *The Mistress*

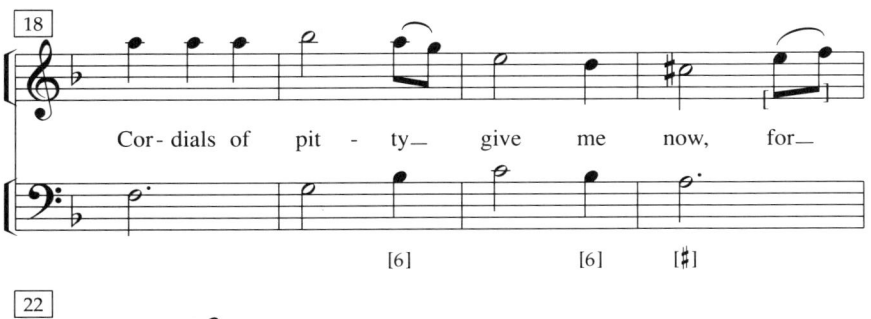
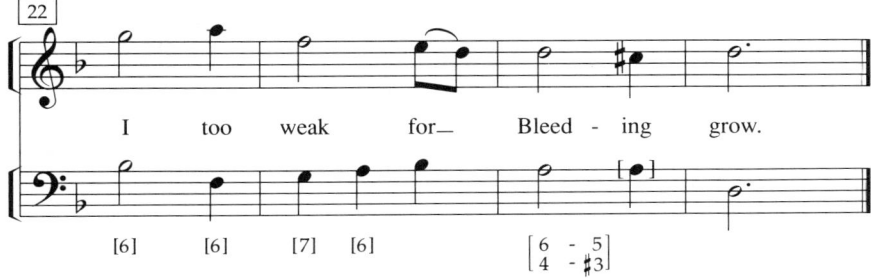

The Discovery.

Songs (1680), II, p. 16.
F1 poem 29.

Pietro Reggio

Settings of Poems from *The Mistress*

Settings of Poems from *The Mistress*

389

390 THE MUSICAL SETTINGS

A SONG: [*The Discovery.*]

Chetham's Library
Halliwell–Phillipps broadside 1929
F1 poem 29.

Nic: Wootton

Settings of Poems from *The Mistress* 391

Settings of Poems from *The Mistress*

LOVE Undiscovered.

Poems (1668), p. 26.
F1 poem 31.

William King

Settings of Poems from *The Mistress* 395

[*Love Undiscovered.*]

BL *ms* Add 19759, f. 26v.
F1 poem 31.

Anon.

396 THE MUSICAL SETTINGS

Settings of Poems from *The Mistress*

Settings of Poems from *The Mistress*

The Given HEART.

Settings of Poems from *The Mistress*

[*The Given Heart.*]

Thesaurus Musicus (1693), I, p. 24.
F1 poem 32.

Mr. John Barrett

Settings of Poems from *The Mistress* 403

The Heart fled again.

Songs (1680), I, p. 39.
F1 poem 37.

Pietro Reggio

Settings of Poems from *The Mistress*

[*The Heart fled again.*]

A Second Booke of Songs (c. 1695), p. 13.
F1 poem 37.

Robert King

Settings of Poems from *The Mistress* 407

408　THE MUSICAL SETTINGS

Settings of Poems from *The Mistress*

The Rich Rivall
out of Mr. Cowley.

BL *ms* RM20.h.8, ff. 174v-173v.
F1 poem 41.

Henry Purcell

Settings of Poems from *The Mistress* 413

Settings of Poems from *The Mistress* 415

Settings of Poems from *The Mistress* 417

*A Song on **Ingratitude**, Words by Mr. Cowley.*

The Theatre of Music (1687), IV, p. 66. Dr. [John] Blow
F1 poem 44.

418 THE MUSICAL SETTINGS

Settings of Poems from *The Mistress* 421

Settings of Poems from *The Mistress*

[Coldness.]

Settings of Poems from *The Mistress*

425

426 THE MUSICAL SETTINGS

The ENJOYMENT.

Poems (1668), p. 6.
F1 poem 47.

William King

Settings of Poems from *The Mistress* 427

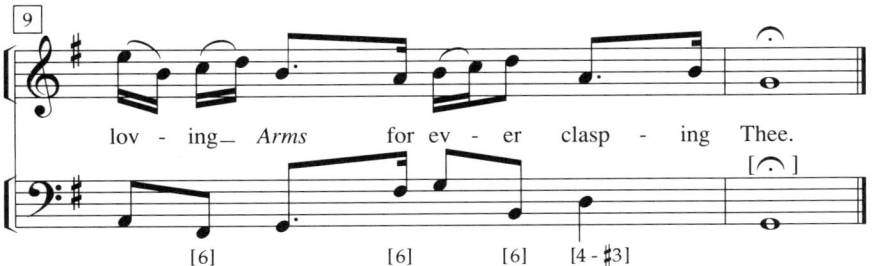

428 THE MUSICAL SETTINGS

[*The Injoyment.*]

Songs (1680), II, p. 9
F1 poem 47.

Pietro Reggio

Settings of Poems from *The Mistress* 429

Settings of Poems from *The Mistress* 431

Settings of Poems from *The Mistress*

The Picture.

Songs (1680), I, p. 30.
F1 poem 51.

Pietro Reggio

Settings of Poems from *The Mistress*

Settings of Poems from *The Mistress* 437

The CONCEALMENT.

Poems (1668), p. 1.
F1 poem 52.

William King

Settings of Poems from *The Mistress*

(The Concealment.)

Settings of Poems from *The Mistress*

Settings of Poems from *The Mistress*

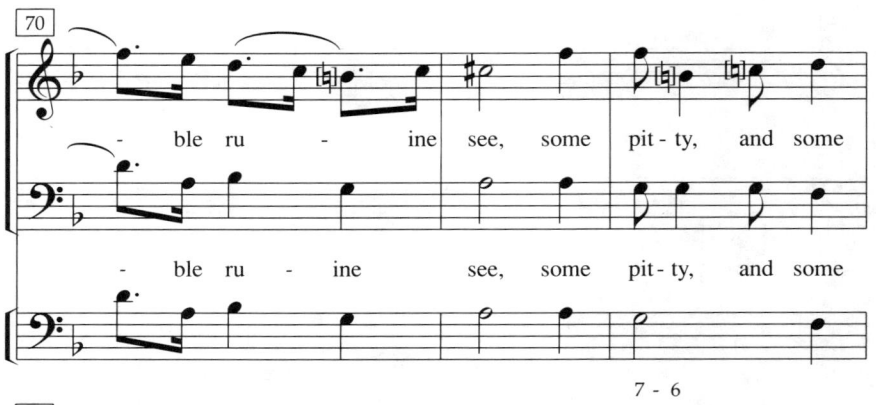
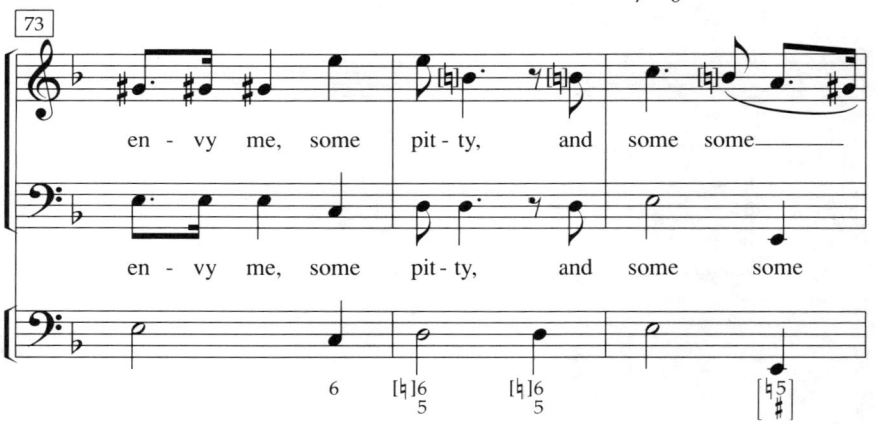
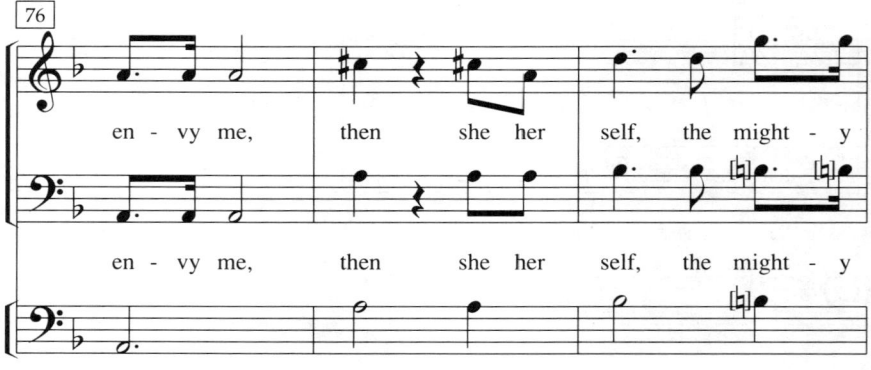

Settings of Poems from *The Mistress*

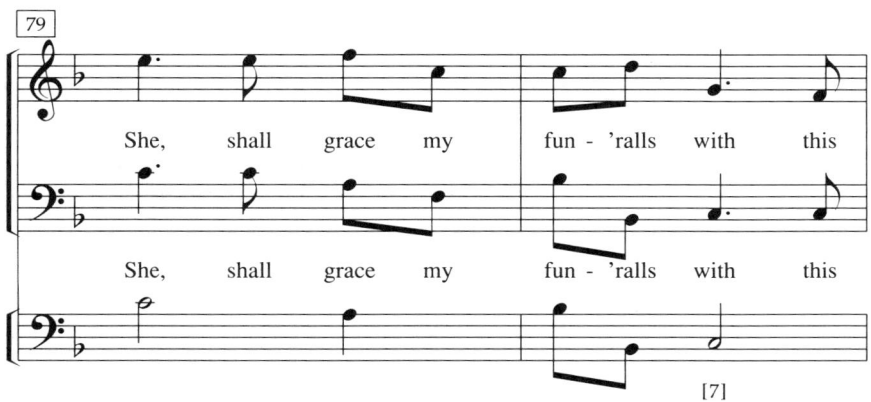
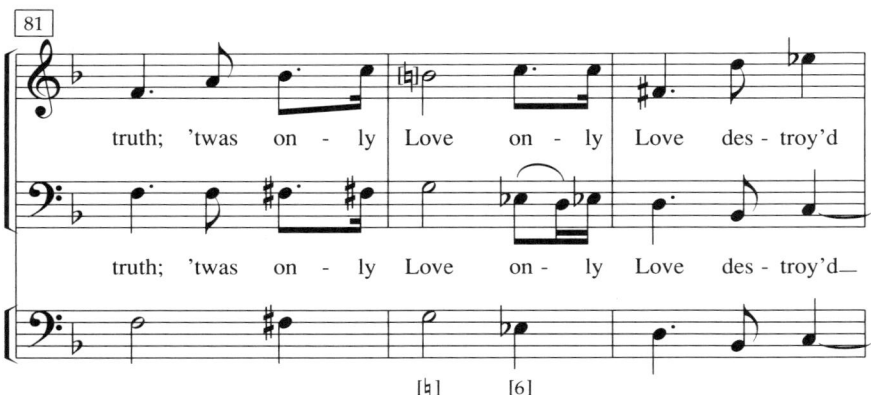
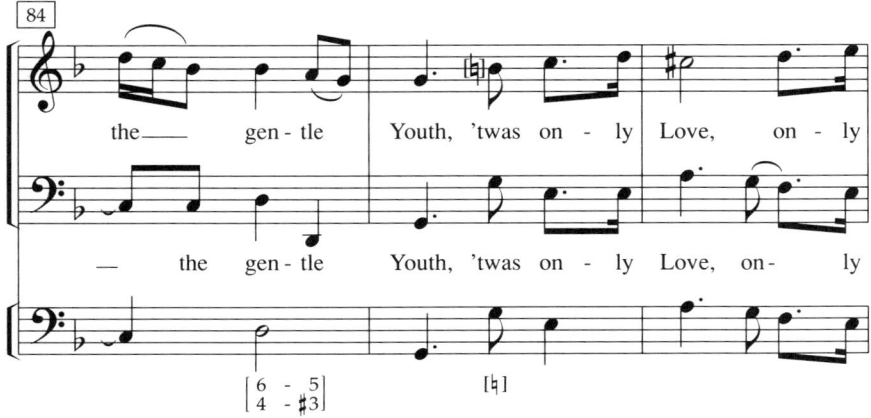

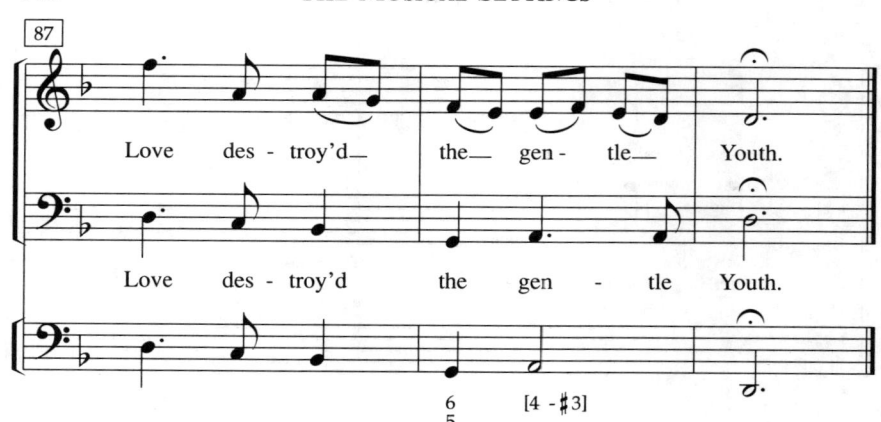

Settings of Poems from *The Mistress* 449

[*The Concealment.*]

A Second Booke of Songs (c. 1695), p. 21. Robert King
F1 poem 52.

Settings of Poems from *The Mistress* 451

Settings of Poems from *The Mistress*

Settings of Poems from *The Mistress*

The MONOPOLY.

Poems (1668), p. 48.
F1 poem 53.

William King

Settings of Poems from *The Mistress*

The DISTANCE.

The Distance.

Songs (1680), I, p. 8.
F1 poem 54.

Pietro Reggio

Settings of Poems from *The Mistress*

The Encrease.

Songs (1680), I, p. 32.
F1 poem 55.

Pietro Reggio

464 THE MUSICAL SETTINGS

Settings of Poems from *The Mistress*

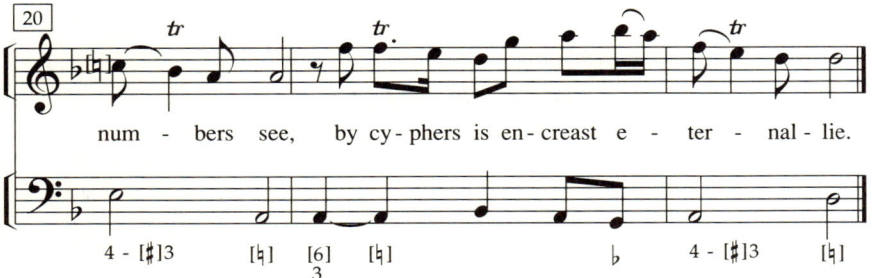

466 THE MUSICAL SETTINGS

LOVES VISIBILITY.

Poems (1668), p. 24.
F1 poem 56.

William King

Settings of Poems from *The Mistress*

Loves Visibility.

Songs (1680), I, p. 13.
F1 poem 56.

Pietro Reggio

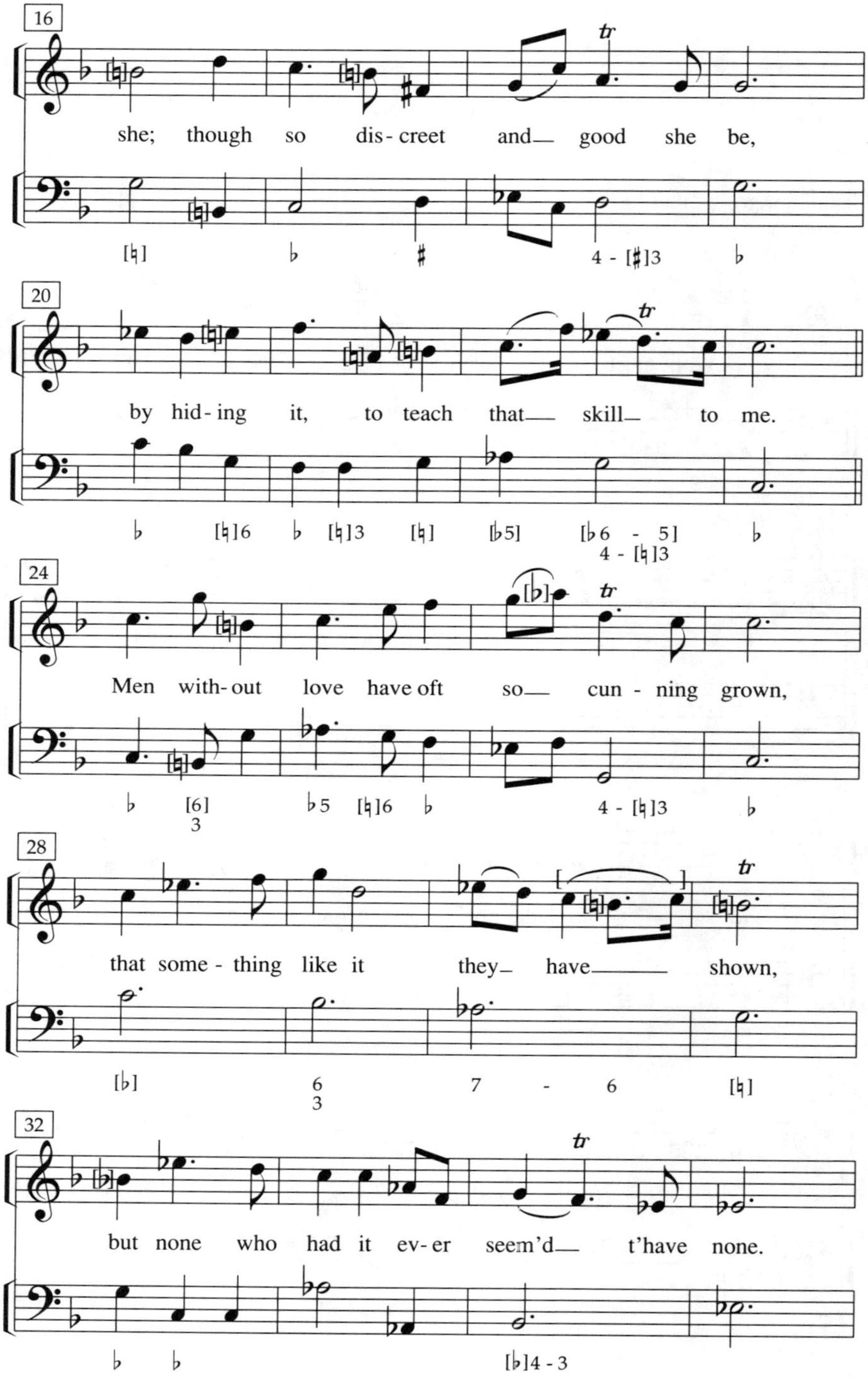
16
she; though so dis- creet and— good she be,
20
by hid- ing it, to teach that— skill— to me.
24
Men with- out love have oft so— cun - ning grown,
28
that some - thing like it they— have—— shown,
32
but none who had it ev- er seem'd— t'have none.

Settings of Poems from *The Mistress*

470 THE MUSICAL SETTINGS

Song: [*Looking on and discoursing with his Mistress.*]

Settings of Poems from *The Mistress*

472 THE MUSICAL SETTINGS

Settings of Poems from *The Mistress* 473

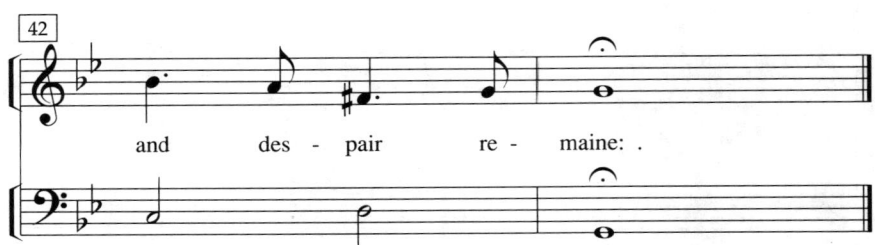

Settings of Poems from *The Mistress*

[*Looking on and discoursing with his Mistress.*]

Vinculum Societatis (1687), p. 18.
F1 poem 57.
Mr. Fran[cis] Forcer

9
Heav'ns de - light as with the blest_ con - verse he
11
might, yet could not get one drop of Wa - ter
by't. Ah wretch I seem to touch her
15
now: but oh, but oh, what bound - less spa - ces
17
[doe] us part! for - tune and Friends and

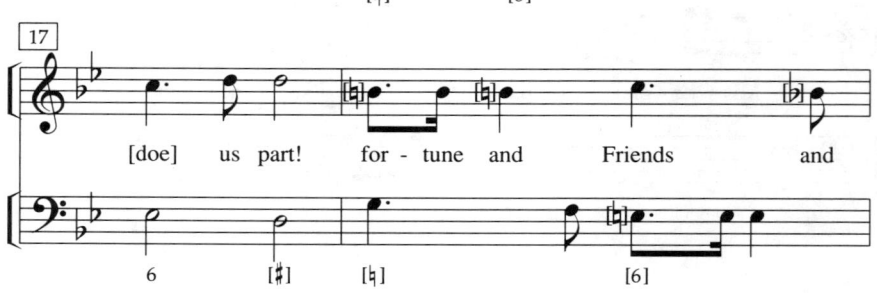

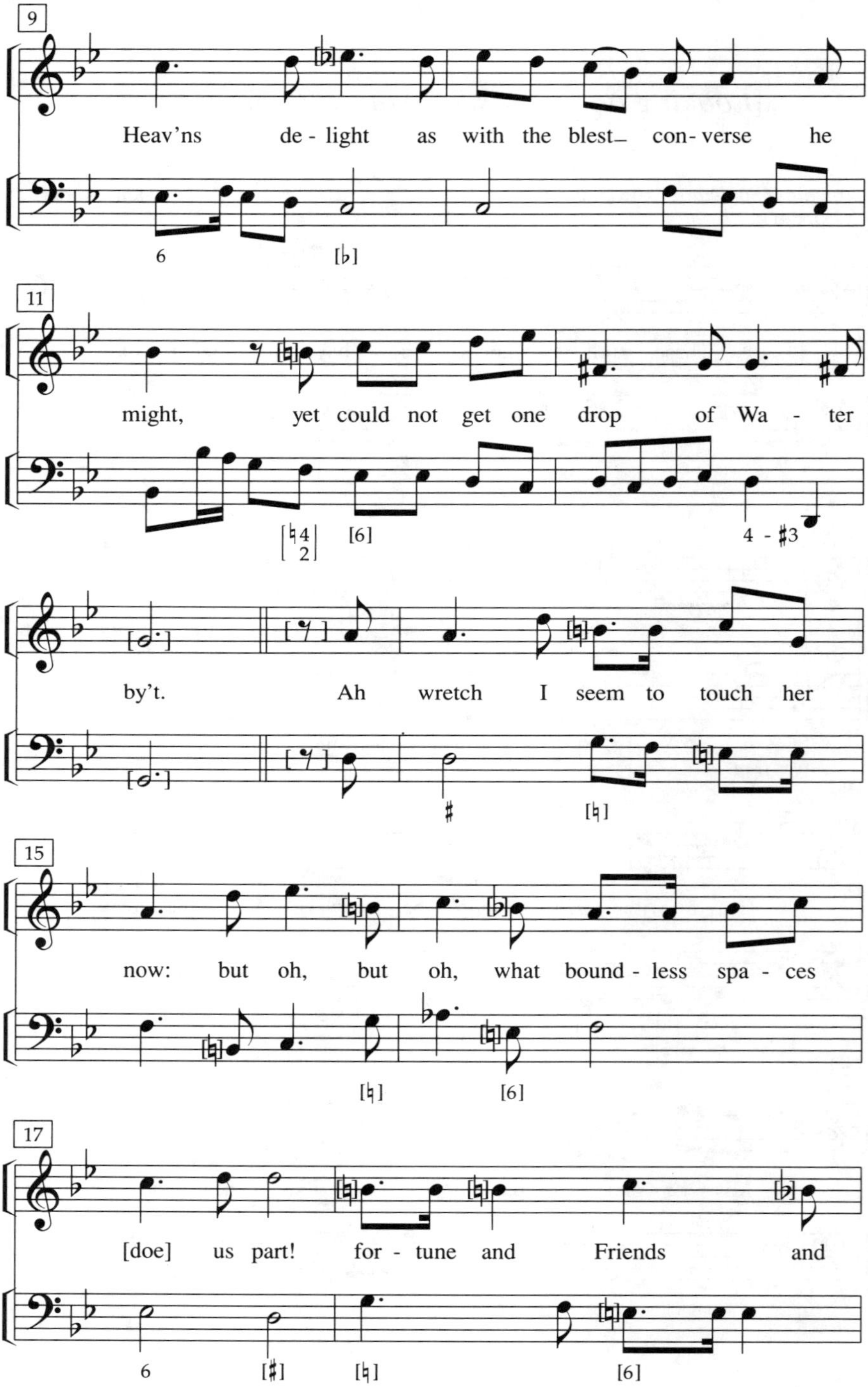

Settings of Poems from *The Mistress*

Settings of Poems from *The Mistress*

Settings of Poems from *The Mistress*

The Heart-Breaking.

Poems (1668), p. 46.
F1 poem 60.

William King

Settings of Poems from *The Mistress*

Silence.

Songs (1680), II, p. 20.
F1 poem 64.

Pietro Reggio

Settings of Poems from *The Mistress* 485

The Dissembler.

Songs (1680), I, p. 29.
F1 poem 65.

Pietro Reggio

4 - 3

Settings of Poems from *The Mistress* 487

Her NAME.

Poems (1668), p. 8.
F1 poem 68.

William King

Settings of Poems from *The Mistress*

Settings of Poems from *The Mistress*

Settings of Poems from *The Mistress*

Song: [Weeping.]

BL *ms* Add 22100, f. 87.
F1 poem 69.

Mr. [William] Turner

Settings of Poems from *The Mistress*

496 THE MUSICAL SETTINGS

Settings of Poems from *The Mistress*

500   THE MUSICAL SETTINGS

[*Weeping.*]

BL *ms* RM 20.h.8, f. 209.
Fl poem 69

Henry Purcell

Settings of Poems from The Mistress

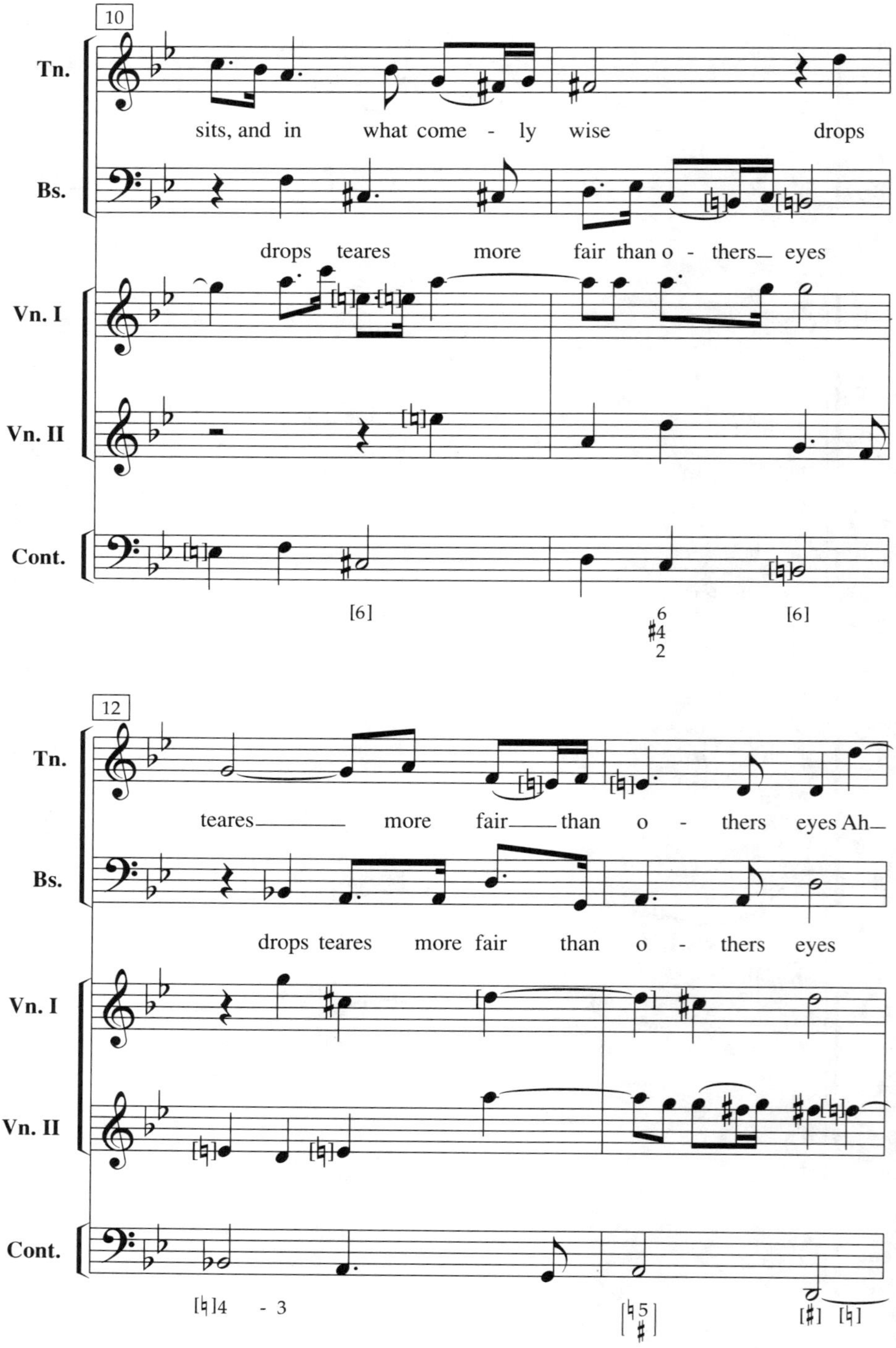
10
Tn.
sits, and in what come - ly wise drops
Bs.
drops teares more fair than o - thers eyes
Vn. I
Vn. II
Cont.
[6] 6 ♯4 2 [6]
12
Tn.
teares more fair than o - thers eyes Ah
Bs.
drops teares more fair than o - thers eyes
Vn. I
Vn. II
Cont.
[♮]4 - 3 [♮5 ♯] [♯] [♮]

Settings of Poems from *The Mistress*

504 THE MUSICAL SETTINGS

Settings of Poems from *The Mistress*

Settings of Poems from *The Mistress*

Settings of Poems from *The Mistress*

Settings of Poems from *The Mistress*

512 THE MUSICAL SETTINGS

Settings of Poems from *The Mistress*

Settings of Poems from *The Mistress*

Settings of Poems from *The Mistress* 519

COUNCELL [II].

Songs (1668), p. 30.
F1 poem 72.

William King

Settings of Poems from *The Mistress* 521

Councel [II].

Songs (1680), I, p. 38.
Fl poem 72.

Pietro Reggio

Settings of Poems from *The Mistress* 523

Settings of Poems from *The Mistress*

The Separation.

Settings of Poems from *The Mistress*

[*The Separation.*]

The Banquet of Music (1688), II, p. 10.　　　　　　　　　　Mr. Fr[ancis] Pigott
F1 poem 74.

528 THE MUSICAL SETTINGS

Settings of Poems from *The Mistress*

The Tree.

Songs (1680), I, p. 3.
F1 poem 75.

Pietro Reggio

Settings of Poems from *The Mistress* 533

Her Unbelief.

Settings of Poems from *The Mistress*

Settings of Poems from *The Mistress* 537

Honour
A Song upon a Ground.

Songs (1680), I, p. 1.
F1 poem 79.

Pietro Reggio

538 THE MUSICAL SETTINGS

Settings of Poems from *The Mistress* 539

Settings of Poems from *The Mistress*

542 THE MUSICAL SETTINGS

Settings of Poems from *The Mistress*

[*Honor.*]
A SONG upon a Ground.

544 THE MUSICAL SETTINGS

Settings of Poems from *The Mistress*

Settings of Poems from *The Mistress*   547

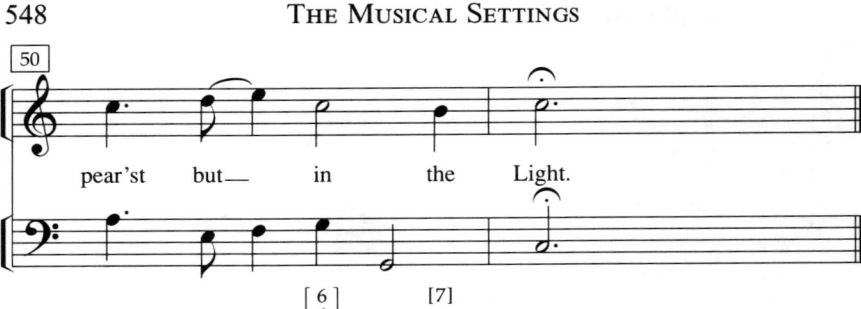

Settings of Poems from *The Mistress*

The Innocent ill.

Songs (1680), I, p. 27.
F1 poem 80.

Pietro Reggio

550 THE MUSICAL SETTINGS

Settings of Poems from *The Mistress*   551

Bathing in the River.

Songs (1680), I, p. 14.
F1 poem 83.

Pietro Reggio

554 THE MUSICAL SETTINGS

Music Copy Texts:
Sigla and Descriptions

BM88 [Day & Murrie no. 97] [double-rule border] THE / Banquet of MUSICK: / OR, / A Collection of the newest and best SONGS / sung at Court, and at Publick Theatres. / WITH / A THOROW-BASS for the *Theorbo-Lute,* / *Bass-Viol, Harpsichord,* or *Organ.* / rule / *Composed by several of the Best Masters.* / rule / The WORDS by the *Ingenious Wits* of this Age. / rule / THE SECOND BOOK. / rule / [engraving, signed "*Gui: Vaughan,*" showing a woman at the harpsichord, a man playing a violin, and a woman singer] / rule / LICENSED, / *May* 3. 1688. *Rob. Midgley.* / double rule / IN the SAVOY: / Printed by *E. Jones,* for *Henry Playford,* at his Shop near the *Temple* Church, 1688.

Collation: 2°: A–M2 ($1 and 2 signed, -A1, K2), 24 leaves, numbered [i–iv] 1–44, copy iii measuring c. 31 cm × 19 cm; watermark, copy iii: a circular border, ornamented at the top, surrounding the figure of a lion, c. 90 mm × 75 mm. The mark is similar to Heawood no. 3142 (London, c. 1689).

Contents: A1 title, A1ᵛ blank, A2 contents, A2ᵛ advertisements, B1–M2 songs. *Selected content*: sig. D1ᵛ–D2 (pp. 10–11), [*The Separation*] set by FR. Pigott.

Copies of selected content collated: i British Library Mus.G.83a; ii Folger P2422; iii Library of Congress M1490 .P58B2 case. No variants.

CA94 [Day & Murrie no. 123] [double-rule border] COMES AMORIS: / OR THE / Companion of LOVE. / Being a Choice COLLECTION / Of The Newest SONGS now in Use. / WITH *Thorow-Bass* to each SONG for the *Harpsichord, Theorbo,* or *Bass-Viol.* / rule / THE FIFTH BOOK. / rule / [engraving, same as TM87 and VS87] / double rule / LONDON, / Printed by *J. Heptinstall* for *John Carr* at his Shop at the *Middle-* / *Temple-Gate* in *Fleetstreet.* 1694.

Collation: 2°: A–K2 ($1 signed, -A1), 20 leaves, numbered [i–ii] 1–38; copy iii measuring c. 32 cm × 19 cm (cropped); watermark, copy iii, foolscap, c. 110 mm × 50 mm.

Day and Murrie note that the sheet signed *I*, which contains one song, is on different paper and has the imprint "Printed for *John Carr* at the *Mid-*

dle-Temple-Gate in *Fleet-street*. 1693 / Price Three Pence'' at the bottom of I2ᵛ. This sheet was probably sold separately. The notice does not appear in copy iii, and the watermark on I1 (p. 31–32) appears to be the foolscap that shows elsewhere. I2 shows watermark initials "MC," c. 15 mm × 30 mm. For this mark combined with the foolscap, see Heawood no. 2051 (undated). Copy i, however, corresponds to Day and Murrie's description. Pages 31–34 are actually numbered [1], [2], [3], [4], and in each case a "3" has been prefixed by hand. The paper for these pages has a different foolscap (though also 110 mm × 50 mm), with three balls. It appears that CA94 exists in two states. The selected content on signature E2 is unaffected by the difference.

Contents: A1 title, A1ᵛ contents, A2–K2ᵛ songs. *Selected content*: sig. E2 (p. 17), [*Counsel*], Set by Mr. *Michael Banfeild*.

Copies of selected content collated: i British Library G. 89; ii Huntington Library (from microfilm S1.5, 136/7); iii Library of Congress M 1740 .A2C73. No variants.

OB98 [Day & Murrie no. 166] [double-ruled border] <u>ORPHEUS BRI-TANNICUS</u> / rule / A / COLLECTION / OF ALL / The <u>Choicest</u> SONGS / FOR / [line set in Gothic Type] *One, Two, and Three Voices,* / COMPOS'D / By Mʳ. <u>Henry Purcell</u>. / rule / TOGETHER, / <u>With such Symphonies</u> for <u>Violins</u> or <u>Flutes</u>, / As were by Him design'd for any of them: / AND / A <u>THOROUGH-BASS</u> to each <u>Song</u>; / Figur'd for the *Organ, Harpsichord,* or *Theorbo-Lute.* / rule / All which are placed in their several Keys according to the / Order of the *Gamut.* / rule / <u>LONDON</u>, / Printed by *J. Hep-tinstall*, for <u>Henry Playford</u>, in the *Temple-Change,* / in *Fleet-street,* MDCXCVIII.

Collation: 2°: *1, 2*2, a2, c1, B–3R2 ($1 signed); numbered [i–vi], (iii)–(vi), [i–ii], 1–248 (166 misnumbered 165; 167 misnumbered 166; 196 misnumbered 199); 130 leaves, copy i measuring c. 32 cm × 19.66 cm; watermark, copy i, a circular figure enclosing an animal, c. 74 mm in diameter, crowned at the top, with the countermark initials "GOB," c. 17 mm × 55 mm—similar to Heawood no. 3158 dated London 1698. Another circular mark enclosing a rampant lion, c. 88 mm top-to-bottom, with the countermark initial "C," 32 mm, appears on some leaves.

Contents: *1 blank, *1ᵛ engraved portrait of the composer, 2*1 title, 2*ᵛ blank, 2*2ʳ⁻ᵛ dedicatory letter to the Lady Howard signed Fr. Purcell, a1 The Bookseller to the Reader signed Hen. Playford, a1ᵛ–a2ᵛ odes and elegies on the death of Henry Purcell, c1 contents, c1ᵛ advertisements, B–3R2 songs. *Selected contents*: sig. S2–T1ᵛ (pp. 67–70) "The Thraldom, the Words by mr. Cowley.", sig. 2I2ᵛ–2K (pp. 124–25) "[Honor] A SONG upon a Ground."

558   THE MUSICAL SETTINGS

Copies of selected contents collated: i Folger P4218; ii Huntington Library (from microfilm S1.5, 158); iii Monuments of Music and Music Literature facsimile (New York: Broude Brothers, 1965; location of copy not indicated); iv British Library Mus. G.100. *Variants*: "The Thraldom," score I, bar 39, note 3: in copy i a "G" is inscribed above the "E"; copies ii–iv show only the "E."

Poems68 [Day & Murrie no. 27] [single-rule border] POEMS / OF / M^r. COWLEY / AND OTHERS. / COMPOSED into SONGS and AYRES / with a Thorough BASSE to the Theorbo, / *Harpsecon, or Base-violl*; / rule / BY / WILLIAM KING Organist of *New-Colledge* / In the University of *OXON*: / rule / [ornament] / OXFORD, / Imprinted by *William Hall,* For the / Author 1668.

Collation: 2°: A–P2 $2 signed (-A1 [title], A2, B2, C2, G2, M2, N2, O2), 30 leaves, numbered [i–iv] 1–55; copy iii (unbound) measures 25.5 cm × 17 cm; watermark, copy iii a small shield, c. 24 mm × 15 mm, shows very faintly.

Contents: A1 title, A1^v blank, A2 epistle "TO ALL / LOVERS OF MUSICK.", A2^v general statement on errata, B1–P2 songs, P2^v blank. *Selected contents*: p. 1 "The CONCEALMENT.", p. 6 "The ENJOYMENT.", p. 8 "Her NAME.", p. 15 "MY FATE.", p. 22 "All-over LOVE.", p. 24 "LOVES VISIBILITY.", p. 26 "LOVE Undiscovered.", p. 28 "The given LOVE.", p. 30 "COUNCELL.". p. 34, "The Given HEART.", p. 36 "Clad in WHITE.", p. 38 "The DISTANCE.", p. 46 "The Heart-Breaking.", p. 48 "The MONOPOLY."

Copies of selected contents collated: i British Library K.7.c.3; ii Bodleian Wood 644(7); iii University of Delaware. *Variants*: copy iii shows the following pen corrections. These do not appear in other copies collated and presumably did not originate at the print shop. All but the last correct obvious errors in the setting. "LOVES VISIBILITY," scores I and II, bar 1, *sig*.: 3 inscribed before the ¢; score I, bar 3, note 2: a half note C♯, slurred to the B, is added to correct the measure. "MY FATE," score II, bar 2, note 1: an F is written under the eighth note G. "COUNCELL," score II, bars 10/11, notes 4/1: a tie is penned in and then apparently crossed out.

SBS [Day & Murrie no. 135] *A Second Booke of* Songs *together* / *with A Pastorall* Elegy *on the Blessed* / *Memory of her Late Gracious MAjESTY,* / *QVEEN MARY, for One Two Three & Fowr* / *Voices, Composed by R King B M;* / *Servant to his MAjESTY;* [This title appears within a wreathed oval panel, in the center of an engraved page, the plate being

19.1 cm × 25.9 cm. In the lower part of the engraving are two cherub/cupids, separated by a harpsichord, playing a viol and hautbois (left and right, respectively) and framed by viols and drums. Above them, in the middle of the engraving and framing the title, are a harp and lyre, then lutes, trumpets, and viols beneath crossed recorders at the top. In the center above the title there is a portrait (Robert King?). A laurel chain, suspended above it and draped downwards on the sides, completes the engraving.]

Collation: *oblong* 2°: unsigned, 35 printed leaves [there are blank leaves at the beginning and ending, one or both of which are missing in some copies], numbered [i–iv], 1–66; copy iii measuring 19.4 cm × 30.2 cm [chain lines running parallel to the longer edge]; watermark, copy iii, situated sideways in the center of the leaf, a lion within a shield, holding a sword upward and seven staves forward, surrounded by a crowned circle and situated above the initials "GG," c. 108 mm × 74 mm (similar to Heawood no. 3141, c. 1685). The watermark initials probably belong to George Gill (see Shorter, *Paper Making in the British Isles*, 50 and fig. 28c, p. 248). If so, the paper is late seventeenth century, made in England. The mark itself represents the arms of the United Provinces; Gill would likely have bought his molds abroad, for home production.

SBS shows no printed date or place of publication. The watermark alone may serve to narrow possibilities to the 1680s and 1690s. The best internal evidence for a more specific date is the featured pastoral elegy on Queen Mary II (pp. 57–66, and announced on the title page). Mary died on 28 December 1694; her funeral was deferred until 5 March 1695. The book was probably published near the time of the funeral. Other internal evidence supports this hypothesis. King includes two untitled songs with texts by Matthew Prior: "Whilst I am scorch'd with warm desire" (p. 8), and "Love has often threatn'd warr" (pp. 29–30). Both are dated c. 1690 in *The Literary Works of Matthew Prior*, ed. H. Bunker Wright and Monroe K. Spears (Oxford: Clarendon Press, 1959). "Whilst I am scorch'd" was first published in 1692, in *The Gentleman's Journal* (first with text alone, and then, in the November issue, with King's setting). The first stanza of the other was initially published in SBS. The composer therefore made use of some material that he had completed in the earlier 1690s, and there is nothing in the volume that can clearly be dated after 1695. Day and Murrie list SBS among their 1695 publications, with only the note "the date is conjectural." Ian Spink (*English Song*, 269) concurs, listing the date c. 1695. The paper appears to be English-made. It is unlikely that English paper would have been purchased and sent abroad, where cheaper paper would have been available, so the book was probably printed in London. It would thus represent an initial stage in King's book-publishing and -selling enterprise (see biographical sketches of the composers), from which he expanded to selling foreign music books.

Contents: blank leaf, [i] title, [ii] blank, [iii–iv] dedicatory letter "To / The Right Honorable the Lord Burleigh", 1–66, songs, blank leaf. *Selected contents*: pp. 13–14 ["The Heart fled again"], pp. 21–24, ["The Concealment"].

Copies of selected contents collated: i British Library Mus. C.411 [showing the handwritten date "1727" on the title page]; ii Boston Public Library M430.2; iii Pepys Library, Magdalen College, Cambridge. *Variants*: In "The Concealment," copy i, score I, bar 3, an errant quarter note D with its line drawn upward shows between notes 3 and 4. This erroneous note does not appear in copies ii and iii.

Songs (1680) [Day & Murrie no. 52] *Songs set by Signor* PIETRO REGGIO. [This title, part of a large engraving on the title page, is set in a banner above the figure of Arion, who is playing an eleven-stringed harp and riding on the back of a dolphin. At the bottom of the page, outside the lower border of the engraving, is the following Latin motto:] UT RElevet MIserum FAtum SOLitosq; LAbores / Ævi; Sit dulcis MUSICA noster Amor. [Capital letters UT RE MI FA SOL LA in the first line of the motto signal the six-note hexachord.]

There is no imprint. The date of publication is known in part through newspaper advertisements. Following its 11 March 1680 announcement of a forthcoming songbook by Reggio, *The London Gazette* no. 1532 (22–26 July 1680) advertises that subscribers for "Signior *Pietro Reggio's* Musick-Book may (as soon as they please)" after 26 July, deliver or send their notes and receive copies of the book "from Mr. Keble, Bookseller, at the *Turk's Head* against *Foster-lane* in *Fleetstreet*." Keble's name does not clearly print in the advertisement, but the address is probably his (see Plomer, *Dictionary, 1668–1725*, 176). Keble's role in the printing and publishing of *Songs*, and the possible involvement of the book's later sellers, is not known. *The London Gazette* no. 1571 (6–9 December 1680) contains a general advertisement describing *Songs* "engraven in Copper in a very large Folio, most of [the songs] out of Mr. *Abraham Cowley's* excellent poems" and advising that copies "are to be had only at Mr. *Thomas Norman*'s, at the *Popes Head* right against the *Castle Tavern in Fleetstreet*, and at Mr. *Lord*'s Shop at the Duke of *Monmouth*'s Head, in *Westminister*-Hall."

John Evelyn records, under the date 23 September 1680, that "*Signor Pietro* a famous *Musitian*" came to his house and "sung *admirably* to a *Guitarr* & had a perfect good tenor and base &c: & had set to *Italian* composure, many of *Abraham Cowleys* Pieces which shew'd extremely well" (*Diary* 4:220). Pepys bought a copy of *Songs* in order to have his music teacher, Caesare Morelli, transpose the treble score to bass and rewrite the accompaniment for basso continuo and guitar (Pepys MSS 2803 and 2804). In his preface, dated 2 November 1680, to *Choice Ayres and Songs* (London

1681), John Playford writes: "I have seen lately published a large Volum of *English* Songs, composed by an *Italian* Master, who has lived here in *England* many Years. . . ."

It appears, then, that *Songs* was available in a subscribers' edition by 26 July 1680. The delay between its 11 March announcement and 26 July may have been occasioned by Reggio's call for pen corrections to the printed sheets (see collation tables, below). Reggio's performances of the Cowley settings on 23 September may well have been intended to promote the book. By 9 December 1680, *Songs* was offered for sale to nonsubscribers at two bookshops clearly distinguished from that of Samuel Keble, the original seller. Day and Murrie (no. 113) report that *Songs* was advertised as "newly Reprinted" and available for sale in *The London Gazette* no. 2813 (27 October 1692). We have discerned no copies of the reprint. If the copper plates from the 1680 edition were used again, this edition will probably show a different watermark and it will probably lack pen corrections.

Collation: large 2°: unsigned; 42 leaves, numbered [i–viii], 1–42, [i–ii], 1–30, [i–ii]. Bound folio, copy iii measuring c. 41.5 cm × 26.5 cm; watermark: copy iii, the initials "IHS," surmounted by a cross, with initials "ET" below, c. 75 mm × 60 mm; on the conjugate leaf there is a shield mark with a large fleur-de-lis in the center, a crown above and below a line descending to shape the numeral "4," beneath which appear the initials "WR." See Heawood no. 1780 (dated 1680), and Churchill no. 428 (dated 1671, identified as the mark of Etienne Touzeau).

Contents: [i] engraved title, [ii] blank, [iii] dedication "*To the* Kings *most Excellent Ma*^{ty}.", [iv] blank, [v] "The PREFACE." and "POSTSCRIPT.", [vi–viii] dedicatory poems, 1–42 texts and settings of songs, [i] title page of part II: [row of ornaments] / THE / SECOND PART. / [row of ornaments, [ii] blank, 1–30 texts and settings of songs, [i] "A TABLE to all the SONGS in this BOOK.", [ii] blank. The texts and settings of songs, on numbered pages, are printed from engraved plates.

Copies collated: i British Library Mus. K 10 b.25; ii Huntington Library (from microfilm S1.5 398/17); iii Folger R754; iv Library of Congress M 1620 .R32 case.

A number of penned alterations, mostly additions to the figured bass, appear in all copies collated. These appear to have been done at the printshop, the penwork being easier than re-engraving the plates. Variants listed below are all in the form of penned alterations. In the table, measure is listed for the system on the page and then as the measure number in the overall setting. Song titles are: (a) "*Honour*"; (b) "*The Distance*"; (c) "*Bathing in the River*"; (d) "*Councel* [II]"; (e) "[*The Injoyment*]".

562   The Musical Settings

Variants in Copies Collated

Title	Leaf/page	System	Score	Measure	Note	Variant
(a)	5ᵛ 2	1	treble	7/53	1	engraved G crossed out and E drawn below it [copy i]; G [copies ii, iii, iv]
(b)	9ᵛ 8	1	bass	4/4	1	flat penned in figured bass [copy iii]; figure *om* [copies i, ii, iv]
(b)	10ʳ 9	1	bass	1/45	1	flat penned in figured bass [copy iii]; figure *om* [copies i, ii, iv]
(c)	12ᵛ 14	2	bass	6/16	1	flat penned in figured bass [copies i, ii, iv]; figure *om* [copy iii]
(c)	12ᵛ 14	2	bass	7/17	1	flat penned in figured bass [copy iii]; figure *om* [copies i, ii, iv]
(c)	12ᵛ 14	5	bass	6/46	1	flat penned in figured bass [copy iii]; figure *om* [copies i, ii, iv]
(d)	25ʳ 39	1	bass	8/25	2	the note E is penned above the B [copy ii]; B [copies i, iii, iv]
(e)	39ʳ pt. II/9	6	treble	1/9	2	flat penned by the note B [copies i, ii, iv]; flat *om* [copy iii]

Readings from copy iv, normative and musically satisfactory, are followed in this edition.

TM87 [Day & Murrie no. 94] [double-rule border] / THE / Theater of MUSIC: / OR, A / Choice COLLECTION of the newest and best *SONGS* / Sung at the COURT, and Public THEATERS. / rule / The *Words* composed by the most ingenious *Wits* of the Age, and set to MUSIC by the greatest Masters in that *Science*. / WITH / A *Thorow-Bass* to each *SONG* for the *Harpsichord, Theorbo*, or *Bass-Viol.* / rule / The FOURTH and LAST BOOK. / rule / [engraving, showing five cupid musicians and a cupid director, as also VS87 and CA94] / double rule / *LONDON*, / Printed by *B. Motte*, for *Henry Playford*, at his Shop near the *Temple* Church, 1687.

Collation: 2°: A–Z2 ($1 and 2 signed, -A1), 46 leaves, numbered [i–iv], 1–88. All copies collated have been rebound as part of collections; copy iii measures c. 31 cm × 19 cm; watermark, copy iii: the initials "IR," c. 13 mm × 22 mm, and on the conjugate leaf foolscap, c. 110 mm × 60 mm; paired with the same initials, another mark—an ornamented pot surmounted by a cross—appears from sig. R to the end. Copy i shows foolscap through sig. R, and then a shield with two rampant lions facing a central cross on sigs. S–Z.

Contents: A1 title, A1^v verse signed Nath. [*sic* Nahum] Tate and imprint: LICENSED, *Rob. Midgley. / October* 23. 1686., A2 epistle dedicatory signed Henry Playford, A2^v contents, B1–Z2 songs. *Selected content*: S1^v–S2^v, pp. 66–68, *A Song on Ingratitude, Words by Mr.* Cowley. *Set by Dr.* Blow.

Copies of selected content collated: i British Library K.7.i.16; ii Library of Congress (from microfilm S1.5, 364/16); iii Folger P2438. No variants. Another issue, British Library R.M. 15.c.9.(1), shows no variants in the Blow setting.

TM93 [Day & Murrie no. 121] [double-rule border] THESAURUS MUSICUS: / BEING, A / COLLECTION of the Newest SONGS / PERFORMED / At their *Majesties Theatres*; and at the Consorts in / *Viller-steet* in York-Buildings, and in *Charles-street / Covent-Garden.* / WITH A / Thorow-Bass to each SONG for the *Harpsichord, Theorbo,* or *Bass-Viol.* / To which is Annexed / A *Collection* of *Aires,* Composed for two *Flutes,* by several Masters. / rule / THE FIRST BOOK. / rule / [engraving showing three cupid musicians and a cupid singer, titled "LESSONS FOR THE RECORDER"] / triple rule / LONDON, / Printed by *J.* Heptinstall for *John Hudgebut.* And are to be Sold by *John Carr,* at / the *Middle-Temple Gate* in *Fleetstreet,* and by *John Money, Stationer* at the Miter / in Miter Court in *Fleet-street.* And at most Musick-Shops in Town. 1693.

Collation: 2°: A–K2, L1 ($1 signed, -A1), 21 leaves, numbered [i–iv] 1–38, copy ii measuring c. 32.5 cm × 19 cm (cropped); watermark, copy ii: fleur-de-lis with the initials "GC" beneath, c. 70 mm × 45 mm.

Contents: A1 title, A1^v contents, A2 dedication signed "*John Hudgebutt.*", A2^v blank, B1–L1^v songs. *Selected content*: sig. G2^v (p. 24), [*The Given Heart*] Set by "Mr. *John Barrett.*"

Copies of selected content collated: i British Library K.2.g.16; ii Folger T870 (missing A2, I2–K2); iii Library of Congess M1619 A2T4 case. No variants.

VS87 [Day & Murrie no. 95] [double-rule border] VINCULUM SOCIETATIS, / OR THE / Tie of good Company. / Being a Choice COLLECTION / Of the Newest SONGS now in Use. / WITH THOROW BASS to each SONG for the *Harpsichord, Theorbo,* or *Bass-Viol.* / rule / The FIRST BOOK of this CHARACTER. / rule / [engraving, same as TM87 and CA94] / double rule / LONDON, / Printed by *F. Clark, T. Moore,* and *J.* Heptinstall, for *John Carr,* and *R. C.* and are / to be Sold by *John Carr* at the *Middle*

Temple-Gate, and *Sam. Scott* at the / *Miter* by *Temple-Barr. Anno Domini,* 1687.

Collation: 2°: A–K2 ($1 signed, -A1; H1 missigned G), 20 leaves, numbered [i–iv] 1–36, copy iii measuring c. 30.5 cm × 19 cm; watermark, copy iii: coat of arms with a cross on the top, lions at either side, and initials "DCH" at the base, c. 112 mm × 93 mm. The mark is similar to Heawood no. 37 (dated 1688).

Contents: A1 title, A1^v blank, A2 epistle dated "*June* the 8th 1687." signed JOHN CARR. R. C., A2^v contents and advertisements, B1–K2 songs. *Selected content*: sig. F1^v (p. 18), [*Looking on, and discoursing with his Mistress*], Mr. Fran. Forcer.

Copies of selected content collated: i British Library K.2.i.25; ii Huntington Library (from microfilm S1.5, 19/2). No variants. Copy iii, M1619 V73, examined at the Library of Congress, is missing sig. F (pp. 17–20) and H1 (pp. 25–26).

Manuscript Copy Texts: Sigla and Descriptions

BL19 British Library Add. MSS 19759. 2° collection, 46 leaves, c. 31.2 cm × 24 cm, watermark foolscap with spiked crown, c. 120 mm × 74 mm, of songs set by Purcell, Blow, Hart, Bannister, Turner, and other composers of the later seventeenth century, with the inscription "Charles Campelman his book, June ye 9, 1681." The transcriptions are in the same hand, presumably Campelman's, up to fol. 15^r. Then a number of other hands enter, along with the first. The settings are inscribed in the vocal score only, suggesting that these are singers' copies.

Selected contents: fols. 26^v–27, a song setting mistakenly titled "The Concealment by Mr Cowley" and listing no composer. The song text is that of "Love undiscovered," F1 poem 31. Fols. 41^v–42, an untitled song, the setting attributed to James Hart. The song text is that of "The Despair," F1 poem 18. These transcriptions are in the same hand, the first hand in the collection.

BL22 British Library Add. MSS 22100. 2° miscellany, 180 leaves (numbered; two sequential leaves are numbered "123"), c. 36.7 cm × 23.3 cm, watermark crowned shield with fleur-de-lis within and the pendant initial "W," c. 154 mm × 64 mm, of songs set by Gibbons, Blow, Purcell, Turner, Hall, and others, generally of the later seventeenth century. Leaf numbered 149^v (actually 150^v) is the last with any text. Leaves 151–78 have only staff lines drawn, and leaves 179–80 are blank. The rear folio is signed "Mr Dolbin^s Book Anno domini 1682/1."

Selected contents: fols. 46ᵛ–48, a song setting titled "Song" and subscripted "Compos'd by Mʳ· Hall." The song text is that of "Looking on and discoursing with his Mistress," F1 poem 57. Fols. 87–89, a setting titled "Song:" ascribed to "Mʳ· Turner:". The song text is that of "Weeping," F1 poem 69.

RM20 British Library R.M. 20 h.8. 2°, Henry Purcell "Score Booke," 246 leaves, plus 28 unfoliated leaves, 40.8 cm × 25.6 cm (trimmed and rebound), watermarks: (1) a crowned shield with fleur-de-lis enclosed, c. 70 mm × 128 mm, and countermark initials "GP," c. 38 mm × 16 mm; (2) another shield enclosing the fleur-de-lis, with countermark "IHS" and the initials "ET" (identical to the watermark on the paper in Reggio's *Songs*, see description). At fol. 85 the volume is reversed, reading from the other end (fol. 246ᵛ), where there is inscribed "Score Booke Anthems, and Welcome songs and other songs all by my father." There is also, on fol. 1, the signature of "Eᵈ H. Purcell grandson to the Author of this Book." Many of the settings are in Purcell's hand, but there are a number of other hands as well. Dated transcriptions are from 1682-89.

Selected contents: fols. 174ᵛ[rev.]–173ᵛ[rev.], a setting headed "(25)" and titled "The Rich Rivall out of Mr. Cowley"; fols. 209[rev.]–207ᵛ[rev.], an untitled duet, headed "(14)", the song text for which is Cowley's "Weeping" (F1 poem 69); fols. 212ᵛ[rev.]–211ᵛ[rev.], "(The Concealment)." RM20 contains other Purcell settings of Cowley lyrics.

Fol51 Folger MS W.b.515. Rebound 2° collection of forty songs, many of them settings of Cowley's lyrics. Fourteen of the settings are by John Blundeville. Other composers include Humfrey, Locke, Blow, Hall, Bannister, and Turner. There is one Purcell setting at the end, "Song upon a ground," which sets Cowley's "Honor" and is considered to be one of Purcell's earliest compositions. There are 48 leaves, measuring c. 30.5 cm × 19.5 cm, numbered 1–53, 53, 54–74, 55–58, 79–82, 82, 83–94. The watermark shows a coat of arms (Amsterdam), c. 105 mm × 95 mm, and on the conjugate leaf the initials "RM," c. 15 mm × 30 mm. See Heawood no. 383 (Amsterdam, 1676-83) and no. 376 (Amsterdam, c. 1683).

Selected content: p. 53, an untitled setting signed "John Blundevile," the song text for which is Cowley's "The Despair" (F1 poem 18).

BL31 British Library Add. MSS 31440. 2°, in sixes, c. 32 cm × 20.6 cm, 195 leaves, showing (faintly) a shield enclosing an animal, c. 40 mm × 42 mm, as the main watermark. Elsewhere there appear larger shield watermarks, 90 mm × 52 mm (see fols. 10, 52, 172, and the ending leaves) and 80 mm × 50 mm (see fols. 48, 99, 148—all indexes that appear to have been added, on different paper). This is a collection of songs and some instrumental compositions. The volume combines material from separately indiced, separately paginated collections, and the transcriptions are in various hands. The first pagination series, beginning with "1" and extending to "95" (fol. 47v), is followed by a blank (fol. 48) and a table of contents ("A una Voce") corresponding to the first run of pp. 1–95. On fol. 49 is a second table of contents ("A due Voci") corresponding to the second run of pp. 1–95. Fol. 98 is a smaller leaf, 29.4 cm × 20.2 cm, showing a shield watermark very nearly the same as fol. 48 but slightly smaller (c. 80 mm × 42 mm), with content listing for songs on pp. 1–61. This index is misbound. It corresponds to fols. 149v–181, or the final pagination series in the manuscript, which is numbered from 1 to 62 (though the song beginning on p. 61 continues through actual p. 64; pp. 63–64 are not paginated). At the end of this index, or table, in a different hand and ink, is "As Water fluid is——15." This p. 15 is on fol. 156v, sharing leaves with another song, "Iesu dulciss," which is also correctly indexed in the table. Fol. 99 is another, smaller (30.3 cm × 19.8 cm) bound-in leaf repeating the index found on fol. 49. It is followed by another smaller leaf, blank, with the shield watermark of fol. 48. Fol. 148, once again a smaller leaf (31.5 cm × 20.5 cm), contains an index corresponding to the preceding pp. 1–95, a third pagination series started on fol. 100v. The songs contained in this manuscript collection are mistakenly catalogued as "to *Italian* words" and by Peter Reggio.

Selected content: the sole English song text, appearing on fols. 156v–157. This duet, "As Water fluid is . . . ," is set to the words of Cowley's "Coldness" (F1 poem 46). It is the only composition in the volume ascribed to Reggio, and it is copied in a hand that appears nowhere else in the collection.

Printed and Manuscript Copy Texts: Sigla Cited Less Frequenty

BL29   British Library Add. MSS 29397

BL31   British Library Add. MSS 31440

BL33   British Library Add. MSS 33234

BL37   British Library Add. MSS 33237

BL87   British Library Add. MSS 33287

CAS83   *Choice Ayres and Songs . . . The Fourth Book*. Printed by A. Godbid and J. Playford, Jr. Sold by John Playford and John Carr. London, 1683.

Music Copy Texts: Sigla and Descriptions 567

CCVI Chichester Cathedral MS V1/1/1

Eg29 British Library MS Egerton 2958

FM18 Fitzwilliam Museum MS 118

FM20 Fitzwilliam Museum MS 120

Fol19 Folger Library MS V.b.197

TM85(1) *The Theater of Music . . . The First Book*. London: Printed by J. Playford for Henry Playford and R. C. , 1685.

TM85(2) *The Theater of Music . . . The Second Book*. London: Printed by J. P. for Henry Playford and R. C., 1685.

TM87 *The Theater of Music . . . The Fourth and Last Book*. London: Printed by B. Motte, for Henry Playford, 1687.

Collations and Notes to the Musical Settings

[Poem 2] "The Thraldom, the Words by Mr. Cowley."

Composer: Henry Purcell

Copy text: *Orpheus Britannicus* 1:67 (OB98), collated with British Library MS Egerton 2598 (Eg29) and Folger Library MS V.b.197, p. 82 (Fol19). OB98 is chosen as the copy text; this first printed edition was set from a manuscript to which Henry Playford granted authority. It also shows readings that would appear to represent Purcell's final intentions and the most comprehensive treatment of the figured bass. An authorial manuscript of the setting was at one time among those that Purcell wanted to have copied into the collection RM20. On fol. 170 a copyist has written the title "The Tharldome [pen-corrected to Thraldome] out of Mr Cowley," and space has been left in the copybook for the setting. It could be that the manuscript to have been transcribed in RM20 or a copy from it supplied Playford with his text for OB98. The setting in OB98, however, contains obvious printer's errors and omissions. Fol19 is a more carefully reproduced setting. It was probably copied from a manuscript very much like the one represented by OB98. Its title is the same, and most of the substantive readings and bass figures are the same. Evidence in bar 70 (see notes, below), along with other clarifications in the setting and song text, suggests that Fol19 was probably not copied from OB98—or, if it was, that the copyist ingeniously corrected careless errors in the printed edition. Eg29, two surviving leaves from a large folio collection that contain only this setting, shows a number of unique substantive readings and some unique performance features. It is subscribed "H.P.," Purcell's initials as they frequently appear at the end of a setting in RM20. The initials could have been inscribed by a copyist as verification of authorship, though Zimmerman lists Eg29 as "late 17th century, supposed autograph" (p. 454). Margaret Laurie does not repeat the supposition in her description of the manuscript (*Works* 25:xviii), although she uses Eg29 as copy text in her edition. In our estimation Eg29 offers little internal evidence to support a case for its representing Purcell's final intent regarding the notes and accidentals. But it is an authentic version of Purcell's setting, probably an early version, and its readings are recorded in the notes below.

Zimmerman notes (p. 186) the reference to another manuscript of this setting, or part of it, appearing in Sotheby's catalogue no. 1398 for a sale held in July 1877. This manuscript has not been located.

Collations and Notes to the Musical Settings (p. 318)   569

Song text: F1 poem 2. Purcell sets the entire poem.

Textual variants: *title*] OB98, Fol19; *untitled (leaf numbered 107)* EG29; *The Thraldome* F1 and Σ   *bar 3* thro'] OB98, Fol19, Eg29; through F1   *bar 7* ev'ry] OB98, Fol19; every Eg29, F1   *bar 10* was] Σ; way Eg29   *bar 13* Angel's] OB98, Fol19; *Angels* Eg29, F1   *bar 30* gen'rous] OB98, Fol19; generous Eg29, F1   *bars 31-32* Conquers] *ed.* and Σ; Conquer's OB98   *bar 32* doth] OB98, Fol19; does Eg29, F1   *bar 65* wea'riest] OB98; weari'st Fol19; weariest Eg29, F1   *bar 70* ted'ous] OB98; tedious Σ   *bars 78-79* sev'ral] OB98, Fol19; several Eg29, F1

Literary source: Agreement among the three song texts against the text of F1 and other printed editions in bar 3 suggests a common source for Eg29, OB98, and Fol19. There is no reason to doubt that it was Purcell's autograph setting. Agreement between the literary text and Eg29 against OB98 and Fol19 in bars 7, 13, 30, 32, 65, and 78–79 (plus the repeat) makes it clear that Eg29 was taken from a setting that represented the literary text regardless of whether it accorded with the vocal score or not. Later elisions in the literary text all work to bring the song text into closer alignment with the notes in score I. The variant in Eg20 bar 10, probably a copyist's error, is enough to show that OB98 and Fol19 did not descend from Eg29. But there is also the fact that Eg29 is untitled, while the other settings show both the title and attribution to Cowley. It is probable that the original manuscript included the title and attribution, as does the inscription on fol. 170 of RM20, and the copyist of Eg29 simply omitted it. Purcell could have adapted his song text from a copy of the poem as it appears in any of the printed editions of *The Mistress* except O1, O2, and F3 (see Literary Collation).

The musical setting: Purcell sets the piece in two sections with the division, a change of meter, at measure 41. The key of the work is A minor, but Purcell explores many key centers during the course of the piece, several of them rather remote. Purcell also uses a number of large intervals in both the vocal and continuo lines, which give the piece an angular characteristic. Minor 7ths, major and minor 6ths, augmented 5ths, and octaves can be found throughout the piece.

Bar	Score	Notes	Comments
3	II	1, 4 *fig.*	Figs. *om* in Fol19 and Eg29.
4	II	5	Fig. *om* in Eg29. Fig. also *om* in Eg29 bars 8–11, 14–21, 25, 29, 34–39, 42–71, 73–84, and 88–91.
5	II	1	Eg29 shows two quarter note Fs.
7	II	3–4	In OB98 bar 7 is broken on the page between two systems. Scores I and II are not clearly aligned, and the printer ties notes 3–4, making it uncertain whether a single sustained tone is intended or not. The bass figure

Bar	Score	Notes	Comments
			at note 3 is 4 3, and the figure at note 4 is 4 ♯3. This edition omits the tie and resituates the bass figures. Fol19 reverses the values of notes 3–4. Eg29 shows two half notes in this bar and omits the bass figures at the second.
10	I	8–9, 10	Eg29 shows a sixteenth-eighth [*sic*] and then a G♯ with ornamentation over.
14	II	2	F♯ in Fol19. Sources represent the bass figure as ♯4/2—here editorially emended to 4/2.
16	II	2 *fig.*	OB98, showing a flat to indicate a natural third, represents the figure as ♭3♭♯—here emended as [♮] 3 - ♯3, the same as the figure at note 3.
18	I	7	C♮ in Eg29.
20	I	5–7	Two sixteenths and an eighth in Eg29.
21	I	5	Eg29 shows a repeat sign above.
22	I–II	*t. sig.*	OB98, Fol19, and Eg29 all reiterate the time signature as ¢, coincident with the word "quickly" in the song text. It may be, as Margaret Laurie conjectures (*Works* 25: 291), that Purcell intended performance of this section at a quicker tempo.
22	II	5–6, 7–8	Slurs *om* in Eg29.
26	II	5–6, 7–8	Slurs *om* in Eg29.
29	II	6	Eg29 shows D.
30	I	9–10	Tie *ed*. Eg29 shows ornamentation over note 10.
31–32	I	9/1	Tie *ed*.
32	II	2	*Ed*. OB98 and Eg29 show C. Fol19 shows a C drawn over to cover the D line.
34	II	10	[♯] *ed.*, to strengthen the cadential move. The F♯ is shown in Eg29.
37	II	5 *fig.*	*Om* in Fol19.
38	II	1–2	Eg29 shows two eighth notes.
41	I–II	[*t. sig.*]	3/4 *ed*. OB98 shows 3 followed by a dotted I; Fol19 shows 3; EG29 shows 3 1.
48–49	I–II	|	Bar line *ed*. OB98 omits bar line here and at 50–51, 54–55, 56–57, 62–63, 69–70, 71–72, 73–74, 75–76, 79–80, 83–84, 88–89, where the editor provides them in this edition.
62–63	II	1 | 1	OB98, showing no bar line, ties these notes. The tie is here *om* (and the bar line provided) to complement the song text. Fol19 likewise omits a tie and capitalizes the *l* in "like," emphasizing the break in the song text and allowing bar 63 to clearly initiate a new stanza.

Bar	Score	Notes	Comments
65	II	2	Eg29 shows both C and A.
70	I	1	This note is missing in OB98, but is here supplied from readings in Eg29 and Fol19.
79	II	1	Eg29 shows a half note E followed by a quarter note D.
83	II	1–2	Eg29 shows a dotted eighth and a sixteenth note.
87	I	5	Eg29 shows a G♮.

[Poem 3] "The Given Love."

Composer: William King

Copy text: *Poems*, p. 28 (Poems68).

Song text: F1 poem 3, stanza 1. William King prints stanzas 2–5 on p. 29, filling the entire page with them; he omits, or does not have room for, stanzas 6–9 of the literary text.

Textual variants: *bar 5.* excepti'ons] exceptions F1   *bar 7.* under Mortalls] *under-mortals* F1; sordid *Mortals* F2ff.   *stanza 2* (F1, l. 10) Since] That F1   *stanza 5* (F1 l. 35) Gold ?] ~ ; F1

Literary source: At the end of stanza 5 as printed in *Poems*, p. 29, King notes: "*vide* Cowley *fol.6.Mist.*" "The Given Love" appears on p. 6 of F1, *Poems* (1656), as well as on p. 6 of F2-3, *Works* (1668). William King's reading in bar 7 makes it clear that he copied the song text from the printed folio edition of Cowley's *Poems* (1656), F1 (see Literary Collation). The variant in stanza 2 is unique to Poems68. This song text is not the one followed in Pietro Reggio's later setting.

The musical setting: The tonality of King's strophic setting is D minor. King achieves a sense of energy by using the *alla breve* sign for meter and a number of rhythmic figures, and he displays some modest word-painting upon the word "enjoying."

Bar	Score	Notes	Comments
–]	–]	scoring	Situated between scores I and II, just below the song text, middle C is indicated by a single note drawn in at the beginning of each system of scores. Here *om*.
–]	II	[*figs*.]	*Ed. Poems* offers no bass figures, throughout.
4	II	1	Poems68 shows a sharp to cancel the flat in the signature.

[Poem 3] "The Given Love".

Composer: Pietro Reggio

Copy text: Songs 1:10

Song text: F1 poem 3. Reggio sets stanzas 1, 2, 3, and 7 of eight 8-line stanzas.

Textual variants: *bars 5–6* vulgar sordid] *thin-sould, under-* F1   *bars 36–37* fore fathers] *Fore-fathers* F1   *bar 79* you] thee F1

Literary source: The variant in bars 5–6 appears in F2–F7; one of these folio editions is the probable source for this song text. The minor variant in bars 36–37 and the altered form of the second person in bar 79 may be attributed to Reggio, a copyist, or the engraver of the setting.

The musical setting: Reggio writes in E major, without indicating this in the key signature. The common meter portion of the setting maintains a sense of energy with runs of eighth notes and dotted eighth/sixteenth figures in the first two sections. Twice in these sections Reggio employs the interesting device of writing a short phrase and immediately repeating it a step higher (see measures 5–6, 12–15).

Bar	Score	Notes	Comments
10	II	3–4	The slur shown in *Songs*, here *om*.
11	I–II	||	Double dots appear on both sides of the double bar in *Songs*.
22	I–II	||	As in bar 11, *Songs* shows double dots here.
29	II	2	[♯] *ed*., as dominant to B-major cadence.
32	I	2	Given the sequence begun in bar 31, an F♯ may be preferred to the F♮ shown in *Songs*.
52	I–II	1	*Ed*., in accordance with the closure of a stanza in bars 11 and 22. *Songs* shows two tied dotted half notes in bar 52.
70	I	2	A C♯, anticipating the forthcoming modulation, may be preferred to the C♮ shown in *Songs*.
71	I	2	[♮] *ed*., following the D♯ in bar 70. *Songs* does not sustain the sharp to bar 71, though perhaps it should be sustained through the phrase initiated in bar 69.
83	I	1	[♯] *ed*., as called for by the bass figure.
84	I–II	1	*Ed*.; *Songs* shows two tied dotted half notes in the bar.

[Poem 9] "The Change."

Composer: Pietro Reggio

Copy text: Songs 1:16.

Song text: F1 poem 9. Reggio sets the first stanza of four in the literary text.

Collations and Notes to the Musical Settings (pp. 328-336)

Textual emendation: *bar 21* [I]n] F1; in *Songs*. Reggio, his copyist, or his engraver characteristically uses lowercase letters for capital letters appearing at the beginning of a line in the literary text. The literary text capital is restored here in the interest of clarity.

A later, unrelated setting of this text appears in R. J. S. Stevens, *Glees*, an autograph score dated 1780, British Library Add. MSS 31810, fols. 3-4; following is a revision, dated 1821, of the same score. John Gay's paraphrase of the text was set by Handel as the air "Love in Her Eyes Sits Playing" (*Acis and Galatea*, c. 1718).

Literary source: Reggio's song text could have been taken from any printed edition of *The Mistress* up to F8.

The musical setting: The composition is in F major. The contour of the melodic line is complementary to the character of the song text.

Bar	Score	Notes	Comments
1	I-II	[*t. sig.*]	The time signature is shown as C 3 in *Songs*.
13	I	1	In *Songs*, the B♮ is indicated with a sharp, to raise the flat in the key signature. Other bracketed naturals in the setting (14.I.3; 15.II.2; 18.II.1) are also represented by sharps in *Songs*.
35	I-II	1	*Songs* shows two tied dotted half notes in score I and two tied, dotted half notes in score II (see headnote on Reggio in the Editorial Principles).

[Poem 10] "Clad in White."

Composer: William King

Copy text: *Poems*, p. 36 (Poems68).

Song text: F1 poem 10. King sets stanza 1 and prints the remaining four stanzas on p. 37.

Textual variants: *title*] Poems68; *Clad all in White* F1   *bar 8* wear For Thou] wear: Thou F1   *bar 11* in] with F1   *stanza 3* (F1, l. 16) the Soul] thy Soul F1

Literary source: The song text shows remarkable fidelity to the text and accidentals in F1, especially in the stanzas printed after the musical setting. The variant in bar 8 expands the line, making it octosyllabic, as are corresponding lines in the stanzas following the setting. King clearly intends that these sequent stanzas be sung to the strophic setting. The variant in stanza 3 could be a printer's error. The bar 8 variant appears again in NAC71, suggesting King's song text as the source for the NAC song text. Pietro Reggio's setting of this poem does not derive its song text from Poems68.

The musical setting: King's strophic setting, in A minor, lacks a key signature.

Bar	Score	Notes	Comments
pickup	I–II	1	The eighth note A appears in the copy text for score I. It is editorially provided in score II. There is nothing in the song text of stanza 1 to accord with this note in the preliminary partial bar, but each of the remaining stanzas shows an extra syllable in the first line. The pickup note accommodates the text of sequent stanzas.
7	I	6	F[♯] *ed.*

[Poem 10] "Clad All in White."

Composer: Pietro Reggio

Copy text: *Songs* 1:6.

Song text: F1 poem 10. Reggio sets stanzas 1–3 of five in the literary text. There are no substantive variants from F1.

Reggio's and William King's settings appear to be unrelated. Another song text, representing all five stanzas of Cowley's poem, appears in NAC71 under the title "Song 108." A major variant in this text in the fifth line of the first stanza (in bar 17 of the Reggio setting; see Literary Collation) establishes that NAC71 and Reggio's song text are independent.

Literary source: The song text could have been copied from any of the printed versions of *The Mistress* up to F8, except for O2, which shows a unique variant in line 18.

The musical setting: Reggio sets his piece in B minor, but without a key signature. The form is ABA′.

Bar	Score	Notes	Comments
27	II	*fig.*	In this bar, as in 42 and 70, the *Songs* engraver has positioned the sharp above and to the left of the 6, leaving some ambiguity as to whether a sharped third plus a sixth or a sharped sixth is intended. The latter is correct.
36	I–II	1	*Songs* shows two dotted half notes, tied, before the double-bar closing this section of the song. This configuration appears neither at the end of the second section of the song (bar 51) nor at the conclusion (bar 87). The note in bar 36 is emended to a single dotted half note in this edition. Double dots appear on both sides of the double bars 36 and 51 in *Songs*, but not, however, at the end of the third section (bar 87).

Collations and Notes to the Musical Settings (pp. 336–347)

Bar	Score	Notes	Comments
42	II	3 *fig.*	See note to bar 27.
51	I-II	||	See note to bar 36.
52	I-II	[*t. sig.*]	The time signature is shown as "3" in *Songs*.
70	II	1 *fig.*	See note to bar 27. A sharpened sixth appears to be the appropriate figure.
87	I-II	||	See note to bar 36.

[Poem 12] "My Heart Discovered."

Composer: Pietro Reggio

Copy text: *Songs* 1:24

Song text: F1 poem 12. Reggio sets all forty lines of this monostrophic text.

Textual variants: *bars 4–7* Clear . . . grew] (Clear . . . grew) F1   *bar 47* the voyce] th'*Voyce* F1   *bar 50* towards] tow'ards F1   *bar 54* [was] *ed.* *Songs*, F1, and all printed editions of the poem until D2 reproduce the grammatically incorrect "were." Alcion [Alcyone] had only one husband and he, Ceyx, only one corpse.

Literary source: Of the variants listed above, only that in bar 50 suggests departure from printed editions of *The Mistress* up to F8. The variant is called for by notation in score I.

The musical setting: The piece is written in G major, without a key signature. There are basically eight syllables to a phrase, though sometimes (as in measures 31–33) two phrases are combined before reaching a cadence. The work is essentially through-composed, though there are repeated figures, two identical measures (19 and 22), and one short sequence (60–61).

Bar	Score	Notes	Comments
3	I	3–5	*Songs* shows these notes as a dotted eighth and two sixteenths, giving one sixteenth too many counts in the measure. The problem arose when the engraver first transcribed the phrase as "transparent to sight," omitting "the," which was later added above the song text line along with the extra sixteenth note in score I. In order to accommodate the song text, note 3 is editorially emended to an eighth note.
32	I	2–3	Slur *ed.*, in accordance with the song text.
42	I	1–4	[♯] *ed.*, though it is conceivable that Reggio intended a dissonance, or possible that the ♯ in the bass figure is an error.

Bar	Score	Notes	Comments
43–44	I	7–8 | 1–2	Slur across the bar line, *ed. Songs* slurs notes 7–8 in bar 43 and 1–2 in bar 44. The relation between score I and the song text in this passage, awkward as it may appear, is true to the copy text.

[Poem 15] "The Soul."

Composer: Pietro Reggio

Copy text: *Songs* 1:22.

Song text: F1 poem 15. Reggio sets the first twenty-two-line stanza, omitting the second and third twenty-eight-line stanzas.

Textual variants: bar 3 they have] They'have O1–2, F1; They've F6–10   bar 11 my abused] my 'abused F1   bar 20 powerful] powe'rful F1   bars 26–27 so epitomiz'd] so 'Epitomiz'd F1

Literary source: Though the variants in Reggio's song text bars 3 and 20 agree with readings in M16 (see Literary Collation), the manuscript title reads "song 148." Reggio probably found the title, the reading in bar 3, and the remaining text of *The Soul* stanza 1 in one of the folio editions of Cowley's *Works* F2–5. "Powerful," in bar 20, is sung on two notes and would therefore elide the second syllable, just as in all printed editions of the poem.

The musical setting: The work is based in G minor with one flat in the key signature. The E-flats in the melodic line and figured bass make possible modulations to C minor and B-flat major. Reggio makes use of sequence in an interesting fashion, with a variant of the sequence figure as a cadence (see measures 14–17). There is also an interesting interplay between the vocal and bass lines in 29–30, followed by a cascading melisma to the final cadence. Despite structural repetitions, the work is essentially through-composed.

Bar	Score	Notes	Comments
1	I	3–4	The eighth rest interrupts the movement of the passage and is not in keeping with subsequent settings of "if" clauses in this song. A dotted quarter at note 3 would promote delivery of the song text.
4	II	4	[♮] *ed.*, indicating the oncoming cadence. *Songs* flats the first E in this bar; there is no accidental at note 4.
13	II	4	[♮] *ed.* The third is flatted in the bass figure at note 1; *Songs* shows no accidental at note 4.
14	II	3	[♮] *ed.* The F is sharped at note 1; *Songs* shows no accidental at note 3.
20	II	2 *fig.*	*Songs* shows ♯3, raising the E♭, note 1, to E♮.

Collations and Notes to the Musical Settings (pp. 347–355)

Bar	Score	Notes	Comments
26	II	3 *fig.*	*Songs* shows a sharp above this note and 7 3 inscribed vertically to the left of it.
29	II	4	[♮] *ed.* The third is sharped in the bass figure at note 1.
30	I	4	*Songs* shows the half note E♭ followed by a quarter rest, giving the measure too many counts. Reggio possibly intended the E♭ as a quarter note.
31	I	5	[♮] *ed.*, as indicated by the bass figure.
31	I	6–7	*Songs* is not clear as to the values of these notes. Both could be sixteenths. The dotted eighth/sixteenth reading is probable.
32	I	11	[♮] *ed.* (the E is flatted at note 1).
34	I-II	1	*Songs* renders the monosyllable with two tied half notes.

[Poem 18] ["The Despair."]

Composer: attributed to John Blundevile [Blundeville]

Copy text: Folger MS W.b.515, p. 53 (Fol51)

Song text: F1 poem 18. Blundeville sets the first of four nine-line stanzas.

Textual variants: *title*] F1; Fol51 *is untitled*   *bar 17* woods] floods F1

Literary source: Blundeville's song text does not derive from the manuscript copy attributed to James Hart in BL19, nor vice versa. Any of the printed editions of *The Mistress* could have provided text for this setting, but the variant in bar 17, unique to Fol51, suggests a manuscript copy of the poem for the composer's immediate source.

The musical setting: Blundeville's setting of a single stanza builds an effective climax from measures 12–16 through chromatic movement. It shares this characteristic with Hart's composition, and both show two flats in the key signature. The settings are otherwise not musically related.

Bar	Score	Notes	Comments
—]	II	[*figs.*]	*Ed.*, throughout.
2	II	2	Fol51 shows a sharp to cancel the key signature here and in the following bars and scores: 2.I; 4.I; 6.I; 8.II; 12.I; and 16.II. A bracketed natural represents the cancellation.
3	II	4	Fol51 shows no accidental by the note.
18	I-II	1	First and second endings, *ed.*, to accommodate the repeat called for in Fol51 bar 11. The copy text shows no repeat sign at bar 18—only the note and fermata as in the present second ending.

[Poem 18] ["The Despair."]

Composer: attributed to James Hart

Copy text: British Library Add. MSS 19759, fol. 41ᵛ (BL19). The transcription is for the vocal part only. As with the transcription of "Love Undiscovered" and others in Campelman's collection, this appears to be a singer's copy, taken from a manuscript setting that would probably have included a figured bass. [Score II] in this edition is editorial, as a reasonable substitute for a performance continuo.

Song text: F1 poem 18. Hart sets the entire poem. As in Charles Campelman's transcription of "Love Undiscovered," this copy is deficient in punctuation. Performers may find it helpful to consult the literary text, p. 43 in this volume, for the F1 punctuation.

Textual variants: *title*] F1; BL19 *is untitled*   *bars 23–24* alass] (alas) F1   *bar 26* that] Which F1   *bar 52* ill Acted] ill-acted F1   *bars 55–56* impertinent] imperti'nent F1   *bar 63* to its] t'his F1   *bar 64* see] saw F1   *bar 65* her] his F1   *bar 66* her] his F1

Literary source: The lack of a title in this manuscript, along with unique variants in bars 23–24, 26, 52, 55–56, and 64 imply a manuscript source for the song text. It was no doubt a manuscript setting, ascribed to Hart, and probably lacking a title. Some of the variants may have appeared in this manuscript source, but it is likely that Campelman created most of them. BL19 is not a careful transcription in either song text or musical setting. Variants in bars 63, 65, and 66 establish that Campelman's source was based on a printed copy of *The Mistress*, F2–3, 6–10, or O3–4, D2. Given the date (1681) of the inscription on BL19, F6–8 are the likely sources for Hart's song text.

The musical setting: This through-composed setting is in some ways similar to John Blundeville's treatment of the text. See notes to the Blundeville setting. Hart's setting concludes (69–84) with a remarkable flat-sharp signature that creates a major/minor ambivalence.

Bar	Score	Notes	Comments
1	I	[*t. sig.*]	*Ed.* Copy text shows ¢, written in a different hand from the setting, in the margin left of score I.
1	I	*pickup*	Dotted eighth rest, *ed.*
2	I	1	BL19 shows a sharp to cancel the key signature here and in the following bars and notes: 5.7; 8.2; 10.3; 16.2; 47.5; 50.3; 51.4; 52.7; 55.4; 56.2; 58.7; 59.6; 60.2; 61.8; 66.3; and 67.1–4. Here a bracketed natural is shown.
2	I	4	BL19 omits the dot.

Collations and Notes to the Musical Settings (pp. 356–363)

Bar	Score	Notes	Comments
6	I	3–7	*Ed.* BL19 shows notes 3–5 as sixteenths and omits the slurs.
9	I	3–4	BL19 omits the slur here and in these bars and notes: 10.4–5; 29.4–6; and 47.8–9.
11–12	I	|	The bar line is *om* in BL19 here and between bars 36–37, 40–41, and 71–72.
14	I	1	BL19 shows a quarter G tied to a half note G, giving three counts. Then there is a double bar preceding the section scored in triple time. The copy text omits a time signature here.
46	I	1	*Ed.* BL19 shows a dotted half note A, as if to carry the musical phrase forward, thus linking "reply" with "no more" in the song text. The double bar and change in the time signature, however, correspond with the end of one textual stanza and the beginning of a new one.
46	I	[*t. sig.*]	6/4 *ed.*, on the evidence of the score following. BL19 shows ¢.
58	I	6, 7	BL19 shows a flat, canceling the F♯, and then a sharp to cancel the signed E♭.
61	I	1	The E♮ would appear to be sustained from bar 60. The note shows as E♭ in BL19.
62	I	1	BL19 shows a whole note G.
63	I	*pickup*/1	Tie *ed.* There would otherwise be three notes against two syllables in "sottish."
		5	BL19 errs in showing an eighth note.
65	I	5–6	BL19 shows a dotted eighth note and a sixteenth note, giving too many counts in the bar.
69	I	|| [*t. sig.*]	*Ed.* The time change is indicated after 69.1 by an elongated 3 and a new key signature indicating B♭ and F♯. The F♯ is drawn twice on the score. The lower sharp is here *om*.
72	I	1	BL19 omits the dot.
81	I	5–6	Slur *ed.*, as phrased in bar 77. BL19 omits the slur.
82	I	1	BL19 omits the dot.
84	I	1	BL19 shows a whole note and no fermata.

[Poem 20] "The Diet of Cowley."

Composer: Pietro Reggio

Copy text: Songs 2:7.

Song text: F1 poem 20.

Textual variants: *title*] *My Diet* F1   *bar 27* captive] *Priso'ner* F1

Literary source: This poem has a rich song tradition. As illustrated in the literary collation for poem 20, there are two song text versions of the poem in addition to Reggio's. One appears in NAC71 and the other in *A Choice Collection of 120 Loyal Songs* (1684; reprinted 1685, 1694). Reggio's musical setting, however, is the only surviving one. Reggio's title is the same as appears in *A Choice Collection*, but the song texts are not the same. The textual variant in Reggio's bar 27 (reading "captive, and your slave" against F1's "*Priso'ner*, and your *slave*") is perhaps anticipated by the variant in NAC71, which reads "pris'ner, and your captiv'd slave." The NAC71 song text, however, adds "captiv'd" to create a decasyllabic line, while Reggio simply replaces "*Priso'ner*" with "captive." We would conclude that, despite the similarities, neither NAC71 nor *A Choice Collection* provided the literary source for *Songs* (1680). Reggio's song text is most similar to the literary text of "My Diet," which does not vary significantly in printings from O1 to F10. One of these printed editions was probably Reggio's source. The coincidence between *Songs* and *A Choice Collection* in the title, however, is difficult to dismiss. It is possible that Reggio heard the song version of this poem, known as "The Dyet of Cowley," before its being printed, and then determined to write a setting of the Cowley poem under the same title. It is just as possible that Reggio, like the song writer whose text appears in *A Choice Collection*, altered the title known from *The Mistress* in order to make specific the pronoun "My."

The musical setting: The setting is in A major, without a key signature. Though the composition is sectional, the first two measures of sections 1 and 2 and the first four measures of section 3 are based on the same harmonies.

Bar	Score	Notes	Comments
6	II	5	[♮] *ed*. *Songs* shows no accidental with note 5.
7	I	4, 6	[♯] *ed*. Harmonies of the passage in bars 6–8 suggest that the D♯ be sustained in bar 7. The accidental here does not appear in *Songs*.
8	II	2 [*fig*.]	*Songs* shows figures for both a natural and a sharped third at this note. We delete the latter.
16	I	1–4	Slur *ed*. Copy text slurs notes 3–4.
34	II	1	*Ed*. (in accordance with bar 17). In bar 34, *Songs* shows the whole note C, thereby ending the cadence on a first-inversion chord.
65	I–II	1	*Ed*. Copy text shows two tied, dotted half notes in the final bar.

Collations and Notes to the Musical Settings (pp. 363-371)

[Poem 21] "The Thief."

Composer: Pietro Reggio

Copy text: *Songs* 1:5.

Song text: F1 poem 21. Reggio sets the first two of four seven-line stanzas.

Textual variants: *bars 46-47* me thinks] methinks F1

Literary source: Variants appearing in printed editions O1-2 and F2 eliminate these as possible sources (see Literary Collation). Reggio's source could have been F1, F3-F7.

The musical setting: "The Thief" is written in D minor, without a key signature. Although the settings of the two stanzas begin with the same basic melody, they are continued and resolved with different musical material.

Bar	*Score*	*Notes*	*Comments*
25	II	1 [*fig.*]	*Songs* shows the figure as a sharp, raising the B from B♭ in bar 23.
29-30	I-II	‖	Double dots at the double bar appearing in *Songs* are here *om*. Reggio reiterates the time signature, 3/4, at the beginning of bar 30.
55	II	1 *fig.*	*Songs* shows a sharp for the third, along with the complex 8/6/4.

[Poem 22] "All-over Love."

Composer: William King

Copy text: *Poems*, p. 22 (Poems68).

Song text: F1 poem 22. Following the setting of stanza 1, King prints stanzas 2-4, completing the literary text, on *Poems* p. 23.

Textual variants: bar 3 short liv'd] short-liv'd F1   Passi'ons] *Passions* F1   *bar 8* though ne're so long] *passage in parentheses* F1   *stanza 3* (F1, l. 11) My *Affection*] My' *Affection* F1

Literary source: King could have taken his song text from O1, O2, or F1 (see Literary Collations). The accidentals in King's stanzas 2-4 are nearly identical to F1. The variant omissions in bars 3, 8, and stanza 3 are probably printer's errors. As is frequently the case in Poems68, the compositor for the setting/song text is less careful with the song text than the compositor for the sequent printed stanzas. F1 is the probable source.

NAC71 prints a song text of this poem that could derive from King's *Poems*. The King text is not related to a later setting by Pietro Reggio.

The musical setting: King's strophic setting is in D major. King produces a very engaging piece by setting the half note pulse against treble notes of short duration.

Bar	Score	Notes	Comments
–]	I	clef	Poems68 presents score I in the soprano clef, here realized editorially in the G clef.
–]	II	k. sig.	Poems68 indicates F♯ in the key signature twice, once on the F line in the score and again an octave lower, below the score. The lower sharp here *om*.
		[*figs.*]	*Ed.* Poems68 provides score II with no bass figures.
5	I	3–4	Slur *ed.* Copy text slurs notes 3–5.
10	II	fermata	The fermata sign appears only over score I in Poems68.

[Poem 22] "All-over Love."

Composer: Pietro Reggio

Copy text: Songs 2:14.

Song text: F1 poem 22. Reggio sets the first two of four stanzas. There are no substantive textual variants in the song text.

Literary source: The source could have been any of the printed editions of *The Mistress* up to F8.

There appear to have been three musical settings of this poem. In addition to the Reggio and William King settings, which are unrelated, the song text alone appears under the title "Song 203" in NAC71 (see Literary Collation).

The musical setting: Reggio writes in D minor, without a key signature. His form is essentially strophic, but there is an interesting structural change in the setting of the second stanza. Instead of bringing the first phrase to a cadence at the end of the fourth measure (as for stanza 1), Reggio delays the cadence to the beginning of the fifth, thereby placing the remaining text one half measure out of phase with the stanza 1 setting, until the final cadence.

Bar	Score	Notes	Comments
2	II	5	The B♮ is *ed.*, inserted to create a strong leading tone to the modulation that occurs in measure 3.
7–9	I	[*slur*]	*Ed.* The slur appears in *Songs* only above notes 2 and 3 in bar 7.
9	I	2–3	Tied Es in this edition supplant a dotted eighth E in *Songs*. Reggio clearly prefers the tie in this setting (see

Collations and Notes to the Musical Settings (pp. 371–376)

Bar	Score	Notes	Comments
			bars 7, 8, 23, and 24). In bar 23, however, notes 8–9 (given the tied form here) are also shown as a dotted eighth.
10	II	5	[♮] *ed.* (the G is suggested as a sharped third above note 1).
13	II	2	The note is, erroneously, a dotted quarter in *Songs*.
14	I–II	‖	Double dots on both sides of the double bar in *Songs* are here *om*.
20	I	2–4	Slur, *ed*. *Songs* slurs only notes 3–4.
21	I	6	[♮] *ed.* No accidental appears in *Songs*. See note to bar 2.
21	II	4 [*fig.*]	[♮] *ed.* In *Songs*, there is a sharp figure here, to change the previously flatted B in the accompaniment to a natural.
22–24	I	[*slur*]	*Ed.* See note to bars 7–9. Notes 8–9 of bar 23 appear as a dotted eighth and a sixteenth in *Songs*.
29	I–II	1	*Ed.* A pair of tied half notes appears in both scores of *Songs* (see headnote on Reggio, Editorial Principles).

[Poem 24] "The Bargain."

Composer: Pietro Reggio

Copy text: *Songs* 1:16.

Song text: F1 poem 24. Reggio sets the first three of six stanzas in the literary text.

Textual variants: bar 6 glitt'ring] *ed. (the vocal score requires this elision)*; glittering *Songs*, F1   bar 41 which] that F1   bars 47–48 nor See] nor ever *see* F1

Literary source: The reading "nor" in bar 5 establishes that O1–2 were not Reggio's source (see Literary Collation). The variant in *Songs* bar 41 may be scribal, echoing "which" in the next line (bar 45). The omission of "ever" in *Songs* bars 47–48 is unique to the song text. It could have been deliberate, a textual alteration to suit the meter and vocal score. Reggio probably copied his song text from one of the folio editions of *The Mistress*, F1–7.

The musical setting: The tonality of the piece is D minor. The form is ABC: a quadruple meter section framed by two triple meter sections containing different musical material.

Bar	Score	Notes	Comments
5	I	1	*Songs* shows a flat by the C, lowering it from the preceding C♯.
24	I-II	||	Double dots in *Songs* are here *om*.
36	I-II	||	As in bar 24, double dots appear in *Songs*.
60	I-II	[||]	The double bar in conclusion is *om* in *Songs*; the engraver has no room at the edge of the plate for it.

[Poem 26] "Counsel."

Composer: Pietro Reggio

Copy text: Songs 2:15.

Song text: F1 poem 26, stanza 1.

Textual variants: bars 23, 27 bleeding] *Purgings* F1

Literary source: Reggio sets the first of six six-line stanzas as printed in all octavo and folio editions of *The Mistress* through F8. The song text variant "bleeding" is synonymous with the reading in the literary text, and it could have been deliberately substituted to create an assonant relationship with "weak," which appears in the same phrase. No manuscript or printed source prior to Reggio's song text shows "bleeding," but the variant reappears in the text of an untitled setting, attributed to Michael Banfield, in *Comes Amoris* 5 (1694). It is likely that Banfield took his text from the Reggio setting. Musical similarities support this conclusion. Alternatively, both song texts could have derived from an undiscovered common manuscript source.

The musical setting: There are remarkable musical similarities between this setting and Michael Banfield's (CA94). Both settings are in D minor; both employ triple meter; both are strophic and treat the same portion of the literary text in a passive, lyrical manner. The only structural difference between the Reggio and Banfield versions is that Reggio extends the work by repeating the final line of the text.

Bar	Score	Notes	Comments
2-3	I	3-4 | 1-2	Slur across bar line *ed*. *Songs* slurs notes 3-4 in bar 2 and ties notes 1-2 in bar 3.
8	I-II	[endings]	In *Songs*, the repeat sign appears above note 1 in bar 1 and again after the second beat in bar 8. The bracketed half note in score I is editorial, for a first ending of the phrase. The second ending is as the notes appear in the copy text.

Bar	Score	Notes	Comments
18–19	I	1 | 1–2	Slur across bar line *ed. Songs* slurs notes 1–2 in bar 19.
26	I	2–4	Slur over the single vowel *ed.*, in agreement with score I, bar 22.

[Poem 26] ["Counsel."]

Composer: Mr. Michael Banfeild [Banfield]

Copy text: *Comes Amoris* (1694) 5:17 (CA94).

Song text: F1 poem 26. Banfield sets only the first of six six-line stanzas.

Textual variants: title] F1; *CA94 is untitled*   *bar 6* wounds] wound F1   *bar 24* Bleeding] *Purgings* F1

Literary source: The variant in bar 6 is unique to CA94; "Bleeding," in bar 24, appears in Reggio's song text and nowhere else. It is very likely that Banfield took his text from Reggio's *Songs*.

The musical setting: Banfield follows Reggio in setting only the first stanza of the poem, by employing triple meter, and by writing in the tonality of D minor. Reggio's use of repeats is the only structural feature that distinguishes these two settings.

Bar	Score	Notes	Comments
1	I–II	[*t. sig.*]	3/4 *ed.* CA94 shows 3 followed by a dotted 1.
–]	II	[*figs.*]	*Ed.*, throughout. CA94 has no figures.
21	I	2–3	*Ed.* A brace is missing between these notes in CA94, leaving the appearance of quarter notes.
24	II	2	*Ed.* The head of the note does not print in CA94. It may have been a middle C, designated for correction during the print run. If so, the correction was left uncompleted.

[Poem 29] "The Discovery."

Composer: Pietro Reggio

Copy text: *Songs* 2:16.

There are four other song versions of this Cowley poem: Nicholas Wootton's sectional setting of stanzas 1 and 2; a song text printed in NAC71; the song text transcribed in M6; and the song text transcribed in M9. None of these appears to be related to Reggio's composition. NAC71, M6, and M9, however, are clearly related on the evidence of their reading from the literary text, line 3 (see Literary Collation).

Song text: F1 poem 29. Reggio sets all four six-line stanzas.

Textual variants: *bar 1* By Heav'n] *ed. (as required by the vocal score)*; By Heaven *Songs*; BY 'Heaven F1   *bar 3* she' asham'd] *ed. (as required by the vocal score)*; she asham'd *Songs*, F1   *bar 18* some times] sometime F1; sometimes O2, F6-10, M9   *bar 23* pow'r] *ed. (as required by the vocal score)*; power *Songs*, F1   *bar 34* towards] tow'ards F1   till 'it] *ed. (as required by the vocal score)*; till it *Songs*; Till't F1

Literary source: The reading in *Songs*, bar 18, coupled with the 1680 publication date of *Songs*, indicates F6-7 or O2 as the literary source for Reggio's song text. Reggio's adherence to the literary text in this setting creates an unusual number of instances (bars 1, 3, and 23) where a single note in the vocal setting aligns with two syllables in the text. In these instances, and in bar 34 where Reggio's departure from the literary text creates the problem, the song text is editorially emended in the present edition.

The musical setting: The composition is in F minor with no key signature. Reggio uses a strophic form, but very freely. As in Wootton's setting (below), there is word painting here; Reggio's is the more versatile.

Bar	Score	Notes	Comments
8	I	5-9	Slur *ed*. *Songs* breaks the slur between notes 6 and 7.
12	I	3-5	Slur *ed*. *Songs* slurs notes 3-4.
14-15	I	1-7 | 1-2	Slur *ed*. *Songs* breaks the slur after note 4 in bar 14, and at the bar line.
15	I-II	| |	Double dots, *om* here, appear on both sides of the double bar in *Songs*.
16	I-II	*t. sig.*	*Songs* reiterates the C time signature at the beginning of bar 16.
23	I	5-9	Slur *ed*. *Songs* breaks the slur between notes 6 and 7.
27-29	I	*slur*	Slur *ed*., in accordance with the song text.
31	I	*t. sig*	*Songs* reiterates the C time signature at the beginning of bar 31.
36	II	4 [*fig.*]	[♮] *ed*. The G♯ calls for a B♮ in the harmony, not B♭ as at note 3.
43-44	I	1-7 | 1-2	Slur *ed*. *Songs* slurs notes 2-3, 5-7 in bar 43 and notes 1-2 in bar 44.
44	I	2	*Songs* shows (erroneously) a dotted quarter G.
45	I-II	*t. sig.*	*Songs* reiterates the C time signature at the beginning of bar 45.
47-48	I	5-7 | 1	Slur *ed*. *Songs* slurs notes 5-6 in bar 47, and shows the tie across the bar line.

Bar	Score	Notes	Comments
48	II	1 *fig.*	*Songs* shows 5, along with the 4–3. The same structure appears in bar 55, where the copy text does not show the figure 5.
51	I	1–4	Slur *ed.*, in accordance with the song text.
56–59	I	*slur*	Slur *ed. Songs* shows only the ties in bars 57 and 58 and the slur of notes 1–2 in bar 59.

[Poem 29] "A SONG" ["The Discovery."]

Composer: Nic. Wootton

Copy text: Chetham's Library (Manchester), Halliwell-Phillipps broadside no. 1929, a single sheet headed "A Song / The Words by Mr Cowley and Set to Mvssick by Nic: Wootton." The first initial and two letters of the engraver's name appear at the bottom right of the sheet: *"engrav'd by I. Ca"*. The remaining letters, along with the bottom right corner of the sheet, are missing. E. Benezit (*Dictionnaire des . . . Graveurs*) lists a possible candidate for the initials, J. Carwitham (active 1723–41). If Carwitham was the engraver, the sheet would have been printed some twenty to forty years after Wootton's death.

Song text: F1 poem 29. Wootton sets the first and second of four six-line stanzas. Stanzas 3 and 4 are printed at the bottom of the broadside.

Textual variants: *title*] A SONG; *The Discovery*, F1   *bars 1–2* Heav'ns] 'Heaven F1   *bars 3–4* boldly tell her] tell her boldly F1   *bars 19–20* Sometimes] sometime F1   *bar 24* being high] being so *high* F1   *bar 26* pow'r] power F1   *stanza 3* (F1, l. 14) nothing] nought F1 (F1, l. 15) by love] by her *Love* F1   *stanza 4* (F1, l. 19) him self] himself F1   (F1, l. 21) t'is he] He F1

Literary source: The variant in bars 19–20 also appears in O2, F6–10, and in Reggio's song text. The elisions in bars 1–2 and 26 also appear in O3–4, D2 (see Literary Collation). Other variants are unique to the song text and, along with the missing literary title, may suggest a manuscript source. If so, the manuscript text was attributed to Cowley. See notes to Reggio's setting for other musical treatments of this text.

The musical setting: Wootton writes this sectional composition in C major. With the exception of the declamatory phrase repeated in the opening measures, Wootton's setting is relatively straightforward as compared to Reggio's.

Bar	Score	Notes	Comments
3	II	1–3	The copy text shows these notes slurred.

[Poem 31] "Love Undiscovered."

Composer: William King

Copy text: *Poems*, p. 26 (Poems68).

Song text: F1 poem 31. King sets stanza 1 and prints the remaining two stanzas on the following page 27.

Textual variants: *bar 2* mode'rate] moderate F1   *bar 8* may] might

Literary source: The elision in bar 2 follows from King's vocal score; the bar 8 variant is a deliberate alteration, possibly King's or Cowley and King's (see notes to William King's setting "The Given Heart") and possibly introduced for greater assonance in the song text. The stanzas printed after the setting are virtually the same, in accidental and substantive regards, as F1—the probable source. The song text printed in NAC71 shows the bar 8 variant and begins (consistent with Poems68 and F1) with the word "I." NAC71 shows two unique variants, but the similarity with King in the reading "may" for "might" suggests that *Poems* was its source. The song text appearing with the anonymous setting copied in BL Add. MSS 19759 does not derive from King.

The musical setting: This strophic composition is based in D minor. There is no key signature.

Bar	Score	Notes	Comments
—]	II	[*figs.*]	*Ed.*, throughout. King's settings are without bass figures.
13	I	2	B♭ *ed*. The flat is sustained through the passage in bars 12-14.
15	I-II	1	Fermata, *ed.*, following King's usual practice.

[Poem 31] ["Love Undiscovered."]

Composer: The composition is unattributed.

Copy text: British Library Add. MSS 19759, fols. 26ᵛ-27 (BL19). As with the setting of James Hart's "The Despair" and others in BL19, Charles Campelman copies only the melody and song text from a manuscript setting that is no longer extant. As the notes to the musical setting below indicate, the copy is none too accurate. It is probable that most of the manuscript settings from which Campelman took the vocal score were written with a bass line; all of James Hart's published settings are. The editor has here provided a reasonable substitution for the missing continuo. It appears in brackets, underlying the manuscript copy of score I.

Song text: F1 poem 31. The setting is of the entire poem. The editorial elisions to BL19 in bars 2, 5, 10, and 29 are called for by the vocal score.

Collations and Notes to the Musical Settings (pp. 393-396)

Textual variants: title] *The bracketed title is from* F1. BL19 *erroneously titles the song* "The Concealment by Mr Cowley."   bar 1 Some] BL19, F2ff.; I 01-2, F1, NAC71   bar 2 mod'rat] *ed.*; moderat BL19; moderate F1   bar 3 that] which F1   bar 5 a] some F1   Med'icine] *ed.*, F1; Medicine BL19   bar 7 ere] ev'en F1   bar 8 loves] Love's F1   bar 10 may] might F1   dang'erous] *ed.*, F1; dangerous BL19   bar 15 cannot] must not F1   bar 23 torment] Torments F1   bar 25 too] *ed.*, F1; to BL19   bar 28 too] *ed.*, F1; to BL19   bar 29 heav'n] *ed.*; Heaven BL19, F1   bars 33-34 rather perish] *perish* rather F1   bar 37 But] Yet F1   bar 50 treasure] Treasures F1   bar 59 you] Thee F1

Literary source: The song text was copied from a manuscript that attributed the poem but gave it the wrong title. The manuscript source may have shown some of the textual variants apparent in BL19, but Campelman, the presumed copyist, probably introduced variants of his own. The musical setting shows a number of errors; so, too, the song text. The reading in bar 1, "Some," suggests that the manuscript source for this song text was based on F2 or a later printed edition. All other variants are unique to BL19 except for "treasure" in bar 50, which coincidentally agrees with NAC71. The BL19 song text is not derived from William King's setting, from which NAC71 may derive.

The musical setting: Like the Hart composition in the same manuscript collection, this piece is sectionally composed. One interesting feature of "Love Undiscovered" is the sudden change of meter, 2/2 to 3/4, nine measures before the end of the first section. This setting is quite compatible to the literary text, moreso than William King's.

Bar	Score	Notes	Comments
3	I	5-6	Slur *ed*. BL19 slurs notes 4-6.
4	I	1	[♯] *ed.*, as sustained from bar 3. BL19 omits the accidental.
5	I	3	*Ed.* The eighth note is dotted in BL19.
6	I	3	*Ed.* The quarter note F in BL19 is not dotted.
8-9	I	–]	The alignment between the vocal setting and the song text is obscure in these bars.
9	I	1-2	Slur *ed.*, accommodating the song text.
9-10	I	5 | 1	Tie *ed.*
12	I	[*t. sig.*]	3/4 *ed.* The time signature change is indicated by an elongated 3 1 between notes 1 and 2 in BL19.
17	I	2-3	Slur *ed.*
19	I	1-2	Slur *ed.*
20	I	[*t. sig.*]	Drawn as ¢ in BL19.

Bar	Score	Notes	Comments
21–22	I	|	There is no bar line in BL19.
22	I	1	*Ed*. The quarter note is not dotted in BL19.
22	I	3	[♯] *ed*. BL19 lacks the accidental sustained from bar 21.
30	I	2–4	Slur *ed*. BL19 shows the slur over notes 1–3.
33	I	| |	*Ed*. BL19 indicates the time signature as ₵ at a single bar line.
35	I	5	BL19 shows a "v" above the note, drawn more or less as the sharp above note 2 in bar 30. Here the accidental is editorially realized as a [♮].
37	I	| | [*t. sig.*]	Double bar and 3/4 *ed*; BL19 shows an elongated 3 1 at a single bar line.
39	I	2–3	Slur *ed*.
47–48	I	|	The bar line is missing in BL19.
54	I	1	*Ed*. A quarter note F♯ in BL19.
54	I	2–3	Slur *ed*.
59	I	2–3	Slur *ed*.
60	I	1–4	The triplet is erroneously drawn as sixteenth notes in BL19, and the slur is above only notes 1–3.
64	I	3–4	Slur *ed*. BL19 draws the slur over notes 2–4.
67	I	4	*Ed*. Campelman does not dot the eighth note in BL19.
69	I	1	First and second endings, the repeat sign (called for at bar 61) and the dotted half in the second ending, *ed*. BL19 ends with the half note shown here at ending 1, preparing for the repeat.

[Poem 32] "The Given Heart."

Composer: William King

Copy text: *Poems*, p. 34 (Poems68).

Song text: F1 poem 32. King sets the first stanza and prints the remaining four four-line stanzas on p. 35.

Textual variants: bar 6 Lovers] *Lover* F1   stanza 2 (F1, l. 12) *Granado-like*] Like a Granado shot F1

Literary source: The variant in bar 6 is unique to Poems68 and NAC71. The variant in stanza 2, read against F1, line 12, has the effect of regularizing a hypermetric line in the literary text. Cowley introduced manuscript changes of this sort in some other poems (see *The Collected Works* 1:184–93), so there is some precedent for authorial emendation that King could have known of only if he either collaborated with Cowley on the changes or if he had access to the manuscript emendations. An association between the composer and the poet is altogether possible, since both were at Oxford during the latter 1650s. Friendship between King and Cowley would certainly help explain why King elected to publish these settings in 1668, as a memorial to the poet. The variant could also have come about by King's independent decision. He reduces the twelve-syllable line from F1 to ten syllables so the text can be sung to the vocal score in bars 8–10, set for the ten syllables "for mine is but a torment to me now."

NAC71, alone of other printed sources, shares the stanza 2 variant (see Literary Collation). It is probable that the NAC71 text derives from King's *Poems*. There appears to be no relation between King's text and that set later by John Barrett, printed in *Thesaurus Musicus* 1, despite the fact that both are strophic settings of just the first stanza of Cowley's text.

Aside from the variants discussed above, the song text closely follows F1 in other regards.

The musical setting: King's setting, musically unrelated to the later setting by John Barrett, is characterized by the composer's word painting upon "wonder" and "torment."

Bar	Score	Notes	Comments
—]	I–II	k. sig.	The F♯ is indicated twice at the beginning of each system in Poems68. The lower sharp is here *om*.
—]	II	[*figs.*]	*Ed.* throughout.
10	II	1	The fermata is shown only above score I in the copy text.

[Poem 32] ["The Given Heart."]

Composer: Mr. John Barrett

Copy text: *Thesaurus Musicus* (1693) 1:24 (TM93).

Song text: F1 poem 32. Barrett sets stanza 1 and prints stanza 2 at the bottom right, filling out p. 24. Stanzas 3, 4, and 5 of the literary text do not appear.

Textual variants: title] F1; TM93 *is untitled*   bars 15–16, 23–24 torment now] *Torment* to me now F1   stanza 2 (F1, l. 7) Courtesies] courtesie F1 *stanza 2* (F1, l. 8) were parted] *parted* were F1

Literary source: The textual variants are all unique to this setting. Those in stanza 2 are probably a printer's, a copyist's, or Barrett's changes. The omission of "to me" in bars 15–16 and 23–24 suits the vocal score, making the last two lines of the first stanza octosyllabic. No effort was made to similarly trim the last line of stanza 2. The song text does not derive from William King's (see variants) or that in NAC71 (see Literary Collation). Any printed edition of *The Mistress* up through F11 could have been the source for the song text.

The musical setting: Unlike William King's similarly strophic setting, Barrett extends the text with a repeat of the first two lines and a *dal segno* at the end, and he employs B flat major for the bulk of the piece.

Bar	Score	Notes	Comments
1	I–II	[*t. sig.*]	3/4 *ed*. TM93 shows 3 followed by a dotted 1.
8	I–II	ǀ ǀ	TM93 shows a tie connecting the note in ending 1 to that in ending 2. It is here *om*. The repeat dots at ending 1 are *ed*.

[Poem 37] "The Heart Fled Again."

Composer: Pietro Reggio

Copy text: *Songs* 1:39.

Song text: F1 poem 37. Reggio sets the first stanza of five in the literary text. There are no substantive textual variants.

Literary source: The song text could have been copied from any printed edition of *The Mistress* to F8 except O2, which omits the word "back" in line 5 (see Literary Collation). The word appears in *Songs*, bar 19.

The musical setting: Reggio's setting is similar in a number of respects to Robert King's later rendition of the same song text. The A-minor tonality and triple time shown in Reggio's setting, for example, are reemployed in Robert King's more expressive treatment. These similarities raise the possibility that King's setting is an elaboration of Reggio's.

Bar	Score	Notes	Comments
—]	I	[*clef*]	*Songs* places score I in the soprano clef. Notes are reassigned to the regular treble clef in this edition.
1	I–II	[*t. sig.*]	The time signature is indicated by an elongated "3" in *Songs*.

[Poem 37] ["The Heart Fled Again."]

Composer: Robert King

Copy text: *A Second Booke of Songs* (c. 1695), p. 13 (SBS).

Collations and Notes to the Musical Settings (pp. 401–409)

Song text: F1 poem 37, stanza 1.

Textual variants: title] *The bracketed title is from* F1. SBS *is untitled; its song text is unattributed.*   text] SBS *spells* "would'st," "wouldst," *and* "woudst" *variously; here normalized as* "would'st."   bar 23 away as] away; / Fled as F1

Literary source: The song text could have been copied from any of the printed editions: *The Mistress, Poems*, or the *Works*. Robert King's departures from the literary text are in the form of repetitions, in the course of which he eliminates a single word, "Fled." Though Pietro Reggio's setting keeps this word from the first stanza of the poem, it also could have been the source for King's song text.

The musical setting: See notes to Reggio's setting for similarities with this composition. As in the SBS setting of "The Concealment," this engraved score shows a number of careless errors in notation and inconsistencies in the drawing of slur lines. It is relatively clear that King wants a slur over sustained vowels in the song text. At such places where SBS omits the slur, the editor provides a slur within brackets. This occurs in bar-score 6.II; 22.II; 37–39.II; 40–42.I; 41–42.II; 43.II; 50.II; and 59.I. In bars 51–52, SBS shows the slur only in score I, ending it on the first note of bar 52. The slur in bar 52 score II is *ed*.

Bar	Score	Notes	Comments
–]	–]	–]	The top vocal line is designated score I, the second vocal line score II, and the continuo score III, throughout.
6	I	rest	SBS shows a faint dot here. We treat bar 6 as bar 8, where King's rest is clearly indicated.
25	I	3	SBS shows a dotted half note E.
26	III	2	SBS copy i shows both the D and a low A. The A does not appear in copies ii and iii, although the stem of the D is extended downwards an extra line.
29	III	1	SBS shows a whole note.
33	III	1	SBS shows a whole note.
35	III	1	SBS shows a whole note.
46	I	1	SBS shows the first B as a quarter note, leaving the bar a count short.
47	II	1	SBS omits the dot to the half note.
53	III	3*fig*.	SBS shows 4-3 with a ♯ drawn off to the right.
54	I	*D.S.*	SBS shows the repeat sign within the top vocal score.
55	II	6	C♮ in SBS.

Bar	Score	Notes	Comments
62	I–III	1,1	Numbered endings and repeat signs are *ed*. SBS indicates the double ending with a double bar between the two As. The A notes are tied, through the double bar, and the repeat sign relating back to bar 54 is missing in SBS. The copy text shows a whole note for the second ending in all three scores. In score III, the first ending note, due to smudged ink, appears to be C over A, and the second ending bass note is given as an undotted C. No dot appears, either, in second endings in scores I and II.

[Poem 41] "The Rich Rivall Out of Mr. Cowley."

Composer: Henry Purcell

Copy text: BL MS RM20.h.8, fols. 174^v–175^v (RM20); collated settings: *The Theater of Music*, Book 2, 1685 (TM85[2]), *Orpheus Britannicus*, 1698 (OB98), and Folger MS V.b.197 (Fol19), p. 1. Differences in the song text and musical setting, outlined below, indicate two versions of this song. Both versions have some claim to authority. RM20, appearing in Purcell's copybook, is perhaps the earlier of the two. The song text in RM20 is substantively closer to F1 and the printed editions of *The Mistress* than versions in TM85(2), OB98, and Fol19. RM20, however, has some errors and omissions in both the song text and the musical setting.

The setting found in TM85(2) was reissued in Henry Playford's *The New Treasury of Musick* (London, 1695), and the text and score in OB98 is based on TM85(2). Most of the bass figures in the present edition are accepted from OB98; those appearing without brackets are from the copy text. Fol19 is very close to OB98 in title, text, most bass figures, and details of the setting. The notational variants in bars 4 and 8 (see below) imply that Fol19 derives from a manuscript source similar to but not the same as that providing copy for TM85(2)/OB98. This hypothesis is strengthened by the fact that Fol19 shows its most significant variant in bar 4 where problems exist in RM20, and presumably in the original score, but not in TM85(2)/OB98. Alternatively, the variants in Fol19 could have been introduced by the copyist.

There are significant musical differences between RM20 and TM85(2)/OB98/Fol19. RM20 has the greater claim to authority. It appears in the copybook Purcell used for his own transcriptions, and there is evidence of the copyist's determination to transcribe only what he could clearly read. Where his source is unclear, both in the song text and in the notation, he leaves blanks—possibly anticipating that Purcell would provide the correct readings. TM85(2), the first printed edition, provides a complete and coherent text. But Playford and Carr's claim to be producing "perfect and exact" printed scores may sound like self-advertising, given the publishers' admitted lack of contact with their "Authors in general" (see TM85[1], sig. A2). Henry Purcell

Collations and Notes to the Musical Settings (pp. 410–411)   595

and John Blow, however, are treated separately from other composers. In a prefatory letter to the first book of *The Theater of Music*, and again in the fourth book, they are thanked by the publishers for serving as unofficial copy editors, "perusing several of the Songs" and "adding Thorow-Basses to such as wanted them." Neither Purcell nor anyone else added bass figures to "The Rich Rival" in TM85(2), and the musical changes that distinguish TM85(2) from RM20 are not obviously corrections or emendations, except in bars 4, 53, and 54. Nevertheless, if the publishers' remarks concerning Purcell's editorial work on the first and fourth books of *The Theater of Music* are given credit, TM85(2) gains some authority by association. Omissions in RM20 are thus supplied with readings from TM85(2), which recur in OB98.

Song text: F1 poem 41. Purcell sets the entire poem.

Textual variants: *title*] RM20; The rich Rival F1; The Rich RIVAL [*Mr. Cowley's words.*] TM85(2); The Rich RIVAL. Words out of *Cowley*. OB98, Fol19   *bar 7* what's] F1 and Σ; w^h RM20   *bar 8* You've] RM20; You 'have F1;   Your] TM85(2), OB98, Fol19   lands] RM20; land Σ   *bar 9* you' ve] RM20; you' have F1; you're TM85(2), OB98, Fol19   *bar 20* whilst] RM20, F1; while TM85(2), OB98, Fol19   *bar 21* word om. in copy text*; Rhet'rick] TM85(2), OB98, Fol19; *Rhetorick* F1   *bar 25* of] RM20, OB98, Fol19; o' F1, TM85(2)   *bar 29* Let's] Σ; lets Fol 19   *bar 34* names] RM20, F1; name TM85(2), OB98, Fol19   *bar 50* "and" *pen-altered to* "but" *in copy text*] RM20; and TM85(2), OB98, Fol19; And F1   *bar 51* she an] RM20, TM85(2), OB98, Fol19; she'an F1   *bars 61–62* "shoud become of me" *pen-altered to* "woud become of yee" in copy text; "would become of thee" *is the majority reading*.

RM20 shows virtually no punctuation marks. TM85(2), OB98, and Fol19, though more fully punctuated, are not exemplary in this regard. Performance of this witty and relatively complex song text would be assisted by reference to the punctuation marks reproduced in the literary text in the first part of this volume.

Literary source: The song text in RM20 was copied from a manuscript. Had it been taken from a printed edition of the literary text or of the setting, the terms "Rhetorick" (bar 20) and "And" (bar 50) would have been easily legible, but the copyist of RM20 apparently cannot decipher these words; he leaves a blank space for the first and shows doubts about the second. The manuscript providing text for RM20 is close to that used for the first printed setting, TM85(2), but there are significant differences in the song texts. Textual errors in bar 25 (affecting RM20) and bars 8, 9, 20, and 34 (affecting TM85[2]) make it clear that neither RM20 nor TM85(2) was derived from the other. Numerous musical differences between the two (see below) underscore this point. A common ancestor may be inferred from the variant readings (bar 51 and perhaps bar 21) shared by all song texts. Variants in the text

596 The Musical Settings

appearing in bars 8, 9, 20, and 34 may suggest a manuscript version of the poem independent of the printed texts and of literary MSS M10, M11, and M24 (see Literary Collation) from which Fol19, TM85(2), and subsequently OB98 were derived. These variant readings are not made necessary by the musical notation, but they could easily have been scribal and/or compositorial errors, such as mistaking "you've" as "you're." Textual variants in bars 21 and 51 are called for by the musical setting. Spelling and accidentals in the song text of RM20 are not consistent with those in TM85(2) and, as discussed above, RM20 is deficient in punctuation. It is likely that the omissions and spelling in RM20 are the copyist's, and that the variant spelling and punctuation in TM85(2) was provided by someone in Playford's shop. On the basis of all textual evidence, we draw the following conclusions as to the literary source: RM20 was copied from a manuscript setting, probably Purcell's autograph, that derived its song text from one of the printed editions of *The Mistress* up through F9 (1681). The TM85(2)/Fol19/OB98 song text derives from a manuscript similar to but not the same as the source for RM20; its song text variants are probably scribal and/or compositorial errors.

The musical setting: This is a through-composed work in ABC form, each section in a different meter. It is pitched in B♭ throughout, although Purcell moves through a number of related keys.

Bar	Score	Notes	Comments
1	I–II	t. sig.	TM85(2), OB98, and Fol19 give the time signature as ₵.
1–3	II	1–3	TM85(2), OB98, Fol19 tie these whole notes.
4	I	1–4	*Ed.*, following TM85(2), OB98, Fol19, which show two sixteenth notes, a dotted sixteenth, and a thirty-second note. RM20 errs in showing a sixteenth, a dotted sixteenth, a thirty-second, and an eighth note.
4	I	5–6	Fol19 reads eighth B and sixteenth A, slurred, and adds a sixteenth B for the song text "as."
4	II	2	G in TM85(2), OB98, Fol19.
6	II	1–2	Score II is less active in TM85(2), OB98, Fol19, all of which show a dotted quarter C and an eighth D. All sources show activity similar to RM20's bar 6 in bar 52, score II.
6	II	6	The figure is accepted from OB98. The bracketed natural represents the copy text sharp, canceling the key signature. RM20, as the other settings, employs the sharp for this purpose here and in the following bars and scores: 14.I; 15.I–II; 16.I, and in the figure accepted from OB98 in II.1; 21.I and in the figure

Collations and Notes to the Musical Settings (pp. 411–412)

Bar	Score	Notes	Comments
			accepted from OB98 in II.1; 22.II; 24.I; 26.I–II; 27.I–II; 28.I–II; 30.I; 32.I; 33.I; 47.II; 48.I, and in the figure accepted from OB98 in II.1; 53.I, and in the bass figure 3 accepted from OB98; 55.I, and in the figure at note 1 and the ♯4 at note 2, score II, both accepted from OB98. In all of these instances, this edition indicates a bracketed natural.
8	I	4	Fol19 reads B.
9	II	2 [*fig.*]	6 accepted from OB98 here; figs. are from OB98 in the following places bracketed beneath score II: bar 15, notes 1, 4; 17.3; 19.3, 20, the 4-♯3; 23.1, 3, 4; 25, the 6 at n. 1; 27, the sharp at n. 1; 29, the 6 at n. 3; 33, the 4-♯3; 39, the 6s at nn. 1, 2; 41, the 6 at n. 3; 44, the ♯6 at n. 1; 48, nn. 1, 2; 51, the 6 at n. 2; 53, the 4-[♮]3 at n. 2; 56, n. 1; 57, the 6 at n. 2; 59, the ♭5 at n. 1; 61, the 4-3 at n. 2. Where a figure from OB98 is *om* or editorially changed, a note is given below.
9	II	3–5	TM85(2), OB98, Fol19 show a dotted quarter E and an eighth D.
12	I–II	[*t. sig.*]	¢ *ed*. All sources show this sign reversed, indicating ¢ at a faster tempo. RM20, unlike TM85(2), OB98, and Fol19, begins the song with the time signature C, or 4/4 (see note to bar 1). Common time is appropriately succeeded by ¢, or 2/2. In TM85(2), OB98, and Fol19, the new time signature is introduced at bar 11. In these settings, bar 11 shows a dotted half and quarter note in score II.
12	II	–]	Reading from TM85(2), OB98, and Fol19; the figure is from OB98. Copy text is blank here.
13	II	1–2	These are quarter notes in TM85(2), OB98, and Fol19.
14	II	[*fig.*]	OB98 gives the sharp figure; [7] *ed*.
15	I	1–2, 3–4	Slurs *om* in RM20; they appear in TM85(2), OB98, Fol19.
15	I	6	Erroneously an eighth note in RM20.
17	I	4–6	TM85(2), OB98, Fol19 show an eighth note followed by two sixteenths.
17	II	1–2	TM85(2), OB98, Fol19 show two quarter notes.
18	I	6	F♯ in TM85(2), OB98, Fol19.
19	I	2–3	Slur *ed*. TM85(2), OB98, Fol19 show a sixteenth and a dotted eighth.
19	II	2–4	Notes lowered an octave in TM85(2), OB98, Fol19.
19	II	4	C in TM85(2), OB98, Fol19.

Bar	Score	Notes	Comments
20	II	1–2	In TM85(2), OB98, Fol19, there is one low D half note.
21	I	2	TM85(2), OB98, Fol19 show two slurred eighth notes, A and G.
22	II	2–3	TM85(2), OB98, Fol19 show a dotted quarter and an eighth note.
24	I	1–3	TM85(2), OB98, Fol19 show notes 1–2 slurred for the word "friends" and two quarter notes for "agree."
24	I–II		TM85(2), OB98, Fol19 show a double bar at the end of this measure. TM85(2) and OB98, but not Fol19, show a repeat sign in bar 23, above the third note in score I, over the word "and." The printed settings thus call for a repeat of the phrase "and our friends agree."
27	II	1–2	TM85(2), OB98, Fol19 show a quarter note A, and two eighth notes, A and G.
28	I	6–7	Slur *ed.* (also in OB98, TM85(2), Fol19).
28	II	3	TM85(2), OB98, Fol19 show a dotted quarter and an eighth note.
29	II	2	E♮ *ed.* (as in TM85(2), OB98, Fol19).
30	II	3–4 [*fig.*]	OB98 shows 4-♯3 here.
31	I	4–5	TM85(2), OB98, Fol19 show two eighth notes.
32	II	1 [*fig.*]	OB98, Fol19 show 5 as the figure. The E in score I raised from the key-signed E♭ to E♮.
33	I	1	Copy text shows ornamentation over the note.
33	I	2–3	Slur *ed.* (as in TM85[2], OB98, Fol19).
34	I	5	TM85(2), OB98, Fol19 show a dotted quarter, omitting the rest.
37	I	1	TM85(2), OB98, Fol19 show two slurred eighth notes, E and D.
37	II	3 [*fig.*]	OB98 shows the figure 4-3.
38	I–II	[*t. sig.*]	3/4 *ed.* Copy text indicates the time signature with an elongated figure 3; TM85(2) and OB98 show 3 1; Fol19 shows 3.
41	I	1–2	Slur *ed.* (as in TM85(2), OB98, Fol19).
41	I	2	An A in TM85(2), OB98, Fol19.
41–42	I–II			RM20 omits the bar line here and in the following bars: 45–46; 47–48; 49–50; 51–52; 53–54; 54–55; 57–58; and 60–61. In these places the bar line is editorially provided.
42	II	1	In TM85(2) the note is D.

Collations and Notes to the Musical Settings (pp. 413–417)

Bar	Score	Notes	Comments
44	I	2–3	Slur *ed.* (as in TM85[2], OB98, Fol19).
45	I	*slur*	TM85(2), OB98, Fol19 slur notes 1–3, for the song text "had," and notes 4–6, for the first syllable of "access." RM20 shows ornamentation over note 5.
47	II	1 [*fig.*]	OB98 shows a ♭5 as the figure.
49	I	5–6	Slur *ed.* (as in TM85[2], OB98, Fol19).
51	I	3–5	TM85(2), OB98, Fol19 show a quarter note F.
51	II	1 *fig.*	2 in RM20; OB98 shows the figure 4.
53	II	2	Reading from TM85(2), OB98, Fol19. Copy text breaks the bar between two systems and shows a dotted quarter G tied to an eighth G.
54	II	1	*Ed.* (as in TM85[2], OB98, Fol19). Copy text shows a half note C followed by a quarter note C an octave higher, then a bar line. The quarter note C actually belongs to the next measure, 55, which otherwise lacks a full count.
57	I	1–2, 5–6	TM85(2), OB98, Fol19 show a dotted eighth followed by a sixteenth in both of these pairs.
62	I–II	[*D.S.*]	*Ed.* Bars 59–62 are to be repeated in all four sources, where the repeat sign is given at bar 59. None of the sources reference the repeat at the end of bar 62.

[Poem 44] "A Song on Ingratitude, Words by Mr. Cowley."

Composer: Dr. [John] Blow

Copy text: *The Theater of Music*, 1687 (TM87), p. 66; reissued in *The New Treasury of Musick* (1695).

Song text: F1 poem 44.

Textual variants: *title*] TM87; *Loves Ingratitude* F1   *bar 23* pow'r] power F1   *bar 40* Flow'r] *flour* F1–7; *flower* F8–10; *Flow'r* O3–4, D2   *bar 56* settl'd] settled F1

Literary source: Blow set the entire text of the poem. There are no substantive and only a few metrical departures from normative readings in the octavo and folio editions of Cowley's *The Mistress, Poems*, and *Works*. The three variants listed above are elisions called for by the musical setting. Blow's reading in bar 40 coincidentally agrees with O3, which was published in 1707. The most significant departure from the literary text is in Blow's title. It is unsurprising that he should have chosen to retitle the poem as a song. The omission of "Love's" from the title is the only evidence that suggests the possibility of an independent manuscript source for the text. Concurrence between the song text and the literary text is far more compelling. We conclude that Blow's source was one of the printed editions; F9 and F10 would perhaps have been most readily available.

The musical setting: The work progresses through four sections, shifting meter and, at the last, changing key. Blow gives a sensitive reading to the text of the poem, repeating some phrases for emphasis and even marking (if it is Blow's marking) a change of dynamic at measure 38. TM87 (and its reprint in *The New Treasury of Musick*) is the only source we have located for this composition. The authority of TM87 is attested by the publisher's claim that settings by John Blow, Henry Purcell, and several others are "true Copies" (that is, autograph copies) that "were by them perused, before they were put to the Press." See the prefatory letter to "All Lovers and Understanders of Musick," TM87, sig. A2.

Bar	Score	Notes	Comments
7	II	1	B♮, *ed.* TM87 shows no accidental in score II, although the Bs in score I are shown with sharps, raising them from the flat in the key signature.
11	I-II	[*t. sig.*]	TM87 indicates the time signature at the beginning of the bar as ₵ 3.
14	II	1	TM87 shows a partial "x," or sharp, by the first F. The sign is fully printed by the second F.
18	I	4	TM87 shows a sharp.
19	I	1	B [♮] *ed.* In TM87 there is no accidental to carry the B♮ from bar 18.
23	II	5	TM87 raises the flatted E with a sharp sign.
28	I	5	TM87 raises the B with a sharp sign.
31	I	3	TM87 raises the B with a sharp sign.
34	II	1 *fig.*	TM87 reads 7-♯6.
38	I	3	"*soft.*" is inscribed above score I in TM87.
40	I	2	"*loud.*" *ed.*, as the text suggests, and following from the marking at bar 38.
41	I	1	TM87 raises the B with a sharp sign.
46	I-II	[*t. sig.*]	TM87 indicates the time signature change as ₵ 3, as above in bar 11. The bar lines in this section are drawn to frame six quarter notes.
46	I-II	*k. sig.*	The F♯ in the key is written twice in TM87, on both Fs in the scores; the [♮] B is inferred but not marked.
48-49	I	5 | 1-2	The slur across the bar line is editorial. TM87 shows only a tie between the two Ds.

Collations and Notes to the Musical Settings (pp. 417–424)

Bar	Score	Notes	Comments
49	I	2,4,6	TM87 shows flats by each of these Cs. No accidental appears by the C at note 3.
49	I	4–5	Slur *ed.*
53	II	1	TM87 shows an "x," or sharp, by the C, which is sharped in the signature.
57	I–II	[*t. sig.*]	TM87 presents this partial measure with no indication of a time change. The word "Throne" is accorded three counts, the bar line is drawn, and then bar 58 resumes 6/4.

[Poem 46] ["Coldness."]

Composer: Pietro Reggio

Copy text: BL Add. MSS 31440, fols. 156v–157r (BL31), subscribed "P Reggio." As others have noted, this manuscript collection is wrongly catalogued as by Pietro Reggio and "autograph" (Pamela Willetts, "A Neglected Source of Monody and Madrigal," *Music and Letters* 43 [1962]: 329-30; Gloria Rose, "Pietro Reggio—A Wandering Musician," *Music and Letters* 46 [1965]: 212n; Rose goes on to claim that neither the signed setting nor any of the other compositions is by Reggio). The setting subscribed as Reggio's, the only one in the collection showing a composer's name and the only one in English, is laterally scored on the bottom half of two folio pages in a sketchy hand that is represented nowhere else in the collection. Above it, on both pages, is the conclusion of a setting ("Iesu dulciss") for four voices. These pages, with three systems lined in advance for up to five parts, had space to accommodate the later transcription of "Coldness." The setting is listed at the end of one of the "contents" leaves (fol. 98, see bibliographical description) in a second hand and different ink: "As Water fluid is - - - 15." The index entry is a late one. Gloria Rose's comparison of fols. 156v–157r with Reggio's handwriting in BL MS Harley 1501 establishes that Reggio himself did not transcribe this setting in BL31. But she is wrong to dismiss the validity of the subscription on the basis of the hand, since it is possible that someone else copied Reggio's setting on these pages. Furthermore, this setting is similar to others that are unquestionably Reggio's.

Reggio writes other duets (cf. *Songs* 2:23, 25, 26, and 29, along with the songs for two voices in Harley 1501), and the great majority of Reggio's settings from *The Mistress* show one flat or sharp less than the tonality of the piece requires with accidentals written into the score where they are needed. Similarly, in the duet "Coldness" B-flats are introduced to indicate a key of D minor, and the sharp is used to naturalize previously flatted Bs in bars 2 and 7. These characteristics are not at all uncommon to the period, and alone they would not establish that "Coldness" is Reggio's composition. Combined with the subscription, however, they strengthen the case for Reggio's authorship. The duet is copied without continuo, so there is no figured bass to compare with Reggio's use of figures in *Songs*. But the song text, *The Mistress* poem 46, is from Reggio's favorite source, and this considerably strengthens the validity of the subscription. It is hard to imagine why a copyist would include Reggio's name unless to verify authorship or, perhaps, to highlight the distinction between this setting and the work of other composers represented in the collection. As no other composer has been identified, we accept the piece as probably by Reggio, transcribed by an anonymous copyist.

Song text: F1 poem 46. Reggio sets the first of three stanzas in the literary text.

Textual variants: *title*] BL31 *is untitled   bars 2–3* doth] do F1   *bar 15 The copyist gives* doth *in the top voice and* does *(here normalized to voice I) in the bottom;* F1 *reads* Does. *The copyist spells both* rigor *and* rigour, restraine *and* restrayne *(here normalized to* rigor *and* restraine*). Ampersands in bars 4 and 18 are here silently expanded.*

Literary source: BL31 is difficult to date as a whole. Reggio's setting was obviously composed before his death (1685), though the transcription could have been later. One of the printed editions of *The Mistress* through F10 could have been the literary source, but there is evidence suggesting a manuscript source for this song text. Unlike most other of Reggio's settings from *The Mistress*, this one lacks a title; the variant in bars 2–3, though a minor one, appears in no printed source; and Cowley, in autograph poems and letters, characteristically spells "woeman" for "woman." Though there are orthographic vagaries in BL31 (noted above), the copyist is consistent in spelling "woeman." As noted in the biographical sketch (p. 314), it is possible that Reggio encountered Cowley in London at some time between 1664 and 1667. The conjecture might follow that Cowley wrote out the verse from "Coldness" for him.

The musical setting: This duet is pitched in D minor. There is no key signature. Reggio employs some imitation between the voices and some independent counterpoint. For the rest of the piece the voices move in a parallel fashion.

Bar	Score	Notes	Comments
–]	I	clef	*Ed.* Soprano clef in BL31.
1	II	4–6	*Ed.* BL31 shows a dotted quarter A, followed by a quarter A. The dotted quarter, requiring that the "i" in "fluid" be elided and the word sung as "flu'd," may be part of the error. While this enunciation is possible, the editor corrects note values to a more probable treatment of the song text, following the treatment of "solid" in bars 3–4.

Bar	Score	Notes	Comments
2	I	4-6	*Ed.* BL31 shows two quarter note As. See note above.
2	II	5	BL31 shows, faintly, a sharp by the B, raising it from the B♭ in notes 1-3.
3	II	1-6	Slur *ed.* The copyist is inconsistent in drawing slurs over extended vowels in the song text. Editorial slurs are added to bar 3, score I, notes 5-7; 8.II.4-5; and 12-14.I-II, all notes, through the first in bar 14.
7	I	3	The accidental is shown as a sharp in BL31 (as in 2.II).

[Poem 47] "The Enjoyment."

Composer: William King

Copy text: *Poems*, p. 6 (Poems68).

Song text: F1 poem 47. King sets stanza 1 and prints the remaining four stanzas on p. 7.

Textual variants: title] Poems68; *The Injoyment* F1   bar 4 *Albi'on*] *Albion* F1   stanza 5 (F1, l. 27) thou hast] thou'hast F1

Literary source: The title appears only in O1-2, F1, and M21 (see Literary Collation). King's title corrects the spelling from "Injoyment" to "Enjoyment," possibly removing a pun. Due to their unique textual variants, M21 and O1-2 cannot be the source. F1 remains as the probable source. The song text printed in NAC71 shows a unique variant in the first line and omits the title. Otherwise, it could have derived from King's *Poems*.

The musical setting: King's setting, in G major and strophic in form, is not related to Reggio's later treatment of this song text. King creates a closely knit piece through the use of a four sixteenth note figure (see bar 1, score I, 3, I; 6, I; 9, I).

Bar	Score	Notes	Comments
–]	I-II	*k. sig.*	The copy text indicates the F♯ twice in each score. The lower sharps are here *om.*
–]	II	[*figs.*]	*Ed.*, throughout.
1	II	1	*Ed.*, following the University of Delaware copy, which shows the note inked over as a quarter. Copy text shows a half note G.
10	II	1	The fermata, *ed.* It is printed only above score I in the copy text.

[Poem 47] ["The Injoyment."]

Composer: Pietro Reggio

Copy text: Songs 2:9.

Song text: F1 poem 47. Reggio sets stanzas 1-3 of five from the literary text.

Textual variants: [title] F1; *the composition is untitled in Songs*   *bar 17* sailers'] Sailors F1   *bar 46* gentlier] gentli'er F1

In addition to Reggio's and William King's unrelated settings of this poem, a song text without music appears under the title "Song 106" in NAC71 (see Literary Collation). The NAC71 song text is independent of Reggio's, but see Notes to King's setting above.

Literary source: Reggio omits the title to this poem, as do all editions of *The Mistress* after F1. Other variants in Reggio's song text are not sufficiently consequential to suggest a source other than one of the printings F2-7.

The musical setting: Reggio uses a D minor tonality with no key signature. The setting is in ABA' form. In sections A and A', Reggio inserts short instrumental responses to the vocal score.

Bar	Score	Notes	Comments
1	I-II	[*t. sig.*]	The time signature is initially given as C 3/4 in *Songs*.
8-9	I	1-3 | 1	Slur is *ed*. Notes 2-3 in bar 8 are slurred in *Songs*.
15	I	2-3	The slur indicates that "Albion" is treated as two syllables.
16	I	2-3	Slur, *ed*.
23-24	I	2-4 | 1-2	Slur, *ed*.; it is broken at the bar line in *Songs*.
29	I	1-3	Slur, *ed*. Notes 2-3 are slurred in *Songs*.
44	I-II	| |	*Songs* shows double dots on both sides of the double bar here and at bar 59.
46	II	3	The B♮ is *ed*. *Songs* omits an accidental here.
52	II	6	The G♮ is *ed*.
59	I-II	| |	*Songs* shows double dots at the double bar (see note to bar 44).
60	I-II	[*t. sig.*]	The return to 3/4 time is indicated in *Songs* with a simple 3/4 signature at bar 60—as contrasted with the C 3/4 at bar 1.
67-68	I	1-3 | 1	Slur, *ed*. Only notes 2-3 in bar 67 are slurred in *Songs*.

Collations and Notes to the Musical Settings (pp. 428–436)   605

[Poem 51] "The Picture."

Composer: Pietro Reggio

Copy text: Songs 1:30.

Song text: F1 poem 51. Reggio sets stanzas 1–2 of four that appear in all printings of the literary text.

Textual variants: title The Picture.] *Songs*, O1–2 (*index*); *My Picture* F1 and Σ   bar 6 I] *Songs*; you F1 and Σ.

Literary source: Reggio's title agrees with the title printed in the index of O1 and the derivative O2 (1647). This title nowhere else appears with the literary or song text. Reggio's variant reading "I" (bar 6; line 2 of the literary text) is unique. In other regards, Reggio's song text is substantially in agreement with printed texts of *The Mistress*. The variant title and bar 6 reading in *Songs* suggest a manuscript source for the song text. The possibility that such a manuscript derived from a source written before 1647 is promoted by the appearance of the *Songs* title in the index of O1 and O2. The index variant is, otherwise, explainable as an error (though it is possible that the manuscript copy from which O1 was set was unclearly titled), and its reappearance in Reggio's title may be mere coincidence. We know of no physical evidence to support the manuscript hypothesis. Alternatively Reggio took his text from one of the printed editions and he or his engraver created the title and variant reading.

The musical setting: The piece is written in A minor and is strophic in form.

Bar	Score	Notes	Comments
1	I–II	[*t. sig.*]	The time signature is shown as C 3/4 in both scores, in *Songs*.
15	I–II	1	In *Songs* the D.S. sign is inscribed above this note in score I only.
20	II	3	The sharp is *ed.*, prompted by the F♯ in score I and the movement toward bar 21.
22	I–II	1	First and second endings, *ed. Songs* shows two tied, dotted half notes, the D.S. sign centered above and between them in score I only, followed by the double bar and double dots.
23	I–II	[*t. sig.*]	After the double bar, the time signature is reintroduced in the copy text as simply 3/4 (contrasting with C 3/4 in bar 1). Double dots are shown at the beginning of this bar.
44	I	1	A D.S. sign appears above the final dotted half note in *Songs*. Uncharacteristically no earlier D.S. sign appears in this section of the song to indicate what phrases are to

Bar	Score	Notes	Comments

be repeated. It is possible that Reggio intended the same kind of repeat here as is indicated for bars 15–22, but then realized that his song text does not allow a coherent statement for repetition in the last eight bars. There are similar instances elsewhere in *Songs*, where Reggio elects a repeat in one section and not in others. The partially rendered *D.S.* here is *om* in this edition.

[Poem 52] "The Concealment."

Composer: William King

Copy text: *Poems*, p. 1 (Poems68). King's setting is later printed, without attribution, in *New Ayres and Dialogues* (1678).

Song text: F1 poem 52. The composer sets stanza 1 and prints stanzas 2–3, completing the poem, on the following page 3. There are no substantive variants from F1 and no accidental variants except in the setting of stanza 1, where the compositor introduces some capital letters and omits some punctuation. It appears that stanza 1, with the musical setting, and stanzas 2–3 were set by different compositors.

Literary source: F1. William King's song text is unrealted to the poetic text in WR50 (see Literary Collation) and to the later setting by Henry Purcell. Robert King's setting could have been dervied from the text in Poems68.

The musical setting: For the suggestion that Robert King used William's setting as a point of departure, see the note to that setting in SBS. Purcell's setting appears to be musically independent of these two.

Bar	Score	Notes	Comments
—]	II	*figs.*	*Ed.* Poems68 shows no figures in the bass score, throughout.
2	I	1–2	Slur *ed.* Poems68 slurs notes 2–3.
2	I	5–6	A rising line, ending with a short crossline, appears in the copy text above the score, between these notes. We cannot identify the form of ornamentation it may designate. Similar lines appear above score I at bar 5, note 1; 10.1; and 21.5
3	I	1–3	Slur *ed.* Poems68 slurs notes 1–2.
3–4	II	3|1	*Ed.* completes the tie between these notes.
12	I	2,4,7	The copy text shows sharps to cancel the key signature, here realized with the natural. The same occurs in bar 13, score I; 16.I; and 17.I.

Bar	Score	Notes	Comments
14-21	II		For the systems containing these bars, the copy text introduces the E♭ twice in score II. The higher E♭ is *om* here.
15	I	3-5	Slur *ed*. Poems68 shows only the tie.
19	I	2-3	Slur *ed*. Poems68 slurs notes 1-3.
24	II	1	Lower fermata *om* in copy text.

[Poem 52] "(The Concealment)".

Composer: Henry Purcell

Copy text: British Library MS RM 20.h.8, fol. 212ᵛ (RM20). Margaret Laurie attests that this is an autograph entry in the copybook. Zimmerman and Laurie both note the occurrence of this setting in Brussels, Bibliothèque du Conservatoire, MS 1035g. We have been unable to examine this manuscript and refer readers to Margaret Laurie's notes on it (*Works* 25:283). On the basis of Laurie's observations, Brussels 1035g has no claim as copy text for this setting.

Song text: F1 poem 52. Purcell sets the entire poem.

Textual variants: title] *parentheses* RM20; The Concealment F1   *bar 34* cens'ring] censuring F1   *bars 46-47* happier] *happi'er* F1   *bars 49-50* not; no tis] not; 'tis F1   *bar 61* ev'ry] every F1   *bar 63* a] an F1

Aside from the exclamation mark in bar 1 and commas in bars 2 and 3, RM20 lacks punctuation. As in the RM20 copy of "The Rich Rival," performance of this song text would be assisted by reference to the punctuation in the literary text printed on pp. 83-84 of this volume. As is the editorial practice in this edition, aspects of the song text, such as capital letters and spelling, are retained from the copy text.

Literary source: The variants in bars 46-47 and 61 are occasioned by the musical setting as slurred in bar 47 and 61. They coincidentally accord with readings in three eighteenth-century printings of *The Mistress*, O3-4 and D2 (see Literary Collation). The major departure from the literary text in bars 49-50 is unique to the setting and called for by the musical notation. Any of the seventeenth-century printings of *The Mistress* could have provided Purcell with the song text, as could William King's printing in *Poems* (1668). Purcell's inscription of the title makes it certain that neither WR50 nor NAC71 was his source. Purcell's song text differs so strikingly from Robert King's as to argue no relation between these two settings, although the duet concluding Purcell's rendition may bear comparison with Robert King's musical setting.

The musical setting: Purcell enploys a number of rhythmic or scalar figures to color the text (cf. measure 5 "till you break"; 26-27 "her anger die"; 37-38 "thunder").

Bar	Score	Notes	Comments
—]	—]	—]	The treble vocal part is designated score I, the bass vocal part (entering at bar 68) score II, and the continuo score III, throughout.
4	I	2	The sharp is used in RM20 to cancel the key signature. The sharp is similarly used in the following bars and scores: 7.I (and in the bass figure, 7.III.2); 19.III; 29.I; 30.I,III; 32.I; 35.I; 36.I; 38.I; 50.III; 62.III; 63.I; 65.I; 66.I; 70.I; 72.I; 74.I (and in the bass figure 6, score III, nn. 1–2); 75.I; 78.II, III; 82.I; 85.I. In these places this edition shows a bracketed natural.
5	I	1–2	RM20 shows a falling line \ between notes 1–2. This backfall would signal a grace note on the preceding tone (see headnote on Purcell, Editorial Principles).
7	I	3–4	RM20 shows a rising line / or forefall between these notes (see note to bar 5).
10	I	1, 3–4	RM20 shows a rising line / before note 1 and a falling line \ between notes 3–4 (cf. notes to bars 5, 7).
20–21	I-II	||	*Ed.* The double bar is *om* in RM20.
20–21	I-II	[*t. sig.*]	3/4 *ed.* RM20 shows 3.
25–26	I	5 | 1	RM20 shows a falling line \ between these notes (see notes to bars 5, 7, 10).
35	I	2	RM20 shows a flat by the C, lowering it from the C♯ in bar 34.
56–57	I-II	||	*Ed.* The double bar is *om* in RM20.
65	I	10	RM20 shows a flat to lower the C from C♯ at note 8.
67–68	I-II	||	*Ed.* RM20 again omits the double bar at the stanza break.
68	I-II	[*t. sig.*]	3/4 *ed.* RM20 shows 3.

[Poem 52] ["The Concealment."]

Composer: Robert King

Copy text: *A Second Booke of Songs* (c. 1695), p. 21 (SBS).

Song text: F1 poem 52. Robert King sets lines 1–6 of the first of three eleven-line stanzas.

Textual variants: *title*] F1; *copy text is untitled*   *bar 3* shou'd] should F1   *bars 13–17* thee] me F1   *bar 18* wou'd] *would* F1   *bars 22, 25, 27, 29, 31* shou'd] *should* F1   *bars 39, 42, 45* thou wilt] they will F1

Collations and Notes to the Musical Settings (pp. 440–449)

Literary source: The variants in bars 3, 18, 22, 25, 27, 29, and 31 appear to be copyist's errors; there is no need for elision in either word. The variants in bars 13–17 and 39–45 are unique to this setting, and they both change the meaning of the text as found in printed editions of *The Mistress*. King's setting is further distanced from the printed editions in that it lacks a title and does not attribute the text to Cowley. This song text does not appear to have been derived directly from F1 or any of the printed versions following it. Nor is it derived from WR50 or NAC71 (see Literary Collation). Robert King's song text is also independent of Henry Purcell's, but there are musical resemblances with the setting by William King, and it is possible that Robert found his song text with the William King setting. If so, the substantive variants in SBS are of his or his copyist's making.

The musical setting: Robert King's other Cowley setting, "The Heart Fled Again," bears some relation to Pietro Reggio's setting; "The Concealment" displays some musical similarities with William King's setting of the same text. Both settings show two flats in the key signature; they begin on the same note in the continuo and vocal scores; and through Robert King's greater elaboration of the text one might perceive melodic resemblances with the more straightforward William King composition.

There are a number of careless errors in this setting, as indicated in the following notes. The setting is also characterized by inconsistencies in slur lines over sustained syllables in the song text. Sometimes a syllable will be slurred in score I but not in score II, or vice versa (e.g., bar 21). At other times, sustained syllables lack slur lines in the copy text (e.g., bars 2, 9–11). In the former instances, it is our opinion that slurs are intended in both scores, and the missing slur lines are provided editorially within brackets. In the latter instances the composer's intention is less clear. In this edition editorial slur lines, drawn in brackets, appear in the following bars and scores: 2.II; 9–11.I–II; 21.II; 24.I; 25.II; 26.I–II; 27.II; 28.I–II; 29.I; 30.I–II; 31.II; 32.I–II; 33.I–II; 34.II; 35.I; 35–37.II; 36–37.I; 38.I–II; 40–41.I; 41.II; 42.I–II; 43–44.I; 44.II; 45.I–II.

Bar	Score	Notes	Comments
—]	—]	—]	The scores are designated throughout as follows: top vocal part score I; second vocal part score II; continuo score III.
3	I	3–4	SBS copy i shows an erroneous D (penned?) between the B and A. This does not appear in copies ii and iii.
5	II	5–6	*Ed.* The copy text errs in showing two eighth notes.
6	I	4	King's setting consists of a series of parallel phrases and phrase-responses. The editorial E [♮] carries out this intent by making this phrase the same as the response in 7.II.

Bar	Score	Notes	Comments
7	II	2	SBS shows a sharp to cancel the key signature, and a ♯4 in the bass figure.
9	I	1	*Ed.* SBS erroneously shows a G.
9	II	3,8	The copy text shows sharps to cancel the key signature and a sharp in the bass figure at note 2.
12	I	2	[♯] *ed.*
14	II	1	Copy text shows a sharp to raise the B, and a sharp in the bass figure at note 1.
15	I	1	Copy text shows a sharp to raise the E, and a sharp in the bass figure at note 1.
15	I	5	The E♭, returning to the key signature, leads to the next bar.
16	I	5	SBS errs in omitting the dot to the eighth note.
16	III	3	Copy text shows a sharp to raise the E.
18	I–III	[*t. sig.*]	3/4 *ed.* SBS reads 3.
18	III	2	The copy text shows a sharp to raise the B.
19	III	2	Copy text shows a sharp to raise the E.
21	I–II	6	The copy text errs in omitting to dot the eighth note.
24–25	I–III	| |	*Ed.* A single line divides these bars in the copy text.
26	II	8	The copy text shows a sharp to raise the E.
28	II	1	SBS shows a sharp to raise the B here, and in score I, note 6. ♯3 appears in the bass figure at notes 1 and 2.
29	II	2	SBS shows a sharp to raise the B and a ♯3 in the bass figure at note 1.
32	II	3	The copy text shows a sharp to raise the E.
35	I	2	The copy text shows a sharp to raise the E.
43	I	3	The copy text shows a sharp to raise the E.
43	I	5	[♯] *ed.*, in accordance with the bass figure shown in the copy text in score III, note 4.

[Poem 53] "The Monopoly."

Composer: William King

Copy text: *Poems*, p. 48 (Poems68).

Song text: F1 poem 53. King sets stanza 1 and prints the remaining four stanzas on p. 49.

Textual variants: *bar 10* hath] has F1   *stanza 5* (F1, l. 25) *woman*] *women* F1

Literary source: The song text appearing with the musical setting shows numerous accidental departures from F1, while the following stanzas are nearly identical to the printed folio F1. It appears clearly that there are two compositors working on this song text. The first, setting the music along with stanza 1, attends to the musical score and evidences marginal attention to the song text. Stanzas 2-5 appear to have been set by someone fully attentive to all aspects of the F1 printing. The variant in stanza 5 likely represents this latter compositor's sole error.

The musical setting: Characteristically William King attempts here to accomplish variety of expression within the short duration of the setting. But his method this time, shifting meter after measure eight, is unusual.

Bar	Score	Notes	Comments
—]	II	[*figs.*]	*Ed.*, throughout.
8-9	I-II	|| [*t. sig.*]	*Ed.* and 3/4, *ed.* The copy text shows no double bar and indicates the time signature with 3.
16	I-II	1	First and second endings, *ed.*, as are the repeat signs. The copy text indicates, at bar 9, that the concluding triple-time segment of the song should be repeated. The fermata is drawn only above score I in the copy text.

[Poem 54] "The Distance."

Composer: William King

Copy text: *Poems*, p. 38 (Poems68).

Song text: F1 poem 54. King sets stanza 1 and prints the remaining three stanzas on p. 39.

Textual variants: *bar 1* I have follow'd] I'Have followed F1

Literary source: In addition to minor variations from F1 in spelling and capitalization (probably compositor's errors), King's song text varies from F1 in the placement of elisions in bar 1. These are not sufficient evidence to suggest a textual source other than F1. Since it is demonstrable by textual variants that some of King's settings were reprinted in NAC71, it is possible that this one as well provided the source for the song text of poem 54 in NAC71. The song text appearing with Reggio's later setting resembles King's in the treatment of the first two words. This is the only evidence suggesting that Reggio may have been familiar with William King's compositions.

The musical setting: King's strophic setting is in A minor. The rhythmic activity of the score is sensitive to the impatient movement stated in the song text.

Bar	Score	Notes	Comments
–]	I–II	[*t. sig.*]	C *ed.* The copy text shows ₵ at the start of the first system. Systems 2–4 show no time signature. The song is scored in 4/4.
–]	II	[*figs.*]	*Ed.*, throughout.
8	II	1	The fermata is drawn only above score I in Poems68.

[Poem 54] "The Distance."

Composer: Pietro Reggio

Copy text: Songs 1:8. ·

Song text: F1 poem 54. Reggio sets stanzas 1 and 2 of four four-line stanzas.

Textual variants: *bar 1* I have] I'Have F1

Literary source: The variant in bar 1 is found in William King's setting of poem 54. This is a minor change, however, and the agreement does no more than suggest the possibility of Reggio's familiarity with King's text and setting. King also produces a further variant in the third word of the text. Both settings, however, are strophic. Reggio's source could have been any of the printed editions of *The Mistress* up to F8. NAC71 prints another song text, omitting the title and reading with F1 in the opening words.

The musical setting: The piece is in D minor, without a key signature. Unlike William King, Reggio is not particularly engaged with the song text. The vocal line and triple meter are characteristic "Reggio."

Bar	Score	Notes	Comments
24–25	I–II	‖	Double dots appear on both sides of the double bar in *Songs*.
25	I–II	*t. sig.*	The time signature is restated in *Songs* as 3, as distinguished from the 3/4 at bar 1. Clef signs are reintroduced as well. The clef sign for score II, applying to bars 25–28, is erroneously a treble clef in *Songs*.
48	I–II	1	*Songs* shows two tied dotted half notes (see headnote on Reggio).

[Poem 55] "The Encrease."

Composer: Pietro Reggio

Copy text: Songs 1:32.

Song text: F1 poem 55. Reggio sets the first two of three seven-line stanzas.

Textual variants: *bar 4* easily] easi'ly F1   *bar 14* would] should F1

Collations and Notes to the Musical Settings (pp. 459–466)

Literary source: Both variants in Reggio's song text are found only in F6–10. Reggio's source, printed before 1680, is F6 (1674) or F7 (1678).

The musical setting: The composition is in D minor. As in Reggio's setting of "The Dissembler," the use of rests, coupled with numerous modulations, gives the work an unsettling quality, complimentary to the song text.

Bar	Score	Notes	Comments
3	I	3	*Songs* shows a sharp, canceling the key signature.
7	I	4	*Songs* shows a sharp, as above.
8	I	5	*Songs* shows a sharp, as above.
11–12	I–II	||	Double dots on both sides of the double bar in *Songs* are here *om*. *Songs* erroneously dots the D in bar 11, score II.
14	I	3	See note to bar 3.
15	I	2	[♯] *ed.*, in compliance with the bass figure at note 1.
18	I	6	[♮] *ed.*, leading to the cadence in bar 19.

[Poem 56] "Loves Visibility."

Composer: William King

Copy text: *Poems*, p. 24 (Poems68).

Song text: F1 poem 56. King sets stanza 1 and prints the remaining five stanzas on p. 25.

Textual variants: *bars 6–7* hither-to] hitherto F1

Literary source: F1 is the source (O1–2 and WR50 show variants against *Poems*). The printer, in this setting, follows F1 relatively closely with regard to accidentals in the first stanza as well as in the stanzas printed after the setting. Usually the set stanza ignores the literary accidentals. (As the following musical notes show, however, the musical setting contains an unusual number of errors.) The variant hyphenation, bars 6–7, is a minor departure from F1, and it follows from the vocal score. The song text appearing with Pietro Reggio's later setting does not derive from King's.

The musical setting: King's strophic setting is in D major. The use of this key and the open, simple vocal line, demonstrate the point of the text: the speaker, or singer, cannot hide anything.

Bar	Score	Notes	Comments
–]	I	clef	The first system is introduced in the standard G clef, but at the beginning of the second and third systems (containing bars 5–12) the soprano clef is indicated. This is a printer's error.

Bar	Score	Notes	Comments
—]	I–II	[*t. sig.*]	3/2 *ed*. The copy text shows ¢ at bar 1, beginning the first system (as usual, the time signature is not repeated for following systems). The time signature has been pen-corrected to 3 ¢ in the copy of Poems68 held at the University of Delaware.
—]	II	*k. sig.*	The F♯ is printed twice at the beginning of each system in score II. The lower sharp is here *om*.
—]	II	[*figs.*]	*Ed.*, throughout.
3	I	2	The second half note C fails to print in Poems68. It is editorially supplied, as is the slur between notes 2–3. This emendation is shown as a pen correction in the Delaware copy of Poems68.
4	II	1	The F♯ represented in the copy text appears to be another error; an A would be better.
12	II	1	The fermata is printed only above score I in Poems68.

[Poem 56] "Loves Visibility."

Composer: Pietro Reggio

Copy text: Songs 1:13.

Song text: F1 poem 56. Reggio sets the first four of six triplet stanzas. There are no substantive variants from F1.

Literary source: The song text was taken from one of the folio editions of *The Mistress*, F1 to F7. The song text reading "who" in bar 32 establishes that the text was not derived from O1, O2, or WR50. There is no likely relation between this and William King's song text or setting.

The musical setting: Cowley's poem is written in lines of 10, 8, and 10 syllables. Reggio, setting the first stanza, alters this to 10, 11, 10; then, he reverts to the syllabic line of the song text. Structurally, the work is ABA'B', with settings of stanzas 3 and 4 appearing as musical variants of 1 and 2. The tonality is C minor.

Bar	Score	Notes	Comments
1	I	3	*Songs* shows a sharp to cancel the key signature here and in the figure at note 2, score II. The same occurs in the second instance of this passage, bar 24.
8	I	1	[♮]. *Songs* shows a sharp here and in the bass figure, as in bar 1 and the parallel passage, bar 31.
14	I	3	[♮], as above, and in bar 37.
16	I	1	[♮], as above and in the parallel passage, bar 39.

Collations and Notes to the Musical Settings (pp. 466-470)

Bar	Score	Notes	Comments
16	II	2	[♮] *ed.*, in accordance with note 1, score I, here and in the parallel passage, bar 39.
20	I	3	*Songs* shows a sharp to raise the E and a sharp in the bass figure, here and in the parallel passage, bar 43.
21	I	2	A [♮] *ed.*, in accordance with the bass figure. The passage recurs in bar 44.
21	I	3	*Songs* cancels the key signature with a sharp and places a sharp in the bass figure at note 3—also in bar 44.
23	I-II	| |	Double dots on both sides of the double bar shown in *Songs* are here *om.*
24	I-II	*t. sig.*	*Songs* reiterates the time signature as 3/4.
26	I	2	A [♭] *ed. Songs* erroneously shows the flat at note 1. Accidentals should accord with the passage in bar 3.
28	II	1 [*fig.*]	*Ed.*, following the figure shown in bar 5.
30	I	3-5	Slur, *ed. Songs* slurs notes 3-4.
30	I	4	*Songs* cancels the key signature with a sharp.

[Poem 57] "Song: [Looking on, and Discoursing with His Mistress.]"

Composer: Manuscript attributed to W[illiam] Hall. The manuscript attribution is written in a different hand from that of the setting. The same is true of the attribution to "Weeping," inscribed later in this manuscript. The hand offering the attributions is the same for both settings.

Copy text: British Library Add. MSS 22100, fol. 46ᵛ (BL22).

Song text: F1 poem 57. Hall sets the entire poem.

Textual variants: title] Song:] BL22; *the bracketed title is from* F1   bar 1 two full] full two F1   bar 6 gulphs] *ed.*; *Gulfs* F1; gulps BL22   bar 9 heav'ns] *Heavens* F1   bar 33 to spye] t'espye F1   bar 34 glimm'erings] *ed. (as called for by the vocal score)*; glimmerings BL22, F1   bar 36 flatt'ring] flattering F1   bar 39 'em] them F1

Literary source: The variant in bar 9 suggests F8-10 or a transcription from one of these as the source, though this elision (like those in bars 33, 36, and 39) is called for by the vocal score. The source cannot be F12 or later printed editions (see Literary Collation). The song text reading in bar 34 makes it especially clear that Hall took his copy from a clear transcription, since the reading does not accord with the vocal setting. Aside from F8-10, there is such a reading in Francis Forcer's setting of this song text (printed in 1687). Forcer's song text agrees with readings from the Hall manuscript in (Hall's) bars 9, 33, 34, 36, and most interestingly in the variant in bar 6, where Hall records "gulps," Forcer records "gulph," and the printed literary texts show "*Gulfs*." Though it may appear that Hall follows Forcer here and creates an error, other unique variants in Forcer make it reasonably clear that BL22 does not derive from Forcer, nor vice versa. Unique variants in other bars in the Hall and Forcer settings show that neither was derived from the other. But agreements in their variant readings show that they derive from the same source, which was probably based on F8–10. The variant in Hall's bar 1 is probably a scribal error.

The musical setting: There are similarities between the Hall and Forcer settings. Both set the entire literary text. Both are composed sectionally (though Hall's is ABA), and both are in G minor, showing two flats in the key signature.

Bar	Score	Notes	Comments
3	I	4	BL22 shows a flat to cancel the previous sharp here and at bar 32, score I, note 4, and bar 36, score II, note 3. The bracketed natural appears in this edition.
3	II	3	BL22 shows a sharp to cancel the key signature here and in the following bars and scores: 6.II; 9.I; 10.II; 11.I–II; 15.I; 18.I; 21.I; 22.I; 26.I; 32.II; 35.II; 38.I; 39.II; and 40.II. The bracketed natural appears at these places in this edition.
3–4	I–II	|	The bar line is not drawn in BL22. It is provided here editorially and in the following places: bars 12–13; 13–14; 15–16; 23–24; 27–28; 33–34; 41–42.
7	II	3	[♮] *ed*. No accidental appears in the copy text.
9	II	2	The measure is split by the end of a system on the page in BL22. A quarter note is drawn in each part, with a tie between them.
22	I	4	[♭], returning to key, *ed*.
31	II	1	In BL22 a tied quarter and dotted half note in a broken measure, as in bar 9.
32	II	3	In BL22 two quarter notes tied across a break in the measure, as in bars 9 and 31.
36	II	3	[♮] *ed*., anticipating cadence in bar 37. No accidental in BL22.
38	II	2	Two quarter notes tied across a break in the measure, as in bar 32.

[Poem 57] ["Looking on and Discoursing with His Mistress."]

Composer: Mr. Francis Forcer

Copy text: *Vinculum Societatis* 1 (1687): 18 (VS87).

Collations and Notes to the Musical Settings (pp. 470-478)   617

Song text: F1 poem 57. Forcer sets all three stanzas of the poem.

Textual variants: *title*] F1; VS87 *is untitled*   *bar 5* gulph] *Gulfs* F1   *bar 7* Miser's] *Misers* F1   *bar 9* Heav'ns] *Heavens* F1   *bar 17* doe] *ed.*; does VS87; do F1   *part !*] ~? F1   *bar 19* empty] *ed.*, F1; emty [*sic*] VS87   *bar 21* those] these F1   *bar 25* the] her F1   *bar 26* of] from F1   *bar 29* when] If F1   *bars 30-31* came to espy] chance t'espy F1   *bar 34* like flatt'ring] Take flattering F1   *bar 35* night] nigh F1

Literary source: Only the reading in bar 9 gives a clue as to which printed version of *The Mistress* might have provided the song text. The contraction appears in F8-10. But the VS87 song text could have been changed to suit Forcer's vocal score in bar 9. Variants in bars 7 and 35 coincidentally agree with F12, printed after VS87. Other variants are unique to VS87, except for those in bar 9 and "flatt'ring" in bar 34. Both of these readings probably occur in a manuscript version of the song text that provided copy for VS87 as well as William Hall's copy recorded in BL22. See Hall's setting, where both variants also appear. This manuscript was very likely derived from F8-10.

The musical setting: See notes to Hall's setting.

Bar	Score	Notes	Comments
1	I-II	k. sig.	VS87 shows the E♭ twice in score I and the B♭ twice in score II in bar 1 and at the beginning of each system. The lower E♭ and the higher B♭ are *om* in this edition.
2	II	1	The copy text shows a sharp to cancel the key signature here and at the following bars and scores: 3.I and in the bass figure; 4.I and bass figure; 5.II; 6.I; 7.I; 8.I and bass figure; 11.I; 14.I-II and bass figure; 15.I-II and bass figure; 16.II; 18.I-II and bass figure at n. 1; 20.I-II and bass figures; 21.II and bass figure at n. 1; 22.I and bass figure at n. 2; 24.II; 29.II; 30.I; 34.I; 35.II; and 36.I and bass figure. The accidental is represented as a bracketed natural in this edition.
5	I	2	*Ed*. VS87 errs in showing a sixteenth note.
13	I-II	1ǀǀ2	*Ed*. VS87 shows a whole note, the double bar, and an eighth note. There is no time change, but a movement from the first to the second stanza of the text.
18	I	5	No accidental appears in VS87.
26	I-II	3ǀǀ1	As at bar 13, the transition is *ed*. VS87 shows a half note G, the double bar, the new (faster) time signature 𝄵, and an eighth note D.
31	II	5-6	*Ed*. VS87 shows a fragment of a score line drawn beneath the brace, making these notes appear to be sixteenth notes.

Bar	Score	Notes	Comments
35–36	I–II	||	*Ed.*, distinguishing the shift to a slower time.
36	II	6	No accidental appears in VS87.
38	I	4–6	Slur *ed.* The copy text appears to slur notes 3–6.

[Poem 59] "My Fate."

Composer: William King

Copy text: *Poems*, p. 15 (Poems68).

Song text: F1 poem 59. King sets stanza 1 and prints the remaining four stanzas on p. 17.

Textual variants: bar 6 Flames] *Flame* F1   bar 8 own] *old* F1

Literary source: Stanza 1 departs from F1 in its accidentals, in addition to the two substantive variants noted above (both of which recur in NAC71; see Literary Collation). The printed stanzas 2–5 are virtually the same as F1. There is no musical reason for the variants in bars 6 and 8. As in most other King settings, the composer for the musical setting and accompanying song text appears to be different from the composer for the sequent printed stanzas, and the variants could be attributable to this composer's focus on the musical setting and relative lack of attention to details of the song text. F1 is the probable song text source.

The musical setting: The work is built on three groups of phrases, the first two of which (measures 1 and 4) begin with the same musical figure. Within the short span of this strophic setting, the composer is acknowledging three moments in the text of stanza 1 with special melodic treatment ("trembling," "Journey upward," and "Go bid . . . t'ascend").

Bar	Score	Notes	Comments
−]	II	[*figs.*]	*Ed.*, throughout.
2	II	1	*Ed.* Copy text shows a G.
3	I–II	1	*Ed.* The copy text shows a bar line after score I, note 6 (II, 3), and again at the end of the full count for the measure—here *om.*
3	II	4	*Ed.* The copy text errs in showing an eighth note.
5	1	2,5	The copy text shows sharps, canceling the key signature.
11	I–II	1	Fermata, *ed.*, following King's usual practice.

Collations and Notes to the Musical Settings (pp. 478-483)   619

[Poem 60] "The Heart-Breaking."

Composer: William King

Copy text: *Poems*, p. 46 (Poems68).

Song text: F1 poem 60. King sets stanza 1 and prints the remaining four stanzas on p. 47.

Textual variants: *bar 2* pit'eous] piteous F1   *bar 4* some-thing it] it some-thing F1

Literary source: As is characteristic with King's settings of Cowley, stanza 1 shows variants against F1 while the following printed stanzas mostly accord with the words and accidentals of F1. The variant "pit'eous" in bar 2 insures that the first line of stanza 1 is decasyllabic, uniform with other first lines except that in stanza 4 (F1, l. 13). The elision would appear to have been introduced so that sequent stanzas could be sung to the same vocal setting. The variant in bar 4 looks like a compositor's inversion. The phrase could be sung in either configuration. F1 is the probable literary source. The song text is not related to the text printed in WR50 (see Literary Collation).

The musical setting: This strophic setting, in G minor, begins on G, moves to a cadence in F major in measure 5, and returns to G.

Bar	Score	Notes	Comments
−]	II	[*figs.*]	*Ed.*, throughout.
9	II	1	The fermata prints only above score I in Poems68.

[Poem 64] "Silence."

Composer: Pietro Reggio

Copy text: *Songs* 2:20.

Song text: F1 poem 64. Reggio sets the first of three stanzas from the literary text. There are no substantive variants from F1.

Literary source: This song text could have been copied from any printed version of *The Mistress* to F8 except F3, which shows a unique variant in line 8 (see Literary Collation).

The musical setting: This is written in D minor without a key signature. At times (e.g., measures 2-3, 5-6, 16-18) Reggio shows a strong relationship between the vocal and continuo lines.

Bar	Score	Notes	Comments
2	II	6 [*fig.*]	*Ed.* B♮ is called for in the accompaniment, following the B♭ at note 5, as note 6 in score I is a B♮.
15	II	2–3	*Songs*, uncharacteristically, shows a slur here. Reggio elsewhere uses ties in the bass line, but not slurs.
19	I–II	1	*Songs* shows a half note D in both scores and what may be a half rest preceding a calligraphic flourish. In light of the ambiguity, the concluding whole note is editorially introduced.

[Poem 65] "The Dissembler."

Composer: Pietro Reggio

Copy text: *Songs* 1:29.

Song text: F1 poem 65. Reggio sets 1 and 2 of five six-line stanzas.

Textual variants: *bar 7* and there is] Ah, There's F1   *bar 14* met with a] met a F1

Literary source: The variants in bars 7 and 14 are unique to *Songs*. It is clearest in bar 7 that the variants from the literary text of F1 and other printed editions are not occasioned by the vocal score—that is, the monosyllables "and" and "Ah" could be sung to the same note in score I. This song text represents substantive variants from the printed editions of *The Mistress*, and its direct source is not likely to have been one of them. A manuscript source is probable, containing the variants and written out in the two stanzas that Reggio sets. We have discovered no manuscript to support this hypothesis.

The musical setting: The work is written in B-flat major, with one flat in the key signature, AA in structure. Reggio enhances the anxiety of the text by his use of quick-note series severed by rests in the vocal score.

Bar	Score	Notes	Comments
6	II	4	*Songs* shows a sharp to cancel the key signature, here and in the parallel passage in this strophic setting, bar 21.
11	I	2	As above, *Songs* cancels the flat with a sharp sign, here and in the parallel passage, bar 26.
15	I–II	‖	*Songs* shows double dots on both sides of the double bar, here *om*.
16	I–II	*t. sig.*	*Songs* reiterates the C time signature at the beginning of bar 16.
21	II	1	Dotted quarter, *ed. Songs* errs in showing only a quarter note.

Collations and Notes to the Musical Settings (pp. 483-489)

Bar	Score	Notes	Comments
30	I-II	1	This is the second of two instances in *Songs* where the piece is closed with an abbreviated measure (see [Poem 64] "Silence," bar 19).

[Poem 68] "Her Name."

Composer: William King

Copy text: *Poems*, p. 8 (Poems68).

Song text: F1 poem 68. King sets stanza 1 and prints the remaining stanzas on p. 9.

Textual variants: *stanza 5* (F1, l. 26) So good] *om* F1

Literary source: The first stanza, included with the musical setting, departs from F1 in a number of accidentals and punctuation marks. These departures appear to be compositorial. The printed stanzas 2-5 are identical to F1, except for the added syllables in stanza 5, introduced to make the line octosyllabic and conformable to the musical setting from bar 4, note 6, through bar 7. This change makes it clear that King intends the printed stanzas to be sung. He could have initiated the change independently, or in collaboration with Cowley. The literary source is clearly F1. NAC71 prints a song text of this poem that cannot be absolutely claimed to derive from Poems68. Yet the coincidence of titles printed in Poems68 and NAC71, along with demonstrable derivation in some cases, suggests that NAC71 may follow Poems68 in this song text as well.

The musical setting: King divides the declamatory opening, set in *alla breve*, from the interrogative text set in 3/2. The strophic setting is formed, overall, by movement from G major through E minor and back to G major.

Bar	Score	Notes	Comments
–]	I-II	*k. sig.*	The copy text prints F♯ twice in both scores. The lower sharp is *om* in this edition.
–]	II	[*figs.*]	*Ed.*, throughout.
7-8	I-II	‖ [*t. sig.*]	*Ed.*, and the 3/2 signature following, in bar 8, is *ed*. Copy text shows 3.
14	I	3	The sharp for the C is misprinted on the bottom line of score I in the copy text.
19	II	2	The note is erroneously printed as a quarter in the copy text.
23	II	1	The dot fails to print by the whole note in score II.

[Poem 69] "Weeping."

Composer: Pietro Reggio

Copy text: Songs 1:15.

Song text: F1 poem 69. Reggio sets the first two of three stanzas appearing in all editions of the literary text.

Textual variants: *bars 26-27* me thinks] methinks F1

Literary source: Reggio could have found his song text in any printed edition of *The Mistress* up through F8, except for O2 (see Literary Collation). A comment on the textual relationship among the Reggio, Turner, and Purcell settings of *Weeping* appears with the notes to the settings by Turner and Purcell.

The musical setting: Unlike either the Turner or Purcell settings of "Weeping," Reggio offers an A-minor tonality (there is no key signature) and writes for single voice and continuo. The Turner and Purcell settings appear to be musically related; Reggio's earlier treatment of this text is independent of either. The form is modified-strophic.

Bar	Score	Notes	Comments
−]	I	clef	*Songs* places score I in the soprano clef.
14	I	2–3	Slur *ed.*, rendering the single syllable in the song text.
17	II	2 [D.S.]	The repeat sign shows only between notes 1 and 2, score I, in *Songs*. Another bracketed repeat is added at bar 37.
20	I-II	1	First and second endings *ed.*, in accordance with the structure of the repeated phrase. The copy text shows double dots as well the D.S. sign for bars 17–20.
21	I-II	*t. sig.*	*Songs* reiterates the 3/4 time signature here.
36	II	1–2	In bar 16, the same passage reads as a dotted half note. The tied half and quarter note rendering here has no readily discernible purpose.
40	I-II	1	First and second endings *ed.*, as in bar 20. The copy text shows two dotted half notes in the final bar of score I, and two tied, dotted half notes in score II.

[Poem 69] ["Weeping."]

Composer: Mr. [William] Turner

Copy text: British Library Add. MSS 22100, fol. 87 (BL22). The ascription to Turner is in a different hand from that of the setting.

Collations and Notes to the Musical Settings (pp. 490–495)

Song text: F1 poem 69.

Textual variants: *title* Song] *Weeping* F1   bar 4 other] others F1
bar 16 ev'ry] every F1   bar 23 such] so F1

Literary source: Turner, like Purcell and unlike Reggio, sets the entire text of *Weeping* as it appears in all printed editions of *The Mistress* except O2, F11, and F12 (see Literary Collation). It is possible, given only the evidence of the song text, that Turner found his text in a copy of the Purcell setting resembling RM20. Turner and Purcell share the minor variant in bar 16 and both settings lack the title that accompanies all printed editions of *The Mistress* and appears with Reggio's setting. If Turner took his song text from Purcell, variants in bars 4 and 23 could be considered errors in transcription or deliberate changes. These readings are unique to the Turner setting. It is less likely that Turner produced these two unique readings in transcribing the song text from one of the printed editions O1, F1–10, and also omitted the title.

The musical setting: Both Turner and Purcell work within the frame of G minor in their respective settings, and their disposition of the text in sections for multiple and solo voices is remarkably similar. Given the evidence of the song texts, Turner could have followed Purcell, but not vice versa. The musical settings are probably related in the same way. In the multivoiced sections, however, Turner treats the voices in a homophonic manner while Purcell pits two voices against each other, in counterpoint based on imitation, and engages the continuo in the linear contest. Further comment on the relation between this setting, Purcell's and Reggio's follows the notes to the Purcell setting.

Bar	Score	Notes	Comments
1	I–III	—]	*Tenor* and *Bass* designations are editorial, as are solo designations at bars 14 and 22, and *Trio* at bar 33. Scores are designated, throughout, as I first tenor voice; II second tenor voice; III bass voice; IV continuo.
1	I–III	[*t. sig.*]	6/4 *ed*. Copy text shows an elongated 3 followed by a dotted I in scores I and II. No signature appears in score III.
5	I	2–4	The slur appears in the copy text; another slur of notes 3–5 is also drawn.
7	II	8	[♮] *ed*., compatible with the E♮ in score I.
12	I–III	1	The copy text shows what may be a repeat sign here. It could indicate that bars 12–13 be repeated, though there is no corresponding sign at the end of bar 13.
15	IV	1–2	The copy text might indicate a tie between these notes. The measure is broken on the manuscript page and is not fully legible.

Bar	Score	Notes	Comments
16	III–IV	[*t. sig.*]	The time signature here, as in bars 18, 19, 20, 21, 22, 39, and 40, is *ed.*, representing the various counts shown between bar lines in the copy text.
24	IV	4	[♮] *ed.*, anticipating the cadence in bar 25.

[Poem 69] ["Weeping."]

Composer: Henry Purcell

Copy text: British Library MS RM20.h.8, fol. 209 (RM20); texts collated: BL Add. MSS 33237, fol. 200 (BL37) and BL Add. MSS 33287, fol. 19^v (BL87). Zimmerman lists a late-seventeenth-century manuscript held by the Bibliothèque du Conservatoire, Brussels (MS 1035). We have not been able to examine it. Zimmerman also reports that the song text alone appears in BL Add. MSS 28644, fol. 36—a manuscript dated c. 1671. This, however, is a parody of Cowley's literary text, beginning "Se where He sits and wth w^t thoughtfull pain / Dos wreck his head and vex his senseless brain." It is not Purcell's song text and sheds no light on the date of Purcell's composition.

Song text: F1 poem 69.

Textual variants: *title*] F1; *untitled* RM20, BL87; Song by Hen:^{y} Purcell—see Cowley's Mistress—Weeping BL37   *bar 51* ev'ry] RM20, BL87, BL37; every F1   bars 62–64 whilst in his flood] Σ; the lovely Boy BL37   *bars 76–78* (for . . . kind)] Σ; *parenthesis om* BL37   *bar 80* beaut'ous] RM20, BL87; beauteous BL37, F1   *bar 84* which] Σ; y^t BL87

Literary source: Purcell sets the entire text of poem 69. A shared variant in the song text, bar 51, suggests that the three manuscripts collated here descend from a common source. This source could have been any of the seventeenth-century printed editions of *The Mistress* except O2 and F11 (see Literary Collation). BL87 is similar to RM20, except for the hasty contraction in bar 85, producing the variant "that" for "which." BL37 is a professional copy dating from the eighteenth century. The most striking variants that it exhibits could be copyist's errors. Parentheses are omitted in the song text, bars 76–78; the omission could have been an oversight. The song text reading in bars 62–64 is probably a lazy repetition of "the lovely Boy" (the copyist gets the normative song text reading in bars 60–61), though it could have been deliberate. BL37, alone among these manuscripts, identifies the literary source in its descriptive title. It also agrees with the literary source against other song text manuscripts in bar 80. The copyist of BL37 could therefore have consulted a printed copy of *The Mistress* in addition to a manuscript song text accompanying Purcell's setting.

Collations and Notes to the Musical Settings (pp. 495–500)

There is a close muscial relationship between Purcell's setting and William Turner's, but textual variants in the Turner song text establish that it could not have been Purcell's source (the inverse, given only the evidence of the song text, is possible). Nor could Reggio's song text have been Purcell's literary source, since Reggio sets only the first two stanzas of poem 69.

The musical setting:

Of the three manuscript sources for "Weeping" collated here, BL87 shows many unique substantive variants. BL37, the professional copy dating from the eighteenth century, shows many unique accidental variants—mostly omitted slurs. RM20 reads with BL87 most of the time with regard to accidentals; it agrees with BL37 most of the time with regard to notes and note values.

Unique substantive readings in each of the manuscripts suggests that none was the source for the others. The relationship of the manuscripts is perhaps clearest in score IV, bar 83 (see brackets in the score and the note below). Here BL87 shows an unrevised state of the passage; RM20 shows both the unrevised and revised state; BL37 shows the revised state. In no other instance does BL37 show a corrected reading against an error in RM20; on the contrary, its unique substantive variants are often errors (e.g., bars 89 and 91) or stylistic modifications (the omitted slurs) perhaps characteristic to the time it was copied. Nor does BL37 derive exclusively from a copy resembling RM20. Readings in bars 90 and 91 make it clear that the manuscript from which BL37 was taken showed some features of BL87. The status of BL87 as representing an earlier, unrevised state of the setting is corroborated by the fact that it shows no figures in score V. The figures that appear in RM20 are carried over to BL37, just as are most substantive changes from readings in BL87. We assume, as the evidence of the clear emendation in bar 83 suggests, that these other substantive changes were made as emendations. Though this setting in RM20 is not autograph, the changes that it exhibits probably reflect an emended manuscript that Purcell provided for the transcription.

RM20 becomes the clear choice for copy text. It appears in Purcell's copy book; it shows evidence of emendation that is probably authorial; it is free from corruptions appearing in the later copy BL37.

Zimmerman (*Henry Purcell*, 225) notes that "Purcell's setting appears to bear a certain melodic relationship to Reggio's composition on the same text." If so, the relationship is very slight and is complemented only by the fact that Purcell and Reggio used a figured bass throughout. In other respects their settings are quite different. Reggio's setting is strophic; he sets only two stanzas of the poem; he composes for a single voice; the piece is in triple meter throughout. In this last regard, William Turner's setting more closely resembles Reggio's. Turner writes in compound triple meter, mostly 6/4 but at times 9/4. Otherwise, Turner's setting is strikingly similar to Purcell's. Both settings are scored in G minor (Reggio's is in A minor). Both are developed sectionally, and both set stanza 1 for multiple voices, stanzas 2 and 3 for single voice, and stanza 4 for multiple voices.

Bar	Score	Notes	Comments
—]	I–IV	—]	The designations "tenor," "bass," "violin," and "continuo" are all *ed*. Throughout these notes the treble voice is designated score I, bass voice score II, first violin score III, second violin score IV, continuo score V.
—]	III–IV	—]	BL87 inverts scores III and IV throughout.
—]	V	—]	No figures appear in the bass score of BL87.
1	I–V	*t. sig.*	₵ in BL87.
4	III	5	The bracketed natural is used throughout where the manuscript indicates, with a sharp, that the accidental is to be cancelled.
5	III	3–6	Slurs *om* in BL37 here, and in the following bars, scores, and notes: 7.IV.6–9; 10.I.5–6; 16.II.4–5; 18.I.3–4; 36.III.1–8; 37.III.1–2; 40.III.3–6; 41.III.3–6; 42.III.1–4; 43.III.1–4; 44.III.3–6; 45.III.3–6; 46.III.2–3; 47.III.1–4, 6–7; 51.I.3–5; 56.I.1–8; 57.I.1–2; 60.I.3–6; 61.I.3–6; 62.I.1–4; 63.I.3–4; 64.I.2–7; 65.I.3–6; 66.I.2–3; 67.I.1–4, 6–7; 74.II.4–5; 75.II.1–3; 88.III.1–4.
6	IV	1–2	No tie in BL37.
7	V	1	BL87 shows B♭.
9	I	3	BL87 shows F.
10	I	3–4	BL87 shows a dotted eighth and a sixteenth note.
11	II	4	BL87 shows B♭.
11	V	2 *fig.*	BL37 shows the 6/4/2 figure aligned with note 3, and with a ♮4.
12	IV	3	BL37 shows the accidental before and after note 3.
12	V	1	BL87 shows the B with no indication by way of an accidental to return to the key signature.
14	I	6	BL87 shows B♭.
14	I	7	No accidental in BL87.
14	III	1–2	Tie *om* in BL37.
14	V	1–2	Tie *om* in BL87 (though note 1 is tied to the previous D in bar 13, and note 2 is tied to the D in bar 15).
15	II	3–5	Two sixteenth notes, C and B♭, and an eighth C in BL87. No slur between notes 3–4 in BL37.
15	II	7–9	Two sixteenths and an eighth in BL87.

Collations and Notes to the Musical Settings (pp. 500–508)

Bar	Score	Notes	Comments
15	V	3–4	Slurred in BL87.
16	II	2–3	Quarter notes in BL87.
17	I	4	An eighth note in BL87.
19	II	4–5	No slur in BL87 and BL37; BL87 shows D♮ for note 5.
20	II	1–2	Copy text shows sharps by both As. The A had been flatted in bar 18; the sharps may remind the singer to return to the natural A.
20–21	V	2 | 1	No tie in BL87.
21	I	5	No accidental shown in BL87.
21	II	4	E♭ in BL87.
21	III	1–2	Slurred in BL87.
21	IV	3–4	No slur in BL87.
21	IV	6	B in BL 87.
22	I	5	[♮] *ed*. Copy text and BL87 show no accidental; BL37 shows a sharp to indicate the A♮, raised from the A♭ that is tied over from bar 21.
22–23	V	2 | 1	No tie in BL87.
24	V	1	Scored as two quarter notes, tied, in BL87.
25	I	1	BL87 lacks the initial eighth-count, tied from bar 24.
25	I	4	E♭ in BL87.
25	II	5–6	Two eighth notes in BL87.
25	V	1–2	BL87 omits the tied quarter G and shows a dotted half note C.
26	V	2	Half note F in BL87.
27	V	1–2	Two half note Fs followed by a half note C in BL87.
32	IV	1–4	Scored as four eighth notes in BL37.
33	IV	7	A♮ in BL37.
35	III	1–3	Slur *om* in BL87, BL37.
35	IV	1–4	Slur *ed.*, to complement violin 1.
35	V	5–6	Quarter notes in BL87.
40	IV	3–6	No slurs in BL87, BL37.
41	IV	2–3	Slur *ed.*, to complement violin 1.
41	IV	5	No accidental by the E in BL87.
42	IV	1–2	No slur in BL87, BL37; note 2 is E♭ in BL87.
42	IV	5–6	Slur *ed.*, to complement violin 1.

Bar	Score	Notes	Comments
42	V	3–4	Dotted quarter and an eighth in BL87.
44	IV	2–3, 5–6	Slurs *ed.*, to complement violin 1.
44	V	1–3	Dotted quarter, dotted eighth, and a sixteenth in BL87.
45	IV	2–3	Slur *ed.*, to complement violin 1.
46	V	3–4	Two quarter notes in BL87.
48	III–IV	1	BL87 gives a half note and a rest. The vocal solo then begins in the same measure of score III.
48	V	1	All sources show a whole note G, sustaining the bass through the first note of the vocal solo.
53	V	3–4	Slurred in BL37.
58	I	3	D in BL87.
60	I	2	BL87 shows no accidental.
61	I	4	BL87 shows no accidental.
61	V	4–5	Slurred in BL87.
62	V	3–4	A dotted quarter and an eighth in BL87.
63	I	1–2	Slur *ed.* (also shown in BL87), in accordance with the song text.
69	II–V	*t. sig.*	BL87 shows no signature indicating a reversion to common time, but bar lines are drawn to show 4/4.
69	II	1–2	Two quarter notes in BL87.
69–70	V	1 | 1	No tie in BL87.
70	II	1–2	Dotted eighth and sixteenth in BL87.
70	III	2	No accidental shown in BL87.
71	V	2	No accidental shown in BL87.
76	II	4	No accidental shown in BL87.
76	IV	1,4	No accidentals shown in BL87.
78	II	5	BL37 adds the flat, indicating a return to the key signature, as does *ed.*
79	II	3–4	D descending to B♭ in BL87.
79	III	6–7	In BL87 there is no accidental by the E, and there is a sharp by the A.
80	III	2	No accidental shown in BL87.
80	III	5	[♮] *ed.* The copy text shows no accidental, to lower the note from F♯ at the beginning of the bar.
83	IV	5–6	*Ed.* These notes are scored as Es in BL87. The copy text RM20 shows oversized notes, apparently first

Collations and Notes to the Musical Settings (pp. 508–520)

Bar	Score	Notes	Comments
			drawn as Es and then enlarged downwards to resemble Ds. BL37 shows Ds.
89	II	2–5	Erroneously scored as a dotted eighth, sixteenth, dotted eighth, sixteenth in BL37.
90	I	5	An A in BL87.
90	III	2–5	The G is not tied over from bar 89, for an eighth-count, and the Cs are scored dotted eighth, sixteenth, dotted eighth, sixteenth in BL87 and BL37. In BL37 note 3 is a B♭.
91	I	2–5	Two sixteenths and two eighths in BL87; eighth, sixteenth, dotted eighth [sic], sixteenth in BL37.
91	II	2–6	Scored as a quarter, dotted eighth, sixteenth, dotted eighth, sixteenth in BL87; quarter, dotted eighth, sixteenth, eighth [sic], sixteenth in BL37.
92	I	4	[♮] ed., avoiding enharmonic relationship in bar 93. All sources show a sharp by the A, perhaps to cancel the A♭ in score II.
92	III	2–3	D, E♭ in BL87.
92	III	6	[♭] ed., returning to the key signature after the E♮ at note 3.
93	I	1–2	Scored as a quarter note B♭ in BL87.
93	II,V	1	[♮] ed., instigating the chromatic movement in this and in bar 94. A sharp sign appears by the Ds in RM20 and BL37. There are no accidentals in BL87.
93	IV	5	A♮ in BL87, BL37.
93	V	2–3	E♮ (indicated by a sharp sign) followed by E with no accidental in BL87.
94	I	2	E♭ in BL87.
95–96	V	3 | 1	No tie in BL87.
98	III	5–6	BL87 and BL37 show the slur clearly, between notes 5–6 reflecting the song text "fall." In RM20 the slur appears above note 6, perhaps to link notes 6–7.
102	–]	*fermata*	Om in BL87.

[Poem 72] "Councell [II]."

Composer: William King

Copy text: *Poems*, p. 30 (Poems68).

Song text: F1 poem 72. King sets the entire poem.

Textual variants: *title*] [II] *ed*.; *Counsel* F1   *bar 5* Physick pot'ions] *Physick*-potions F1

Literary source: Probably F1. In this setting, unlike most of William King's other treatments of poems from *The Mistress*, the entire text of a comparatively short lyric is set. The compositor for the setting appears to have been more attentive to the music than the words; perhaps he specialized in musical typesetting. This compositor is characterized in other of the settings by a disregard for accidentals and punctuation marks in his copy text, most of which are scrupulously followed in printed stanzas following strophic settings of a first verse, perhaps set by someone else. True to form, in this setting the song text diverges from F1 in accidentals (spelling, capitalization, use of italics) and omits most of F1's punctuation marks. This song text is not the one used later by Pietro Reggio.

The musical setting: King's composition, in D minor and using a number of dotted eighth-sixteenth figures, is not related to Reggio's setting of the same text. King's through-composed setting treats the three short stanzas of Cowley's text as a continuous statement.

Bar	Score	Notes	Comments
−]	II	*scoring*	What appears to be a middle C is drawn above score II at the beginning of each system in the copy text. It may be a misplaced reference to the B♭ in the key signature. *Ed.* has omitted this designation in this edition.
−]	II	[*figs.*]	*Ed.* throughout.
3	I	1	The copy text shows a sharp to cancel the key signature here and in the following bars and scores: 4.I; 5.I; 9.II; 12.I; 15.I; 17.I; and 18.I. The accidental is represented in the present edition by a bracketed natural.
7	I	3	*Ed.* The copy text shows a G.
10	I	5	*Ed.* Copy text shows a sixteenth note.
10	2	4	In Poems68 the ♯ appears in bar 11, where the tie is continued.
16	I	5	Copy text shows a flat, returning the note to C♮.
19	II	1	In Poems68, the fermata is drawn only over the note in score I.

[Poem 72] "Councel [II]."

Composer: Pietro Reggio

Copy text: Songs 1:38.

Song text: F1 poem 72. Reggio sets all three four-line stanzas, though his setting makes no distinction between stanzas 1 and 2.

Textual variants: *bar 34* I am] I'm F1

Literary source: The variant in bar 34 is unique to *Songs*; it suggests a manuscript source probably derived from one of the printed editions of *The Mistress* up to F8 (since there are no other variants from the literary text that remains unaltered through all these editions) but copied out with this change. Reggio's setting is developed sectionally, and he could have scored for either the elided "I'm" or "I am," the latter of which appeared in the song text he had before him.

The musical setting: Reggio's setting treats the three stanzas of the text in an ABC form, in G major. It is not related to William King's treatment of the same text.

Bar	Score	Notes	Comments
1	I-II	[*t. sig.*]	3/4 *ed. Songs* shows a C 3.
28	I-II	1	First and second endings *ed.*, for the repeat of bars 25–28. At the double bar, *Songs* shows double dots on both sides. These are here *om* (see headnote on Reggio in Editorial Principles).

[Poem 74] "The Separation."

Composer: Pietro Reggio

Copy text: *Songs* 1:18.

Song text: F1 poem 74, stanza 1.

Textual variants: *bars 11–12* Separated] sep'arated F1   *bars 22, 26, 28* I am] I'm F1

Literary source: Reggio sets the first of two six-line stanzas appearing in all printed versions of *The Mistress* through F8. The variants listed above are both syllabic expansions, made to suit Reggio's setting. If these variant readings derived from an independent manuscript of Cowley's poem, it was not M26 or a copy of it (see Literary Collation). The existence of M26, however, establishes that this poem circulated in a single-stanza version. Reggio's song text is not the same as the one found with an untitled setting, attributed to Mr. Francis Pigott, in *The Banquet of Musick*, vol. 2 (1688).

The musical setting: The piece is in B minor without a key signature. Reggio's forward movement is accomplished by structural imbalance, two nine-measure phrases followed by a fourteen measure phrase. Reggio's setting and Francis Pigott's are not related.

Bar	Score	Notes	Comments
22	I-II	[*t. sig.*]	[6/4] *ed.*, as is the return to [3/4] in bar 23. Reggio expands bar 22 without notice.
31	I-II	endings	*Ed*. In *Songs*, the final bar shows two dotted half notes in score I and two tied, dotted half notes in score II. The D.S. sign, for return to bar 25, note 2, is positioned above the second dotted half note in score I.

[Poem 74] ["The Separation."]

Composer: Mr. Francis Pigott

Copy text: *The Banquet of Musick* 2:10 (BM88).

Song text: F1 poem 74. Pigott sets the entire poem.

Textual variants: *title*] F1; BM88 *is untitled*   *bars 7–8* separated] sep'a-rated F1   *bar 30* as they say;] as, they say, F1

Literary source: The variants are unique to BM88. As to accidentals, the song text is relatively close to F1 and other printed editions of *The Mistress* up through F11 (1688). The song text is not derived from Reggio's earlier setting.

The musical setting: Pigott writes in a modified strophic form, in D minor. Pigott appears not to have been influenced by Reggio.

Bar	Score	Notes	Comments
—]	II	*k. sig.*	The B♭ is printed twice at the beginning of each system for score II. The higher flat is here *om*.
—]	II	[*figs.*]	*Ed.*, throughout.
7	II	4	BM88 shows a sharp to cancel the key signature here and at the following bars and scores: 11.I; 12.I; 15.I; 25.II, note 4; 29.I; 30.I; and 33.I. A bracketed natural is shown in this edition.
15	II	5	[♮] *ed*. No accidental appears in BM88.
18	I-II	||	BM88 inserts the double bar between notes 5 and 6 in score I and in score II at the end of the measure, as here represented, following the pickup to the second stanza of the text.
33	II	5	[♮] *ed*. No accidental appears in BM88.

[Poem 75] "The Tree."

Composer: Pietro Reggio

Copy text: *Songs* 1:3.

Song text: F1 poem 75. Reggio sets stanzas 1 and 4 of five six-line stanzas.

Textual variants: *bar 2* flourishingst] flour'ishingst F1   *bar 10* violent] vi'olent F1   *bar 11* they have] They'have F1

Literary source: The variants in bars 2 and 10 agree coincidentally with copies of the folio *Works* (F10–12) published after 1680. Reggio's source could have been any of the printed editions of *The Mistress* except O2, disqualified for its variant reading in the first stanza (see Literary Collation).

The musical setting: The work, composed in a modified strophic form, is in C minor.

Bar	Score	Notes	Comments
2	I	4	[♭] *ed.*, in accordance with the C-minor tonality.
4	I	3–4	Slur *ed.*
10	I	5–6	Slur *ed.*
13–14	I–II	‖	Double dots on both sides of the double bar in *Songs* are here *om.*
16	II	1–2	*Songs* shows a tie between these notes. It is here *om.*
20–21	I	6–7 | 1	Slur across bar line, *ed. Songs* slurs only notes 6–7 in bar 20.
24	I	5	[♮] *ed.*, in accordance with the harmony made explicit in the bass figure.
25	II	1–2	*Songs* shows a slur. It is not characteristic of Reggio's treatment of the bass line and is here *om.*

[Poem 76] "Her Unbelief"

Composer: Pietro Reggio

Copy text: *Songs* 1:19.

Song text: F1 poem 76. Reggio sets stanzas 1 and 3 of six five-line stanzas appearing in all printed editions of *The Mistress*.

Textual variants: *bar 2* ignorance] *Igno'rance* F1   *bars 9–11* and] but F1   *bars 16–17* them-selves] themselves F1

Literary source: The variant in bars 9–11, "and" for "but," coincidentally agrees with the reading in M26, an extract of two lines that cannot be the source. The variant in bar 2 suggests F4–7 as the literary source (see Literary Collation).

The musical setting: The tonality is G minor, with E-flats supplied as accidentals. The form is strophic, with modifications in the melody to accommodate the text of the second verse (stanza 3 of the literary text). There is more activity in the bass line and a greater incidence of figures than usual for Reggio.

Bar	Score	Notes	Comments
1	II	3	*Songs* shows a flat, lowering the F.
3	II	1–2	*Songs* shows a sharp, to cancel the B♭ in the key signature.
4	I	2–4	Slur, *ed. Songs* slurs notes 2–3.
8	II	1–2	*Songs* shows a sharp, as in bar 3.
10	I	6	*Songs* shows a sharp, canceling the key signature.
10	II	1–2	*Songs* shows a sharp, canceling the key signature.
10	II	5 *fig.*	*Songs* shows a sharp, as in score I, note 6, raising the B.
11	II	3	[♯] *ed.*, consistent with *fig.* note 1 and the treble score.
12	II	1 *fig.*	[♭] *ed.*, to be compatible with the implied retention of the E♭ from measure 11.
13–14	I–II	‖	Double dots, appearing on both sides of the double bar, are here *om* (see headnote on Reggio in Editorial Principles).
14	I–II	*t. sig.*	*Songs* reiterates the time signature C to begin the second stanza.
14	II	3	*Songs* shows a flat, lowering the F.
16	II	1	*Songs* shows a sharp to cancel the key signature, as in bar 3. No accidental appears at note 2, but the passage is the same as in bar 3 and the second B should be played as a natural.
17	I	2–4	Slur, *ed.* (compare bar 4); *Songs* slurs notes 2–3.
21	II	1–2	*Songs* shows a sharp, canceling the key signature.
23	I	5	*Songs* shows a sharp, as above.
23	II	1–2	*Songs* shows a sharp, as above.
26	I–II	1	In *Songs*, two tied whole notes appear (see headnote on Reggio in Editorial Principles).

[Poem 79] "Honour. A Song upon a Ground."

Composer: Pietro Reggio

Copy text: *Songs* 1:1.

Margaret Laurie notes that Henry Purcell's "A Song upon a Ground" sets Cowley's "Honour" to the same ground as this Reggio composition. Reggio's score, in its printed form as the first score in *Songs*, was advertised in *The London Gazette*, no. 1532, by way of a notice that subscribers could receive their copies of *Songs* after 26 July 1680. Laurie can date Purcell's setting as late 1680 if Purcell wrote "in direct response" to Reggio (*Works* 25:277). Ian Spink also maintains that Purcell borrowed Reggio's ground (*English Song*, 218). Reggio's placing this song first in the volume may suggest something of its popularity.

Song text: F1 poem 79.

Textual variants: *title*] Honor F1   *bar 32* what is] What's F1   *bar 85* Devilship] Devi'lship F1-3; Devilship F4-10

Literary source: Given the 1680 publication date and the reading in *Songs*, bar 85, Reggio's song text was taken from one of the printed editions of Cowley's *Works*, F4-7. A comparison of the textual variants above with those listed for Purcell's "A Song upon a Ground" reveals that both Reggio and Purcell sought Cowley's literary text for their song scores. Purcell does not follow Reggio's song text, nor vice versa. Reggio calls attention to the literary source by including its title, "Honor," in his own. Purcell omits the literary title and (if Laurie and Spink are correct in assessing Purcell's song as a response to Reggio's) perhaps calls attention to Reggio's composition by using its subtitle. "Song upon a Ground," however, is a very common title for this kind of composition.

The musical setting: Reggio sets the ground in a four-measure phrase, in triple meter. Purcell sets the ground in a two-measure phrase, in sextuple meter. Both versions are in the key of C. Reggio employs thirty repetitions of the ground, plus two one-measure cadences. Purcell has twenty-five repetitions of the ground (he does not repeat bits of the song text, as Reggio characteristically does) and a final measure of cadence. Reggio begins by working the phrases so that they agree with one statement of the ground, but by measure 32 he is beginning the text on the fourth measure of the ground, on the second measure in 38, and so on. Purcell does much the same thing in matching the text with the ground. Both Reggio and Purcell offer opportunities for the continuo to function in a solo capacity. In the melodic line, both composers employ some word painting; the more expressive examples are in Purcell.

Bar	Score	Notes	Comments
1	I-II	[*t. sig.*]	The time signature is indicated as C 3 in *Songs*.
—]	II	[*figs.*]	Reggio writes figures for the bass score in all settings published in *Songs* except for this one. This is also the only song in the collection that is set upon a ground. All bass figures in this text are set in brackets and are *ed*.
20	I	2-4	Slur *ed*. Notes 3-4 are slurred in *Songs*.
47-48	I	2-4 | 1-2	Slur *ed*. The slur is broken at the bar line in *Songs*.

Bar	Score	Notes	Comments
101	I–II	bar	We place a double bar line here, indicating the end of a stanza, as Reggio has done at bars 29 and 65. The double bar line is *om* in *Songs*, as is a two-bar interlude before the text and vocal score resume, as after bars 29 and 65.
102	I–II	*t. sig.*	In *Songs* the time signature is reintroduced here, with a simple 3 sign.
124	I	3–5	Slur *ed*. Notes 3–4 are slurred in *Songs*.
128	I	2–4	Slur *ed*. Notes 3–4 are slurred in *Songs*.
130	II	*D.S.*	*Songs* shows the D.S. sign above score I only, here and at bar 127.

[Poem 79] "A Song upon a Ground"

Composer: Henry Purcell

Copy text: Orpheus Britannicus 1:124 (OB98) (based on the printing in *Choice Ayres and Songs . . . The Fourth Book*, printed by A. Godbid and J. Playford, Jr., Sold by John Playford and John Carr; London, 1683 [CAS83], p. 42); collated with Fitzwilliam Museum MS 118, p. 74 (FM18); Fitzwilliam Museum MS 120 (FM20); Chichester Cathedral MS VI/1/1, fol. 411 (CCVI); BL Add. MSS 33234, fol. 124ᵛ (BL33); BL Add. MSS 29397, fol. 69ᵛ (BL29); and Folger MS W.b. 515, p. 92 (Fol51).

This is the most frequently copied of all the Cowley poems set by Henry Purcell. OB98, the memorial edition based on the earlier John Playford edition CAS83, is the copy text. Though it is further removed from the manuscript source for CAS83, OB98 shows bass figures that could be authoritative (see Henry Playford's prefatory letters to TM85[1] and TM87) and it corrects an error in bar 44. CCVI, FM18, and Fol51 are manuscripts of particular interest since they are based on the earliest authorial manuscript or copies of it (see below). Variants in the song text suggest that the composition was revised. Notational variants suggest that it was revised twice. BL29 and Fol51 both mention CAS83 in their index listings, though neither appears to have been copied from this printed edition. See notes to Reggio's "Honor: A Song upon a Ground" for its relationship to this Purcell setting.

Song text: F1 poem 79. Purcell sets the entire poem.

Textual variants: title] OB98, CAS83, Fol19; A Song upon A Ground: Made 1680 CCVI; A Song upon a ground. She Loves and She Confesses too FM20; untitled, Fol51; *(listed as* "She loves Purcell" *in index)*, BL29; *(listed as* "She loves & she confesses" *in index)*, FM18; *Honor*. F1   bar 6 Work's] Σ; works CCVI, FM18, FM20   bar 16 what] Σ how Fol19   bar 17 still]

Collations and Notes to the Musical Settings (pp. 541–543) 637

Σ; yet BL33   *bar 19* up in] Σ; upon Fol 51   *bar 22* Have] Σ; Here FM20   *bar 23* this] Σ; thy Fol 51   *bar 28* what] Σ; that Fol19   *bar 30* thou] Σ; *the word does not appear in F1, in other printed or manuscript versions of the literary text, or in Reggio's song text*   *bar 31* cause] Σ; shade CCVI   *bar 33* But] Σ; yet FM18   *bar 36* Devilship] Σ; *Devi'lship* O1-2, F1-3, O3-4, D2; *Devil-ship* F11-12   *bar 37* this] Σ; the FM18   *bar 42* Night's] OB98, CAS83, Fol19, BL29, BL33, CCVI, F12, O3-4, D2; *Nights* Σ   *bar 46* ev'ry] OB98, CAS83, Fol19, Fol51, BL29, BL33, CCVI, FM20; every FM18 and Σ   *bar 47* Sprite] Σ; sight BL29   *bars 47-48* attempt'st] Σ; attempts CCVI, Fol 51   Men] Σ; *om* FM18   *bars 48-49* to affright] OB98, CAS83, Fol19, Fol51, BL29, BL33, CCVI, FM20; to' affright FM18; t'affright *all versions of the literary text*   *bar 51* Light] Σ; night CCVI, Fol19, Fol 51; night *pen-corrected to* Light FM18

Literary source: Very near agreement in the song text of all the musical settings in bars 30, 36, 46, and 48–49 implies a common manuscript source for this tradition of the text. Two of the readings add a syllable to the literary text and the other elides a vowel; all three are occasioned by the musical setting. We can infer that the original manuscript setting contained these readings. Manuscripts CCVI, FM18, Fol51, and Fol19 read "night" in bar 51; it is probable that the first setting showed this error in the song text. The text was corrected (as was FM18) in the manuscript copy sponsoring BL33, BL29, and FM20, as well as the manuscript provided for CAS83. The reading "Devilship" in bar 36 suggests that song text is based on one of the printed editions of Cowley's *Works*, F4-7. Reggio's setting also shows this reading.

The musical setting:

Variants among the sources in bars 3 and 23 indicate a manuscript tradition for the composition independent of the printed settings and including all manuscripts except Fol19 and FM20. These last manuscripts mostly agree with CAS83 and OB98 (though curiously the song text of Fol19, in bar 51, agrees with the earlier manuscripts). The manuscript tradition is complex. Fol51 mostly agrees with CCVI and/or FM18; the evidence argues a common ancestor for all three (as does the song text reading in bar 51). Unique readings in CCVI bars 6, 11, 34, 48, and especially 41, and the unique reading in FM18, bar 18, establish that neither is the source for the other or for Fol51. Fol51 shows some singular readings in the song text, but no unique readings of major consequence in the musical setting. It thus appears to represent the early manuscript setting most closely. BL33 and BL29 are harder to align, as they agree in some places with the early manuscripts, elsewhere with CAS83, and elsewhere with one another. BL33 is distinguished by unique readings in bars 3, 5, 13, 29, and 39, while BL29 shows no unique readings of major con-

THE MUSICAL SETTINGS

sequence. BL29, then, may be said to represent most closely a source that it shares with BL33 and which, as Margaret Laurie has offered (*Works* 25:277), stands chronologically between the early manuscripts and the printed texts. Many of the variants recorded below reflect copyists' attempts to align the vocal score with the song text by way of slurs. The differing solutions suggest that the song was performed in a variety of ways. The emendation in bar 31 of the present text follows CCVI rather than Fol51 because, in our estimation, CCVI best solves the problem of relating the vocal score to the song text.

Bar	Score	Notes	Comments
–]	–]	t. sig.	FM18, BL33, and BL29 are in 3/4 time. CCVI and Fol51 are in 6/4, though signed "3 1." Fol19 and FM20 are written in and signed 6/4, like OB98. CAS83 is in 6/4 and signed ¢3.
2	I	2–3	A quarter note A in CCVI, FM18, BL29, and Fol51.
2	I	4–8	Dotted eighth and sixteenth slurred, quarter and eighth slurred, and an eighth note in CCVI; two eighth notes, a quarter note, and dotted eighth slurred, and a sixteenth note in BL33; dotted eighth, sixteenth, and quarter slurred, and two eighth notes slurred in Fol51 and FM18.
2	II	1–2	FM18 shows a quarter note and dotted eighth here and at recurring points in the ground, throughout.
3	I	2–3	A dotted eighth and sixteenth note in BL33; no slur, CCVI and Fol51.
3	I	4–5	A half note G in CCVI, FM18, BL33, BL29, and Fol51.
3	I	6	Two eighth notes, slurred, A and B, in BL33.
4	I	2–3	Two eighth notes in CCVI and Fol51.
5	I	3–4	Two eighth notes in BL33.
6	I	1–3	Half note C and quarter note A in CCVI; a half note A, eighth B, and eighth A in BL33.
11	I	2–3	No slur in CCVI, Fol51, FM18, and FM20.
11	I	9	An F in CCVI.
11–12	I	4–9 | 1–5	No slur in FM20.
13	I	1	A dotted half note in BL33.
18	I	4	The note is B in FM18.
20	I	4–6	The slur is drawn over notes 5–6 in FM18, Fol51.
20–21	I	4–6 | 1–2	The slur extends from notes 5–6 in bar 20 to note 2, bar 21, in CCVI and BL33. In FM18 and BL33 notes 1–2, bar 21, are a dotted eighth and a sixteenth note, slurred.

Collations and Notes to the Musical Settings (pp. 543–548)

Bar	Score	Notes	Comments
23	I	4–5	Two eighth notes in CCVI, FM18, BL33, BL29, and Fol51.
28	I	*half rest,* 2,3	A quarter rest, eighth rest, eighth note, and quarter note in CCVI, FM18, and Fol51.
29	I	1	B♮ in BL33.
31	I	–]	The reading is accepted from CCVI. CAS83, OB98, Fol19, and FM20 give notes 1–3 to the word "cause," note 4 to "of," and the word "solid" is sung on notes 5–10. FM18, BL33, BL29, and Fol 51 give notes 1–3 to "cause," 4–5 to "of," and 6–10 to "solid." Notes 6–8 and 9–10 are slurred in FM18; notes 6–9 are slurred in BL33 and BL29.
33	I	*t. sig.*	The measure is in 3/4, though not signed, in CCVI.
34	I	1–2	A half note and a quarter in CCVI.
37	I	*t. sig.*	The measure is in 9/4, though not signed, in CCVI and Fol51.
37–38	I	4–9 | 1–8	No slurs in FM18 and FM20.
39	I	1	A dotted half note in BL33.
41	I	2–5	A quarter note, dotted eighth and sixteenth, and a quarter note and slur over notes 3–5, in FM18, BL33, BL29, Fol 51; a quarter, two eighths, and a quarter, slur over 3–5 in CCVI; a dotted quarter and three eighth notes, slur over 3–5 in Fol19 and FM20.
44	I	2	An F in CAS83.
44	I	1–4	Two eighths, a sixteenth and dotted eighth in CCVI and Fol51; two eighth and two sixteenth notes (omitting an eighth-count) in BL29.
46	I	1–2	A dotted quarter, and an eighth B slurred to a quarter A in BL33.
46	I	3–6	No slur in FM18.
48	I	2	An eighth note E and an eighth D in CCVI and BL33.
48	I	3–6	Dotted quarter B, eighth A in CCVI.
48	I	6–7	Notes slurred in FM18. Following the FM18 song text variant in bar 48, alignment between text and notes in score I differs from other settings through bar 50.
51	I	1	OB98 concludes with a dotted half note; CAS83 shows a dotted half under a fermata.

[Poem 80] "The Innocent Ill."

Composer: Pietro Reggio

Copy text: Songs 1:27.

Song text: F1 poem 80. Reggio sets stanzas 1 and 4 of this four-stanza poem.

Textual variants: *bar 16* the ear] th'*Ear* F1   *bar 18* every] ev'ery F1   *bars 29-30* well natur'd] well-*natur'ed* F1   *bar 39* e'en] e'ven F1

Literary source: Variants in bars 18 and 29-30 establish the literary source as one of the folio editions of Cowley's *Works*, F5-8. F8, published in 1680, is not a likely source. Given the dates for preparation and publication of *Songs* (see bibliographical description), it is probable that none of the settings was composed later than 1679.

The musical setting: The work appears to be in D minor, with B-flats used to modulate to the key of F. The work is essentially strophic, with modifications in the melody in measures 26-27 and a reverse procedure in measures 29-30.

Bar	Score	Notes	Comments
20	II	3-4	These continuo notes are slurred in the copy text.
21-22	I-II	| |	The copy text shows double dots on each side of the double bar. These are here *om* (see headnote in Editorial Principles).
37	II	3 [*fig.*]	[♭] *ed.*, following the figure in the same passage at measure 17.

[Poem 83] "Bathing in the River."

Composer: Pietro Reggio

Copy text: Songs 1:14.

Song text: F1 poem 83, stanzas 1 and 3 of six seven-line stanzas.

Textual variants: *bar 8* treacherous] treach'erous F1   *bar 13* can] might F1   *bar 25* every] ev'ry F1   *bar 30* am'rous] *ed. (as required by the vocal score)*; amorous *Songs*; amo'rous F1   *bar 36* amorous] am'orous F1

Literary source: The variant in bar 13 is unique to *Songs*, and it suggests a manuscript source for these two stanzas from Cowley's poem. All other variants involve elisions, and it is apparent that the vocal setting dictates departures from F1 and other printed versions of the text up to F8. As there is no extant manuscript to confirm a literary source independent of the printed editions, as the other variants can be attributed to the setting, and since Reggio found other of his *Mistress* texts in one of the printed folio editions, it is likely that the literary source for this song is one of the folio editions printed before 1680.

The musical setting: The setting is in F major; the form is modified strophic. Reggio's simple rhythmic movement in the melody complements his relatively candid song text.

Bar	Score	Notes	Comments
13	I–II	1	*Songs* shows a sharp in score I to cancel the flat in the signature and a sharp in the figured bass to the same effect.
16	II	1 [*fig.*]	Some copies omit the figure. See collation (cf. bar 17).
17	I	2	[♮] *ed. Songs* retains the B♭ here; where the same figure occurs in bar 46, Reggio cancels the flat.
17	II	1	Some copies show a flat figure, above the note. See collation in the description of *Songs*, p. 562.
29	I–II	—]	First and second endings *ed.*, for the repeat of bars 25–29. *Songs* shows two tied, dotted half notes at bar 29.
30	I–II	*t. sig.*	The time signature is reintroduced as 3 in *Songs*, as distinguished from 3/4 at bar 1.
36	I	2–3	*Songs* slurs these notes. We recognize the difference in the treatment of the word "amorous" in measures 30 and 36.
41	I	rest	Elsewhere in this setting, Reggio maintains a continuous movement in the vocal line. The anomalous break here does not follow from the sense of the song text; it could be a copyist's error. It may be preferred to render the measure with a half note and quarter note, expressing the song text "current."
42	I–II	1	*Songs* shows a sharp, to cancel the flat in the signature, and a sharp in the bass figure.
43	I	3	*Songs* shows a sharp to cancel the key signature. The bass figure 3 is emended accordingly.
46	I	2	*Songs* shows a sharp to cancel the key signature. See note to bar 17.
46	II	1	Some copies show a flat figure, above the note. See collation (cf. bar 17).
59	I–II	—]	First and second endings *ed.*, for the repeat of bars 55–59. *Songs* shows two tied dotted half notes in bar 59, with the D.S. inscribed between them above score I only.

Index to the Commentary, Explanatory Notes, and Notes to the Musical Settings

This selective index lists proper names appearing in the literary Commentary, Explanatory Notes to the text, and Notes to the musical settings. There are a limited number of references to pages in the Textual Introduction, Analysis, and bibliographical sections where historical information appears. Where works by Cowley not yet printed in this edition have been cited, the index provides reference under the titles of first printed editions. Where a name appears in discrete references that occur on each page of a sequence, the first and last page of the sequence are listed.

Addison, Joseph, 219, 238, 278
Agrippa, Cornelius, 286, 291
Aiken, Pauline, 241, 281, 294
Amphion Anglicus, 311
Anacreontea, 274-75
Apuleius, Lucius, 301
Aquinas, St. Thomas, 301
Ashley, Maurice, 250
Ausonius, 243, 263
Ayres, Philip, 233-34, 253, 257, 259, 269, 274, 287, 289, 293, 298
Ayton, Sir Robert, 246, 273, 274

Bacon, Francis, 240, 252, 262, 270, 283-84, 287
Bampfield, Joseph, 161-62, 208
Banfield, Michael, 311, 382, 557, 584-85
Bannister, John, 564-65
Barnes, Barnabe, 270
Barnes, Joshua, 271
Baron, Robert, 231-32, 246, 254, 266, 278, 284
Barrett, John, 236, 311, 315, 401, 563, 591-92
Beggars Opera, 311
Behn, Aphra, 312
Bernærts, Balthazar, 157
Blount, Sir Thomas, 174

Blow, John, 179, 229, 236, 240, 311-15, 417, 563-64, 595, 599-600
Blundeville, John, 235-36, 257, 311, 315, 354, 565, 577-78
Bold, Henry, 263
Boydill, Thomas, 174
Broghill, Roger Boyle, baron Broghill and first earl of Orrery, 272
Brome, Alexander, 171, 234, 237, 245, 261, 263, 289, 290
Browne, Sir Thomas, 251, 254, 273, 284, 286, 297, 300
Buckingham, George Villiers, second duke of, 234, 242; as author of "Abrahamus Couleius Anglorum Pindarus," 171-72
Bullen, A. H., 248
Burton, Robert, 239, 248-49, 260, 264, 268-70, 280-81, 284, 293-94, 296, 298
Butler, Martin, 255-56
Butler, Samuel, 234, 264, 295-96
Buxton, John, 278
Byrd, William, 285
Byron, George Gordon, sixth baron, 284-85

Cambridge, 9, 168, 224
Campelman, Charles, 564, 578, 588-89

Campion, Thomas, 237-38
Car, Thomas, 188-89
Card of Courtship, The: Or, the Language of Love, 235
Carew, Thomas, 231, 238, 240, 242, 248, 250, 261, 276-78, 290, 297-301
Carey, John, 243
Carr, John, 236, 594-95
Carrington, Philip, 260
Cartwright, William, 169, 224, 235, 248, 251, 263, 291
Carwitham, J., 587
Cary, Lucius. *See* Falkland, Lucius Cary
Cary, Patrick, 234, 257
Catullus, Gaius Valerius, 233, 238-40, 272, 281-82
Cavendish, Margaret. *See* Newcastle, Margaret Cavendish
Cervantes, Miguel de, 234
Chapel[s] Royal, The, 236, 311-15
Chapman, George, 251
Charles I, King, 226, 256, 313
Charles II, King, 311, 313
Chaucer, Geoffrey, 241
Cherbury, Edward, lord Herbert, 270, 277
Choice Collection of 120 Loyal Songs, A, 180, 580
Choice Collection of 180 Loyal Songs, A, 180, 580
Clarendon, Edward Hyde, earl of, 229
Clark, Mary, 156
Claudian [Claudius Claudianus], 251, 276, 284
Clayton, Thomas, 246, 295
Cleveland John, 168, 172, 187, 242, 251, 266, 269, 273, 276, 295, 297
Constable, Henry, 283
Cooke, Henry ["Captain"], 311-12, 315
Cooper, Samuel, 279
Cotton, Charles, 231, 234, 265-66, 277-78, 280-82, 291, 293
Cowley, Abraham (*titles from "The Mistress"*): "Against Fruition," 58; "Against Hope," 71; "All-over, Love," 48, *settings* (W. King) 371, (Reggio) 373; "Answer to the Platonicks," 37; "The Bargain," 50, *setting* 376; "Bathing in the River," 122, *setting* 553; "Beauty," 79; "Called Inconstant," 63; "The Change," 32, *setting* 334; "Clad all in White," 34, *settings* (W. King) 336, (Reggio) 338; "Coldness," 77, *setting* 424; "The Concealment," 83, *settings* (W. King) 437, (Purcell) 440, (R. King) 449; "The Constant," 103; "Counsel," 53, *settings* (Reggio) 380, (Banfield) 382; "Counsel [II]," 109, *settings* (W. King) 520, (Reggio) 522; "The Cure," 110; "The Despair," 43, *settings* (Blundeville) 354, (Hart) 356; "Dialogue, After Enjoyment," 119; "The Discovery," 57, *settings* (Reggio) 384, (Wootton) 390; "Discretion," 106; "The Dissembler," 99, *setting* 485; "The Distance," 86, *settings* (W. King) 459, (Reggio) 460; "Eccho," 69; "The Encrease," 55, *setting* 463; "For Hope," 72; "The Frailty," 75; "The Gazers," 113; "The given Heart," 60, *settings* (W. King) 400, (Barrett) 401; "The Given Love," 23, *settings* (W. King) 326, (Reggio) 328; "The Heart-breaking," 92, *setting* 482; "The Heart fled again," 65, *settings* (Reggio) 403, (R. King) 405; "Her Name," 104, *setting* 458; "Her Unbelief," 112, *setting* 534; "Honor," 116, *settings* (Reggio) 537, (Purcell) 543; "Impossibilities," 97; "Inconstancy," 30; "The Inconstant," 101; "The Incurable," 115; "The Injoyment," 77, *settings* (W. King) 426, (Reggio) 428; "The Innocent Ill," 117, *setting* 549; "Leaving Me, and then loving Many," 35; "Looking on, and discoursing with his Mistress," 89, *settings* (Hall) 470, (Forcer) 475; "The Long Life," 52; "Love and Life," 49; "Love given over," 124; "Love undiscovered," 59, *settings* (W. King) 393, (anon.) 395; "Loves Ingratitude," 74, *setting* 417; "Loves Visibility," 88, *settings* (W. King) 466, (Reggio) 467; "Maidenhead," 95; "The Monopoly," 84, *setting* 457; "My Dyet," 46, *setting* 363; "My Fate," 91, *setting* 480; "My Heart

discovered," 36, *setting* 343; "My Picture," 82, *setting* 434; "Not Fair," 30; "The Parting," 81; "The Passions," 41; "Platonick Love," 31; "The Prophet," 61; "The Request," 19; "The Resolution," 62; "Resolved to be beloved," 55; "Resolved to Love," 90; "The rich Rival," 70, *setting* 411; "The Same," [i.e. "Resolved to be beloved II"] 56; "The Separation," 110, *settings* (Reggio) 525, (Pigott) 527; "Silence," 98, *setting* 483; "Sleep," 78; "The Soul," 39, *setting* 350; "The Soul [II]," 68; "The Spring," 26; "The Thief," 47, *setting* 368; "The Thraldome," 21, *setting* 318; "The Tree," 111, *setting* 531; "The Usurpation," 93; "The vain Love," 38; "Verses lost upon a Wager," 121; "The Waiting-Maid," 108; "Weeping," 105, *settings* (Reggio) 490, (Turner) 493, (Purcell) 500; "The Welcome," 64; "Wisdom," 42; "The Wish," 44; "Womens Superstition," 66; "Written in Juice of Lemmon," 28

Cowley, Abraham (*works cited not appearing in this volume*): *Anacreontiques* 237, 241, 260-61, 275, 281-82; *The Civil War*, 140, 146, 188, 224, 252, 255, 265-66; *Cutter of Coleman Street*, 157; *Davideidos, Liber Primus*, 9, 161; *Davideis*, 148, 224, 234, 241, 246-47, 252, 276, 285; *Essays*, 173, 179, 199, 225, 256-57, 271-72, 283; *The Guardian*, 168-69, 187, 229, 257, 297; *Miscellanies*, 174, 257, 267, 274, 289, 292; *Plantarum*, 257; *Poems* [1656], "Preface," 220, 228, 238, 266, 288-89; *Poetical Blossomes*, 241, 243, 246, 251-52, 256, 271; *The Puritan and the Papist*, 241, 255, 265, 315; *The Puritans Lecture*, 238, 255-56, 315; *Pindarique Odes*, 173, 233-34, 239, 251-52, 255, 259, 284, 292-93; *Sylva*, 170, 174, 257; *Verses*, 239-40, 267. [*Works attributed to Cowley: Davideis . . . Libris Quatuor*, 144-45, 161; "Epigram. On the Power of Love," 158-59; "The Force of Love," 158; *The Rehearsal*, 234, 242]

Crashaw, Richard, 167-68, 172, 186-89, 224, 238, 272-74, 291, 298
Curtius, Ernst, 261

Daniel, Samuel, 269, 273, 276-77, 279, 288
Dante Alighieri, 240, 301
Davenant, Charles, 169
Davenant, William [W.D.], 169, 171, 222, 242, 255, 273, 300
Davison, Francis, 227, 237, 249
Day, Cyrus, 556-57, 561
Democritus, 240
Denham, John, 171, 273
Digby, Sir Kenelm, 249, 271, 284
Disraeli, Isaac, 262, 285, 287
Donne, John, 168-69, 171, 227-29, 234, 238, 240, 243-51, 254, 257-61, 264-66, 272, 276-79, 281, 283, 285-87, 289-91, 294-95, 297-302
Dowland, John, 237, 240, 291
Drayton, Michael, 245, 261, 264-65, 281, 291
Dring, Thomas, 235
Drummond of Hawthornden, William, 263
Dryden, John, 171, 173, 228, 238, 265
DuBartas, Guillaume, 250
Dunton, John, 301
d'Urfe, Honoré, 245, 288, 295

Earl of Oxford. *See* Vere, Aubrey de
Eitner, Robert, 312, 316
Elisbury, Edward, 171, 222-23
Ellrodt, Robert, 273
Elys, Edmund, 219-20
Empson, William, 283
Erasmus, Desiderius, 270, 286
Etherege, Sir George, 276
Evelyn, John, 256-58, 560
E.Y., 313

Fairfax, Edward, 301
Falkland, Lucius Cary, second viscount, 224, 242
Fanshawe, Sir Richard, 301
Ferrabosco, Alfonso, 291
Flatman, Thomas, 12, 234, 273, 315
Fleming, Robert, 170

Fletcher, Phineas, 171
Fontenelle, Bernard Le Bovier de, 287
Forcer, Francis, 236, 312, 475, 564, 615-17
Fortune, Nigel, 218
Fotherby, Robert, 279
Fowler, Alastair, 246, 260, 293-94, 299
Further Considerations about mix'd Dancing, 193-94

Galileo, 271
Gay, John, 247, 311, 573
Gibbons, Orlando, 564
Gill, George, 559
Godolphin, Sidney, 238, 299
Gongora, Luis de, 301
Gosse, Edmund, 220, 247
Greaves, Thomas, 277
Greene, Robert, 297
Greg, Walter W., 156
Greville, Fulke, lord Brooke, 237, 240
Grierson, Herbert J. C., 243, 248, 250, 300-301
Grosart, Alexander B., 159, 194, 220, 284, 298
Grotius, Hugo, 233
Guarini, Giovanni Battista, 241

Habington, William, 269, 290, 299
Hall, John, 253, 277, 291, 293
Hall, William, 236, 311-15, 470, 558, 564-65, 615-17
Handel, George Frederick, 236, 247, 573
Hanmer, Lady Elizabeth, 12
Harington, John, 228, 232, 249, 301
Harper, Charles, 156
Hart, James, 235-36, 257, 311-15, 356, 564, 577-78, 588-89
Heath, Robert, 231-32, 237-38, 241, 275, 280
Henrietta Maria, Queen, 16, 223-24, 255-56, 266, 282-83, 313
Herbert, George, 172, 234, 270, 273, 291
Herrick, Robert, 168, 235, 250, 275, 289
Herringman, Henry, 156, 164, 186
Hesiod, 252
Heywood, Thomas, 286-87
Hill, Richard L., 244
Hinman, Robert, 271
Hobbes, Thomas, 225, 254, 284-86
Holland, Philemon, 292, 295

Hookes, Nicholas, 231, 233, 241, 247-48, 270, 277, 283
Horace [Quintus Horatius Flaccus], 171, 241, 243, 248, 299
Hoskins, John, 279
Howell, James, 284
Humfrey, Pelham, 312, 315, 565
Humphries, Rolfe, 302
Hutchinson, Lucy, 266
Hyde, Edward. *See* Clarendon, Edward Hyde

Jenkins, John, 315
Jermyn, Henry, first earl of St. Albans, 223, 282, 313
Johnson, Samuel, 158, 219-20, 224, 227-28, 234, 262, 264, 271, 291, 293
Jonson, Ben, 227, 229, 237-38, 240, 243, 245, 248, 263, 279, 281-82, 290, 298-99
Jordan, Thomas, 227, 245, 249, 289, 297, 299
Juvenal [Decimus Junius Juvenalis], 264

Keble, Mr. [Samuel], 560-61
King, George, 313
King, Henry, 168, 253, 263, 273
King, Robert, 236, 311-13, 315, 411, 449, 558-59, 592-93, 603-4, 606-14, 618-19, 621, 629; Robert King's *Consort*, 313
King, William, 235, 313, 315, 326, 336, 371, 393, 400, 426, 437, 457, 459, 466, 480, 482, 488, 520, 571, 573-74, 581-82, 588-89, 590-92, 603-4, 606-7, 609-14, 618-19, 621, 629-31
King's Music, The, 236, 311-12
Knight, Gowin, 259
Korshin, Paul J., 284

Laurie, Margaret, 568, 570, 607, 634-35, 638
Lawler, Justus, 248
Leake, William, 144
Leigh, Jo., 224-25
Leigh, Nicholas, 286
Leishman, J. B., 242, 248-50
Lionardi, Alessandro, 291
Livy [Titus Livius], 292
Locke, Matthew, 312, 565

Index 647

Lodge, Thomas, 267
Loiseau, Jean, 160, 223, 246, 258
Longus, 295
Lovejoy, Arthur O., 290
Lovelace, Richard, 227, 245, 249, 263, 289-91, 299, 301
Lucas, F. L., 270
Luckett, Richard, 314
Lucretius [Titus Lucretius Carus], 245, 284
Lyly, John, 286-87

Macocke, John, 164, 186
Madan, Falconer, 169, 173
Magus, Simon, 260
Mandeville, Sir John, 268
Margoliouth, H. M., 254, 259, 291
Marino, Giambattista, 243, 256-57, 270, 289
Marlowe, Christopher, 238, 289
Martial [Marcus Valerius Martialis], 171, 250, 263-64, 280, 286
Martin, L. C., 160, 168, 186, 242, 247, 259, 276
Marvell, Andrew, 234, 243, 253-54, 259-60, 278-79, 281, 287, 291, 295
Mary II, Queen, 559
May, Thomas, 226, 295
Mennes, Sir John, 234
Milton, John, 251, 269, 277, 301
Montagu, Walter, 246
Montalvan, Juan Perez de, 291
More, Henry, 247
Morelli, Cesare, 560
Moseley, Humphrey, 9, 134, 139-46, 161, 188, 224-26, 232, 235, 274, 297
Motte, Benjamin, 157, 562
Munday, Peter, 268
Murrie, Eleanore B., 556-57, 561
Mysteries of Love & Eloquence, The, 167, 197-98, 220. See also Phillips, Edward

Naps upon Parnassus, 233, 244
Nashe, Thomas, 301
New Academy of Complements, The, 167, 179-80, 182, 194, 196-97, 201, 222, 573-74, 580-82, 585, 588-92, 603-4, 607, 609, 611-12, 618, 621. See also Davenant, William [W.D.]
New Ayres and Dialogues, 606

Newcastle, Margaret Cavendish, duchess of, 251
Newcomb, Thomas, 145-46, 163-64
Nethercot, Arthur H., 233, 264, 272, 284
Nicholas, Sir Edward, 243
Nicholas [Nichols], John, 187
Nicholson, Marjorie Hope, 262

Oldham, John, 263, 283
Orpheus Britannicus, 557, 568-69, 594, 636
Osborne, Dorothy, 225, 279, 287-88
Otway, Thomas, 312
Ovid [Publius Ovidius Naso], 272, 295; *Amores*, 229, 237, 245, 248, 253, 260-61, 271, 275-77, 281, 289, 293-94; *Ars Amatoria*, 243, 265-66, 293; *Metamorphoses*, 157, 227, 238, 241-42, 245, 250-52, 267-68, 270-71, 277, 280, 288, 301-2; *Remedia Amores*, 237
Oxford, 168, 170, 224-25, 244, 259, 313, 315, 591

Packwood, H., 172
Paris, 188-89, 223-25, 242-43, 266, 313
Parry, Graham, 221, 223
Pepys, Samuel, 314, 560
Peters, Helen, 286
Petrarch, Francesco, 238, 240, 242, 247, 262, 287, 296, 302
Petrarchan tradition, 227, 283
Petronius, Gaius [Arbiter Elegantiarum], 263
Philipott, Thomas, 226, 276, 293
Philips, Katherine, 171-72, 263-64, 269, 295
Phillips, Edward, 167, 219-20, 225
Pigott, Francis, 236, 311-15, 556, 631-32
Playford, Henry, 311-13, 556-57, 562-63, 568, 600, 636
Playford, John, 236, 311-13, 315, 560-61, 594-95, 636
Pliny [Gaius Plinius Secundus], 243, 277, 286, 295
Plotinus, 301
Plutarch, 239, 287
Pope, Alexander, 219, 242, 272, 287
Pope, Walter, 179
Porter, Walter, 242

Prior, Matthew, 559
Propertius, Sextus, 246, 289, 294
Prujean, Thomas, 226
Purcell, Henry, 229, 236, 298, 309–15, 318, 411, 440, 500, 543, 564–65, 568, 594, 600, 606–9, 622–26, 634–36
Purchas, Samuel, 268, 278–79

Quarles, Francis, 261

Rabelais, Francois, 234
Ralegh, Sir Walter, 285
Randolph, Thomas, 172, 227, 237, 248, 280, 284, 299, 301
Reggio, Pietro, 180, 222, 229, 235–36, 298, 308–9, 311, 314–15, 328, 334, 338, 343, 350, 363, 368, 373, 376, 380, 384, 403, 424, 428, 434, 460, 463, 483, 485, 490, 522, 528, 531, 534, 537, 549, 553, 560–61, 566, 571–72, 574–76, 579, 581–85, 587, 592–93, 601–2, 604–5, 609, 611–14, 619–20, 622–23, 625, 630–32, 634–37, 640–41
Reynolds, Rowland, 143–44
Richmond, Hugh M., 242, 263, 269
Rochester, John Wilmot, second earl of, 171, 273, 298
Ronsard, Pierre de, 241
Roscommon, Wentworth Dillon, fourth earl of, 171
Rose, Gloria, 314, 601
Roxburghe Ballads, 248–49
Royal Society, The, 233, 242

Saintsbury, George, 247
Salusbury, Oliver, 172, 222–23
Sancroft, William, 169
Sandys, George, 172
Scarborough, Charles, 161–62, 251
Scarron, Paul, 234
Shadwell, Thomas, 312, 315
Shakespeare, William, 239–40, 244–45, 247, 260–62, 279, 286, 295
Shaw, Watkins, 313
Shelley, Percy Bysshe, 277
Sherburne, Edward, 235, 289
Shirley, James, 168, 226, 237, 242, 246, 258, 260, 267, 271, 279, 296–97
Sidney, Lady Dorothy, 241
Sidney, Sir Philip, 227, 232, 237, 240, 247–48, 270, 276–77

Smith, John, 251
Smith, William, 270
Sole, William, 236
Sparrow, John, 142, 159–60, 164, 166–67, 194, 246, 248, 258, 263, 265, 275
Spence, Joseph, 272, 287
Spenser, Edmund, 246, 249, 256, 260, 267, 274, 277, 286, 290, 296, 301
Spink, Ian, 313–15, 559, 635
Sprat, Thomas, 144, 154, 189, 225, 230–31, 233–34, 241, 253, 272, 276; English *Life*, 162–64, 174, 219, 264; Latin *Life*, 161, 272
Stanley, Thomas, 226, 235, 237, 245, 256–57, 267, 270, 275, 289, 291
Stephen, Leslie, 219
Stevens, R. J. S., 573
Strode, Ralph, 242
Stubbe, Henry, 233–34
Suckling, John, 169, 171, 226, 231, 237, 242, 251, 253, 263–64, 271, 273
Suetonius [Gaius Suetonius Tranquillus], 239, 287
Swift, Jonathan, 234, 248, 264
Sylvester, Joshua, 250

Tasso, Torquato, 238, 242, 278, 301
Tassoni, Alessandro, 234
Tate, Nahum, 173, 563
Temple, Sir William, 234, 279, 287–88
Theater of Music, The, 594–96, 599–600
Theocritus, 301
Thurloe, John, 161–62
Tibullus, Albius, 241
Titian [Tiziano Vecelli], 249
Tofte, Robert, 247, 291–92
Tonson, Jacob, 156
Trotter, W. David, 282, 293
Tudway, Thomas, 316
Turner, William, 236, 311–15, 493, 564–65, 622–23, 625–26

Vaughan, Henry, 226, 234, 242, 244, 273
Veen, Octavio van, 157
Veer, Gerart de, 278–79
Vere, Aubrey de, twentieth earl of Oxford, 161
Virgil [Publius Vergilius Maro]: *Aeneid*, 230, 252, 262, 268, 302; *Georgics*, 267, 288

Waller, A. R., 142, 159
Waller, Edmund, 169, 171–72, 226, 241–43, 247, 263, 277, 279, 294–96, 301
Wallerstein, Ruth, 251
Walsh, William, 241, 256
Walton, Geoffrey, 224, 243, 272
Walton, Izaak, 252, 279, 301
Warner, William, 268
Warren, Austin, 269
Watson, Thomas, 270
Webster, John, 270
Weir, Peter, 265
Wesley, John, 233
Wesley, Samuel, 231, 233–34
West, John E., 315
Whiting, Nathaniel, 260
Willetts, Pamela, 601
Willis, Francis, 276

Wilson, William, 134, 138, 143
Wither, George, 289
Wits Interpreter, 243
Witts Recreations, 160, 167, 174, 196–98, 607, 609, 613–14, 619
Woodford, Dr., 171
Wootton, Nicholas, 222, 315–16, 390, 585–87
Wyatt, Sir Thomas, 240, 262
Wythorne, Thomas, 273

Yalden, Thomas, 276
Yates, Frances, 254
Younge, Nicholas, 291

Zephiria, 249–50
Zimmerman, Franklin, 312, 314–15, 568, 607, 624–25